HONKY TONK ANGEL

The Intimate Story of

PATSY CLINE

ELLIS NASSOUR

CHICAGO
REVIEW
PRESS

An A Cappella Book

Cover design: Scott Rattray
Cover photo © GAB Archives/Redferns
Photograph appearing on half title page collection of Connie B. Gay.

This book was first published as *Patsy Cline* by Leisure Books in 1981, then
as *Honky Tonk Angel* by St. Martin's Press in 1993. This updated edition is
published in 2008 by
Chicago Review Press, Incorporated
814 North Franklin Street
Chicago, Illinois 60610
ISBN 978-1-55652-747-0
Printed in the United States of America
5 4 3 2

for
Hilda Hensley and Charlie Dick
and
Dottie West

... thanks for the memories

CONTENTS

	Foreword by Dottie West	ix
	Author's Note	xiii
Side One	"SWEET DREAMS"	3
	"HONKY TONK MERRY-GO-ROUND"	17
	"JUST OUT OF REACH"	31
	"AIN'T NO WHEELS ON THIS SHIP"	43
Side Two	"PICK ME UP ON YOUR WAY DOWN"	61
	"I'M MOVING ALONG"	71
	"HUNGRY FOR LOVE"	80
	"LOVE, LOVE, LOVE ME, HONEY, DO"	94
Side Three	"STOP, LOOK AND LISTEN"	109
	"THAT'S HOW A HEARTACHE BEGINS"	123
	"(WRITE ME) IN CARE OF THE BLUES"	141
	"GOTTA LOT OF RHYTHM IN MY SOUL"	162
Side Four	"IMAGINE THAT"	175
	"I LOVE YOU SO MUCH, IT HURTS"	183
	"NEVER NO MORE"	204
	"TODAY, TOMORROW AND FOREVER"	236
	Afterword	252
	Patsy Cline Discography	286
	Bibliography	294
	Acknowledgments	295
	Index	297
	About the Author	306

FOREWORD

$\mathcal{P}$atsy Cline could never be summed up easily. The closest I'd come is to say that she was *real*.

I first met Patsy in Nashville, my home town, in 1961 backstage at the Grand Ole Opry down at the Ryman Auditorium. In 1957, after I saw her on "Arthur Godfrey's Talent Scouts" and bought her record of "Walkin' After Midnight," I wrote Patsy a fan letter—the only fan letter I've ever written. And she answered it, saying she hoped we'd get to meet.

We did, after I finished Tennessee Tech, got married, and came back to town for Starday Records. I saw Patsy at the Opry and made a point of bumping into her. Before long we were good friends. Patsy would come in off the road, or I'd return home from a date, and we'd get together to talk shop. When I wasn't working, Patsy took me on the road with her to help with her wardrobe.

More than anything, I watched her. And I learned from her. It was unbelievable the way I looked up to her. Patsy not only put feeling into her music but also her entire self. Until I studied Patsy onstage, I just sang songs. I knew I'd never be able to duplicate Patsy, and I became determined to try.

Patsy taught me how to show emotion, how to say the words with the feeling they deserved. She'd say, "Find one person to sing to and sing to just that one." When I got that down, Patsy added, "Now make each person out there think he or she is that one and cast a spell over them."

That was the best advice anyone ever gave me.

Patsy was born for show business. Her life was singing. When you saw her perform, you knew that nobody else came close. There's no one around today who can! She had a charisma that was equal to Elvis or Johnny Cash, both of whom she admired.

She wasn't just good. Patsy was sensational. I wish more of her had rubbed off on me. When she sang a ballad—you know, a real tearjerker—and you'd see her crying, Patsy wasn't faking. She was into her music that much. She knew how to touch an audience. Patsy sang with such heart and feeling. Nobody could sing the blues like Patsy. Her troubles might have added to her greatness as a singer. And she didn't have to have a microphone. Her voice was strong.

By the end of her set, she'd have the audience so wound up they were on their feet. She said, "When you depend on the public for your future, you must be real with them."

She enjoyed the recognition of stardom. When it came, she said, "Damn, it's about time. I've paid my dues." She loved signing autographs and posing with her fans for pictures. When she had a new record, we'd get the trade magazines and look for her song and watch it progress each week.

Like everyone, she had ego, but what amazed me was how she wasn't afraid of competition. She knew how good she was and encouraged all of us. Patsy had a heart of gold offstage. She was always giving to all of us just starting out. The stories are endless—she gave advice, food, clothes, costumes, furniture. Once when she noticed I didn't have anything special to wear around the house before going to bed, she bought me a bright royal-blue robe. It was the most gorgeous robe I ever owned. I lost it when my house burned.

About the only thing I saved was the scrapbook Patsy gave me the year before she was killed. We were crying over the trying times in the business and the ones our men put us through, and she suddenly said, "Hoss, I want you to have these." When I got home, I was leafing through the clippings and mementos and a check for seventy-five dollars fell out with a note saying, "I know you been having a hard time." It was the money we needed to pay the rent.

In the era we came up through, the women singers didn't have the clout or the money-making potential they do today. And these were women who were stars in their own right. We were mainly used for window dressing. Patsy broke the boundaries. Her massive appeal proved women, without men by their side, could consistently sell records and draw audiences.

Patsy was bright. If anyone thought differently, they were in for a surprise. She made the men—singers, musicians, record executives, promoters—respect the success she achieved. She was outspoken for our time. You never had to guess or read between the lines with her. You always knew where you stood. If you were her friend, she'd step in front of a locomotive to save you.

Patsy could be soft and feminine, but she could hold her own against any man. It was common knowledge that you didn't mess with "the Cline." If you kicked her, she'd kick right back.

Patsy's voice was a unique one in the late fifties, when her impact was first felt. She didn't birth the new Nashville sound, but followed close on the heels of Jim Reeves and Eddy Arnold in bringing it out of diapers. Hers were the first country female's records to cross over into pop. She was discovered by an audience that most likely never would have found time to listen to our music.

Patsy was always so full of joy—on the outside. On the inside, she dealt with a lot of hurt and unfulfilled promises. She brought everyone such happiness, the saddest thing to me was that Patsy never found it in her own life except in her children. She worked so hard and was a star—I mean, a really big star—three years.

I recall Patsy's last date in Kansas City as if it were yesterday. We shared a dressing room for the benefit concert. Though suffering with a terrible cold, Patsy went on and was so terrific she defied anyone to remember who'd been on before her. In between the three shows, she tried to rest but we talked.

That night she was exhausted, yet she went on and, as always, had the audience on its feet. Watching from the wings, I could see she was moved. She tried to quiet them to a roar and shared some emotional things. At one point she said, "I never could have gotten this far without your support. I love you all!" It was obvious from the ovation that they loved her too. Patsy came offstage into my arms, crying.

The next morning, her manager/guitarist Randy Hughes's plane was delayed indefinitely because of fog, but Patsy was impatient to get home. I talked her into driving back in the car with us. At the last minute, she changed her mind and decided to wait out the weather with Randy. Hawkshaw Hawkins and Cowboy Copas, veteran stars of the Grand Ole Opry, were to fly with them.

Two mornings later, I woke to a nightmare. We got news of the crash on the radio. Losing three prized entertainers hit hard, but for me it was worse. My Patsy was gone.

At Patsy and Charlie's house she was laid out in the living room, according to her wishes. I put my hand on the bronze coffin and was cold and numb. I could hardly stand. I wanted to reach out to Patsy. She had been like my sister and there was so much I wanted to tell her. But it was too late.

I miss Patsy. I know she's dancing with the angels and singing in heaven's band. I think of her often but try not to cry. I cherish the past, yet I can't live in it. Patsy prepared me for the future, making me a better person, a better singer. I thank God she was a part of my life. I hope that's the way people remember me.

I wouldn't exchange what we shared for anything. Patsy was the consummate artist and human being. There'll never be another like her. She's probably listening to me right now and laughing, "Oh, Hoss!" I can hear her.

—DOTTIE WEST

AUTHOR'S NOTE: After sustaining life-threatening injuries in an automobile accident en route to the Grand Ole Opry, Dottie West died during surgery on September 4, 1991.

AUTHOR'S NOTE

*W*hen I began researching Patsy Cline's life, I envisioned telling the story of a simple girl from the Shenandoah Valley and the Apple Blossom city of Winchester, Virginia, who came up the hard way—determined to become a star. I was in for a surprise.

Most of my knowledge of Patsy came from working with Loretta Lynn in 1970. Through Loretta, I met Patsy's second husband, Charlie Dick, a remarkably affable guy. In 1977 I wrote a magazine series to commemorate Patsy's forty-fifth birthday. I had several interviews with Hilda Hensley, Patsy's bright, charming, and devoted mother, and Charlie. Then came Loretta's autobiography, *Coal Miner's Daughter*, and the movie adapted from it. Suddenly there was an explosion of interest in Patsy Cline. I spent the summer of 1980 in Nashville, Dallas, Houston, and the Virginia/ Maryland area where Patsy lived. I interviewed a hundred family members and friends from Patsy's early days through her final years of stardom. I returned to many of these same places and sources in 1991 and 1992 for this new, revised, and much expanded edition.

Patsy was simple, yet complex; gentle, yet volatile; smooth, yet rough; sweet, yet bittersweet; shy, yet outspoken. She had great strengths and weaknesses. Here was a woman not only twenty years ahead of the pack musically—the female singer responsible for changing the course of country music—but also twenty years ahead as a feminist.

Patsy was a woman who enjoyed life as it came and with great gusto. She wasn't a beauty in the traditional sense, but, over and over, I heard of an inner beauty, warmth, friendship, and loyalty to those she considered dear. She was the first Nashville female superstar, equally at home in the recording studio, onstage, or on television. She was an innovator, though not always willingly, in what she recorded and how she recorded it. She set trends in style and dress that were mocked behind her back, then quickly copied. As a singer, Patsy had great range. Songwriter Harland Howard noted that writers couldn't take full advantage of Patsy, since they didn't have the ability to write for her voice. He noted that, had she set her mind to it, Patsy could have sung operetta.

This is a candid retelling of Patsy's life—a story of the total woman. There are many wonderful memories and a few ugly incidents. It was important to me to present the full story, because in learning of the complete woman that Patsy Cline was, not just the record artist, we see the fire that burned within her to create the trailblazer she became. I discovered facets of Patsy Cline that those closest to her—even her husbands and mother—weren't familiar with. Some of these revelations haven't set well with Charlie Dick and Hilda Hensley. I apologize for any unintentional hurt. It was the furthest thing from my mind. In fact, at all times I have gone to extreme lengths to be fair and objective to all parties. For especially troubling passages, I substantiate facts from at least two additional sources. Concerning controversial or questionable situations, I present an alternate take from another person or persons. Often I heard the same story from different people but the time frame and details weren't consistent. I have made every effort to separate truth from fiction. Conversation between Patsy and others is quoted. In some instances, this is direct conversation to the best of an interviewee's memory; in others, a conversation is used to flesh out scenes in keeping with the stories I was told. Some people recalled exact bits of Patsy's conversation; in other cases, conversations were remembered in an interviewee's words and not verbatim as they originally transpired.

Faron Young's observations and recollections, for instance, are judiciously edited from eighteen pages of transcripts from our interviews in his office in Nashville in 1980.

This book wouldn't have been possible without the selfless cooperation of the musicians, artists, writers, fans, friends, and family who knew Patsy Cline, Charlie Dick, Gerald Cline, and Bill Peer. They came forward with warm welcomes into their homes, offering remembrances, long-forgotten facts, and photographs. These wonderful people provided the oral history of Patsy Cline that I have edited and shaped into book form.

No one was more supportive of this project than Dottie West, who, on several occasions before her tragic and untimely death in September 1991—once during a crisis in her own life—interrupted her hectic schedule to give generously of her time and Patsy Cline artifacts.

Recording session and release dates came from the Decca Records archives I was allowed access to and Nashville's Country Music Foundation.

March 1993 marks the thirtieth anniversary of Patsy Cline's death. Her phenomenal revival in popularity across age groups and lifestyles proves she was no mere shooting star. In fact, Patsy's more popular today—not only in the United States and Canada but also around the world (Australia, Britain, Scotland, France, Germany, Austria, Japan, Argentina, and Brazil)—than she was at her peak.

Patsy was the personification of the word original. Her life is testament to the saying "Where there's a will, there's a way." I feel this is the story, with its inspiring ups and gritty downs, Patsy, had she lived, would have told.

. . . Love that runs away,
Dreams that just won't
let me be,
Blues that keep on
bothering me,
Chains that just won't
set me free . . .

—"Just out of Reach" by V. P. Stewart
(© 1958 Four-Star Music Company; copyright
renewed by Acuff-Rose Music, Inc.)

"SWEET DREAMS"

VIRGINIA HENSLEY: "Mama, we got company."
HILDA HENSLEY: "It's eleven o'clock!"
VIRGINIA HENSLEY: "It's Wally Fowler. He's in the living
  room."
HILDA HENSLEY: "What? Now listen, Virginia!"

The anguish of Patsy Cline, Hawkshaw Hawkins, Cowboy Copas, and Randy Hughes as their Piper Comanche crashed straight into the Tennessee hill country in March 1963 was so intense it is all but unimaginable. Their pain has returned to haunt their loved ones throughout their lives.

Charlie Dick, Patsy's widower, has a deep love for Patsy that nothing and no one has ever been able to fill. He had a hard time accepting her death, especially under the rocky emotional circumstances of their marriage. Charlie kept the living room of Patsy's dream house locked. He left their bedroom as it was, and slept in another room. Her clothing remained in the closets. He left her makeup, hairspray, and combs in the bathroom. Friends who visited had the eerie feeling that Patsy was in the house.

But with two children to raise, Charlie remarried in 1965. Still, he could not forget his Patsy. Especially when drinking heavily, he would play Patsy's records over and over, which led to friction with the new Mrs. Dick, singer Jamey Ryan.

On one occasion, Charlie repeatedly played Patsy's recording of the Bob and John Wills classic "Faded Love." At the end, Patsy sang:

I miss you, darlin', more and more ev'ry day,
As heaven would miss the stars above.

With ev'ry heartbeat, I still think of you,
And remember our faded love.[1]

On the final repeat of the word "love," Patsy, who had bet Charlie she could reach the high note without modulating, took a very audible deep breath, then sang out.

This particular night, as the record kept playing, Jamey asked Charlie to shut the phonograph off and come to bed, but he continued to replay the song. Finally, she said, "Honey, it's late. Come to bed. Patsy's dead. I'm your wife now."

As Patsy sang that last, sustained note, Charlie yelled, "Listen, she's not dead! How can she be? Here she is living, breathing!"

Mrs. Hilda Hensley of Winchester, Virginia, feels she disappointed her daughter, Patsy Cline, only once.

"Singing was Patsy's life," she reflected. "Country singing. I know, more than anything, Patsy would have considered her election to the Country Music Hall of Fame the greatest honor of her career. It's the one I treasure, but on the night of her election I let her down. When Johnny Cash read her name, I fainted. When I came to, that part of the Country Music Association awards show was over. I was angry that nobody told me about her election. Since the bronze plaque which hangs in the Hall in Nashville had to be cast, someone had to know. No one said anything on Patsy's behalf. That was the very least I could have done after all she did for me."

Each year an active and inactive member of the country music industry are inducted into the Hall of Fame. Though five nominees in each category are announced in advance, only the company that produces the plaques, the executive director (then Mrs. Jo Walker) of the C.M.A., and the accounting firm that tabulates ballots know the names of the inductees. They are sworn to secrecy. During the broadcast, a previous honoree reads the nominees' names and unveils the plaques. Acceptance remarks are not made.

At the seventh annual awards, on October 15, 1973, one exception was made. Cash, not yet a Hall of Fame member, was selected to do the presentation. Chet Atkins, the internationally renowned guitarist and record producer, was named in the active category. Then Cash read Patsy Cline's name.

As Charlie remembered, a hush fell over the audience. Patsy's membership was another break with tradition. She was the first solo woman artist to be so honored—a tribute to her trailblazing career in country and pop music. Sylvia Mae Hensley, Patsy's sister, let out a scream of shocked surprise. No one recalls Mrs. Hensley fainting, only that she sat silently in shocked disbelief.

That night Mrs. Hensley relived "a lot of heartaches and some beautiful memories." She said, "It wasn't at all sad. She was a wonderful daughter. I saw her start from nothing and watched her accomplish great things. She made her dream come true. All she ever talked about and wanted was to be a country singer. God in heaven knows she did it the hard way, and had very little to show for it except her children."

Everybody has asked Mrs. Hensley how Patsy got interested in country music. "It must have been in her blood," she explained. "She didn't take after me or her daddy. Patsy's love of music accounted for her drive to become a singer."

Before setting her goal, Patsy Cline was quite impressionable. As a child, Virginia Hensley, as Patsy was then called, idolized Shirley Temple. All the way home from the one-hundred-seat Elkton Theatre in Elkton, Virginia, where she and her mother had seen a Shirley Temple movie twice, she would tap dance down the streets.

For hours, then days, afterward, she'd say, "Mama, I want to be a dancer just like Shirley Temple."

"What?" replied her mother. "Now listen, Virginia, you know we can't afford dance lessons."

But it didn't do any good. Before Mrs. Hensley could get the words out, Virginia was tap dancing all over the house.

"I'd stand, watch her and shake my head," her mother recalled, "and couldn't help but laugh."

Mrs. Hensley hoped and prayed that dancing was a phase her daughter would soon pass through, but at age four Virginia still hadn't given up the dream. When Mrs. Hensley saw a notice for a children's dance competition, she entered her precocious child: "To my amazement, she took first prize. Without any formal training! Then something funny happened. That was the end of dance. Now came the music phase. Not singing, but playing the piano."

Virginia had a half sister, Tempie Glenn, from Mr. Hensley's first marriage, who was being groomed by Elkton music teacher Sally Mann into an accomplished musician. (She later went on to the Shenandoah Conservatory of Music.) When Virginia visited, she spent hours listening to Tempie Glenn play the piano and came home mesmerized. "Mama, I want to play the piano just like Tempie Glenn!"

"What?" exclaimed Mrs. Hensley. "Now, listen, Virginia, you know we can't afford piano lessons."

But Virginia drove her parents crazy until, on her seventh birthday, they bought her a piano. It was either that or having her go to any house in town with a piano to "visit."

"Virginia played by ear," Mrs. Hensley said. "When I took her for lessons, right in the middle of the practice the teacher said, 'She's got a natural gift. You'll be wasting your money. I don't think I could teach her to play.'"

Mrs. Hensley noted that from the time she was ten, Virginia had a new fascination. "She never missed the Grand Ole Opry and knew every detail about each singer."

Saturday nights Virginia sat in front of the radio and sang along with tunes on the broadcasts. She'd get excited and burst out, "Mama, I want to be a singer just like Ernest Tubb"—or Mother Maybelle (Carter) or Roy Acuff or Tennessee Ernie Ford or Rose Maddox or Red Foley, or she wanted to yodel like Patsy Montana.

Mrs. Hensley uttered her standard reply: "What? Now, listen, Virginia!" She hoped and prayed that this phase, too, would pass. But it was a lost cause. Virginia wouldn't let go. She really and truly wanted to be a country star.

Her cousin Herman V. Longley, Jr., of Elkton remembers that "even from an early age [Virginia] was a go-getter. If she wanted something, she set her goals and went after it with a vengeance."

Mrs. Hensley discovered that nothing could defeat Virginia. "When she told the children at school that she was going to be a country music singer, even they took her seriously."

Patsy Cline's grandfather, Solomon Job Hensley, was born at Hensley Hollow in Virginia's Blue Ridge Mountains on April 12, 1858, the sixth of eleven children. Sol, as he came to be called, was, for his time, an educated man. Mountain schools went only to the seventh grade, and it is believed he completed his education. He was an avid reader. "Grandfather looked forward to the daily newspaper," said Longley, "which he not only read but thoroughly digested. He was a man everyone respected and looked up to. They had to." He stood at least six feet tall and weighed approximately 250 pounds.

He met Margaret Elizabeth Shifflett when she was nineteen, a year older than he. They married September 26, 1878.

Sol, thanks to land acquired by his father and mother, Benjamin and Rebecca, became a massive landowner. According to Longley, a son of Sol's daughter Lelia Ann, "He wasn't the wealthy man some in the family have presented him as. Today, I hear the grandchildren talk about Sol and Margaret having maids and servants. I have to laugh. The only maids they had were the daughters, and the only servants were the farmhands. Grandfather had money, but lived a simple, Spartan life."

In quick succession, Margaret gave birth to Ida, Bess, Lelia, and Cicero, who died in 1884 at age six. Sol and Margaret left Hensley Hollow with his father in the spring of 1888. Together, they bought a farm of more than 200 acres approximately two miles west of Elkton in Rockingham County. They named it Solsburg and grew wheat and corn there. They built two homes, which still stand on State Route 981: one is a stone bungalow and the other a simple frame house that became the homestead. It was here that the other children—Mattie, who died at six months at the end of 1888, Samuel Lawrence, James, Alice, Ruth, and Ashby—were born.

When Benjamin Hensley decided to end the partnership with his son in 1889 after Rebecca's death, his son bought his share of the farm. Benjamin bought another farm a mile west of town while Sol increased his landholdings, slowly at first and then more rapidly.

In 1907 he purchased a 130-acre farm near Penn Laird. Hensley eventually added 460 acres of grazing land in the Blue Ridge Mountains (now a part of Shenandoah National Park), which he named Cedar Falls, and 640 acres, known as Allendale, on the James River near Scottsville.

Sol had a great appetite for land, and, it appears, ladies. One encounter with the latter was to change the course of his life and respectability. He was on his way from Solsburg to Cedar Falls and stopped to water his horse at a spring.

Resting near the water was an attractive girl, Polly Shifflett (no relation to Sol's wife). That meeting led to a tempestuous affair. A few months later, Polly was pregnant. She was fifteen.

A scandal errupted, not so much over Polly's age—in that era, men much older than Sol married young girls—but over the fact that Sol described himself as a "hit and miss man." He claimed the baby couldn't be his. Sol was married and a respected family man, with no intention of divorcing his wife. The matter went to trial at Harrisonburg, the seat for Rockingham County, and became a sensation. After weighing the testimony, the judge decided, "No matter your past performance record, you, Solomon Hensley, have obviously scored a run this time. And you'll pay up." Sol settled a fortune on Polly and her family but staunchly denied being the father.

Sam, the father of Patsy Cline, was born August 16, 1889. As a teenager, he showed a love of his father's land and great promise as a farmer. He stopped growing at five foot seven but was extremely strong. He carried his 175 pounds well. Sam, said Longley, was an outgoing, energetic, and mechanical-minded man.

He, too, developed a reputation as a ladies' man but, suddenly, in 1912 quietly settled down and married Wynona Jones. In 1914, he signed up for World War I. He did service as a blacksmith on the front in France's Argonne Forest and was discharged in November 1918 after the Armistice.

Sam returned home a different man. He lost interest in farming. On one of his father's farms there was a limestone quarry used for grinding rock for mountain-road surfacing. Sol offered his son a job as one of the foremen, but Sam turned it down. He moved to the hamlet of Gore, Virginia, about thirteen miles from Winchester on Highway 50, and found work in a quarry where sand was processed into glass.

He and Wynona had two children, Randolph, born in 1919, and Tempie Glenn, born in 1921 and who died in 1989.

In 1927 Wynona caught pneumonia and died. Not long after, Sam, forty, met thirteen-year-old Hilda Patterson of Gore at a Sunday school picnic. According to Hensley's diary, they married in 1929 after a whirlwind engagement. The couple settled on Solsburg and Sam reluctantly went to work for his father.

Tempie Glenn, eight, and Randolph, ten, went to live with and were raised by Sally Mann, their Elkton music instructor.

Randolph "Hobby" Robinson, an Elkton raconteur and the owner of Robinson's Department Store, got to know the family well. He described Sam as "a hard-drinking, mean son-of-a-gun and hell-raiser."

However, Longley said, "Sam was a complex person, but he was ordinarily not a heavy drinker and hell-raiser. A pint of liquor would last him two or three years and the only time I ever saw him raise hell was on the rare occasion when he got really mad. Sam was just plain folk, but he could put on the dog and be refined."

Hilda became pregnant in December 1931. She returned to her family in Gore, where Virginia Patterson Hensley was born September 8, 1932. (A family member made the contention that Patsy may have been born two years earlier.) When Virginia was ten days old, Hilda returned to Solsburg.

Robinson has vivid memories of Virginia Hensley. "I can still see her now, as a five- and six-year-old, skipping down the street, singing at the top of her voice. I adored Virginia and would wait on her personally when her mother and father brought her in, especially when Virginia needed shoes. I remember the friendly, rough time she gave me. Already she possessed a sassiness and the knowledge that she was someone special.

"Virginia was a bit high-strung and temperamental. She only wanted what she wanted, which was always Mary Janes, those black patent leather shoes with the strap. I'd tease her with another kind, saying, 'Well, Virginia, I have these in your size. They're very nice. Don't you like them?' She'd tell me in a minute, 'No! I want the Mary Janes.' And that's what she got."

When she was in the third grade at Elkton Elementary School, her parents began a series of moves. The first was to the Allendale farm, which Sam was to oversee. Then Sam bought a small house on Elkton's main street, East Spotswood Avenue.

Virginia was given to daydreams and flights of fancy inspired by Saturday afternoons spent in the Elkton Theatre. When Virginia wasn't accompanied by her mother, she'd climb the ladder to what was called the balcony and take one of the six seats in front of the flickering light. It was on the screen of the tiny theatre that Virginia saw a very wealthy woman in a luxurious bath. It was something she never forgot, something she'd always envy.

Sam found work as a fireman at the Virginia Military Institute in Lexington, where he stoked the boilers. The family relocated once again.

Margaret Hensley, Sam's mother, died in 1938. That same year, Sol suffered a series of debilitating strokes that partially paralyzed him. Sam and Hilda returned often to Solsburg.

Sam and Hilda moved to Grottoes, about thirty-three miles northeast of Staunton in a region of the Shenandoah Valley famous for its natural caverns. Sam worked for the Duplan Textile Mill.

In 1941, Sam relocated his family in Portsmouth, where he worked as a master blacksmith and engineer at the nearby Norfolk, Virginia, Navy Yard. The Hensleys' son, Samuel Lawrence, Jr., whom everyone was to call John, was born here.

Longley has a photo of Sol at eighty-four with his two-year-old grandson on the front porch of the stone bungalow. Sol has a full head of beautiful silver hair, which, according to Longley, would sparkle in sunlight.

Sol Hensley died November 27, 1943. Daughter Lelia was the executor of his estate. Because of mounting bad debts and the financial slide that began with the settlement of the paternity suit, she decided to sell off the various properties and divide what was left among the siblings.

After the war, Sam and Hilda returned briefly to Elkton with Virginia and Sam Jr. and lived on Rockingham Street. Not long after, Hilda gave birth to Sylvia Mae.

When times got tough, fourteen-year-old Virginia, passing for sixteen, got a job at a Rockingham poultry factory, where she plucked and cut chickens. She told friends about wearing hip boots because of the wet, bloody floors and complained about the foul smell and working conditions.

While Virginia, whom the family called Ginny, was in the eighth grade, the

Hensleys ended their nomad existence and settled in Winchester. Though Sam Hensley came from a monied background, the money was gone.

The house at 608 South Kent Street between Monmouth and Germain was in a working-class section a few blocks from downtown. It was a small, two-story frame structure with a living room, dining room, and small kitchen on the first floor and bedrooms on the second. A former neighbor described it as a clapboard house.

People who knew Sam and Hilda well reported "they often were on the outs and would separate." Like millions of Americans, Sam was a hard-working laborer always looking for the next and best opportunity. That often meant a job far away from home. Hilda wanted a stable environment in which to raise her children. From time to time, Sam went his way, as was the case shortly after the move to town.

Virginia was often reminded by the kids in school and various townspeople that she came from the other side of the tracks, but her abundance of raw, natural talent compensated for her lack of material wealth. She said over and over again, "Just you wait. I'll show you. I've made my wish on a shooting star. Someday I'll be a country singer on the Grand Ole Opry. I'll make records and everybody'll know my name."

When her mother, girlfriends, and boyfriends told her how difficult becoming a star would be, Virginia only became more determined. Like her grandfather, she was curious, adventuresome, and had the pioneer spirit. There was nothing she couldn't overcome. Even the obstacles became advantages.

"I had a serious bout with rheumatic fever when I was thirteen," Patsy Cline related in 1957. "I developed a terrible throat infection and my heart even stopped beating. The doctor put me in an oxygen tent. You might say it was my return to the living after several days that launched me as a singer. The fever affected my throat and when I recovered I had this booming voice like Kate Smith's."

Virginia sang in the Baptist church choir, where she did duets with her mother, and at socials. "Virginia had a lovely voice," her mother said, "and people always made comments. She loved gospel and religious songs. Often she'd play them at home and church on the piano."

But, at fourteen, when Virginia marched into the kitchen and told her mother she was going on the radio, Mrs. Hensley did a double take. "You're doing what? Now listen, Virginia!"

"Mama, I'm tired of waiting," she replied. "It's time I made my move."

Joltin' Jim McCoy, a disc jockey on station WINC, did a live show with his band, the Melody Playboys, on Saturday mornings. It became a favorite of Virginia's, so it was natural she singled him out to introduce the phenomenon that was to become Patsy Cline.

"Someone buzzed me to say this girl was waiting to be on the show," said McCoy, laughing. "We were getting set up to go on and I asked the band members if they knew anything about a girl singer. They didn't, so I went to see what was going on."

As he came into the reception area, there was this smiling girl all dressed up.

Since she looked a couple of years older than she was, McCoy had no idea she was only fourteen. "Can I help you?" he asked.

"I'm here to see Joltin' Jim."

"That's me. What can I do for you?"

"You're Joltin' Jim?"

"Yes. Who are you?"

"Virginia Hensley from here in Winchester. I listen to your show all the time. I'm more than a fan. I'm a singer myself and I want to be on your show. If you give me a chance, I'll never ask for pay."

"Honey, you think you're good enough to sing live on the radio?"

"Yes, sir."

Impressed with her naiveté and determination, McCoy decided to audition Virginia. As she sang, he wondered if anything, least of all a microphone that broadcast to thousands, could scare this girl. "Someday this gal's gonna be a star!" McCoy thought.

She finished her song and stood before him.

"Well, if you got nerve enough to stand before that mike and sing over the air live, I've got nerve enough to let you."

Hilda Hensley couldn't believe what she was hearing on the radio that morning.

Philip Whitney, general manager of the station, recalled, "Virginia was quiet, a wide-eyed youngster. She wasn't good, and her inexperience was obvious. Eventually, she developed a good style. Patsy always wanted advice and actively sought it. When you gave it, she took it seriously."

She became a regular with the Melody Playboys. "Here was this child who walked in off the street one day," McCoy observed, "and none of us knew what a find we had. How she'd impress and thrill us! But, to be a star, she knew she had to work hard, and she didn't mind one bit."

Mrs. Hensley concurred. "Virginia was dedicated. She had to be. I told her she was picking the most competitive business in the world. In those days it was difficult for a woman no matter what she wanted to do, but country music was dominated by men. It would be especially tough for a woman, but there was no talking her down."

Virginia said, "Mama, others have done it. Why can't I?"

Mrs. Hensley decided if Virginia was going to sing, she'd need more experience. She took her to meet a young pianist she knew from Winchester, William R. "Jumbo" Rinker, who played at the Melody Lane Club not far away in Martinsburg, West Virginia. "I was awfully robust as a child," Rinker explained, "and that's how I got that nickname. Even after I grew up and became quite skinny, the name stuck."

Hilda asked Rinker to back Virginia on local dates whenever possible. "She was as pretty as could be," he said. "When I asked her for a date and she told me she was fourteen, I gulped real hard and said, 'I can't believe it. No way.' She looked so much older. I told myself, 'Watch it, boy! You're messing with trouble.' But I plunged right ahead and asked her out anyway. When I told her I was eleven years older, she didn't blink an eye."

As Virginia began establishing herself locally, Hilda's marriage to Sam was deteriorating. A family member stated, "From the way Hilda talked, Sam's heavy drinking might have contributed to the matter." Years later, Patsy Cline gave the impression more than once to friends that her father tried something with her one night when he was drunk.

In September 1947, when Virginia was fifteen and her mother was thirty-one, Sam and Hilda, according to Herman Longley, had conflicts they couldn't resolve. "He said there wasn't another woman and hinted that Hilda was seeing another man, but I didn't put much faith in that." Sam deserted the family.

Patsy Cline's early home life has often been described as unhappy. Except for those circumstances, it was far from it. She had a beautiful relationship with Hilda, whom she turned to time and again for support. "Virginia was born when I was sixteen, so even as she got older, we were more like sisters than mother and daughter. We had the type of relationship where we could discuss very personal things. If I never let her down, I can truthfully say she never let us down."

Patsy told record artist, honky tonk pianist and Grand Ole Opry member Del Wood, "If I made a list of the people I admire, Mom would probably fill up half of it. She can do anything and everything, and she does for me. She's the one person I know I can always depend upon."

"I heard so much about Mrs. Hensley," Wood said, "I thought I knew her. Patsy sang her praises so often I felt her place in heaven was all arranged. Once I kidded her, 'Hon, I bet your mother never once took a switch to your behind!' Patsy replied, 'No, that's not true. She whipped me many times!' I said, 'Thank goodness, she's not perfect. She's a child beater!' Patsy apologized for talking so much about Hilda. I said, 'Don't be silly.' Patsy gushed, 'It's just I love her so much.'"

Mrs. Hensley, an expert seamstress, couldn't earn enough to support the family. The burden of helping out financially fell on Virginia, the oldest. "I could never have asked for a better daughter," said Mrs. Hensley. "Virginia quit Handley High School early in her sophomore year and went to work at Gaunt's Drug Store on Valley Avenue and South Loudoun downtown as a clerk and fountain attendant. She considered it her obligation, but I don't know what we'd have done if it hadn't been for her. It was terrible she had to leave school, but there was no other way. And the Gaunts became more than Patsy's employer. They were true, understanding friends."

Winchester photographer Ralph Grubbs met Virginia at Gaunt's and played a small part in helping her get her career started. "I was thirty-six, but every afternoon I'd go in for a milkshake. I listened when she talked about her singing and she often asked for advice." He first heard her in 1948 when he was on a committee of the 40 & 8, a civic organization sponsoring a talent contest at the high school. "Virginia and her friend Virginia Taylor put together a song-and-dance routine. They had Uncle Sam costumes Mrs. Hensley made. After I heard her sing, I told her she'd have a better chance of winning if she did a solo. But she insisted she couldn't break up the act and lose a friend."

They were runners-up. Not long after, Virginia showed the photographer a letter she'd written to the Opry to ask for an audition. She said, "A friend thinks I'm crazy to send it. What do you think?"

"By all means, do it," Grubbs replied. "You've got everything to gain and nothing to lose. You're better than some of the singers I've heard on the Opry!"

A couple of weeks later, Patsy got an answer from the Grand Ole Opry asking for pictures and a recording. She went to Grubbs and asked how much he'd charge to take her picture.

"I can't rightly figure until I know exactly what you want and how much I'll shoot. But it'll be reasonable."

"Will it be okay if I pay you something each week when I get back?" she pleaded. "I've got just enough money saved to make the trip, but I don't know what Mama's going to say about all this."

Grubbs agreed. They did the session one afternoon and Virginia was in the studio the next day to select the prints.

"Hey, Virginia," Grubbs said, "I told you a couple of days'!"

When he saw how disappointed Patsy was, Grubbs told her to return the next day and he'd have everything ready. She was there at the appointed time and selected her pictures.

"Okay, Mr. Grubbs, now tell me the bad news. How much?"

He looked at her real serious and said, "Well, let's see." Grubbs flipped through the pictures, as if tabulating the cost. "Virginia, I hope you agree this is fair." He paused, then handed her the pictures. "This is a gift. It's my contribution to getting you started in your career."

"Oh, Mr. Grubbs, thank you! Thanks so very much!" And she reached up and hugged him.

Now Patsy worried about getting a recording. Grubbs told her he'd speak to Bob Gaines, a partner in the G&M Music Store on West Boscawen. He agreed to make the recording for free. There was no tape then. Gaines had a machine that fed a guitar string–type wire over a magnetized head.

Wally Fowler, an all-but-forgotten pioneer of the gospel caravans that traveled across the Midwest and Southeast, and his Oak Ridge Quartet were famed for their hillbilly and gospel All-Night Sings broadcast live from the Ryman Auditorium following the Grand Ole Opry. His appearance at Winchester's Palace Theatre on South Loudoun was an event among country fans and one fan in particular. Virginia had mapped out her route to Nashville, and was about to put it into effect.

It was a night Mrs. Hensley would never forget.

"I was preparing supper when Virginia came in and put her arm around me. I thought, 'What's she got up her sleeve?' She said, 'Mama, Wally Fowler's in town and I'm going to see if I can get on his show.' I looked at her and asked, 'You're going to do what? Now, listen, Virginia!' But she was used to that. I could see no force on earth could stop her."

At the Palace stage door, Virginia asked to see Fowler and the attendant laughed. No way! She knew an usher, who sneaked her past the ticket taker and pointed the way backstage. Suddenly, there he was coming toward her.

"Mr. Fowler, can I audition for you?"

"Who's this girl?" he assailed one of his entourage.

"My name's Virginia Hensley."

"What do you want?"

"I sing."

"Is that right? Boys, she sings!"

"Mr. Fowler, let me—"

"So you think you can sing?"

"Yes, sir. I know so. I'd like you to tell me what you think."

"Okay, young lady, you sing and I'll tell you what I think!"

"Oh, Mr. Fowler, you mean it?"

"Yeah. Sing!"

"Just like this?"

"Just like this."

"But—"

"But *what?* You wanna back down now that I'm giving you your big chance?"

"Well—"

"Are you gonna sing? I got a show to do."

"Okay."

She sang. Fowler listened. And that very night Miss Virginia Hensley made her theatrical debut. When Fowler introduced Virginia as his discovery from Winchester, she entered to a wild burst of applause for the hometown girl. She sang and captivated everyone.

When Patsy got home, Mrs. Hensley was in bed. "She came into my room very quietly and told me, 'Mama, we got company.' I said, 'What? Now, listen, Virginia, it's eleven o'clock!' She replied, 'It's Wally Fowler.' I answered, 'Wally Fowler. You've got to be kidding.'

"I got up, put a robe on and went into the living room. And there was Wally Fowler. I nearly dropped dead!"

"Now don't let me interrupt anything, ma'am," Fowler said. "I just wanted to talk to you about Virginia. She wants to be a singer on the Grand Ole Opry."

"Yes, sir."

"She has an amazing voice. I'd like to arrange an audition for her in Nashville with WSM Radio and the Opry officials."

As Fowler explained what he would do, Virginia got more and more excited. Mrs. Hensley wasn't in favor of the plan but finally capitulated.

"He left that night and I honestly never expected we'd hear from him. It was all Virginia talked about for days and days. She kept saying, 'Mama, if Wally Fowler came over here, he must have liked the way I sing.' I prayed that God in His eternal wisdom would have Mr. Fowler call so I could have some peace."

Of course, Mrs. Hensley didn't know Fowler had a reputation of "discovering" young girl singers in the towns he played. He'd audition them and they'd never hear from him again.

"When I next saw Virginia at Gaunt's," said Grubbs, "she was preparing to go to Nashville. I didn't know whether the audition was a result of her letter or Wally Fowler's visit."

Mrs. Hensley reported, "Mr. Fowler was a man of his word. He took a genuine interest in Patsy. He called and asked if I could bring Virginia to Nashville for an audition at WSM Radio. We were to see Jim Denny, the general manager of the Opry. I knew I'd be a goner if I said no, so I agreed. Mr. Fowler called back in a few days with the arrangements."

It was two weeks later, on a Friday morning. "The trip was nearly eight hundred miles and our old car wouldn't make it. A friend took us. The Gaunts gave Patsy the day off. I had no one to leave Sylvia Mae and Sammy with, so we took them along. Since we had no money for a motel, we drove all Thursday night.

"Oh, dear, what a mess it was! Virginia was fidgety, the kids were fidgety, I was fidgety and we drove our friend fidgety."

They arrived on the outskirts of Nashville as the sun was rising and pulled into a picnic area. Virginia saw the tables and said, "Mama, I'm tired. I'm gonna take a nap." On the way into town, they stopped at an Esso station to wash up.

"There we were in this tiny cubicle," Mrs. Hensley recalled, "with the kids doing one thing or another and Virginia trying to change into her good dress and put on makeup."

Patsy spoke of the incident later to Del Wood. In the Ryman Auditorium "girl singers' dressing room" (nothing more than a tiny restroom), she joked, "Before I ever came to the Opry, I had a better dressing room than this. And it was a crapper, too!"

The Grand Ole Opry, since its inception on November 28, 1925, has been a revered institution and show-business phenomenon.

The National Life and Accident Insurance Company's Nashville radio station WSM—its call letters reflecting the firm's goals: "We Shield Millions"—began broadcasting that October with a thousand watts of power, one of only two such stations in the South. George D. Hay, a Chicago announcer calling himself "the solemn old judge," had originated the WLS Barn Dance. When he joined WSM, he launched the WSM Barn Dance.

WSM, an NBC affiliate, carried "The Music Appreciation Hour" hosted by composer and Metropolitan Opera conductor Dr. Walter Damrosch. Hays followed with three hours of country music. One night, Damrosch, citing the need for realism in classical music, presented a young Iowa composer who, with symphony backing, depicted the onrush of a locomotive.

Judge Hay, not to be outdone by a Yankee, said to his listeners upon signing on: "Dr. Damrosch told us it is generally agreed that there is no place in the classics for realism. However, for the next three hours we will present nothing but realism. It will be down to earth for the earthy." At the close of a solo by DeFord Bailey, a black harmonica wizard, Hay intoned, "For the past hour we have been listening to music taken largely from grand opera, but from now on we will present the Grand Ole Opry."

Crowds from throughout Tennessee and the South clogged the corridors of WSM at Seventh Avenue and Union Street in downtown Nashville. This popularity led to the construction of the 500-seat Studio C.

When WSM could no longer accommodate the throngs, the Opry moved to the

Hillsboro Theatre in southwest Nashville. The Opry's next home, in 1929, was the Dixie Tabernacle across the Cumberland River in east Nashville.

The setting of splintery benches and sawdust on the floor was ideal but within two years the Opry was on the move again. At the new War Memorial Auditorium, near the state capitol, twenty-five cents admission was charged in an effort to curb the ever-growing crowds. It was no deterrent. The weekly fans averaged more than three thousand and many in the overflow crowds had traveled long distances.

In 1943, the Grand Ole Opry relocated to Fourth Avenue near lower Broadway in the Ryman Auditorium. Riverboat captain Tom Ryman had built it in 1831 as a tabernacle for a preacher he heckled and who subsequently brought him to the Lord. The Opry quickly became the most popular and strongest single voice for the propagation of country music. (It remained there until 1974 when it moved to a 4,400-seat theatrical and television facility in the Opryland music theme park, now owned by Oklahoma-based Gaylord Entertainment.)

So it was with trepidation that Virginia Hensley came to her audition with "the biggest country music program in all of the United States." "But," noted Mrs. Hensley, "if she was nervous, you could have fooled me."

Virginia had to see the Ryman Auditorium and take pictures.

"Mama, I thought it would be bigger."

"Honey, maybe it is. This is only the outside."

At the stroke of nine in the WSM Radio offices, Mrs. Hensley asked for Jim Denny, who ushered Virginia into a studio and introduced her to pianist Moon Mullican. She screamed, "Oh, my God, Moon Mullican."

"Yes, ma'am, that's me—the Moon Mullican part anyway!"

Mullican, a deft Texas musician who adapted the blues to suit a swinging country beat, had the tag King of the Hillbilly Piano Players. In over six hundred releases, he had numerous best-sellers, including the standard "New Jole Blon," written with Lou Wayne. Ernest Tubb noted that Mullican's playing style became synonymous with country music.

"Don't let all these big shots running around scare you," Mullican advised Virginia. "They're just like me and you. Stay calm and just be sincere."

When she began singing, Mullican looked up from the piano in great surprise. Denny, having auditioned other Wally Fowler "finds," was impressed. She sang another song, and then Denny and Mullican conferred. Denny asked the Hensleys to return the next morning so other executives could hear Virginia. Mrs. Hensley stated her situation with the children, her friend, and the borrowed car but was too embarrassed to say she didn't have the money to stay over. Nor did Denny volunteer any.

"It wasn't an easy decision," she admitted. "I felt I was holding Virginia's future in my hands. It was obvious their reaction was positive." Mullican even remarked that Virginia would be one of the youngest performers to appear on the Opry.

Roy Acuff came in and asked Mullican whom he'd heard singing. "Roy, I want you to meet Miss Virginia Hensley from Winchester, Virginia. Y'all, this is Roy Acuff." Mrs. Hensley noted that, for once, her daughter was speechless.

"Virginia, that's one of the sweetest voices I've ever heard," Acuff said. "I'm hosting 'Noon-Time Neighbors.' Will you do me the honor of singing a little song?" Virginia managed to utter, "Oh, Mr. Acuff! Yes, sir!"

After the show, Denny and Mrs. Hensley spoke. He needed more time. She told him it wasn't possible to spend the night. Denny advised them to stay put while he tried to locate some people.

"I knew Virginia had her heart set," she said. "I thought maybe the others could go back and we'd take the bus, but I only had enough money for gas to get us home. Things began to drag into late afternoon. It looked like whatever Mr. Denny wanted to do would take a while. Finally, when we hadn't heard anything, I took Virginia aside and told her we'd have to leave but that we could always come back. She took the news better than I expected." They returned to Winchester. "We never got a letter or call from Mr. Denny or anyone," Mrs. Hensley said, piqued. "I thought that was a shame. He let us down."

Virginia worked at the drug store and continued her singing dates. She waited and waited for the call from WSM and the Grand Ole Opry. Through nine years of ups and downs, she remained undaunted.

"After all, Mama," she told her mother, "Wally Fowler, Moon Mullican, and Roy Acuff thought I was great!"

"HONKY TONK
MERRY-GO-ROUND"

BILL PEER: "The first thing we gotta do is change your
   name."
VIRGINIA HENSLEY: "I kinda like what I'm stuck with."
BILL PEER: "Virginia just ain't right for a singer. Patsy.
   Patsy Hensley! Like it?"
VIRGINIA HENSLEY: "Yeah. I do. Patsy it is!"

Virginia's job at the drug store didn't put an end to her singing ambitions. With Jumbo Rinker on keyboards, Virginia sang at church socials, benefits, fraternal parties, carnivals, and minstrels. As her reputation spread, other singing dates were offered. Gene Shiner, her neighbor on South Kent Street, formed the Metronomes, a pop music band, and hired Virginia as lead vocalist. She held that job for about four months, but it wouldn't be the last time she worked with Shiner.

Mrs. Hensley was busy making western costumes for her daughter's singing engagements. The Gaunts, like family now, let Virginia off early to perform. Like most artists starting out, Virginia worked some rough places—everything from taverns to honky tonks. In addition to Gaunt's Drug Store, she had part-time jobs at Winchester's Greyhound terminal and Front Royal's Virginia Gentleman restaurant, where she also sang. Though not quite five foot four, Patsy knew how to take care of herself. What she didn't know, Rinker taught her. "The guys knew not to manhandle her," he said.

Patsy later told Del Wood, "Nothing men do surprise me. I'm ready for them. I know how to whack below the belt." In 1960, Patsy Cline spoke of those days of working day and night. "Mama would pick me up and take me to wherever I had a job. We had the one car, so she dropped me off and came back to get me later or she'd stay the whole night. Mama didn't trust me with anyone! Knowing me, it was probably just as well. We'd get home about one in the morning, totally exhausted. At six I was up with Mom fixing breakfast for the kids, then off to work. And, you know what, we loved every minute of it!"

"Though she wasn't a beauty," said Rinker, "men fell at Virginia's feet. She possessed much allure. She was well-endowed and had the right moves. Virginia had pretty brown hair and sparkling brown eyes. She'd smile and guys would be hog-tied, but Virginia was chasing rainbows. She liked to get serious without having to get serious. She had no plans to get tied down. She enjoyed playing the field and having a good time. She liked the fast crowd. If anything scared her, I didn't know about it. As far as Virginia and me, we were romantic friends but not headed for any altar."

Besides Rinker, Virginia dated Elias Blanchfield of Martinsburg, to whom she was briefly engaged at seventeen, and Ray Horner of Le Gore, Maryland.

Not everyone liked Virginia, according to her early friends, nor did she make it easy to like her. "She was aloof," Rinker observed, "which a lot of people misunderstood for being conceited or thinking she was better than they were."

"The Hensley gal," as she was often referred to, could be tough and tomboyish. She was notorious for her vulgar mouth, but could turn around and be the perfect genteel lady. Part of the perceived problem was that Virginia didn't always make the "correct" or acceptable choices for her day and age. She wore tight-fitting sweaters, dresses and jeans, red lipstick, lots of makeup, and long, dangling earrings. More often than not, she chose gaudy colors and styles. It didn't take long for her to earn a reputation as a "loose woman, a hard-boiled teaser out only for herself." The men with whom she flirted and teased nicknamed her the "Honky Tonk Angel."

In 1951, Virginia, nineteen, became a regular at George and Katherine Frye's Rainbow Inn on Greenwood Road south of town. Virginia wore a colorful array of cowgirl outfits made by her mother. Sonny Frye, who played guitar, and the Playboys (a frequently used tag for bands in the region)—Bobby Lee, Jimmy, and Del—were sons of the owners and, along with Harold Senseny, made up the house band.

The club has been described as "an old henhouse of a dive," but it was a rather tame Texas-style dance hall, famous locally from the 1940s for its country ham sandwiches. Sonny Frye said, "People came out on Saturday night and let their hair down. There was plenty of beer and live country music. We also had a jukebox with about twenty records. People played them over and over again and everybody sang along."

Frye said there was hardly ever time to rehearse, especially with Virginia Hensley. "She impressed us with her talent and how well she knew her material. We didn't have music stands or sheet music. Usually, with Virginia we went on cold turkey. She'd just tell us what key she wanted and we took it from there."

The Virginia that Sonny, brother Bobby Lee, and Bobby's wife, Betty, knew differs greatly from her honky tonk angel persona. "She was a down-to-earth, good ole country girl," Betty Frye observed. "There wasn't anything smart about her.

Virginia was everybody's friend. We'd sit and talk for hours. Virginia wasn't fancy or full of herself. She liked mashed potatoes and fried chicken just like I did."

The Winchester area had numerous dance halls, and the Playboys played them all—Bert's on Route 50 West, the Shamrock on Route 7, and Chuck and Ray's on Route 11. They were regulars on the club and drive-in theater circuit within a hundred-mile radius of town. Usually, wherever the Playboys appeared, Virginia Hensley would show up to sing.

"We had a reputation for knowing all the best songs," Bobby explained. "We played by ear. Unlike today, there weren't a whole slew of new songs coming out every week. A handful of established artists put out records. When a new one came along that the public liked, we were right on it, thanks mainly to the jukebox at the Rainbow. And Virginia was right in touch with the latest hits, sometimes maybe a step ahead. She'd snap out the tempos and guide us if we hit a snag."

In the summer of 1952, the Fryes built an outdoor stage adjacent to the Rainbow Inn for Sunday afternoon family concerts. People brought picnic food and drink and relaxed on the grass. The shows, many of which featured Virginia, attracted crowds of one to two hundred. Often before she performed, Virginia would ride the Fryes' horses.

Interestingly, Bobby said, the band knew Virginia "simply as a local girl who wanted to entertain and who could sing her heart out. She never said anything to give us a clue she wanted to go to Nashville."

That was before Virginia met Clarence William Peer.

Peer, virtually uncredited for what he did for Patsy, was a guitarist, well known by Nashville artists whom he'd sometime play for. At thirteen he joined WFMD Radio's Log Cabin Boys in Frederick, Maryland. He relocated to Charles Town, West Virginia, where after ten years with other groups, he formed the Melody Boys and Girls in 1941. His was one of the first country bands to use female musicians. The band was a regular at the Charles Town Racetrack, Washington's Joe Turner Arena, the Mount Vernon Showboat which cruised the Potomac, and the tri-state Moose Lodge and American Legion circuit.

Bill Peer's full-time avocation was country music, but it didn't earn him enough to support his family and his career. He worked two day jobs in order to be free weekends to accept band dates. He was employed by Goode Motor Company in Charles Town, where he ran the parts department and was a part-time Buick salesman. Evenings would find him at McGaha's Appliance Store selling washers, dryers, kitchen ranges, and refrigerators. On weekends he was a West Virginia deejay on Martinsburg's WEPM Radio, where he and the band appeared live on Saturday mornings.

Band members recall Bill "as an excellent salesman, one of the best" they knew. They also found him a talented musician and leader.

"He was intelligent with street smarts," said Roy Deyton, a member of the band with his brother Ray. "He knew how to survive. Bill was a good organizer. When it came to music, he was always trying to teach us something, especially about how to make sure you get the music across to the listener. He'd say, 'If they look like they're enjoying it and get up and dance, you're doing it right. If they don't, then you got to weed out the bad material.'"

The first Mrs. Peer, Jenny, remembered Bill saying he first met Virginia Hensley when she approached him for an audition at work at Goode Motors. The second Mrs. Peer, Dolly, recalled Bill saying they met at WEPM Radio in the summer of 1952.

"She wanted to sing with the band and told Bill of her goal to get to Nashville," Dolly said. "He suggested if she was serious to get some material ready."

Rinker claims that in late summer 1952 he introduced Virginia to Bobby Carper, Peer's steel guitarist, who ran a Winchester body repair shop. "She kept after me to get Bobby to arrange an audition," Rinker explained. "One day we pulled in and Virginia told me to put some pressure on Bobby. So I told him, 'Hey, she's driving me nuts! When you gonna set her up with Bill?' He spoke to Bill, who said, 'If she's ready, bring her over.'"

Whatever her route, on September 27, a half hour before the band began to play, Virginia Hensley arrived at the Brunswick, Maryland, Moose Lodge on Potomac Street at Fourth Avenue, across from the Baltimore & Ohio railyard.

She walked up to Peer, who, like Jumbo Rinker, was eleven years her senior. "Hey, there, you remember me?"

"I sure do."

"I'm ready."

"We'll see about that."

Virginia sang as Bill played the guitar. He couldn't take his eyes off her. Like many before him, Bill was smitten.

"You impressed the hell outa me."

"Me? Or my singing?"

"Both. And you've driven Bobby and me nuts for two months, so I better hire you and get it over with! But the first thing we gotta do is change your name. Got any ideas?"

"I kinda like what I'm stuck with—"

"Virginia just ain't right for a singer."

"Let me think about it."

"Did you say your middle name's Patricia?"

"No, Patterson after my mother's."

"Oh . . . Wait a minute!"

"What?"

"It'll still work. Patsy. Patsy Hensley! Like it?"

"Yeah. I do. Patsy it is!"

"Now, it's only ten dollars a show."

"I accept!"

At the Moose Lodge, Patsy was an instant hit. Bill told everyone what a bundle of talent his discovery was. "She's got a voice that's gonna take her places." The first place it took her was into his arms.

As Jenny Peer remembered, "The first time I saw her, I knew there was trouble ahead. Patsy was a woman any man would take a second look at. I warned

Bill, 'Be careful. You know what she's like. She'll use you and dump you.' But Bill fell in love and love's blind.

"He saved everything from two jobs and went into debt to help Patsy. He became her manager, bought her clothes, and attempted to get her a record contract. He was on the phone constantly to friends in Nashville about taking Patsy there."

Did Patsy fall in love with Bill? "I knew she was never in love with Bill, but he wouldn't let her alone. Patsy was complex. She had these two quite interesting sides. She was tough as nails and tender-hearted, too. She wanted to get ahead. She had her dreams. Her goals were set. With Bill, she saw an opportunity."

It's alleged by several local people that Patsy, to advance her goals, would "avail herself for special favors." A rampant rumor is that "some of her best performances" took place in front of the camera, posing with male companions. A Moose Lodge regular and early owner of a Polaroid, who was often asked to snap pictures for friends, denied knowledge of Patsy doing such things.

Another person, who enjoyed an intimate friendship with Patsy, said, "Quite frankly, Patsy was accused of doing a lot of things. It was just talk. Sometimes it was a way of getting back at her. A lot of guys came on to Patsy and, if she wasn't interested, she made no bones about telling them where to go. That wasn't the way things were done. On the other hand, if Patsy was interested, she'd grab your hand and lead the way."

Roy Deyton, who played upright bass, lead guitar, and fiddle in the band, noted, "Patsy was a great asset to the band. The way she sang and moved, she brought a whole new dimension to what we did. Audiences loved her, but Patsy wouldn't necessarily win any Miss Congeniality awards. If you stood in the way of something she wanted, she'd either sweet-talk you or bulldoze right over you. But it soon became quite clear never to say anything the least bit detracting about Patsy. Bill wouldn't stand for it."

Bill and Patsy became inseparable. He urged her to follow her dreams and told her she was a born star. Peer began grooming her for that big day. Those close to them describe how Bill took the rough-hewn singer that was Virginia Hensley and transformed her into a dynamic country belter.

Peer made many promises. Realistically and financially, he was able to deliver on very few of them. He was a small fish in a big pond. Though he had contacts with Nashville stars when they toured through the area, to them he was a respected local musician whom they could call on in a jam or use for backup. Regionally, however, Bill was well known and had connections. It was his goal to record Patsy. He produced and circulated a number of demonstration tapes of Patsy's vocals.

If Patsy was to be a star, he wanted her to be his star. He talked endlessly of how crazy in love with Patsy he was, how much he wanted to marry her. Patsy pointed out that there was his wife and son. Peer called Patsy several times a day. He wanted to spend every possible moment with her. Late at night, after he'd worked two jobs, he'd drive to Winchester just to sit in the car and talk to Patsy. When he couldn't be with her, he'd mope and say how much he missed her.

Bill became obsessed with Patsy. He wanted to get a divorce and marry her. She wouldn't hear of it. Many times Bill told her, "Honey, I can't live without you." Patsy would reply, "Oh, Bill! Stop carrying on. You know my career comes first."

There are several mutual friends who said Patsy led Bill on. Others point out that she constantly reminded him that marriage wasn't something she was contemplating. Or was it?

Suddenly, in December 1952, Patsy shocked her mother and friends with the news that she had decided "to mend [her] evil ways and settle down." She announced she was getting married.

Everyone knew Bill was in love with Patsy, but he was already married.

"I know that," she told friends. "But it ain't Bill."

It was someone none of Patsy's intimates knew. To most of them, he was a most unlikely candidate. Peer was stunned and felt betrayed.

Gerald Cline was, perhaps, the most fascinating man in Patsy's life. One can only be puzzled by her attraction to him, especially at a time when she was involved in a torrid affair with Bill.

Gerald was born in 1925, the son of Earl Hezekiah and Lettie Viola Cline. His father owned a contracting and excavating company in Frederick, Maryland, and had an impressive home at 436 East Patrick Street.

Cline's brother Nevin stated, "Gerald liked flashy cars and women. He gave the impression he owned the family business and had plenty of money. He never had anything until Dad died. He was Saturday night rich—after payday—and Monday morning poor. He'd take the girls out one night a week. That's all he could afford.

"He never lifted a finger to help us. Gerald was supposed to drive one of the trucks, but he'd only do it if he was forced. Dad finally gave up on him and, in the end, made him secretary of the company, but I don't know what he ever did even in that position. He was good at one thing, being a ladies' man. Gerald sealed the bonds of matrimony several times and, I think, each time with invisible glue."

"When you boiled away all the grandiose bravado—b.s., in other words," observed Patsy's friend Fay Crutchley, "you had to like Gerald. He was always good for a laugh. There was only one problem. You never knew when he was telling the truth. He'd be carrying on and I'd be laughing and calling him a lie bag."

In 1943, Gerald marched Ruth Moser up the aisle only because he was forced to by both families. She was three months pregnant. "Gerald immediately went to live on the Moser farm to avoid the draft [through a farm exemption]," reported Nevin. "Gerald and Ruth were divorced in late 1947—after the war, please note!" Ruth took him to court a few months later, suing him for nonsupport of their son, Ronnie.

"Dad never paid much attention to me when I was growing up," charged the son. "Hardly anybody knew he was my father. I haven't seen or heard from him in years."

Gerald began dating Evelyn Lenhart before his divorce from Ruth was final. They moved into the second floor of Nevin and Dorothy Cline's two-family house in Braddock Heights.

"We're total opposites," noted Nevin. "Gerald was like Dad, I was like Mom. But Dad had drive and ambition. Gerald had none. He'd have been perfect for the hippie movement. He never liked to stay in one place long, or with any one person. He was a swinger."

The relationship between Gerald and Evelyn was shaky at best. While she was at work, he thought nothing of bringing women to the house. "Evelyn set traps to catch him," Nevin reported, "and when she'd find him fooling around or hear that he was, she'd beat the tar out of him. Then, when she'd leave for work, Evelyn would push Gerald into the closet and lock him in. He'd yell and cry like a baby, but neither Dorothy or me dared let him out until Evelyn was way down the street."

The couple stayed together four years. When they split, Gerald played the field, spending part of Saturday nights at the Moose dances. On October 11, 1952, the five-foot-eight, 220-pound Gerald, dressed as usual to the nines, arrived to find an addition to the band.

"It may not have been love at first sight when Patsy saw me," Gerald Cline said, laughing, "but it was for me. I walked into the party room on the second floor, the band came on, and there she was. She knocked me out! During the first break, I went to meet her and see if she'd join me for a drink. When I was finally able to get her to one side, Bill was right behind her hanging on to Patsy and our every word."

Gerald didn't let that deter him.

"Hi, I'm Gerald Cline," he told Patsy, taking her by the hand. "I think you're fantastic."

"You do, huh?"

"Yeah."

"My, you're quite a big man."

"Yeah, and I got a new car."

"Which of you is fastest?"

"Want me to show you?"

"We'll see. Hang around."

Later, telling Bill she was joining some friends, Patsy had several drinks with Gerald.

"Let me take you out," he pleaded. "You won't regret it!"

"Is that a fact?"

"Yeah."

"I better not, big fellow."

Gerald admitted going berserk over Patsy. After their first date, he couldn't get her out of his mind. He said, "If nothing else, Patsy admired my persistence."

Though Patsy and Bill were an item, she began seeing Gerald on a regular basis. He'd drive often to Winchester, pick Patsy up, and they would travel around the area. He even brought her to work at the Lodge, right under Bill's nose. Gerald had another way of endearing himself to Patsy—through her mother. He would bring large supplies of kerosene to the Hensley house to heat the kitchen stove and heaters. Mrs. Hensley sang his praises.

In early 1953, Fay returned to the Moose dances with her husband, Harry. She was impressed with Bill's new singer. She spotted Gerald.

"Hey, you know all the pretty gals," Fay said. "Who's that fantastic singer?"

"Hi, Fay. Why that's Patsy Cline!"

"Cline? Any kin to you?"

"You could say that. She's my wife."

"Gerald, you're crazy! You're already married. Come on, who is she?"

"I told you. She's my wife. We just got married!"

"I can't ever believe anything you say—"

"Well, you can believe me this time!"

He was telling the truth. On Saturday afternoon, March 7, Patsy and Gerald were married in the presence of the Reverend Paul L. Althouse in the Frederick Evangelical Reformed Church (United Church of Christ). It was a small wedding—Gerald didn't even invite his family. Nevin didn't know about the marriage until after the newlyweds moved into their new apartment on the second floor of 824 East Patrick Street, Frederick, a block from the Cline family home.

Close friends such as Doris Fritts of Mechanicstown, West Virginia, and Dolly Huffmeister (a future Mrs. Peer) couldn't help but wonder why Patsy married Gerald. It soon became obvious that Patsy thought marrying Gerald would give her respectability and access to money to advance her career.

Several years later, another reason came to light.

"Patsy and I were just sitting around talking," revealed Lois Troxell, with whose family Patsy was to live for several months, "and it came up. I asked and wasn't prepared for the answer. Patsy said she married Gerald because he was so in love with her that he threatened to kill himself if she didn't."

Fay Crutchley recalled her friendship with Patsy, whom she and several other girlfriends called Pat. "I can sit right here in my living room and still see Pat sitting on the couch, laughing and doing all sorts of crazy things. Doris Fritts and I were two of Pat's closest friends. We were buddies, confidantes, the girls she ran around town with. Pat was a down-home person—no phoniness or pretensions. If Pat wasn't here, she was either visiting or eating supper with Doris and her parents, Melvin and Beulah, at their country store and gas station. They had a house behind and upstairs of the store.

"Doris and I idolized the way Pat sang. She had warmth and a lot of heart in her music. From the night Gerald introduced us, Pat and me had a bond that lasted until the day she died. I never got tired of being with her. Some people thought of Pat as a hard woman. Not me. For that period of the fifties, I guess Pat, as far as the way men and some women look at women, was wild and brassy. I thought of her as colorful and unique.

"Saturdays we'd spend almost the entire day together. I'd leave Frederick about twelve-thirty and meet Pat at the Moose Lodge, then sit while they rehearsed. I'd bring clothes, go to a friend's, and change, then come back at night to meet my husband. If Doris wasn't already there, she'd pull in and join us. We'd have a long table near the stage, and Pat would be with us off and on throughout the evening. On special occasions, like New Year's Eve or an anniversary, Pat, Gerald, Harry, and me would have dinner before the dance. Other times, Pat would eat with Doris, who'd then drive her to the Lodge.

"Gerald was at least eight years older than Pat if he was telling the truth. I never did ask, but I could see what attracted her to him. As cocky and boastful as he was, he was fun and Pat loved a good time."

According to Mrs. Hensley, "I thought, with her career drive, marriage would have been the furthest thing from Patsy's mind. I liked Gerald. He was nice and considerate. Patsy seemed to have no misconceptions about a husband slowing down her goals or sidetracking her career."

Songwriter Lee Burrows, also a record and song promoter, got to know Patsy well. "She didn't seem the marrying kind. Her career came first. After she married, Patsy'd say, 'I sure surprised everybody.' So did her choice. Here was a girl who could've had the pick of the crop. When I met him, I could've mistaken Gerald for her uncle. He was overweight, only a bit taller than Patsy, and not much in the looks department.

"But he doted on Patsy, so who's to say he didn't sweep her off her feet? Since Patsy's father deserted the family when she was so young, maybe it was the age difference that attracted her. As I got to know him, he was anything but a father figure! I never heard Patsy say she loved him. She'd say things like 'Oh, Gerald's real nice. He wants to take care of me' and give her this or give her that."

It wasn't long, given Patsy's determination to be a star and Gerald's personality, before problems developed. Fay explained, "Pat was the type of person who liked to travel and get around. She never lost sight of becoming a country singer. She knew she was good and that she was going to make it. Many times Pat would say, 'I'm going to the top.' I don't think anything in the world could have stopped her.

"Pat's working didn't bother Gerald—at first. He'd even travel from date to date with her, drinking, dancing, having a good time. When he got tired of that, Pat didn't seem to mind. She had Bill. He was always in the picture. Yes, it gets complicated! Some things that went on were ridiculous. There weren't too many well-kept secrets in Frederick, Brunswick, or the road in between. People knew what others were up to and loved to talk. Pat, Bill, and Gerald were the subject of much of the gossip."

Lois Troxell explained how distasteful and embarrassing Gerald's mother, who was very stern, found the gossip. "It didn't endear her to either one of them," she said.

Roy Deyton heard that Patsy and Lettie Cline didn't get along. "Mrs. Cline was tight with a dollar. She thought Patsy married Gerald for the family's money and became fairly determined she wouldn't get any. Gerald never helped Patsy with her career. It was Bill who put out the money. In spite of her marriage, Bill was still mad about Patsy and made good on his promise to get her to Nashville."

On April 10, 1953, Bill and Jenny drove Patsy and Gerald to Music City. "We had adjoining rooms at the Colonial Motel," Jenny recalled. "Bill got Ernest Tubb to invite us to the Opry, where Bill introduced Patsy around. We knew Mr. Tubb from appearances in our area, when Bill's band would either play or he'd play guitar for Mr. Tubb. We went to WSM Radio, then to the Ryman for the Opry. We circulated backstage and sat in the onstage pews."

That night they saw Ernest Tubb's special guest, Elvis Presley, in one of his rare Opry appearances. The audience didn't take to him—some even booed—but Patsy loved him. Gerald criticized his "colored singing," leading Patsy to ask, "What do you know about singing, anyway?"

When Elvis came offstage in tears, Tubb took him aside, put his arm around him, and said consolingly, "Don't worry about that now, boy. You did a fine job.

They don't know. They just don't know." Elvis replied, "Thanks, Mr. Tubb. Just you wait. I'm gonna show 'em. I'm gonna make 'em eat all those words."

After the Opry, with Patsy still talking about Elvis, the Clines and Peers went next door to Tootsie's Orchid Lounge, the famed Opry hangout that fronted on Lower Broadway but had an entrance from the side of the auditorium to an artists' room on the second floor. Just before midnight they crossed the street to the Ernest Tubb Record Shop.

Tubb came off a farm in Crisp, Texas. He was a fan of Jimmie Rodgers and developed honky tonk, a fusion of western swing and country, as well as popularizing the electric guitar. He was soon dubbed the Texas Troubadour. He was the first country star to play New York's Carnegie Hall, where he made the oft-quoted remark, "My! This place sure could hold a lot of hay."

In 1932, after two forgettable Durango Kid westerns, Tubb had a smash with "I'm Walking the Floor over You." He relocated to Nashville and joined the Opry. During the 1950s, before record clubs, when mail-order country and gospel records were big business, Tubb virtually monopolized this product through his Opry advertisements and plugs on his own show, the "Mid-Nite Jamboree," broadcast live from his store after the Opry. It was traditional for the stars to make periodic visits to the record store and Tubb introduced them with great fanfare—making sure to mention their latest release was "in a record bin right here before my eyes." Tubb would receive promising newcomers for a quick number with his band.

That Saturday night, Tubb introduced Patsy as his discovery and she sang two songs. Afterward, while Patsy and Jenny stargazed, Bill and Gerald spoke with Tubb about what direction Patsy should take. As a result of the trip, Patsy and Jenny drew closer. However, after they were home a while, Mrs. Peer had a feeling funny things were going on. "Bill was always making excuses about why he wouldn't be home," Jenny said. "He'd tell me one thing and Patsy'd say something else. I didn't believe him and didn't know whether or not to believe her. It didn't take long before I didn't believe anything. They were lying constantly."

Patsy had another secret she was keeping from Gerald and Bill. She'd fallen in love with a twenty-year-old sailor based at the Little Creek Amphibious Station near Norfolk. Alexander Groves's best buddy in his barracks at Little Creek hailed from Winchester and invited him home for a long weekend that summer of 1953. "We went out to a club and I was introduced to a dark-haired, sexy girl about my own age named Pat Cline," Groves recollected. "When I got back to base, I wrote her. She answered and asked me to come back soon. I did. Several times.

"Pat never mentioned anything about being married, nor did any of her friends. My friend said something that I thought real strange. He told me, 'I don't like her. Her real name's not Pat Cline. Stay away from her. She's crazy!' He said that she was from Winchester but really living at the time in some small country place forty or fifty miles away."

Groves didn't know that Patsy was a singer until one night when Doris Fritts mentioned that Patsy was quite serious about a music career. He asked, "What do you mean?" When she told him, Groves was flabbergasted.

The facts as we know them don't always match up, but, according to friends,

Patsy and Gerald were often separated and she would return to her mother's house or stay with girlfriends.

"Pat introduced me to an older couple in Winchester whom she said were her parents," said Groves. "But when I'd go to pick her up, Pat would be at the house with a woman not much older than her who had small children. I thought she was her older sister." Groves eventually discovered she was Patsy's mother, who was raising Sylvia Mae and Sam.

The romance between Patsy and Groves ended with the coming of fall. He and his Winchester friend from base went separate ways. "About a year later, I ran into him," reported Groves. "He told me that Pat was traveling around the region entertaining in small clubs. But our paths never crossed."

With Groves off in the navy, Patsy went back to her old juggling routine with Gerald and Bill without skipping a beat. "It was really something, the way they carried on," Jenny related. "Gerald would drop Patsy off at Fay's and Bill would pick her up and they'd go off to 'rehearse.' Bill would bring Patsy back to Fay's and come home to me and she'd go home to Gerald. None of this seemed to make Patsy uncomfortable when she was around me. That September she even invited me to her twenty-first birthday party."

Nevin Cline commented, "Whatever happened between Patsy and Bill, Gerald allowed. Patsy'd ask him to take her places where she and Bill were working and stay with her through the show. Dad spoke to him and asked, 'Son, why don't you take your wife where she needs to go when she's working? Don't use coming to the office on time as an excuse 'cause you ain't doing a damn thing around here.'"

Gerald wanted Patsy home with his supper and slippers waiting when he got there. That wasn't Patsy! Their arguments were legend with the downstairs neighbors. They recalled one particular bout, early on a Thursday morning. Bill brought Patsy home. She went up the stairs and opened the door quietly, but Gerald was waiting.

"Home at last! It's two in the morning."

"Gee, Gerald, you can tell time."

"Where the hell you been?"

"None of your damn business!" Patsy would yell back. "You're not my father—"

"No, I'm your husband! I want to know what you been doing and who you been doing it with."

"Gerald, I've been rehearsing, if you must know. Ain't no way of getting around it. You knew I was lead vocalist in Bill's band when you married me."

"It's time you start being a wife! You're spending more time with Bill, a married man with kids, than your own husband. Don't forget you're Mrs. Gerald Cline."

"I'm Patsy Cline and don't you forget it."

"I want a wife."

"I can't quit now. I've got to have my music."

"I'm not asking you to give it up. Just stay at home and be with me sometimes. Baby, I need you! I want to take care of you."

"Take care of me? You're so tight with a buck you make Jack Benny seem like Rockefeller."

"No more gallivanting. You're staying home."

"I ain't gonna."

"But, Patsy, honey."

"Not that 'honey' stuff, Gerald. I can't be a singer and have supper on the table at five-thirty."

"Tell me what you need."

"I don't need you to get in my way. Don't you understand? I'd just die if I couldn't sing. It's my life."

But Gerald didn't understand. He told everyone Patsy was driving him insane.

"There wasn't any one problem with the marriage," Fay said. "Pat simply had her goals, and Gerald wanted a wife. As far as any romance between Pat and Bill, they fooled me at first. When we'd go out, Pat and Gerald were one big happy family. After the dances, when Bill had everything packed away, Pat, Gerald, Bill, Jenny, Harry, sometimes our son Harry Lee, and me would go to Hagerstown, Maryland, to a Chinese restaurant that stayed open all night. We'd get chow mein to take out or sit there for hours and have a great time.

"At the dances, Pat and Gerald would occasionally dance together. I don't think it was something she really enjoyed, but they seemed to have a marriage like just about anyone else's, except Pat was in show business. They didn't have children and I don't know if they wanted any. Pat was concerned with one thing: becoming a star. I don't remember Pat ever saying that she and Gerald fought."

One day, speaking to Lee Burrows of how mixed-up she was, Patsy explained, "Things have been rough between us and I don't know what to do. I don't want to hurt or leave Gerald. I haven't fallen out of love. He's been a good husband. He wants me to be happy, but he doesn't want me in show business. He's real thoughtful. Oh, he's not the type to buy you surprises all the time, but anything I ask for or want, he'll try to get for me."

Patsy hated Gerald's bragging and showing off. She described to Fay the night she and Bill were returning with Gerald from a gig.

"Gerald, you better slow down," she urged. "Hey, babe, you're speeding."

"The cops patrol this area all the time," Bill pointed out.

"Cops! Screw them. I ain't scared of any cops. They know who I am and how important my family is."

"Just the same, Gerald," replied Bill.

"Ain't no cop going to give me a ticket!"

From out of nowhere, a siren started blaring. Everyone was quiet as Gerald pulled over. The officer came to the car and asked for his driver's license.

"Mr. Cline, do you know how fast you were going?" he asked.

"I wasn't speeding, was I, officer?" Gerald sat, scared to death.

The officer recognized Bill, who leaned over and did the talking. The patrolman let Gerald off with a warning.

Starting the car, Gerald snapped loudly, "You see, it was just like I said. I guess I showed him!"

Patsy yelled, "Quick, Gerald, pull over. I think I'm going to puke!"

On a Saturday in June 1954, Fay was at the Lodge for the rehearsal when Patsy complained of not feeling well. She rushed to the ladies' room. Fay followed.

"My God, I feel like I'm going to die!"

"Pat, let me take you home so you can get some rest."

"Naw, Hoss, it ain't that bad. I can't miss a night's work and let my public down."

"Your public can do without you one night. Bill can always get another singer, but I'll never find a friend like you. What you need is to get off your feet and take it easy."

"Oh, quit worrying. It's only some little kind of virus."

Patsy was hardheaded, said Fay. "She went on with the band at nine o'clock but I could tell she wasn't her normal self. Whenever she was onstage, Pat would move all over the place. But not that night. She stood at the mike all pale and drawn."

During her first two breaks, Patsy had stomach cramps and spent a good deal of time in the restroom. When the pain became so bad she couldn't bear it, she asked Fay to get Elias Blanchfield, her former fiancé, to take her home. When Fay got to the apartment, Patsy had had a miscarriage.

"My God, Pat! You're still bleeding. I'm calling an ambulance."

"I'm all right now, but I thought I was going to die. The pain was so sharp, it felt like a knife was stuck in me! I'm okay. Take that worried look off your face. A couple of aspirin'll do the trick. I took care of everything. It was just a miscarriage. Now we know what the problem was."

"What's Gerald going to say? What's Bill going to say?"

"What they always say if they find out, which they ain't."

Patsy was back singing at the Lodge the following Saturday night, and, as far as Fay knew, no one ever spoke of the incident. Patsy was determined not to have any more accidents, as she put it, which may have caused the further disintegration of the Clines' marriage. Soon, Gerald was making no attempt to hide his many indiscretions.

☆

On August 7, Patsy was a contestant in the fourth annual National Championship Country Music Contest, an annual Jaycees (Junior Chamber of Commerce) fundraiser held at Warrenton, Virginia. It was sponsored by entrepreneur and broadcaster Connie B. Gay. Patsy won a hundred dollars as Best Female Vocalist and a weekday job at Gay's WMAL Radio in Washington doing commercial jingles. In addition, at Gay's WARL Arlington station, she was a fifty-dollar-a-day regular on the afternoon show "Town and Country Time," starring Jimmy Dean and his Texas Wildcats.

"When I met Patsy," Dean recalled, "I was working a D.C. club with Roy Clark. She came up packing a dress bag and said 'Hi, Mr. Dean. I'm Patsy Cline. I want to sing for you.' She had a great body, and I thought, 'If she can sing, too—great!' She went to change and came out in full western regalia. Roy looked at me and I looked at him. I thought, 'Holy cow.' I looked around and said, 'What the shit! Nothing but a bunch of drunks.' We moseyed to the piano, she sang and just knocked everybody's hat in the creek."

Under Gay's contract with the U.S. Army recruiting program, fifteen minutes of the daily radio show was transcribed on sixteen-inch long-playing acetate disks and sent to 1,800 stations. Though the recording was done in a small studio, there was an attempt to make the listener think an audience was present. In late September 1954, Dean introduced Patsy:

"Well, sir, it's guest time here on 'Town and Country Time.' And our guest is a mighty pretty girl that sings a real fine song. Here's a girl that's kinda just making a start here in country music. And sooner or later, I know that you're gonna hear a whole lot about a real fine young'un by the name of Patsy Cline. And we'd like to say hello to her. Patsy, how are you, honey?"

"Just fine, Jimmy."

"You're looking real good."

"Why thank you."

"Uh-hummmmmm," said one of the band members. "Mercy!"

"All the guys 'round here're standing, drooling down over the bibs of their overalls," cracked Dean. "As lazy Jim Day would say, 'My overalls drawed up till my feet wouldn't touch the ground for three days, by golly!' Patsy, what you gonna sing for the folks?"

"I'm gonna walk a li'l bit of dog!"

"That's fine!"

She was referring to the Cliff and Tex Grimsley tune, "I'm Walking the Dog," which began:

I'm a walking the dog and I'm never blue.
I'm walking that dog, I'm not thinking of you.
I don't need no one to tie me down
'Cause I'm walking that dog and painting the town . . .

Patsy wanted stardom. To achieve this, Bill advised, she needed to make records. As far back as the end of 1953, Bill began producing and circulating a number of demonstration tapes of Patsy's vocals. Nothing came of it until the day when Gay played one for a man with a spotted reputation, who nonetheless got things done.

William A. McCall, president of Pasadena, California–based Four-Star Records, crisscrossed the nation on talent-hunting expeditions. The tight artist rosters at the major labels made room for independents, some not always scrupulous.

McCall's biggest prize had been signing Jimmy Dean, who, at the first opportunity after a Four-Star hit, went with Columbia Records. McCall knew of Patsy from demos sent by Bill and her work for Gay. When Bill caught up with McCall in Washington, he told him he was missing "the opportunity of a lifetime" in not signing what was essentially a prize package: Patsy Cline and Bill Peer and the Melody Boys.

When McCall met Patsy, he definitely saw possibilities. Bill told him, "And she's a dream to work with." Almost three weeks after her twenty-second birthday, on September 30, 1954, with Bill as her manager and in the presence of Gerald, Patsy signed a two-year recording contract with Four-Star. They were so excited, they didn't bother to have a lawyer review the fine print.

It was probably the single biggest mistake Patsy made in her professional life.

"JUST OUT OF REACH"

PATSY CLINE: "It's Gerald! Quick, hide."
BILL PEER: "He couldn't have seen my car!"
GERALD CLINE: "Hi, honey! I'm home."

*I*n Nashville music annals, Bill McCall is an enigma. By those who found him less than honorable, he has been termed a "shrewd businessman who maintained the upper hand," "devious and cunning," and "a first-class son of a bitch" and "con artist." Jimmy Dean reminisced, "Bill was the craftiest operator I'd seen in my life. A Californian in the truest sense of the word—suave, delightful, and he could charm the pants right off your behind while he stabbed you in the back. Anyone who signed with him—writers, singers—he nailed to the wall. He was a shyster from the word go."

"There're two sides to every story," said songwriter Donn Hecht. "Bill was honest, hard-working, and there when you needed him."

Four-Star was basically a music publisher, but McCall signed artists, recorded them at their expense, then leased product to a major label, such as Decca.

Pioneer record producer Milt Gabler, for years A&R (Artists & Repertoire) chief at Decca, claimed McCall "operated just this side of the law. You didn't envy anyone who dealt with him."

Just about everyone considered McCall a nuisance, yet he made good economic sense. The label distributed his product and reaped nice commissions. "Nashville is full of Bill McCalls," Hecht said. "They're hard-driving, profit- and loss-minded executives who know how to recoup their investments. No one thinks of them as suspect. Writers, some desperate for money, went to McCall. He'd say name a price for the publishing rights, then he'd buy the song. He didn't twist any arms. When that song would become a hit, McCall was found guilty. He couldn't see into the future. A lot of what he bought didn't even make it to the bottom of the charts."

Patsy's contract was a standard American Federation of Musicians (AFM) form, specifying "a minimum of 16 (sixteen) 78 rpm record sides, or the equivalent thereof ... and additional recordings shall be made at our election. The musical compositions to be recorded shall be mutually agreed upon between you and us, and each recording shall be subject to our approval as satisfactory."

Her services would be exclusive with Four-Star for two years with a one-year renewal option. Any recordings made would remain the property of Four-Star. Patsy's royalty of 2.34 percent of the retail list price on records sold in the United States was about half the royalty paid to established stars. Session musicians would be paid within fourteen days of services and such payments, at scale, would be deducted from Patsy's royalties—the industry norm.

After the contract signing, McCall took Peer, Gerald, and Patsy for drinks and dinner. Years later, Patsy remarked, "McCall paid that night, but it ended up being on me. I paid for every goddamned thing from then on. I didn't know how much till it was too late."

Patsy went into the new phase of her career with guns blazing. Either on her own or with Bill in tow, she covered the region, going anywhere such stars as Ernest Tubb or Webb Pierce performed. Her reckoning was that she had to be seen and heard to advance her career.

Teddy Wilburn, just home from the Korean war, and his brother Doyle met Patsy when they were singers and musicians in Pierce's band and did the "Town and Country Time" show. "Patsy was someone we thought of as a fan rather than someone with star potential," Teddy noted. "She was well-meaning and you couldn't help but like her. She was a bit aggressive, but in a bubbly, exciting sort of way. She wasn't offensive. And she had quite a sense of humor. Musicians loved her. From how she talked of becoming a star, you might think she was putting you on.

"As it turned out, her talent was real. We hit it off. After that, if we were anywhere close, you could bet she'd show up to say hello, then ask if she could sing. We'd talk to Webb and get him to put her on. It was hard to say no. You could see how much it meant."

Bill had a better idea to bring Patsy stardom: a trip to New York. McCall urged Bill to assemble a more experienced, pop-oriented band for the trip. He set up a demo session with Decca Records' chief of country A&R, Paul Cohen. In addition to the Melody Boys, Bill added Gene Shiner, his brother-in-law who had the Metronomes; former Melody Boy Pete O'Brien who formed his own band; and Leo Miller, one of his musicians. Bill arranged for Patsy and the band to try out for CBS's half-hour, prime-time show "Arthur Godfrey's Talent Scouts," which introduced promising amateur artists.

Traveling in two cars, they arrived in New York in late November and checked into the Dixie Hotel (now the Carter) on West Forty-second Street in the heart of Times Square. Bill immediately took Patsy shopping for new dresses. According to Leo Miller, he spent more than eight hundred dollars. The audition, conducted by Janette Davis, a featured vocalist on the show and Godfrey's administrative right hand, took place on the sixteenth floor of the old CBS headquarters on Madison Avenue between Fifty-first and Fifty-second streets. Their big competition was a young girl dressed in petticoats and a white ruffled dress, who was a violin virtuoso playing on a prized Stradivarius.

"Miss Davis was polite," Shiner recalled, "but she wasn't too taken with the band. She told us she'd be happy to book Patsy, whom she felt transcended country and was more a blues singer. All Bill and Patsy knew and wanted was country music. We ultimately decided that if it had to be that way, then Patsy should accept. The reason for coming was to try to get the band and Patsy on the show, but we knew getting Patsy on was Bill's number-one goal. Patsy's dream was to become a star and here was her big chance. She completely stumped us. She told Miss Davis we were a package and it was 'all or nothing.' I thought Bill would kill her! But it was no deal and the girl with the violin went on that night and won."

Davis took Patsy and Bill aside and made a commitment that if ever Patsy wanted to come back and audition, she'd see to it. According to Shiner, Davis contacted Richard Lisell, who managed Teresa Brewer, and suggested he meet Patsy and the band. When they met at Lisell's East Side apartment, Roy Deyton remembered, Bill touted Patsy as "the second greatest singer in the whole U.S.A." It became clear Bill was pushing Patsy and not the entire package. To some of the band it seemed Lisell got the idea of prying Patsy away from Bill and signing her himself.

The band Bill put together was solid, and impressed everyone. Lisell quickly had them working—singing and playing, not pop, but country after all. It was a novelty in New York. In one night, the band managed one-hour sets at four clubs, including the famed Latin Quarter.

Peer and Lisell supervised Patsy and the band's taped demos at Decca's studios on West Fifty-seventh and Seventieth streets. There were two Four-Star songs, "Turn the Cards Slowly" and "Three Cigarettes (in an Ashtray)" plus "Crazy Arms" (later a hit for Ray Price)[1] and "This Ole House," which was a number one pop hit that summer for Rosemary Clooney.

The session went smoothly until they got to "This Ole House." Peer had his ideas, Patsy had hers, and Lisell had his. Shiner says there were twenty-seven takes before it proved acceptable to Lisell. Members of the band could now tell they were not being considered for a record deal. This was all for Patsy. They felt used, there were words, and Patsy and Lisell argued. When Patsy didn't show that night for a booking he had arranged, Lisell washed his hands of the whole affair.

McCall and Cohen were still in the picture. Cohen liked the band, and was prepared to offer them a year's contract, but it meant they'd have to stay in New York. Because of jobs and families, the musicians didn't pursue the deal.

Finally, after eleven days, it was time to head home. Patsy overslept, and, as everyone was anxious to leave, she packed quickly.

Patsy returned to Frederick and to Gerald and his early Christmas present—to himself—a sporty 1955 Buick Roadmaster. She took to wearing a flattering New York-style coiffure, pulling her hair up and over her head.

Besides the cowgirl outfits Mrs. Hensley made, Patsy now sported her New York "originals," the most glamorous being a "shocking" semi-strapless two-piece

---

1. Members of the band contend that when the first three songs were commercially released by Decca, it was with their instrumental backing, for which they were never officially paid.

black gown with silver highlights and a sequined bodice that she tied with a chiffon sash.

☆

The Saturday before Thanksgiving, as Patsy, Bill, and the band rehearsed, Mrs. Peer arrived and sat with Fay. Shortly after, a delivery arrived from the Dixie Hotel. It was a large box addressed to Mrs. Bill Peer. Jenny thought it was a surprise from Bill and hurried to open it.

"Why on earth is the hotel in New York sending me Patsy's coat?" she inquired.

She read the attached note: "Dear Mrs. Peer, we are happy to inform you that the coat you left behind in your room was turned over to this office by your maid. We are returning it herewith. Sorry if your oversight caused you any inconvenience. It was our pleasure to serve you. We hope you had a nice trip."

As Patsy told Del Wood later: "I looked at Bill, he looked at me and Jenny looked at both of us. The music stopped and you could hear a pin drop. Bill said, 'Oh, shit!' and almost did. Then all hell broke loose!"

Fay noted that thereafter the various goings-on in what she called the Brunswick Triangle slowed notably. Gerald suddenly started following Bill and Patsy everywhere they went. Jenny was always "dropping in" on rehearsals unexpectedly and staying all night at the dances. She never let them out of her sight. Yet Bill and Patsy found a way.

McCall contacted Cohen, who reviewed the tapes and saw Patsy's potential, not exclusively as a country singer. He felt that she had great pop potential. "Bill, I want to sign her," he said to McCall. "How much?"

"No," McCall told him. "What I'm offering is a leasing deal. I retain all artist and publishing rights."

Cohen was suspicious of such an arrangement and felt the stipulation that Patsy only record Four-Star songs would limit selectivity. In the end, he bought it. But he had one reservation about Patsy: "She's two handfuls. Can you control her?" McCall assured him, "Don't worry about her. I'll take care of her."

McCall advised Bill to whip Patsy and the band into shape. He sent new material, which, when sufficiently rehearsed, was tried out on the Saturday night Moose regulars. The first weekend in December a Fredericksburg, Virginia, radio station studio was booked for a demo session.

"It was the only facility with decent equipment," Roy Deyton explained. "Patsy, really primed for the occasion, recorded 'Honky Tonk Merry-Go-Round,' 'Hidin' Out,' 'A Church, a Courtroom and Then Goodbye' and 'Turn the Cards Slowly,' which we did in New York. The band was paid, but we really all pitched in to help Bill. It seemed he wouldn't rest until he made Patsy a star."

It was obvious that Bill's goals were not the same as those of the band members. The following Saturday at rehearsal, Patsy stopped the music and yelled, "Goddamn it! Can't you guys ever get the beat right? Bill, do something. They're awful."

Grover Shroyer, the drummer, expressed the general consensus, "That's right, Patsy, treat us like dirt. You got what you wanted. You don't need us anymore."

Before the dance, Patsy apologized and smoothed Shroyer's feathers, but it seemed that the fun was gone.

☆

Patsy's first Nashville session under the auspices of Paul Cohen and Bill McCall was scheduled for Wednesday, January 5, 1955. Cohen reviewed the tapes and was mesmerized by Patsy's voice, but he didn't know what to have her record. He consulted every artist on Decca from Webb Pierce to Ernest Tubb, except the Reigning Queen of Country Music, Kitty Wells, who was Patsy's chief rival.

Tubb asked, "Has Decca signed Patsy Cline?"

"No," Cohen replied. "We've got her under a Four-Star deal. E.T., do you know her?"

"Yeah, of course. From Bill Peer's band. Sweet little gal with a great big voice."

"E.T., that's the problem. I've hit a snag. Patsy's got the potential to have broader appeal than Kitty. I think she's got a pop sound. It's there. I just know it."

"Heck, Paul, if she's got a pop sound, why don't you get Owen Bradley to work with her?"

Bradley, who was in his late thirties, was at home in any music field. As a businessman—with ethics, yet—he became one of Music City's wealthiest, dabbling with brother Harold in real estate and recording studios while others chose song publishing.

As a producer, he was years ahead of his rivals. Bradley wasn't afraid to be innovative at a time when country had become static. (He was elected to the Country Music Hall of Fame in 1974.)

Downtown Nashville still had the Ryman, Tootsie's, Tubb's record store, and assorted taverns, but farther out toward the West End, what has come to be known as Music Row was taking shape. Some of its prime movers were the Bradleys, who in 1952 built a studio on Twenty-first Avenue South behind McClure's Department Store. In 1955, when Cohen considered moving recording operations to Dallas, where better technology was available, the Bradleys bought a house in the rundown neighborhood along Sixteenth Avenue South and installed a studio. They later added an adjacent metal Quonset hut (now part of Sony-Columbia) that was quickly dubbed Bradley's Barn.

On the main floor was a studio for filming such syndicated TV as "The Stars of the Grand Ole Opry" and the U.S. Army's "Country Style, U.S.A.," which pitched military recruitment. In the basement, the Bradleys created one of the most technically advanced recording studios in the region.

At that time, Bradley had no magic formula for Patsy's voice. As he noted later, even if he'd thought to record her pop, it wouldn't have been accepted. Whatever everyone's second thoughts about her voice, Patsy was being sent to Nashville to record, and that's where they did country. Tubb and Pierce were called in to review the song choices McCall sent. Tubb recalled, "Webb and I sat down with Paul and those Four-Star folk and picked out the best four songs they had to offer. Webb didn't think any of them approached what he could write."

After ringing in the New Year at the Moose Lodge with their respective mates and revelers, Patsy and Bill left Sunday, January 2, for Nashville. It was their first plane ride. Gerald claims he was also along on the trip, acting as official chaperon. Bill was terrified of flying and held on to the armrests, his face pale. He told Patsy, "I'm so nervous, I'm about to wet my pants!"

She pulled out a flask and said, "No problem. Have a couple of swigs. It'll do the trick."

"You know I don't drink."

"Hoss, there's a first time for everything."

"And this is it!"

It didn't take long for Patsy and Bill to be sailing through the friendly skies. She even offered to help the crew with their duties.

Bill later told Roy Deyton that as the plane approached Nashville, the stewardess came on the speaker.

"Ladies and gentlemen, the captain has lighted the fasten seat belt sign."

Suddenly Patsy jumped into the aisle, straddled her legs across it and yelled, "All right, ladies, you don't want to ignore the captain. Fasten your sanitary belts!"

At first there was shocked silence, then everyone broke out laughing.

"Madam," the stewardess began.

"Hey, watch what you call me!"

"Please take your seat. Where are you going?"

"To help the captain fly this thing!"

Bill grabbed Patsy and pulled her back into her seat.

Bill's hope that the previous sessions would yield a "package deal" for Patsy, himself, and the band was dashed. The tapes weren't country enough and proved unacceptable. Cohen informed Peer they would use studio musicians, "the best money can buy." According to Deyton, Bill didn't understand that to mean it would be his money.

Wednesday morning, as he waited in Bradley's studio for the session to begin, Bradley approached Bill and asked, "Hey, Bill, who's going to make the financial arrangements for this? We have to pay the musicians."

He replied, "According to Patsy's contract, McCall pays."

"Well, Four-Star has made no arrangements with us. What are we going to do?"

"Call McCall!"

Bradley took the responsibility of making the call. McCall told him he was in no position to pay session costs. "Bill says you'll have to lay the money out," Bradley repeated.

Frantically grabbing the phone from Bradley, Bill asked, "What the hell's going on? If I'd known this, we could've stayed home. You're trying to screw us!"

"Calm down, Bill," McCall told him. "Lay the money out and I'll reimburse you within two weeks."

Bill conferred with Patsy, who said, "If you've got the money and he says he'll pay you back, let's do it, as long as we're here."

As a result of his mother's death, Bill had come into a sizable inheritance, which he was using to bankroll Patsy's career. It's said he pulled out a roll of hundred-dollar bills and paid Bradley fifteen hundred, adding, "Don't forget my receipt!"

Deyton said, "I knew someone would take a shellacking, and it was Bill. Patsy didn't have it at the time, but he told me she never made an attempt to pay him back. There's no fool like a fool in love!"

Bradley wasn't looking forward to meeting Patsy. Cohen told him Patsy had a mind of her own, which no producer likes to hear. And McCall warned that Patsy "was mean as hell and hard to get along with."

"I expected the worst," Bradley said. "I figured Patsy would tongue-lash me, then beat me to death. She was exactly the opposite. In fact, she didn't open her mouth. If I told her to do something, she did it."

Patsy recorded "I Don't Wanta," written by D. Haddock, W. S. Stevenson, and Eddie Miller, who had the 1954 hit "Release Me" and a long association with Patsy; Miller's "I Love You, Honey," a funny, bouncy standout, which he claimed to have written at fourteen; and Tubb's favorite, "I Cried All the Way to the Altar," a weeper that told a marvelously concise story, showcased Patsy's natural voice and her hiccup growl, or yodel, as she called it, on the high notes; and "Come On In," in its original length a gospel song and later Patsy's opening number for live engagements.

Even with Bradley producing, Cohen was unhappy with the cuts and shelved them. "I Love You, Honey" and "Come On In" came out in February 1956 as a back-to-back single.

W. S., for William Shakespeare, Stevenson (after Robert Louis Stevenson) was none other than Bill McCall. It was the pseudonym he affixed to hundreds of songs in Four-Star's massive catalog. McCall, who couldn't read music, usually found a way to make some type of lyrical contribution on material from writers who had no power base.

Patsy, Bill, and Gerald left for home immediately after the session. Now it was a matter of waiting. Patsy walked on air. She told everyone, "I'm beginning to realize my dreams! I've been taking it one step at a time and it's finally going to happen."

Winchester's big event, held the last weekend of April or the first weekend of May, is the Apple Blossom Festival, which is kicked off by two huge parades of dignitaries, celebrities, bands, cavalry, and floats. Patsy and Bill and the Melody Boys, popular throughout the area, were invited to participate in the Grand Feature Parade (as opposed to the Fireman's Parade).

Bill secured a handsome 1955 black Cadillac convertible that was decorated with crepe paper streamers, music notes, and a horseshoe for the front of the hood. Patsy and the musicians, in their finest western costume, sat on the rear of the car and its seats, waving. The crowd, well-dressed adults and children holding balloons three and four abreast on the sidewalks of the parade route, didn't seem that impressed. As Mrs. Hensley has pointed out, everyone in Winchester was used to seeing Patsy Cline.

Paul Cohen, increasingly frustrated at not finding the right material for his singer, scheduled another session with Owen Bradley for June 1.

Bob Gaines of Winchester's G&H Music Store related that, to prepare for the second session, Patsy came to the shop several times a week to practice. She would ask questions about recording techniques and go into a booth to make a record, listen to the playback, and record the song again until she got it the way she wanted.

The June 1 Nashville session was made up of songs Patsy first did in the Fredericksburg, Virginia, radio station demo. McCall sent a Four-Star pitch letter to disc jockeys. It read: "We think Patsy Cline sings better than any female vocalist we have heard. Her diction, sense of timing, and phrasings are exceptionally good. We hope that you will agree with us and will give her first record a chance to be heard."

On July 20 a single of "A Church, a Courtroom and Then Goodbye" and "Honky Tonk Merry-Go-Round" and her first Extended Play 45, *Songs by Patsy Cline*, with "Turn the Cards Slowly" and "Hidin' Out" added, were released.

"Patsy was exceptional," Owen Bradley said. "Paul Cohen would say again and again, 'Owen, she's got it. She's special. We're going to hit it. It may take some time, but we'll do it. All we need is the right combination.' That was the hardest thing. We were limited in what Patsy could record."

It's ironic that the songs Patsy recorded usually reflected what was happening in her life at that very moment.

A CHURCH, A COURTROOM AND THEN GOODBYE

by Eddie Miller and W. S. Stevenson (© 1955 Four-Star Music Company; copyright renewed by Acuff-Rose Music, Inc.; all rights reserved; used by permission)

The first scene was the church,
Then the altar
Where we claimed each other;
With tears of joy we cried.
Our friends wished us luck there forever,
As we walked from the church
Side by side.

My next scene was a crowded courtroom,
And like strangers we sat side by side.
Then I heard the judge make his decision,
And no longer were we man and wife.

I hate the sight of that courtroom,
Where man-made laws pushed God's laws aside.
Then the clerk wrote our story in the record,
A church, a courtroom and then goodbye.

We walked from that courtroom together,
We shook hands and once again we cried.
Then it was the end of our story,
A church, a courtroom and then goodbye.

HONKY TONK MERRY-GO-ROUND

I'm on a honky tonk merry-go-round,
Making every spot in town;
Starting out early, coming home late,
Every night I'm with a brand new date.

I'm on a honky tonk merry-go-round,
Acting like a foolish clown;
Still racing those blues that they leave with me,
A wondering if I'll ever be free.

'Round and 'round and 'round I go,
Riding high and feeling low;
'Round and 'round just like a top,
Well, I'm a-getting dizzy but I can't stop.

I'm on a honky tonk merry-go-round
Acting like a foolish clown;
Still racing those blues that men leave with me,
Wondering if I'll ever be free.
Yes, I'm wondering if I'll ever be free.

Patsy and Bill were missing from the Moose Lodge the weekend of June 24. They returned to Nashville, taking advance copies of her record to as many music people as possible—Ferlin Husky, Faron Young, Porter Wagoner, and Eddy Arnold. On June 26, in Nashville's Centennial Park, Patsy was a special guest star of Ernest Tubb and his Texas Troubadours, featuring Tommy Jackson on fiddle. She performed for a crowd estimated at better than fifteen thousand. *Billboard* listed her as Patsy Kline.

Fay and Harry Crutchley, Elias Blanchfield, and his fiancée Frances Null, Fay's sister, joined "the Peers" on July 1 at the Drake Hotel Courts on Murfreesboro Road. After supper, they went to the Ryman Auditorium, where Patsy joined up with her discoverer and mentor Wally Fowler. She was a guest on his All-Night Gospel Sing broadcast from the hall, singing "Just a Closer Walk with Thee."

"It was quite a thrill," Fay remembered. "Bill drove us by Bradley's studio, took us sightseeing, and then, like bigshots, we just pulled up to the backstage entrance and were waved right on in by the security guard. If that wasn't enough, we were back the next night for the Opry and Pat's first time singing on it. It seemed almost everyone knew Bill. He said he was Pat's manager and he introduced her to nearly everybody. We mingled with the stars and took loads of pictures."

Ernest Tubb hosted the Ralston-Purina portion of the Opry. He brought Patsy on with a flourish: "Here's a little lady with a powerful voice. I've been predicting big things for her. Make welcome Coral Records'[2] newest star, singing her debut recording, 'A Church, a Courtroom and Then Goodbye.'"

---

2. Coral was to be the company's country label.

When he commented he'd never seen Patsy nervous, she told Tubb about her Opry audition when she was sixteen and how she was snubbed. This would be her revenge. Alas, there wasn't much response even when Tubb rushed onstage to pump the audience for more applause. He put his arm around her, leaned into the microphone and declared loudly: "Folks, Miss Patsy Cline. Isn't she terrific!" As she went to walk off, he called her back. "Patsy, honey, take another bow."

Crying, Patsy ran off into Bill's arms. "Oh, Bill, how can I thank you? I don't care what they think. Appearing on the Opry's my biggest dream come true! You made me the happiest woman in the world."

"You were in fine voice," Tubb assured her. "It was that damn song. It would bring a pall over an Irish wake." And this was the very tune he had recommended.

Tubb's manager, Gabe Tucker, told him, "E. T., we've found us a female Red Foley. She sounds like nobody'll believe. Everybody's talking about her voice." Tucker cornered the Opry general manager and told him how impressed he was. Denny, perhaps not remembering how he had once snubbed Patsy and her mother, replied, "Then maybe you ought to sign her."

After a stop at Tootsie's to see and be seen, Patsy and Bill went to Tubb's music store to do the "Mid-Nite Jamboree," where Tucker spoke at length about her career. He arranged for her to sing with Tubb the next day, and after the broadcast had Patsy go in an audition booth and record several acetates singing a cappella.

He played the acetates for Tubb. "Good God, Gabe, you're right. That gal can reach out and get it. This stuff's better than what she's recorded."

"E. T., I'd love to manage Patsy, but I can't talk to her without that guy butting in."

"That guy is already her manager and a lot more. Leave it alone for now."

"She's saying how low on money they are."

"Can you do anything?"

"She's going to sing with us tomorrow and I'll see if I can get her on at the cave in the afternoon. Told her it would only be fifty dollars, but they were agreeable."

"When you ain't got it, fifty's agreeable."

Tucker called Claude "Spot" Acuff, who ran his brother Roy Acuff's Dunbar Cave Resort near Clarksville, at the Tennessee-Kentucky border, which was once a Big Band mecca for the GIs at Fort Campbell, and said, "There's a girl here—"

"You don't say. Is she pretty?"

"Yes, sir."

"Is she good?"

"Goddamn right, she's good! And she needs money."

"If she's good 'n' pretty 'n' needs money, I'll put her on the afternoon show. Will that do?"

"It's all taken care of."

"Then why the hell did you call?"

On Sunday, Patsy and Bill drove forty-two miles northwest to Dunbar Cave, where Patsy did a whole set.

Tubb explained, "It was near impossible not to adore Patsy—or resist her charms. That gal was dedicated. She had a good voice and was trying so hard to make it. She knew exactly how to get to me! Years before, Patsy had started coming around to where I was playing and flattering one of my musicians till they introduced her to me. Then she'd ask me to let her sing a song."

On Monday, the Fourth, after their friends left Nashville for home, Bill and Patsy happened to be passing through Memphis. She "dropped in" on Tubb and Faron Young at the ballpark, where the temperature was over a hundred degrees.

"Faron asked, 'You know who's here?' and I turned and there she was," Tubb said. "I told her, 'Patsy, honey, I didn't know you was coming.' She said she wanted to go on the road with me. I replied we didn't have room in the cars. She started bawling so bad none of us knew what to do. 'It's just I been having a real hard time, but it don't matter, Mr. Tubb. Only if I could just sing one song. I'll even do it free, for the exposure.' Finally, I said okay. Patsy wiped her eyes and waited on pins and needles to go out on that stage. I gave her a big introduction. There must have been fourteen thousand people, and they loved her. Afterwards, she hugged and thanked me and they were on their way."

A day after their return, Gerald was at work and Bill and Patsy spent a lazy afternoon together. Bill didn't park on Patrick Avenue but in the lot of a five-and-dime store temporarily located down the street at the fairgrounds. He'd stand on the corner to await Patsy's signal that the coast was clear, then hurry across to the apartment. He and Patsy were in the throes of passion when she heard a car door slam.

"Holy shit!" she screamed. "It's Gerald! Quick, hide."

"What? He couldn't have seen my car."

As Gerald began his ascent up the shaky flight of stairs, Bill ran into a closet. Patsy thought better and hid him under the bed.

"As soon as he comes in," she whispered, "he'll head to the refrigerator for a beer. Then you get the hell outa here!"

"Surprise!" Gerald proclaimed. "Hi, honey! I'm home."

"Hi," replied Patsy, unnerved.

Gerald looked around.

"What you looking for, Gerald?"

"Nothing." Under the bed he saw movement and went to sit on it.

"There's cold beer in the fridge."

"Thanks. Want to get me one?"

"Why don't you get it yourself?"

"Naw. I'll just sit till I cool off." He flopped down on the bed. "Oh, by the way, driving around town last night, guess who I spotted in Bill's car?"

"I give up."

"You—"

"You must be seeing things. I was at Fay's."

"You really must think I'm an idiot! Up to your old tricks, huh?"

"Talk's cheap!"

"You think about that while I rest awhile."

As Patsy watched nervously, Bill sweated. Gerald lay back and finally dozed off. Patsy signaled Bill frantically, who crawled out from under the bed slowly and tiptoed to the door. "I ran down the stairs like a bat out of hell!" he told one of his Melody Boys. His movement on the creaky stairs woke Gerald.

"What was that?" But he drifted back to sleep.

☆

The next weekend at the Lodge, Bill and Patsy performed. However, something was different. They weren't smiling and stayed apart. Two days earlier, Bill's wife Jenny sprung quite a welcome-home surprise. He'd made her the laughingstock of the area for the last time. She filed for divorce on the grounds of adultery.

"A Church, a Courtroom and Then Goodbye" received little public response, even from the Brunswick Moose regulars, but on that point no explanation is necessary.

"AIN'T NO WHEELS ON THIS SHIP"

☆

PATSY CLINE: "I'm going to light a fire under your
  goddamn ass."
GEORGE HAMILTON IV: "Yes, ma'am."
PATSY CLINE: "You walk out there like you're
  embarrassed. You ashamed to be singing with us?"
GEORGE HAMILTON IV: "No, ma'am."

S ome people might get the idea our tri-state area is a Peyton Place within a
  Peyton Place," Fay Crutchley said, laughing. "And they'd be about right."
  "You could say we were a friendly area," Lois Troxell commented. "If you
made the circuit of Moose Lodge dances, you'd see couples from throughout the
area, happily dancing and enjoying themselves. You'd think they had ideal marriages. Before you knew it, they'd be divorced and remarried to each other or
friends' spouses. Sometimes, it was astonishing to me what went on when good
friends got together. First, it was a few drinks, then dancing and one thing led to
another."
  Because of some of her escapades, Fay explained, "Pat had a reputation for
being a bit loose, but what she was doing was going on all over the place. To my
knowledge, the Moose wives didn't consider Pat a threat and weren't hostile to her."
  Mrs. Peer filed her action July 11, 1955, in Jefferson County Chancellory Court,
Charles Town, West Virginia. A date of September 22 was set to hear *Virginia M.
Peer* v. *William Peer*. Divorces and spouse swapping was so commonplace, Jenny's
action hardly caused a stir except to those intimately affected.
  "It wasn't all Patsy's fault," Jenny observed. "Bill was older; she was only

twenty-two. He was persistent and insistent. I blame him as much as her. I knew what was going on but didn't have solid evidence. They never told the truth. I didn't even know about them going to Nashville alone. I was terribly hurt by it all. From the way they carried on, I felt sure Bill would marry Patsy as soon as the decree was final."

Gerald was the winner by default. Once again he was squiring Patsy around and, according to Doris Fritts, "They seemed as happy and in love as two peas in a pod. Patsy would show off the wallet-size wedding photo of them on the steps of the Frederick Reformed Church. But, since gossip spread like wildfire, everyone knew the truth."

However, when Gerald passed the five-and-dime, Bill's car was nowhere to be seen.

"Before the divorce," Lois Troxell reported, "Patsy and Gerald would be separated one month and she'd be either living at her mother's or staying with my family and me. We lived next door to Gerald's parents on Patrick Street. She didn't have a car, so Doris Fritts and I took turns chauffering her back and forth to work in Washington."

"And," Fay noted, "Pat was dating Bill—until the next month when she'd be back with Gerald. You needed a score card. One month they—Pat and Bill—were hot; a month later, they weren't. One month they—Pat and Gerald—were on; a month later, they weren't. When Pat told me she was going home, I never knew just where she meant. Sometimes when Pat would tell me what was going on, my head would spin. I said, 'You're always talking about your career but all I hear are hims, hims, hims and this ain't church. If you want to get ahead, put men on the back burner.'"

Jenny's words returned to haunt Bill after the divorce, when he intensified his efforts to marry Patsy. "You know I love you," Patsy would say, "but it'll take some time." He kept after her to divorce Gerald, but she put him off. In spite of the precarious financial situation brought on by his divorce costs, Bill lavished Patsy with gifts.

Melody Boy John Anderson (he became vocalist and electric bass guitarist when band member Mark Johnson quit to marry Jenny Peer as soon as the decree was final) remembered that Bill "finagled a deal where he worked, Goode Motor Company in Charles Town, to get Patsy a new Buick. Band members John Neal, Gene Shiner, and me helped her break it in on a trip to Rhinehold, outside Philadelphia, where we backed Patsy in her appearance at the county fair."

Enjoying the big-city whirl of D.C. and playing the field, Patsy, now appearing with Jimmy Dean on the local weekday "Town and Country Time," quickly cooled on Bill.

On October 15, Patsy and the band played for the opening of a Chevrolet dealership in Martinsburg, West Virginia. On the way to the Moose Lodge, Patsy announced she was leaving the band. That night, she took close friend Roy Deyton aside and told him, "Once I helped you make up your mind about getting married. You were torn between your girlfriend and going [with brother Ray] to Nashville for a career. Remember you told me she made you happier than your music. It's different with me. Ain't nothing I love more than my music, so it's time I moved on. Staying here ain't going to help matters any or my career."

"I didn't like what Patsy did," Deyton explained, "but maybe he asked for it. Poor Bill. It wasn't the type of thing you wanted to see."

Peer went off the deep end and came close to having a nervous breakdown. He couldn't sing without getting upset. He'd moan and groan about how Patsy had dumped him. One night, Anderson found him on the floor crying. At a restaurant after one of the dances, he broke down.

"Where's Patsy? She didn't show tonight and that's not like her."

"Bill, Patsy's not with the band anymore," Deyton said.

"Why's Patsy doing me this way?" he sobbed. "Why's she treating me so damn mean and cold? Don't she see I gave up my wife for her? Don't she even care?"

Grover Shroyer exhorted, "Bill, you can't let Patsy get to you like this. You're going to destroy yourself. We're going to have to take you to the hospital."

But he just sat there with his head down, bobbing and shaking. "You'll make yourself awfully sick, Bill," Deyton advised. "You've got to stop carrying on like this."

Bill didn't hear a word. He had the lovesick blues.

Gerald Cline pointed out that Patsy's popularity was a double-edged sword in their marriage. "When I could, I took Patsy to her one-nighters and stayed to bring her home. Everywhere she'd sing, people would come up to me and say, 'Hey, you've got some wife! We've never heard anybody like her.' They were right. Patsy was unique. None of her records had made it, but, live and in person, no one came close to touching her.

"I had to get up early for work, so I couldn't always go on the Jamboree one-nighters. It eventually got to the point where when she was home, I'd be working. She'd either be sleeping or rehearsing. When I was home, she'd be working the show, on the road with Jimmy or doing band dates.

"Before too long, there wasn't much of a marriage. Patsy wanted to have her cake and eat it, too. She was all for Patsy. It was all for one and one for *one*. She couldn't bend. She wasn't flexible. It was her way or not at all. And that wasn't fair to me. For a long time, I tried but I got nothing in return."

Patsy told Fay, "In the beginning Gerald and I had a good marriage, as marriages go. My problem was that I don't think I knew what love was."

The couple moved from Patrick Street into a mobile home in Dutrow's Trailer Park on Bowers Road in Frederick. Though Gerald claims he and Patsy lived together until the end of March 1957, Patsy's friends note he was out of the picture, except for appearances' sake, by as early as 1956.

"Although they lived in the same house," Lois Troxell observed, "they weren't getting along worth a plug nickel. Gerald didn't understand Patsy's unrelenting drive to sing, sing, sing. Things got worse when Gerald, thinking it might bring he and Patsy closer, decided they'd live with his folks. But the two Mrs. Clines clashed. Patsy was a free spirit and only the devil could get along with Lettie.

"Patsy had her goal to go up, up, up but she felt Gerald was holding her down. She was so mixed up. Patsy wasn't in love with Gerald and wished she wasn't married. If love is blind, marriage is an eye-opener."

In a matter of weeks, Patsy and Gerald separated unofficially. She was commuting between her mother's house and the Troxell home in Brunswick. Patsy maintained a good relationship with Earl Cline but Gerald's mother snubbed her terribly and was quite mean on several occasions.

Washington, D.C., had become as big a country music entity as Nashville, minus the recording industry, and Jimmy Dean was the big cheese. He was as popular as anyone at that time. But it was Connie B. Gay's empire.

Town and Country Time became a lucrative service mark for Gay, "the country bumpkin from Lizard Lick," North Carolina, who had a shrewd eye for talent and was an innovator in the use of television to sell country music. (Founding president of the Country Music Association, he was elected to the Country Music Hall of Fame in 1980.) In addition to the afternoon radio and TV series on D.C.'s WMAL (now WJLA) headlining Dean and army transcriptions of the radio series, Gay produced a Town and Country Barn Dance, Town and Country Time live shows, and "Town and Country Jamboree," America's first live, late-night television musical variety show. Sponsored by Gunther Beer, Briggs Hot Dogs and Ice Cream, L&M Cigarettes, and the Otha Williams Buick dealership, "Jamboree" was on the Town and Country Network, a lineup of capital, Virginia, and Maryland stations airing Saturdays from 10:00 P.M. to 1:00 A.M. With fifteen thousand music lovers at the Capitol Arena, it was the place to be for a good time. There were stars galore and lots of singles, so it was an instant hit with the masses.

Patsy was added to the television shows in October 1955, as she was distancing herself from Bill Peer. For her radio work, she received scale. "It was sixty dollars and eighteen cents a week, double for TV," Gay explained. "Jimmy made twice as much. But I paid the regulars on both shows an average of fifty dollars a day for a six-day week."

"Connie B. Gay, Mr. Generosity himself!" asserted Dean. "Don't be fooled! After a USO tour and a radio show I did for Connie in Silver Spring, Maryland, I went to work for him at WARL. Sy Bloomenthal, who owned the station then, tried to put me wise to Connie. He pulled me aside and advised, 'Jimmy, watch out for him!' But did I listen? No! I thought of Connie as a father, but look what he did. When we did the radio transcriptions, we were led to believe nobody was making any money. It was suggested we should do the show as a public service. Connie only paid us scale. What we didn't know was that Connie and this army major had the whole thing figured out. We did the work, they got the money.

"Connie had us working like slaves—doing this show, doing that show. Plus we were trooping everywhere on the live package shows. Before you knew it, it all started to run together in your mind. He had all these artists from the Opry stopping by to do the army transcriptions and I thought, 'Ah, great. How patriotic.' Then I found out what they got paid.

"Television was still a novelty. We were greenhorns. It amazed me how we came off so good 'cause it was a gigantic mess. I'd get the gang together and we'd fill in the tunes to the allotted time. I'd ask Patsy, 'What you gonna sing, doll?' She'd tell me and I'd say, 'Great. What key you gonna do it in?' She'd reply, 'Hell, I don't know,' so I'd jump in with the guys and say, 'Okay, let's try this one. You know all the words? ... Good ... Sounds like it might be conducive to have a fiddle kick in. Hey, pardner, you wanna try that? You missed a chord. That goes *kerchunk*. *Kerchunk*, got it? Let's run it down again and use a diminished chord.' That's the way we did it till we got it right. No choreographer. No arranger. Just the bands, and we used head arrangements."

Audiences were diversified: politicians in limousines, hillbillies in pickup trucks, young hipsters in Corvettes. Local bands appeared alongside Grand Ole Opry stars and name recording artists. Any musician working the area would come to the arena at midnight when the bars closed. The regular cast included Roy Clark on banjo; Quincy Snodgrass, bass and rube comedy; Mary Klick, rhythm guitar/bass and vocals; Buck Ryan, fiddle; Dale Turner, vocals; Marvin Carroll, steel guitar; Alec Houston, ventriloquist; Billy Grammer, guitarist; Herbie Jones, rhythm guitar; George Hamilton IV, vocals; and Patsy.

"We had Tiny Jenkins, a huge guy who always smelled bad," Dean recollected, "and, oh, my God, Texas Jim Robertson, a fine singer who wore cowboy outfits topped by this big ole white Stetson. Under that hat was a real bad rug, in a pompadour style yet. He'd come to the mike and cock the hat back of that pompadour and just sing away. But it was hot in the arena. We used three cameras and many more lights than today. Jim used to sweat down two, maybe three outfits a night. Once, his sweat melted the stickum on his rug and everything started to go. He was singing and at the same time trying to give it a shot to get it all back in place. The more he tried, the worse it came down. I went into a tailspin of shock. Ah, live TV. I took a flying leap to the [video] truck in the street and shouted 'Shoot the crowd! Shoot the crowd, damnit! Whatever you do, stay off Jim.'

"But, oh, those were good times! There musta been twenty dozen cups of coffee on that stage if there was one. A cup of coffee could be all the way across the stage and it would somehow work its way over to get spilled on me. By the end, I was a big stain. I had it spilled on my sleeves, pockets, pants, even on my crotch. There I was playing the piano and smiling into the camera. Some folks might have wondered what I had to be smiling about."

Patsy Cline? "She was something else, cocky as hell about her ability. She knew she could sing and enjoyed listening to herself. Patsy was brash to the point where, if you didn't know her, you'd say she was arrogant. You'd not construe Patsy to be a polished lady 'cause she had a mouth on her that'd embarrass a truck driver." Few of the Jamboree regulars knew she was married. "Patsy didn't go on about what a wonderful guy she was married to. Gerald came around occasionally on the package shows. I just remember he was short and heavyset."

"Patsy flirted with anything in pants," said a band member. "Sometimes you had to pull her off you. She flirted with one musician incessantly and finally decided she was going to have him. He talked about how she was in bed for days, until one of us had to shut him up. He said after they finished, Patsy looked him straight in the eyes and asked, 'Now, Hoss, wasn't that the best fuck you ever had!' He couldn't get over the way she visualized it as something you should get a testimonial about."

Others cite her talent and self-possession. Teddy Wilburn said, "Doyle and I were with Webb's band playing the home furnishings show. When we finished, we hightailed it to the 'Jamboree,' the only live place in town after everything else closed. Patsy, dressed in one of her cowgirl outfits her mother made, slapped me on the back. She said, 'Hoss, I'm on my way. I'm making records. I'm going to do one of my songs now, so let me know what you think.' I was amazed at how relaxed she was and her natural rapport with the audience. That night we talked. We had a few drinks and things got looser and looser. By the time we parted, we'd become best buddies and it was that way until she died."

George Hamilton IV, at nineteen "a bit wide-eyed and bushy-tailed," wasn't prepared for the woman he met when he joined the "Jamboree" in 1956. "Patsy came on strong and I said, 'Who's this woman?' Having just completed my freshman year at the University of North Carolina at Chapel Hill, I was confronted by words I'd never heard. Patsy shocked me, which was what she set out to do. She talked tough and was. She was putting me to the Patsy Cline Worthy-of-My-Friendship Test. I must have failed I don't know how many times before I passed.

"I was six foot to her five feet four inches, but Patsy had an overpowering presence in her cowgirl outfits. She was bemused by me, this lanky kid from the sticks. Patsy liked people to stand up to her, and I never did. I was the youngest of the group and she kind of tolerated me. I was bashful and wet behind the ears, yet she took great delight in embarrassing me. But she never put me down or poked fun at me to the point of hurting me in front of others. In private, it was another thing. She'd find me backstage—usually hiding from her—and hit me across the back and go to town."

Patsy sternly admonished Hamilton. "Hoss, I'm going to have to light a fire under your goddamn ass. You're going to have to learn to go out there in front of those cameras and hold your head up. Take charge when you're singing!"

"Yes, ma'am."

"You say the only thing in life you want is to be a country singer and then you walk out there like you're embarrassed to be on that stage. Are you ashamed to be singing with us, Chief?"

"No, ma'am."

"What kind of singer are you, anyway, college boy? You ain't going nowhere with that kind of attitude. You don't learn everything from books, you know. If you're trying to be humble, goddamnit, that's not humility. That's weakness. Let me tell you something, you got to get up there and show 'em! You want 'em to eat right out of your hands. You're the star. When you're doing your songs, take command, Hoss!"

It was good advice. In the end, Patsy helped Hamilton and they became friends.

"Everyone eventually saw Patsy's crass exterior," Dean said, "but it concealed a warm heart. If she was your friend, you didn't have a worry in the world. She'd go to the wall for you.

"Patsy wasn't a great showman, though she had a fantastic personality. She couldn't talk. But she could sing! She really ripped up a lyric. Patsy sang her butt off. She was a huge fan of Kay Starr's and had a lot of her style.

"All Patsy could think of was getting away from Winchester and making it big—getting away from anything that might hold her back. She knew she was good. You betcha! She was gonna make it and that was that. Nothing could have stood in the way. Nothing! In Patsy's mind, there was no price too big to pay for it. I don't know if I ever saw anyone that wanted stardom more. Maybe Dottie West. Dottie was that way.

"There was little I could find wrong with Patsy. She had two things that, if you're going to be associated with me, you must have: punctuality and professionalism. Patsy laughed a lot and had a good time. That was important to me, too. But when it came to career time, no one could have been more deadly serious or deliver the goods the way she did.

"A lot of guys thought she was the sexiest thing they'd ever seen. I could never see it. We were in our twenties and at our peaks, but Patsy was totally devoid of sex appeal. Still I loved her to death. There was just no physical attraction. We became the closest of friends. I was already married, so she didn't have an affair with me. I might have been one of the few. I'm not easily shocked, but Patsy got to me one time. We were working in Canada and checking into a hotel. She looked around the lobby and saw this big Canadian Mountie. Right out loud she snapped, 'He's a big, good-looking son of a bitch! I want him! I'm screwing the boots off him tonight.' And she took off across to him and did what she said she was going to do."

Lois Troxell, who was especially close to Patsy during this period, explained, "Patsy's truck-driver mouth was a way of venting her anger and hostility. She was always hurting and at odds about what direction she should go in. There was something very sad about her. Patsy came from what we'd now call a dysfunctional family. She needed real friends. I found her to be sincere, gentle, and warm. She was aware of what a wonderful gift God gave her. I got the biggest kick out of her sitting in our living room and playing the piano and singing. I was in awe of her voice."

Dale Turner first saw Patsy when she sang at a D.C. club where Dale worked. "I saw this girl in a big, white western hat, red cowgirl outfit with white fringe and white boots. As soon as I heard her name, I realized I'd heard people speak of her. Patsy sang and at the end, she whipped off that hat and held it up in the air. I said, 'You can learn from this gal.'

"When I came to work on the 'Jamboree,' I thought I'd be the only girl singer. And there was Patsy and I sighed, 'This is really all you need!' But we became friends. Patsy not only wanted records, she wanted hit records. Everything revolved around her career. It was that way with most of the cast. They got married and had children but music was more than a livelihood. It was their world. To me, it was like being part of a family and getting paid to do what I liked doing best.

"I had six months' experience when I came on. Patsy was determined I'd become a star. She'd point out my bad habits: 'Dale, when you sing, you keep your right hand moving in time. You look like you're beating eggs. Keep that hand still or I'll come out and tie it behind your back.' Patsy had the tools and knew how to use them. I never liked camera work. I was fine just singing. Connie used two cameras, high up on dollies. I saw them moving up and down, back and forth, but they were far enough away not to scare me. There was little time for rehearsal. Jimmy could talk off the cuff for three hours, always knew the next cue and where to be. Audiences loved him. If he thought of something, he just sent you out to do it. I wasn't good at the ad-lib stuff. The commercials were the worst part. I had to do the jingles for Gunther's Beer or the cigarette commercial. They never let me forget the time I had the L&M box upside down.

"Patsy had a determination and power that made her shine. Everything was so effortless. When you saw her once, you knew she'd be a star. I've never known a singer as amazing and exciting. I'd watch her and say, 'She's giving it her all.' But she always held something back. You knew it when she got to the last note."

When Patsy wasn't performing, she ran around in her fringed or sequined cowgirl outfits causing mischief. When she wasn't telling somebody off, she was driving the stars crazy for pictures and autographs. She'd do anything to avoid the square dances with audience members that followed the show.

Dale toed the line. If Gay and Dean said to do something and the others balked, she'd say, "Connie says we have to" or "Jimmy told me to do this."

"If Connie says jump off the goddamn roof," Patsy would reply, "you going to jump?"

Though Dale doesn't remember Patsy telling dirty jokes, several cast members recall her cringing at Patsy's language, which made it all the more fun for Patsy. If Patsy was telling one of her risqué jokes to the guys and saw Dale coming, Patsy yelled, "Well, hush my mouth, here she comes. Hello, Your Highness!" As Dale walked by, everyone laughed, including Dale.

Patsy and Jimmy often thought Dale was praying for them. At particularly rough moments in the run-throughs or the show, Dean would look at Dale and, if he thought she was praying, he'd say, "Honey, please stop praying. Everything's going badly enough. I don't want you to make it worse." Then Patsy would yell, "Dale, promise me you ain't praying for me!"

Bill was back with Patsy, but, according to Peer's son Larry, solely on a professional basis as manager or adviser. As Jenny Peer explained, "Bill wasn't so much bitter about what Patsy did as he was hurt. He and I became friends again. I loved Bill and had two children with him. (After her divorce from Mark Johnson, they remarried.) I thought he'd straighten up with Patsy out of his life, but he didn't."

"Bill reentered Patsy's life hoping the old sparks would ignite. He did everything but grovel," a band member said, "but Patsy rejected his advances and just wanted to be friends. That's not what Bill wanted."

In Nashville, Paul Cohen issued Patsy's Coral single of "Hidin' Out" backed with "Turn the Cards Slowly" in November to coincide with the annual WSM Birthday Celebration and country disc-jockey convention. This was several days of artist showcases, interviews, cocktail parties, award dinners and product giveaways—culminating with the announcement of the best in country music at the Saturday Opry.

Patsy came with her new "manager" Gerald Cline, who told everyone how great a star he was going to make her. After hours upon hours of interviews for the home town stations in the WSM studios to promote herself with jockeys more interested in getting to the hotels and the next hospitality suite for the next drink, Patsy was tired. Lee Burrows picked Patsy and Gerald up at the Colonial Motel and they had dinner at an out-of-the-way spot.

"He talked incessantly," observed Lee, "and I couldn't wait to get Patsy alone to see how everything was. It surely seemed fine. Gerald was most charming. He even picked up the tab. Patsy was eager to get to the Opry, which was brimming with stars."

In the wings, Patsy shone with excitement. "It's always such a thrill being here. When I stop and think of all the great names that have played on this stage. It makes me proud to be a part of it."

The audience roamed the aisles, and while the show was in progress they approached the stage to shoot flash pictures. Anyone with a connection had a backstage pass and mingled with the stars. Amid constant travels, this was the place where the singers and musicians saw each other. Coca-Colas were dispensed constantly from the machine, and after too many drinks spiked with bourbon, bottles rolled across the floor.

Patsy was worse than the fans about autographs and being photographed with her idols. On December 26, Lee received this letter:

Dear Lee,

Just thought I'd drop you a line to let you know we got home okay and loved every minute down there and the time with you. It's a visit I'll never forget! I guess I'll see you real soon. I'm supposed to be back the 6th and 7th for the Opry coast-to-coast TV show. I'm so thrilled, I don't hardly know how to act. I didn't think I'd have a chance at this kind of deal so quickly.

After Nashville, I'm off to Missouri and the Ozark Jubilee and the Big D Jamboree in Dallas. Between all this, I'm supposed to get another session in. It looks like I'm set for a big winter!

Gerald's fine and says to tell you hello. The pictures I took at the Opry came out just grand. Mr. McCall called today and said he has the contract you sent for me on your song "Red-Blooded Man." I love it and can't wait to record it. If you have any other red-hot blues, Lee, send them to him. I want some on my next session.[1]

Write and tell me how you are. Merry Christmas and Happy New Year.
Your friend,
Patsy Cline

Springfield, Missouri, was home to the "Ozark Jubilee," the leading Midwest country music show. Broadcast from the 1,200-seat Jewel Theater on radio and, beginning in January 1955, weekly for an hour on ABC-TV, it starred pioneer recording artist Red Foley of Blue Lick, Kentucky, with regulars Wanda Jackson and Leroy Van Dyke.

After her January 1956 appearance, Patsy sat down with Foley, mentor to countless stars. "Red," she told him, "I got some records out there. I'm working with Jimmy on TV and hotter than a pistol on the Town and Country circuit. I'm doing everything I can and ain't going nowhere."

"Well, gal, you sure got it, so just keep singing and you're gonna get there."

"But when?"

"If it's gonna happen, it's gonna happen."

1. McCall refused because it was not a Four-Star song.

Patsy would tell Del Wood and Lee Burrows over and over, "But it sure as hell ain't happening."

In Washington and the surrounding area, Patsy Cline was a star. In a March 18 *Washington Star* Sunday magazine cover story she was dubbed "the hillbilly with oomph." Gay was quoted: "Patsy has brought a brand of showmanship and rhythm to hillbilly music that's as welcome as a cool country breeze in springtime. We call her a country music choreographer. She creates the moods through movements of her hands and body, and by the lilt of her voice, reaching way down deep in her soul to bring forth the melody. Most female country music vocalists stand motionless, sing with a monotonous high-pitched nasal twang. Patsy's come up with a throaty style loaded with motion and E-motion."

As her success on the "Town and Country Time" shows grew, Patsy developed quite a following. As far as she was concerned, she was underpaid. "She referred to her contract with Mr. Gay as a Hitler contract," reported Mrs. Hensley. "Patsy went to him and asked for a raise. He informed her she was being paid more than enough for a woman in the business."

Gay wouldn't budge, so Patsy went to Bill McCall. "No problem, young lady. But what are you going to do for me?"

"What do you mean? I'm asking for an advance against my royalties!"

"You don't have any. Your records haven't earned one red cent! What about this? In exchange for some ready cash, you sign on for another year to give me time to recoup some of my costs."

Patsy agreed. When she returned the contract renewal, dated March 30, 1956, McCall sent her $200. Patsy was now tied to Four-Star through September 29, 1957.

Connie B. Gay, according to Dean, wasn't known for his generosity. "He could pinch pennies. For our package shows, Connie broke down and spent some money. He bought what Patsy and me referred to as the Kidney Buster, an old bus with springs so shot it was like a produce truck. You couldn't sleep, you couldn't relax. The only reward was a sore butt! We'd travel eighty-five to a hundred miles in an evening, work till two in the morning and then have to drive home and go in to do the damn afternoon TV show. But it was a living. Two hundred and fifty bucks a week and all the pictures we could sell."

The headliners had publicity photos of themselves solo and with each other in various poses. These were sold six in a pack for one dollar. It was the only sideline Gay didn't share in.

In between Patsy's career struggles, love was suddenly in the air. Friday, April 13, Patsy met Charlie Dick, who was infamous in the area as a flamboyant ladies' man. Her life would never be the same. "I grew up in Winchester," Charlie explained. "As Virginia Hensley, I saw her in a play at Handley High but never really knew her. I dropped out at the end of the tenth grade and eventually got a job at the *Winchester Star*[2] as a Linotype operator.

---

2. Owned by Harry F. Byrd, former Virginia governor and Democratic senator.

"Friday nights I went to Berryville, Virginia, about eight miles east of Winchester, to the Armory dances. My friend Bud Armel had a good-time band called the Kountry Krackers. This particular Friday night, I was hanging out and saw this gal go up onstage. Bud introduced her as Patsy Cline. I thought she looked familiar, but the name threw me.

"This was the first time I'd heard her sing and she literally bowled me over. She sang every kind of song imaginable. She was a real belter. Nobody could do a song like Patsy, and I still don't think there's anyone who can compare to her. Man, how she moved! Patsy couldn't stand still. She was all over the place! That's what made her so great and created the impact she had.

"She not only sang well but was also a knockout. The moment I saw her, I decided I was going to make my move. During the first break I asked Bud who this Patsy Cline was. He said she was a Town and Country regular but was going to be working with him on Fridays."

Armel cracked, "I probably didn't say too much because I'd waited long enough to get her and, knowing Charlie, I didn't want to lose Patsy." The popular musician and bandleader first met Patsy as Virginia Hensley at age fourteen, when she sang with Winchester's Don Patton and the Playboys. Later, playing briefly with Peer and the Melody Boys, he worked with her again as Patsy Hensley.

"I formed my own band, the Kountry Krackers, in 1952. Although we played throughout the area, we were Friday regulars at the American Legion dances at the Berryville National Guard Armory. When I heard that Patsy and Bill split, I asked Patsy to sing with us.

"My wife Geraldine and I'd known Charlie for years. Charlie's aunt and uncle, Pete and Myrtle Braithwaite, were her next-door neighbors on Highland Avenue."

"Charlie was something!" Mrs. Armel said, smiling. "He was five years younger than me but used to pester the daylights out of me. He gave me an especially hard time when I got my own bicycle. He wanted to ride it and I'd never let him. The more I said no, the more he'd try to drive my resistance down! He came from a fairly poor family and didn't have a lot of things. Eventually, I gave in. Funny thing, after he rode the bike, he never bothered me again!"

Armel remarked, "Charlie was good at getting into trouble. He was pretty wild and had a reputation for drinking, picking fights, and being a ladies' man. Patsy tamed him a bit."

In 1949, when his father committed suicide,[3] it fell on Charlie to help support his mother, Mary, and his younger brothers, William and Mel. (A third brother was deceased.) He worked and excelled at various jobs—including selling newspapers and clerking in the *Star*'s mailroom. He graduated to the paper's composing room, where, because of his speed and accuracy, he became a valued employee.

Mel Dick, forty-five, said, "I don't have a lot of detailed impressions of Charlie because I was the youngest. When I was a kid, he was already a teenager running around. When he and Patsy married, I was nine. Then Charlie went off to the army and, not long after he got out, they moved to Nashville. We've gotten to know each other better later in life and have a good relationship.

---

3. Many family members didn't know this until they saw the 1985 biographical film *Sweet Dreams*, starring Jessica Lange as Patsy Cline.

"Growing up, William and I were quiet. Charlie was the exception. He had so much in common with Patsy, Charlie could've almost been a blood relative of hers. They were always on the go and looking for excitement. That's why they got on so well together."

That particular April night in Berryville, Charlie was about to meet his match in every department.

"I got Bud to introduce us," Charlie said, "and Patsy played it cool. I tried talking to her and she didn't seem interested. I didn't let that stop me."

At the next break, he tried again, determined not to take no for an answer.

"Excuse me, Miss Cline, would you like to dance?"

"Thanks, but no thanks," she replied.

"Just thought I'd ask."

"I can't dance while I'm working. Okay?"

"Sure thing."

The next time Charlie spotted Patsy, she was on the floor dancing. A few minutes later he went up to her again.

"Maybe now you'd like to dance?"

"Hey, didn't I tell you that I can't dance while I'm working?"

"Sure you did, but I just saw you dancing with some guy."

"That guy happens to be my husband!" snapped Patsy.

"Well, excuse me!"

Charlie didn't let her out of his sight the rest of the night. The following Friday, there she was again.

"Hello, Patsy," he said politely.

"Howdy, Hoss," she replied.

"Hoss" really grated on him, but he detected a hint of interest in her greeting. Charlie observed her for a while and decided to give Patsy another shot. She still played it cool.

Charlie was already two weeks more patient than he was with other women. Not seeing Gerald, he approached Patsy a third time.

"Hello, Patsy. Would you like to dance?"

"You don't take no for an answer, do you?"

"Guess not. I'd like to get to know you."

"Oh, you would, Hoss?"

"Yeah. My name's Charlie. Charlie Dick."

"Nice to meet you, Hoss."

"My name's Charlie—"

"I know. Charlie *Dick.*"

"That's right."

"Well, I call everybody 'Hoss.'"

"Call me Charlie."

"Okay, *Charlie.* But it's against policy for me to dance with the customers. See you around."

At the next break, Charlie asked Patsy if he could buy her a drink.

"I can't drink while I'm working." His spirits were deflated. He wanted to tell her to go to hell. Patsy turned and walked away, then stopped, turned around and said, "*But* if you'd like to go outside for a little fresh air, that would be nice."

Charlie explained they went to his car and "just sat and talked." He saw the intense feeling of attraction was mutual. However, he admitted, "When I asked her for a date, I thought she'd say no. But she didn't."

The next night Charlie picked Patsy up at her mother's in Winchester and drove her to the "Jamboree."

Patsy was dating—among others, Jumbo Rinker. "I'd moved to Baltimore," Rinker said, "but one weekend in Winchester I ran into Patsy and she told me she and Gerald had broken up. She said, 'Maybe we can go out sometime.' I started coming down weekends and we'd go up in this single-engine plane I flew. Patsy loved it. She was a daredevil. Nothing scared her. She loved to laugh and we talked of the old days. It was never anything serious. I guess you could call us music buddies."

Melody Boy John Anderson noted that Rinker wasn't exactly an expert aviator. "My wife Frances and me used to run around with Jumbo. I'll never forget the Sunday, not long after he took Patsy for a ride, he rented a spanking brand new Aero Coupe from George Schrader, the owner of the local airfield. We were at the Winchester Speedway attending the jalopy races. Jumbo took off about five-thirty and only a matter of minutes later, as the races were breaking up, made a left bank over the speedway to observe the goings-on. His left wing clipped a telephone wire and he cracked up in the field across from the track. He broke a leg, had some serious bruises, and totaled the plane."

Charlie—two years younger than Patsy, cocky, oozing with personality and sex appeal, with a distinct nose, wavy brown hair, and chiseled good looks—immediately became the pivotal object in her life. Patsy and Charlie were totally enamored of each other. Bill, if even remembered, was totally forgotten by Patsy; Gerald was all but permanently put on the shelf.

To anyone who'd listen, Patsy would say, "There's only one man in my life, Charlie. He's a man, all man." Fay reported, "Pat carried on something terrible about Charlie and how he excited her. I'd listen and say to myself, 'Uh-huh, uh-huh, uh-huh. She's singing another him!'"

Patsy described Charlie's lovemaking techniques in great detail. "He satisfies all my wanton desires," she told Fay. "Yes, ma'am, there's quite a bit of life in my man." Recounting his physical attributes, Patsy bragged to Fay, her hands extended, "Charlie's bigger than life and twice as hard!"

Fay recalled Patsy telling her that once, when she and Charlie were making love, he called out, "Baby, you take me halfway to heaven." Patsy yelled, "Hoss, what do you mean, 'halfway'?"

On April 21, 1956, backstage at the Opry, Patsy visited in the ladies' dressing room with Del Wood.

"Hi, hon," Del exclaimed. "How you doing?"

"Awful," replied Patsy. "I still don't have a hit."

"You got to have patience in this business. Just don't let 'em tie you down. How's Gerald?"

"Who?"

"Gerald, your husband?"

"Oh, him! Hoss, I got some news. I met a boy my own age who's a hurricane in pants! Del, I'm in love and, this time, it's for real."

The next day, in her third session, Patsy recorded the hilarious rockabilly "Stop, Look and Listen," about current trends in music, Eddie Miller's poignant, crying-in-your-beer ballad "I've Loved and Lost Again," plus two gospel numbers,[4] "He Will Do For You (What He's Done for Me)" and "Dear God."

Musicians remember Patsy in tears at the end of the gospel takes. Opry announcer Grant Turner recollected Patsy's visits to the Ryman Auditorium on Wally Fowler's all-night sings. "She'd do those sacred songs with such feeling, there'd be silence at the end. Patsy's face'd be covered in tears. She was as moved as the audience."

After the session, as Patsy, Owen, and Cohen listened to playbacks, Teddy Wilburn, who with brother Doyle emerged from Webb Pierce's band to record for Decca, came in. Patsy pleaded, "Hoss, stick around and listen with us. Let me know what you think."

Wilburn reported that everyone had something to say. "Listen to 'em, Hoss!" Patsy said. "Everybody knows what I should and shouldn't do, but nobody listens to me. It's all in the material and I ain't got no decent material."

Patsy went home and back to the Town and Country shows.

The Lion's Club didn't invite her to ride in the 1956 Apple Blossom Festival Parade. She took it as a snub from her home town.

Gay had a solution. "Hell, Patsy, if you want to ride in the parade, why didn't you say so? I'll take care of everything—or they won't get any more cars from my showrooms."

In the Fireman's Parade, which began May 4 late in the afternoon and ran into the night, Patsy—wearing one of her mother's finest cowgirl creations—waved to the crowds lining the sidewalks. Sister Sylvia Mae was at her side. The banners on both sides of the convertible read "Town & Country T.V. Star PATSY CLINE ... Courtesy Gay Oldsmobile, Warrenton, Va."

She was back in Nashville for the July 8 release of "I've Loved and Lost Again" and "Stop, Look and Listen," her first Decca single.[5] With help from Ernest Tubb, the label arranged for Patsy to debut her record that weekend on the Prince Albert Tobacco–sponsored portion of the Opry carried on the NBC Radio network.

She also appeared twice with friend Faron Young on "Country Hoedown," a fifteen-minute show transcribed in Bradley's studio for U.S. Navy recruitment promotion on several hundred radio stations. On the first program, Patsy plugged her new release and sang "Come On In," "Turn the Cards Slowly," and "The Wayward Wind," a big hit that summer for Gogi Grant. On the second, she performed Sonny James's hit "For Rent" and Webb Pierce's "Yes, I Know Why."

Later that month Patsy was on the West Coast in Compton, a suburb in southeast Los Angeles, to sing the A-side of her single on the syndicated "Western Ranch Party," hosted by Tex Ritter. On an excursion to downtown Hollywood, she met someone who would play an important role in her career.

4. Not released in Patsy's lifetime.
5. Cohen had put aside his plan to make Coral a country label.

On her return to Winchester she waited and waited. Finally, seeing zero response from disc jockeys and record buyers on her latest efforts, Patsy decided she'd been patient long enough. She told her mother she'd been backed into a corner by McCall and Decca. "Something's wrong and I don't think it's me. I'm trying to run forward and they're holding me back. It's time I took the initiative."

That came in October, when Patsy was so fed up she talked Charlie into driving her to New York for another audition for "Arthur Godfrey's Talent Scouts." Janette Davis still thought Patsy's style was all wrong for her voice. Anyway, the show was booked for weeks. Before she left, Patsy told Davis not to forget her.

Charlie noted, "They gave us a song and dance which I took to mean, 'Don't call us. We'll call you.' I figured, 'That's the end of that.'"

Patsy knew better.

Shortly afterward, George Hamilton IV auditioned for "Talent Scouts," was selected to go on, and won. "That this kid, whom Patsy had criticized over and over, beat her to the punch was too much for Patsy," commented Del Wood. "She was madder than a wet hen. I thought she'd bust a gut."

That only made Patsy more determined. She expected a call any minute, any day, any week. It didn't come, but she was used to waiting. Mrs. Hensley prayed that God in His eternal wisdom would let the Godfrey people call so she could get some peace.

... I'm hungry for love,
Like a hobo for food,
Like the devil hunts for bad,
Like the angel looks for good ...

—"Hungry for Love" by Eddie Miller and W. S. Stevenson
(© 1957 Four-Star Music Company;
copyright renewed by Acuff-Rose Music, Inc.)

"PICK ME UP ON YOUR WAY DOWN"

PATSY CLINE: "Daddy, I've been accepted on 'Arthur
    Godfrey's Talent Scouts.'"
SAM HENSLEY: "I don't want you going off to New York.
    It's too big and it's not safe."
PATSY CLINE: "After being out of my life for seven years,
    you sure picked a fine time to start showing
    concern."

In 1956 Donn Hecht was trying very hard to make it in Los Angeles. "I probably wore out four pairs of shoes carrying my song folder to every music publisher in Hollywood. In those days Coffee-Dan's, near the corner of Sunset and Vine, teemed with every would-be songwriter and singer in the world. The country singers hung out there, too, but weren't considered part of the family. They were thought of as hicks who sang through their noses and couldn't read music.

"It was there I first met Patsy Cline. Not often, but enough to remember her without knowing her name. She had quite a presence and would be hard to forget. Not beautiful, not plain, she walked like a dancer and something played off her that made her stand out from the crowd. We were two unknown fish in the same lake.

"Later on [June, 1956], I was thin and broke and sitting before Bill McCall at Four-Star Records at 500 South Fairoaks Avenue, Pasadena, California. 'You're a comer, boy,' he told me. 'I think you've got real talent, and I'm gonna gamble on you, *but...*'

"That 'but' meant a seven-year contract, guaranteeing a six-hundred-dollar monthly draw against royalties. It stated McCall could fire me anytime, but that I couldn't quit! My car was up for repossession, my rent past due, and I had less than three dollars in my pocket. I signed."

By the time Hecht met him, McCall's hair was thin and half gone over the forehead. His once stocky build was pouched and wrinkled from weight loss to keep down an aggravated heart condition. His small, steel-gray green eyes peered from his small-framed glasses so coldly and without feeling they seemed artificial. His thin lower lip had a distinct downturn from years of smoking cigars, and his cheap suits looked "a little carny."

"But a speaker he was!" the songwriter declared. "His delivery, tone, and emphasis could charm a grape from the vine and make you wonder why he wasn't sitting in some governor's chair or a seat in Washington.

"A cheat? A thief? Perhaps. I've heard this stated by virtually everyone. From what I witnessed, I can't say he was. Do I believe I should have made more money than he paid? Yes. However, I saw the good things he did, such as help writers who were down on their luck.

"Eddie Miller, for example, would haunt the Four-Star offices and regularly confront McCall with urgent pleas for money. Others came, offering to sell songs for twenty-five dollars, eighty dollars, a hundred and fifty dollars. If they were alcoholics, Bill took them across the street for a meal, handed them ten dollars and ordered, 'Go dry out.' They'd return the next morning, soused, angry that he didn't do a 'buyout.' Bill would finally agree, in disgust, and call in Ruth, his Oriental secretary, and dictate a release of all title for the demanded amount of money.

"Bill would sulk. 'What the hell's the matter with you people? That stupid bastard signed away everything! A genius of a man pissing his money away on booze, destroying his liver, fucking his life away. And you can bet your ass, I'm the one everybody'll say was responsible.' McCall would tear a contract to shreds and say, 'After the booze does him in and if the song hits, don't you know he'll be surprised when some money rolls in.'"

When Hecht inquired why McCall would offer to buy all rights to a song, he replied, "What the hell you expect me to do? Don't you know the jackasses'll go to [competitor] Hill & Range and sell their goddamn songs for pennies? And that Jew'll add six or seven more songs to the contract for less money!"

"Of course," noted Hecht, "Bill didn't tear up all such agreements, but there is that other side. Though I didn't always agree with him, he possessed instincts which I've never witnessed the equal of."

In September, McCall had Hecht set up to produce for his country artists. "I groaned, 'Me? A writer of semi-classical music?' He told me, 'Yeah. No problem. Nothing to worry about.'

"My assignment was to pick a star from among the hopefuls and write that person a hit. I told McCall, 'Sorry, I need the money, but I'm afraid I can't write this stuff.' He glared at me and barked, 'You've heard the worst, now listen to this, and listen good.'"

McCall put a record on the phonograph, and before it made ten revolutions, Hecht was hypnotized by the girl's voice.

"Who is she?" the lyricist wanted to know.

"Her name's Patsy Cline."

"I've never heard anyone sing like that before."

"There's a problem. Her contract's about to expire and I don't know if I want to renew. I've spent a fortune releasing her stuff and she's bombed every time. Can you tell me why?"

"Hell, that's easy. She's not a country singer."

"She's got the same tear in her voice you have in your material."

"Bill, that's the problem. The stuff you've got her singing. She shouldn't be doing hillbilly. You really have something there."

"Not if she bombs out one more time. I'll have to drop her."

"Let me give it some thought."

"Bring me in something and I'll give it the test."

Hecht explained that McCall had a "sure-fire" method of knowing whether songs were good. "He played them for his 'chief A&R executive,' Truly, the night cleaning woman. His theory was 'This woman mops my floors for a living and knows as much as I do about the business. You bet your ass I've got to be interested in any song she likes well enough to go out and spend her hard-earned money on.'

"And so they'd sit, in the light of a desk lamp, McCall in his high-back executive chair, and Truly, her mop and bucket resting nearby, from eight to often past midnight, listening to demos offered by an army of writers."

The writer went home and searched through a stack of unpublished songs until he came across a yellowed lead sheet of a song nobody wanted. He'd cowritten it with Alan Block, an electronic engineer, who composed mainly as a hobby. The song was for Kay Starr, but Capitol Records' A&R chief wouldn't let her do it.

Hecht couldn't get Patsy's voice out of his head. He sat down with the sheet music and made minor changes. A day or two later, he had a singer come in and do a demo session. He took the tape to McCall. When he heard it, McCall "almost fell off his chair," and Truly loved it.

"Let me call that gal in Virginia," McCall said, rushing to the phone.

"It's about time you had some exciting news for me," cracked Patsy. "What's the title?"

"'Walkin' After Midnight.'"

"I don't like it."

"Not so fast! Not so fast! You ain't heard it yet. Hell, gal, give it a chance."

McCall played it with the receiver next to the hi-fi's speaker.

"I hate it!"

He played it again.

"I still hate it!"

McCall was so angry, he almost swallowed his cigar. "Listen, goddamnit, you work for me. I'm sending you a ticket and you're coming out here all expenses paid. We'll talk about it—"

"Ain't nothing to talk about—"

"I said, we'll talk about it!"

In early October, Patsy arrived in Los Angeles to meet with McCall. On the side, she contacted the Town Hall Party representatives in Compton to appear on the popular three-hour country music variety show, which was telecast regionally. She was a featured guest Friday and Saturday, October 12 and 13.

At the Four-Star meeting on Monday, McCall, Hecht, and Patsy clashed. Hecht reported that McCall played "Walkin' After Midnight" again and again, making Patsy angrier and angrier.

"I won't do it!"

"You'll do what I tell you to do," yelled McCall. "I've spent a fortune on you and got nothing to show for it."

"But it's nothing but a little ole pop song."

"And you're nothing but a little ole pop singer who lives in the country," countered Hecht.

"Now I'm going to leave you two alone," McCall informed emphatically, "and let you work out the details."

He stormed out. Patsy looked at Hecht. He looked at her. Silence. She glared. He glared. Then Hecht broke out laughing and Patsy did, too.

"I'm sorry," she said.

"No. I'm sorry," he said.

"Look, Mr. Heck—"

"It's pronounced like Hector without the o-r."

"Look, Mr. Hector without the o-r, it's just that for two years I been singing what everybody else wants, and when it flops, who gets the blame? Me! It ain't fair."

"I've got to tell you, the song's perfect for you. Your voice is pure B-flat blues. It'll work."

"I don't think so. It ain't country."

"Why don't you try this on for size. You say you been singing what everybody else wants. Okay, tell McCall you'll do this one if he lets you pick one you like for the flip side."

"Don't think I haven't been through this before. He never lets me pick a song."

"I'll back you. He likes me!"

"I still hate the song. But I like you."

"I'll consider that a compliment, but that other part won't do."

"What do you mean?"

"You singing a song you don't like will never come over to the audience."

"Okay, I'll try to like it."

McCall returned with coffee and doughnuts.

"Bill, Mr. Hecht and I have decided. I'll do one side I really like along with 'Walkin' After Midnight' and you release them back to back."

McCall nearly knocked his coffee over. He arched his eyebrows and studied Patsy and Donn.

"Then if your side sells, I'll never argue about material again. But if my side sells—"

"This is blackmail!"

"If you say so."

"What if neither side sells, what then?"

"Then you just get yourself another singer. Is it a deal?"

McCall bit into his doughnut. "It's a deal."

Before returning home, Patsy saw McCall again. Chronically short of money, she asked for an advance. Gladly, he replied, in exchange for an additional one-year renewal. It was dated and signed July 2, 1956. Patsy got two hundred dollars. She was tied to McCall through September 29, 1958.

Everything was set. Patsy would go to Nashville the week of November 4 for her fifth recording session and to attend the WSM Birthday Celebration and disc jockey convention for Decca and Connie B. Gay Enterprises. Charlie would join her.

Doyle Wilburn and brother Teddy saw Patsy Monday and Tuesday at WSM, where they did interviews, posed for photographs, and handed out product, and at the old Andrew Jackson Hotel, where Decca had its hospitality suite.

"On the second night," recalled Doyle, "my voice was shot. I needed a break from all the hand-grabbing, so I headed for my room for a catnap. I ran into Patsy in the hall. She was real upset. I invited her to the room for a drink."

Patsy sat on the bed and started to cry.

"Hey, what's the matter?" Doyle asked. She couldn't stop crying to answer him. "Patsy, honey, you got to stop. This ain't good. Now, come on." Doyle gave her some water and a towel to wipe her face. "What's got you so bothered?"

"I'm madder than hell at that bastard McCall!"

"That bald-headed runt's the biggest crook in the business. He steals us country folk blind!"

"He's making me record this song I just can't stand. It's awful. I hate the goddamned thing! Doyle, it's pop and I don't want to sing pop. I'm a country girl!"

"Patsy, just tell him you don't want to do it."

"What do you think I been doing? I've told him till I was blue in the face. He says I don't have a choice. One of the little stipulations in my contract states I can only record Four-Star songs. He's got me over a barrel. He and Owen got the session set for Thursday night. What am I going to do?"

"Sue the bastard!"

It was too late. November 8, Patsy was in Bradley's studio. She and Donn Hecht spoke by phone.

"We talked about her Blue Ridge Mountains in Virginia and how she loved to go fishing and hunting," he reported. "She was upset she wasn't able financially to do things for her mother. She really got to me. Here was a girl, simple but complicated, with a heart as big as those mountains that made her eyes shine each time she spoke of them.

"She told me, once again, of her intense dislike of 'Walkin' After Midnight.' She didn't take the session lightly and was under a lot of pressure. I didn't envy Owen. I knew Patsy could tax a truck driver.

"She was stubborn, and any material she recorded had to be pure country. She considered everything she recorded like an entry in her diary. 'It's like writing a lot of personal things down on the page,' she told me, 'and wanting them just right so that when other people see it, they'll see how it was and how you really felt. Doing something I don't believe in makes me feel like a whore.'"

Patsy recorded two country songs, "The Heart You Break May Be Your Own" and "Pick Me Up on Your Way Down" in addition to "A Poor Man's Roses (or a Rich Man's Gold)" by pop writers Bob Hilliard and Milton Delugg. The latter was "her song"—the non Four-Star Music tune—in her pact with McCall. Then came "Walkin' After Midnight."

It didn't go smoothly. Patsy told Bradley her heart just wasn't in it. When they listened to the playback, Patsy begged, "Please, Owen, let's try it one more time." He assured her it was fine.

Bradley and Charlie observed that Patsy was never completely happy with anything she recorded. "No matter how close to perfection she came," the producer said, "she felt she could do it better."

At the end of convention week, Patsy was back in Washington on "Town and Country Jamboree." Gay had her booked on enough package show one-nighters to keep her busy through Thanksgiving and into the Christmas season. The season for giving was at hand and Patsy, who had extravagant tastes, was flat broke.

She called McCall and asked for money. He reminded her she had yet to earn a penny in royalties, but since Patsy's recording of "Walkin' After Midnight" flushed him with the $weet $mell of $ucce$$, he offered her five hundred dollars and a two-year renewal, dated November 29, 1956. Patsy was contractually tied to him until September 29, 1960.

On December 8, there was an atmosphere of great expectancy at the rehearsals and final run-through for the "Jamboree" telecast. Gay was hanging about more than usual. Dean was "a more hard-driving commander in chief" than ever. Attention was paid to things that never had attention paid to them. No one knew what was going on.

Minutes before the show went on, Dale Turner rushed into the dressing room. "Everybody do your best tonight!" she exclaimed. "Arthur Godfrey's at home watching the show."

Godfrey, a Virginian, maintained a residence in Leesburg, about thirty-five miles from the capital, and was tuned to the Town and Country Network.

Since she was never allowed to audition for the TV star, this would be Patsy's moment. She went onstage and sang like she never sang before. When she got home to her mother's house in Winchester, she told Mrs. Hensley, "Arthur Godfrey was watching the show tonight." There was no response. "Mama, Arthur Godfrey was watching the show tonight!"

"I heard you, honey."

And Mrs. Hensley knew it would start all over again. Once more she said her prayer.

When she came back from a Front Royal club date Sunday night, Patsy was exhausted. She'd worked hard all weekend. Monday was her day off. She told Mrs. Hensley she wanted to sleep late. When the phone rang at 11:00 A.M., Mrs. Hensley ran to answer so it wouldn't wake Patsy.

"Oh, my goodness!" she blurted. "Just a minute. I'll see if I can get her." She ran to Patsy's room. "Patsy, it's long-distance. It's the Godfrey people!"

"Who?" she asked, half asleep.

"It's the Arthur Godfrey show! They want to talk to you."

"Here, a major television show was calling with the call we'd been hoping for," Mrs. Hensley said later. "But, oh, that girl was cool."

Patsy shot up. "Let them wait a few minutes. They let me wait. Tell them I'm next door."

"What?" asked Mrs. Hensley. "Patsy, are you crazy? You get to the phone!"

Patsy enacted a charade. As Mrs. Hensley told the caller she was on her way,

Patsy went to the front door, opened it, and slammed it. When she took the receiver from her mother and began to speak, she spoke very matter-of-factly.

"Hello . . . Yes, this is Patsy Cline . . . 'Arthur Godfrey's Talent Scouts?' Oh, hi, Miss Davis. How ya'll doing? . . . You remembered me."

Davis said, "We want you to come to New York and do the show."

"Well, okay," replied Patsy.

"Who will be your talent scout?" Davis inquired.

"My mother—"

"Oh, no, you can't do that—"

"How come?"

"It might prejudice the audience. See if you can find someone to bring with you. We'd like to have you on in January."

"That's next month."

"Is that a problem?"

"No. No, I think it'll be all right."

Mrs. Hensley jabbed Patsy in the arm. Patsy told Davis about her latest recording session and asked if she'd received her new record. Details were discussed and a date set. When Patsy hung up she nearly soared right through the roof. She and Mrs. Hensley huddled to think of who they could get to sponsor Patsy. Patsy told Hilda she wanted it to be her.

"But," advised Mrs. Hensley, "there's no way around it. Rules are rules." There was silence as Patsy thought. "Patsy, what's running through your head?"

"Mama, I'm Patsy Cline and you're Mrs. Hilda Hensley of Winchester, Virginia. You'll be my talent scout, *not* my mother!"

"I should've known I could depend on you for some kind of scheme!"

Patsy mapped out her conspiracy. When Davis phoned the next day, she gave the name of her talent scout.

"Mrs. Hilda Hensley?" repeated Davis.

"That's right."

"Is she a friend?" Davis asked.

"Yes, ma'am. My best! She's known me all her life."

Patsy and Charlie were hotter than the coals on a fire. He'd be the first to admit he's "one hell of a partying man." He was, in the words of one of Patsy's colleagues, "a connoisseur of booze and gave Patsy an appreciation of it." From other accounts, Patsy may have taught Charlie a thing or two.

Theirs wasn't always the perfect relationship. Charlie may have swept Patsy off her feet, but, according to close friends and associates, he sometimes did it with strong doses of male chauvinism.

"Patsy and I became quite close on the 'Jamboree,'" Jimmy Dean related. "We'd be in a dressing room talking and she'd go into tirades about Charlie, calling him names and saying things like 'That no-good so-and-so treats me like you-know-what.' I asked, 'Do you love the son of a gun?' and she'd tell me how much they loved each other. 'But, Jimmy,' she'd say, 'all we do is fight.'

"One day they'd be happy as a barrel of monkeys and on the outs the next.

Patsy carried on about how she was going to leave him, then two breaths later tell you how much she was in love with Charlie. I told her, 'Hey, make up your mind!'"

Dean reported that more than once Patsy showed up "bruised from where Charlie had whipped hell out of her." He remembered an incident when Patsy and Charlie were cruising around Winchester in Patsy's car. "He'd been drinking and when they began battling, she stopped and kicked him out. And he didn't go voluntarily."

When Patsy came to work with a black eye, Dean thought it was sad but had to laugh. "He hit her and she had him arrested. Then Patsy mourned about it all night and got him out the next day. When he drank, Charlie was a different person. They were rough on each other. Sometimes that can be a form of love. Patsy'd take anything Charlie dished out and had no problem standing up to him. She had a way of getting back at Charlie. She'd embarrass the daylights out of him in front of others. To me, it didn't sound dirty. It was vernacular with Patsy."

Dale Turner reminisced, "Patsy and I were friends but not bosom buddies. She didn't cry on my shoulder. Personal things were personal. We were a close-knit group, so there were things you couldn't hide. But everybody minded their own business.

"All I remember about Patsy and Gerald was there was an age difference and they didn't have the same interests. When Patsy and Charlie started dating, he didn't so much hang out with us as he was just always there. They were boyfriend and girlfriend. There weren't a lot of questions. She never talked about his getting drunk and beating her."

Everyone but Herman Longley of Elkton had lost track of Patsy's father, Sam Hensley. All vestiges of the great dynasty that his grandfather Benjamin and father Sol Hensley had begun were stripped away. After deserting his family in 1947, Hensley went to Ohio and lived a vagabond existence for a year. When he returned to Virginia, he lived in a boardinghouse in Harrisonburg.

Having worked around coal most of his life, starting back when he was a boiler fireman at the Virginia Military Institute, he developed lung cancer. As the illness became graver, it fell on Longley, now a public accountant in Elkton, to care for Hensley. Finally, in late 1956, he admitted him to Newton D. Baker Veteran's Administration Hospital in Martinsburg, West Virginia. On his way home from the hospital, Longley stopped in Winchester to visit Hilda and tell her the news. Mrs. Hensley informed Patsy.

"Mama, I know what-all he did," said Patsy, "but it seems he's real sick and may not make it. In spite of everything, I want to visit him."

To her surprise, Mrs. Hensley told her she'd accompany her. During the visit, Patsy excitedly informed Sam Hensley, "Daddy, I've been accepted on 'Arthur Godfrey's Talent Scouts.'"

Though he could hardly talk, he admonished her, "Now, Virginia, I don't want you going off to New York. It's too big and it's not safe. You don't need to be running off up there. You stay right at home."

"Daddy, just think what this could do for my career! Appearing on nationwide TV with Arthur Godfrey!"

"I don't care. I don't want you going up there."

"Daddy," she replied angrily, "after being out of my life for seven years, you sure picked a fine time to start showing concern. I've been to New York before and I'm going. And you ain't going to stop me!"

When she saw she was frightening her frail father, Patsy backed off, telling him she'd be extra careful. Before she left, she asked him to be sure and watch her. "Daddy, you've never really heard me sing. I'm pretty good!"

Patsy Cline said her good-byes to the father she was so ambivalent about. Sam Hensley never got to hear his daughter. He died December 11, 1956. On the night of the funeral, Hilda Hensley asked Herman Longley to reserve a plot next to Sam's in Winchester's National Cemetery.

Jimmy Dean's favorite dictum was "Time is a man's most valuable asset." He considered punctuality next to godliness, and Patsy upset his apple cart. Suddenly she was constantly late for rehearsals, then defied Gay by refusing to do the square-dance segment following the "Jamboree."

In the argument with Gay over not dancing with audience members, he fumed, "People who start at the top, young lady, usually end up at the bottom, so I advise you to watch your step. You're going too far. You're late, you won't dance, and then you have the gall to come and ask Jimmy and me if you can have time off to go to New York to be on Arthur Godfrey!"

Patsy told Gay that appearing on Godfrey would be good for the show. He shot back, "I'll decide what's good for the show!"

However, Gay knew the extent of Patsy's popularity. She was the main attraction for the male viewers, who went out and spent money on his show's sponsor's products.

If there was doubt, it was erased the next Sunday, December 30, when, with Dean, Dale, and Mary Click, Patsy was on the cover of the *Tele Vue* magazine of the *Washington Star*. She was a valuable asset. Godfrey's national telecast would make her more valuable. And he needed Dean and Patsy now more than ever.

CBS was planning to cancel its 7:00 A.M. "Will Rogers Jr. Show" and create a new country program. It would be a gamble. Was coast-to-coast America ready for country music that early in the morning? As CBS vacillated, everybody wanted in on the action. Competition became fierce among the WLS "National Barn Dance" in Chicago; Shreveport's "Louisiana Hayride"; the "Ozark Jubilee," already a proven TV success; the Grand Ole Opry; and Connie B. Gay's empire. WTOP, the network's D.C. affiliate, had alerted executives of the popularity of "Town and Country Jamboree" in that region, and they were already in touch with Gay.

On Friday night, January 4, Patsy sang in Berryville and spent the night at Charlie's house. Mrs. Dick didn't know to wake Patsy. When Patsy woke and saw she was late for "Jamboree" rehearsals, she and Charlie ran down the street to Grayson's Grocery since the Dicks had no phone. Patsy called the Arena and asked for Dean. "Jimmy, I'm awfully sorry," witnesses at the store reported Patsy as saying. "I had to work real late last night and I just got up. The alarm didn't go off. I'll be there as soon as I can. I'm leaving right now—"

"Hold on a minute, girl!" Dean yelled. "You can go right back to sleep. Don't bother to come, you hear? If you can't make it on time for rehearsals, there's no need to come for the show, because there won't be a spot for you."

"What do you mean, Jimmy?"

"I mean, consider yourself fired!"

Patsy turned white and seemed to be in a state of shock. She turned to Charlie and moaned, "Jimmy just fired me. I can't believe it. Jimmy just fired me!"

On the telecast, Dean didn't mention Patsy by name, but got his digs in. "People on the way up should be especially nice to those they pass, because they might need them when they come tumbling down. I'd like to dedicate this song to a girl you all used to see a lot of." Dean sang "Pick Me Up on Your Way Down," which Patsy had just recorded and which Bill McCall had tried to get him to record while he was on Four-Star. At the end, Dean waxed, "On my way up, I'll pass you on your way down."

At least Patsy had "Arthur Godfrey's Talent Scouts" on the horizon. She went to the Cline apartment in Frederick to gather clothes and belongings for her trip to New York. She later described her meeting with Gerald to her friend, country singer Pearl Butler.

Gerald, in T-shirt and boxer shorts, was watching TV and eating a TV dinner when she arrived.

"Look who's here!" he snapped, quite surprised to see Patsy.

"Good news, Gerald!"

"You moving back? Your mother kick you out?"

"No."

"Then what's the occasion? Need a change of clothes?"

"I'm picking up some things. It's happened. I'm going on 'Arthur Godfrey's Talent Scouts'!"

Gerald grew red-faced and flushed with anger. "Seems if I want to see you, I have to look at TV! You just won't face it, will you? You're wasting your time."

"Why's everyone always trying to hold me down? Dammit, Gerald, look what I've accomplished! This is the break I've prayed for."

"You ain't sold a nickel's worth of records. Country music ain't got no place for a woman. And I'm sick and tired of what's going on behind my back! You played Bill along and now you're playing me along. Why don't you come home and stop running around with every Tom, Dick—"

"If you're talking about Charlie, don't hand me your pious bullshit!"

Gerald became furious and, according to Patsy, went to slap her.

"Don't you dare!" she warned him. "What the hell's got you so upset? Please don't try and make me feel sorry for you, Gerald. How can you stand there and throw stones when you've been seen with another woman?"

"Wouldn't have had to if you'd been where you belong. This ain't right! I can't sleep. I can't eat. The business is going down. I want a wife!"

"It's too late for that, Gerald. This marriage's been like a bad dream with no tunes in it."

"But, Patsy, honey!"

Gerald broke down and cried. Patsy gathered her things for the trip to New York. The world was waiting and Patsy Cline was ready.

"I'M MOVING ALONG"

JANETTE DAVIS: "Why were you hiding 'Walkin' After Midnight'?"

PATSY CLINE: "I hate it because it makes me feel like a prostitute! It's nothing but a little ole pop song."

JANETTE DAVIS: "But it just might make you famous."

The day before Patsy and her talent scout left Winchester for New York City, she called Donn Hecht in Los Angeles.

"Can you believe it?" she said. "It's finally happening. God! Arthur Godfrey! New York! Donn, that town scares me to death."

"It's just another town with a few more people," he replied. "You'll do fine."

"It's all those people I'm worried about."

"People are alike the world over."

"Maybe, but New York people aren't like country folks. They dare to make you like them."

Patsy and Mrs. Hensley arrived at LaGuardia Airport on Friday afternoon, January 18, 1957. They took the airport bus into Manhattan, to the hotel where Patsy had stayed with Bill Peer. Patsy contacted Al Gallico, general manager of Shapiro & Bernstein Music Company. It was their "A Poor Man's Roses (or a Rich Man's Gold)" that Patsy had picked as "her song" in her deal with McCall, and Gallico had paid Mrs. Hensley's airfare.[1]

"Hello, Al. We're here!"

"Hey, Patsy, where the hell are you staying? I've called every hotel in town and I couldn't find you registered."

1. Since the Godfrey show sent Patsy two tickets, she may have made money on the deal.

"You didn't call the Dixie."

"That dump? I know Godfrey's cheap, not sending you a ticket for your mother, but not that cheap! You shouldn't be there. It's not for you."

"It's very nice, Al. I like it. It's my kind of people. And, furthermore, it's only thirteen dollars a night."

Gallico picked up the Hensleys and took them on a guided tour. They didn't make a long night of it, since Patsy had shopping to do the next day.

The Monday, January 21, 1957, *Winchester Star* carried an article headlined PATSY CLINE SINGS ON GODFREY SHOW:

> Patsy Cline, Winchester's top contribution to the world of television, will appear on the Arthur Godfrey show at 8:30 tonight.
>
> The singing gal from South Kent Street has been a constant performer with Jimmy Dean on the Saturday night television show "Town and Country Jamboree." Tonight's appearance on CBS will mark her first time on national network television.

Early Monday morning, Patsy went to the CBS studio and met with Janette Davis. They went through the sheet music McCall and Gallico had given Patsy.

"Do you have anything else, Patsy?" Davis asked.

"That's about it. There're over thirty songs there."

"Your voice has such a wide appeal. You're not just another hillbilly singer."

"What's wrong with being hillbilly?"

"Oh, my goodness, nothing. But look at it this way, you've got the potential to reach a far vaster audience."

Davis introduced Patsy to music director and conductor Bert Farber. Patsy was telling him all about the western outfit her mother made for her to wear on the show. As they looked at material, Patsy would say, "That's country. I can sing that" or "That's not country. I can't do it."

"Patsy," Davis interrupted, "what makes you special is the magic your voice weaves. It's really unique. We need a song to match that quality. Bert, we've got to find the right song for her to sing." They settled on "A Poor Man's Roses (or a Rich Man's Gold)."

Davis, still not satisfied, asked, "Is there anything else in the portfolio I haven't seen?"

Patsy threw her arms into the air. "Okay. Okay. There's just one more." She showed Davis "Walkin' After Midnight."

"Ah! Now we're getting somewhere," Janette said. "Why were you hiding this one? It's wonderful. The blues sound fits your voice and style perfectly."

"Let's go with 'A Poor Man's Roses.'"

"'Walkin' After Midnight' would be much better, I think."

"You'll get me in trouble."

"Trouble? How?"

"It's Decca policy not to allow their artists to publicly perform a song before it's released."

"But 'A Poor Man's Roses' isn't out yet."

"Then let's not do either one."

"You're talking about a technicality. We can easily get around that. Now sing this for me, Patsy."

She complied reluctantly. When she finished, Davis requested, "Now sing it again as if you meant it." Patsy sang it again. "That's it! That's the one you've got to do on the show."

"I hate it because it makes me feel like a prostitute!"

"Patsy, you have a vivid imagination. It's fine. You did it beautifully."

"It's nothing but a little ole pop song."

"Maybe so, young lady, but it just might make you famous."

On her break, Patsy called Hecht. "Guess what they want me to sing?"

"'Walkin' After Midnight'?"

"What else?"

"Wow! That's fantastic!"

"For you, but not for me."

"Come on, Patsy."

"Okay, I give up. I surrender! It's four against one now."

"What do you mean?"

"There's Owen, Bill McCall, you, and now Janette Davis. First thing I'm going to do when I get back to Nashville is record that song again!"

"Why?"

"Because I like it. I really like it now! And we're going to win with it."

Patsy arrived for the run-through that afternoon in her finest cowgirl attire, which sent Davis into a tailspin.

"You can't wear that outfit and sing 'Walkin' After Midnight'!"

"I don't know why not!" Patsy rebuffed her.

"You just can't! And that's final."

Davis took Patsy to wardrobe and personally selected a cocktail dress for her to wear.

"I'll be on top of you every step of the way, Patsy. Don't pull any fast ones and change into Dale Evans!"

She marched her to the orchestra rehearsal and told Mrs. Hensley what she would do.

"Where's Mr. Godfrey?" Patsy wanted to know.

"Mr. Godfrey never comes to rehearsals. We use a stand-in. He never meets the performers before going on the air."

As the 8:30 P.M. airtime approached, Patsy and Mrs. Hensley became nervous wrecks.

"We were worried whether our little play-acting was working," revealed Mrs. Hensley. "Oh, my, it nearly killed me, having to keep quiet. And I felt a bit guilty about being deceptive—or only telling half the truth. Whenever Patsy would want to speak to me, she'd call out, 'Oh, where's that nice Mrs. Hensley? You know, my talent scout.' And I'd look to see who she was referring to! I wasn't used to Patsy calling me anything but 'Mama.' I must have looked awfully suspicious!"

The theater filled with people and the show began. About 8:15 Davis called Patsy and Mrs. Hensley onto the stage and positioned them for Godfrey's introduction. Then the lights hit them. Mrs. Hensley joined Godfrey at his desk and told all about her "find" from Winchester, Virginia. Godfrey said he was a Virginian and mighty proud of anyone from that state. Then he announced, "Ladies and gentlemen, Miss Patsy Cline."

As the orchestra began, Mrs. Hensley moved offstage to watch Patsy on a TV monitor. She was wringing her hands. "What happened was just unbelievable. Patsy sang her heart out for over two minutes. Then there was an eternity of applause."

WALKIN' AFTER MIDNIGHT

I go out walkin' after midnight,
Out in the moonlight,
Just like we used to do.
I'm always walkin' after midnight,
Searching for you.

I walk for miles along the highway
Well, that's just my way
Of saying I love you.
I'm always walkin' after midnight,
Searching for you.

I stop to see a weeping willow,
Crying on his pillow;
Maybe he's crying for me.
And, as the skies turn gloomy,
Night will whisper to me,
I'm lonesome as I can be.

I go out walkin' after midnight,
Out in the moonlight,
Just hopin' you may be
Somewhere walkin' after midnight,
Searching for me.

"Patsy cried," Mrs. Hensley remembered, "and I cried. I wanted to run out and throw my arms around her, but I knew I couldn't. This moment was everything Patsy'd ever dreamed of—the recognition and receiving such fantastic exposure over national television. Patsy told me later she had a strong impulse to holler out 'Mama!' but got control of herself. The response was overwhelming. People were standing and yelling for more."

Godfrey finally had to calm the audience. He put his arm around her. "Congratulations, Patsy. Something unbelievable has happened. For the first time in our history, the applause has frozen the meters. It looks like you're the winner!" All Patsy could do was smile and cry. "Little lady, you sure know how to sing. Will you do another song for us?"

The audience went wild again. Patsy got to do a country song after all, the Hank Williams hit "Your Cheatin' Heart."

"And when she finished," exclaimed Mrs. Hensley, "the audience went crazy again! It was one of the most memorable occasions of my life. And Patsy's!"

Godfrey congratulated Patsy once again. "There's surely stardust on you, Patsy Cline!" As was the custom with the winners, she was invited to return the following Monday as special guest.

As excited as she must have been, that night Patsy wrote in her diary, simply "Went on the Godfrey Talent Show ... Won." Now Mrs. Hensley was feeling more deeply ashamed of their deception and made Patsy promise that when they saw Godfrey the next morning they'd tell him the truth.

In his office at the CBS building, after they exchanged pleasantries, Patsy told the host there was someone special she wanted him to meet. "Mr. Godfrey, Mrs. Hensley is really—"

"My God, girl, I know this lady is your mother!"

They had been found out, but Mrs. Hensley was immensely relieved, especially when Patsy wasn't disqualified.

Godfrey scolded Patsy, "I'd be ashamed to show my face back in Winchester if I had my mother with me and didn't introduce her to everybody watching!"

"But Miss Davis told me it wasn't allowed."

"Normally it isn't. But I make the rules and I can break them! Patsy, let me tell you something. You may not always be the wide-eyed little country girl you are now, but, for goodness sake, don't you ever change from the girl you really are. If you do, no one will ever love or respect you. Now, I have a surprise for you and the nice Mrs. Hensley. Patsy, how would you like to go to work for me?"

"Oh, Mr. Godfrey! I don't know what to say."

"And I bet that doesn't happen often. And, Patsy, listen to Miss Davis and Mr. Farber. They're talented people and know what best suits your voice. Work with them. Don't fight them."

"Oh, yes sir!"

Mrs. Hensley went home the next day, while Patsy was received at Decca by an elated Paul Cohen.

"Finally something's happened," he told her. "What a great voice and a great song! Orders are pouring in! Young lady, looks like we've got an unreleased hit on our hands."

Patsy told Cohen she was broke and asked if she could receive an advance.

"That's between you and Bill McCall," Cohen said. When Patsy told him she'd be working as a Godfrey regular, he saw the potential for bigger sales and a promotional campaign around a record star with TV recognition. "Well, Patsy, how much do you need? I'll speak to McCall."

"Mr. Cohen, could I get an advance of twenty-five dollars?"

"Is that all? Most artists with a potential hit record would come in here demanding two to three hundred dollars."

"Well, that's all I need to get by on till Mr. Godfrey pays me."

On Wednesday Patsy began on "Arthur Godfrey Time," broadcast to an audience of ten million from the CBS studio at 49 East Fifty-second Street. Godfrey introduced her: "Now, ladies and gentlemen, I want you to meet one of the finest country-western-blues singers in the world. Here's a gal that can sing just about any kind of song that was ever written and make you love it. We think she's got everything—sincerity in the delivery of a song, poise, finesse. Welcome, Miss Patsy Cline."

She sang "Walkin' After Midnight" and the audience saw everything Godfrey stated to them was true. As Patsy bathed in applause at the end of her number, Godfrey asked, "By the way, Patsy, what do you attribute your success to?"

Patsy hesitated, then answered, "I don't know, Mr. Godfrey. I guess it's just me!"

"Well, just leave it like it is!" replied the host. "Don't ever change it."

Later, in Godfrey's office, she said, "I've given it some thought."

"What?" he asked.

"You know, what you asked me this morning—about what do I attribute to my success. I owe it all to the wonderful people who have given me a helping hand along the way."

"That's great, Patsy. Never forget that, but, hon, don't sell yourself short. You've evidently done some work, too."

At home, everyone patted Gerald on the back and congratulated him on his wife's TV success. He'd seen "Arthur Godfrey's Talent Scouts" and was impressed. "But I always knew Patsy had it in her," he noted. "Finally the timing was right." As much as he enjoyed basking in her glory, Gerald fired his own salvo. On January 23, in the Frederick, Maryland, courthouse, he filed a bill of complaint for divorce.

"When it came to Pat and Gerald's divorce," Fay said, "we weren't shocked, just taken by surprise. I never heard Pat or Gerald speak of any problems. The obvious one about Bill never came up. Sure, everyone knew. When Gerald filed his petition, most of us assumed Bill had come between them again. I figured Gerald and Pat, too, realized it wasn't going to work. Lord knows, they'd done it the trial-and-error method enough to know the answer."

Patsy Cline was heralded an "overnight sensation." Mail poured into CBS and Decca. The public was clamoring for copies of "Walkin' After Midnight." Everyone wanted to know about this incredible new star.

No one expected the type of response Patsy elicited. Or were they prepared for it all along? Rumors circulated that "Talent Scouts" "was often predictable in the outcome"—in other words, that the show was rigged. If that was the case, Mrs. Hensley says she and Patsy were totally unaware of any fraud. Donn Hecht says such allegations "are unfounded and absolutely false." He pointed out that if Decca knew Patsy was going to be a sensation, "Walkin' After Midnight" would have been pressed and distributed to stores.

Patsy was on cloud nine, but there were realities to face. She had to move to a cheaper residential hotel on West Forty-fourth Street. It was all she could afford. And what would this instant stardom do to her relationship with Charlie? They talked nightly on the phone and arranged to see each other weekends and on her days off.

On her next "Talent Scouts" appearance, Monday, January 28, she performed "Walkin' After Midnight" and followed with "A Poor Man's Roses (or a Rich Man's Gold)." At the end, Godfrey called out, "Hey, Patsy, how's your mother?" Before she could answer, he cracked, "There, that'll let the world know who that nice Mrs. Hensley was last week!"

Godfrey's daily morning show came on the air at 10:00 A.M. A half-hour format ran on TV but the entire ninety minutes went out over CBS radio. There were fifteen-minute segments and each regular had his or her slot with Godfrey. The TV shows were a favor to the network. When CBS offered to transfer his radio shows to the small screen, Godfrey wasn't interested. He finally agreed, informing executives, "I'm not going to cater to the camera. If you want to put us on television, just shoot the radio show the way we do it."

Remo Palmier, a guitarist in the Godfrey orchestra for twenty-seven years, observed, "And that's exactly what CBS did. Cameras were positioned in the back of the auditorium and they shot straight on. There were no sets or costumes, just down-home chit-chat and good music. Mr. Godfrey might have indulged the network by wearing a tie." Rehearsals were the afternoon before and from 8:00 to 9:30 A.M. on the day of the program. Patsy went over her numbers with the staff arrangers, then did a run-through, as the cameras rolled, with the orchestra under music director Norman Leyden for sound check and camera blocking.

"Arthur arrived at nine fifty-nine," Leyden reported, "only a minute before showtime. He came in his chauffeur-driven car, sauntered into the studio, and very nonchalantly walked in just as we were hitting the airwaves. The first time we saw him was when he came out after being introduced by announcer Tony Marvin.

"There were times when we wondered if he might not make it, but then in he'd walk. Arthur was casual, very relaxed. He didn't use a script. Everything was spontaneous. The morning show was a forerunner to 'Tonight' and the Merv Griffin–type shows." Patsy and Godfrey, described as a ladies' man, got on famously. "Arthur sat at his desk and would talk to Patsy about her work and what was going on in Nashville. Then Tony would introduce her and she'd sing. When she finished, Arthur would have the last word. Her first week, after she sang, he told her, 'Patsy, you're the most innocent, the most nervous, most truthful and honest performer I have ever seen.'

"Patsy was as professional as they come," Leyden apprised. "You'd have thought she was a seasoned artist. I was impressed with her range and abilities. If hit records had eluded her to that point, I felt it had to be the material she was recording. I saw what she could do with a good song. She had a driving style—country western but with a good, solid beat. We thought she was a natural for jazz and blues numbers. But Patsy had a mind of her own."

For one thing, she wanted to sing country. Davis and staff tried to sway her toward pop music, even rock 'n' roll. It never worked. She'd bring one of her cowgirl outfits, talk about her roots, her love of the Opry, and try to slip in a country tune.

Davis told Patsy she was "wasting [her] time recording in Nashville. That's just the wrong place. New York's where it's happening. Why limit yourself to only country music?"

"I don't want to be a pop star," Patsy would reply.

"Think of the money. You could make so much more."

"That I wouldn't mind."

"Anybody else would've been happy on the Godfrey show," songwriter Lee Burrows said. "Not Patsy. She was miserable."

"I hate every minute," Patsy cried. "I want the Grand Ole Opry, not Arthur Godfrey."

"But," countered Lee, "Godfrey's thrilled with you and you should be thrilled to be on with him. You could have quite a future on TV."

"But all they want me to sing is MOR [middle of the road]. Janette won't let me yodel!"

Patsy bugged Davis again to let her wear a western outfit her mother had made. Davis remained adamantly opposed. Patsy pouted all day.

"Patsy," asked Davis, "what's wrong?"

"You know what's wrong. No one lets me do what I want to do."

"It's not your show."

"Janette, please let me do a country song!"

"I'll think about it, Patsy."

"You promise?"

"I'll see!"

Patsy was also driving Godfrey crazy, and he spoke to Davis. When Pat Boone came on the Wednesday night "Arthur Godfrey and Friends," Davis paired Patsy with him for a duet. According to Burrows, "They wore white western everything. Patsy was in heaven!"

But Davis had let the cow out of the barn. From then on, Patsy fought Davis and Godfrey each time they wanted her to sing pop. After two weeks, things became increasingly difficult.

Godfrey told Patsy, "You've got to do the songs Janette selects. That's her job."

"I won't do it!" Patsy exploded.

"Then, young lady, you leave me no choice. You're fired."

"What?"

"You heard me! You can come back and see us every once in a while, but, Patsy, you can't buck Janette and the music staff and be a regular. We're a team. They've been with me for years. I depend on them. And they do their jobs damn well. Why don't you go to Nashville or go wherever you want?"

Patsy called Charlie with the news and packed her bags.

Winchester went wild over its native daughter. The city sent Godfrey a bushel of its red apples and a Patsy Cline Day was planned.

"We were a bit surprised at all the to-do," Mrs. Hensley observed. "Everyone bragged incessantly and declared how proud they were. Suddenly, they were taking credit for her success. I thought it funny, because when she needed them they never knew she was there. Everything quickly got back to normal. Patsy may have been a celebrity elsewhere, but at home they were used to her. She'd walk up and down the streets with her hair in rollers and no one paid any mind."

It was a time of whirlwind activity for Patsy, and some intrigue. Out of work and waiting for the release of her hit record, Patsy went to see Gay and humbled herself. She wanted her old job back, but with a raise. He kept asking why he should take her back "after you deserted us—the very ones who helped make you a star!"

"But you fired me!" Patsy exclaimed.

When the dust settled, Patsy said, "He rehired me. He needed me, I needed money, and so I promised to turn a new leaf."

What she didn't know was that the executives from CBS had informed Gay they thought Patsy Cline was "quite the little darling" and, with Dean, the potential cohost of their new morning TV show.

"HUNGRY FOR LOVE"

ARTHUR GODFREY: "I heard you got married."
PATSY CLINE: "Yes, I did."
ARTHUR GODFREY: "Are you happy?"
PATSY CLINE: "As happy as if I had good sense."

own and Country Jamboree" was filmed Saturday, February 2, as an audition for CBS. But, though she'd been rehired by Gay, Patsy didn't participate. Her diary entry for that date reads: "Supposed to do kinescope[1] for C.B.S. Didn't do Town & Country Jamboree." The next day's entry simply states: "Stayed home."

Patsy wasn't on the "Jamboree" the following Saturday. Friday, February 8, she left Winchester to appear on the Ozark Jubilee, telecast Sunday, the ninth, on ABC as "Country Music Jubilee."

Decca finally rush-released a single of "Walkin' After Midnight" on February 11. It became an immediate hit across the charts, country and pop.

Saturday night, February 16, Patsy was invited on the Grand Ole Opry as a special guest star on the half-hour segment sponsored by Prince Albert Smoking Tobacco and carried on the NBC Radio Network. In the dressing room with Roy Acuff before her segment, Patsy told him, "This is the crowning moment in my career. It took me almost nine years, but I'm here."

For the occasion, she traded in her cowgirl outfit for a more urban look. She received a rousing response when Ernest Tubb announced her. At the end of "Walkin' After Midnight," there was deafening applause. Tears rolled as she thanked the audience and came offstage. Patsy was hugged, kissed, and congratulated on her hit record by every star in the wings.

1. The technique used for recording a live TV program on film.

Jim Denny, still general manager of the Opry, told Patsy, "You were terrific. Come back and see us real soon."

"Mr. Denny," she gushed, "this has been unbelievable. And definitely worth the wait.[2] I've never seen anything like it. There ain't no place like the Opry!" Patsy didn't remind him he'd let her slip through his fingers in 1948.

Meeting western-swing bandleader Pee Wee King, who with his vocalist Redd Stewart wrote "The Tennessee Waltz," Del Wood reported, "Patsy strutted right up to him and said 'Hey, Pee Wee, "The Tennessee Waltz" is my favorite record! When are you going to write me a hit like that?'"

She looked around and found herself staring at the price tag on the straw hat of comedienne Minnie Pearl, who praised her delivery, confidence, and style.

"Cousin Minnie!" Patsy sighed. "It ain't nothing. I love to work."

"But it *wasn't* work to her," observed Pearl. "We all say that, but Patsy got a kick out of performing. Patsy was a sexy girl. She had a full figure. Patsy wasn't overweight, but a big girl. She went in for a little shorter dresses than most of the girls. Her wardrobe had a lot to do with her being known as a sex symbol. Patsy wore her clothes tight around the hips. She liked sequins and gold and silver lamé. And she could wear 'em. And high-heeled shoes. It kind of went with her. It was the package."

By February 20, "Walkin' After Midnight" was number three on the *Billboard* country charts and zooming up the pop charts, an unprecedented first for a female country artist. On March 3 it became *Billboard*'s number two country hit. In April, it attained a high of 12 on their pop charts. It was listed a total of nineteen weeks on *Billboard*'s country charts, sixteen on the pop.

Again, there was no "Jamboree" on her schedule. On Saturday, March 9, Patsy left for California, accompanied by her seventeen-year-old brother Sam, Jr., whom she introduced to McCall as a potential teen heartthrob. At his studio in Pasadena, McCall, perhaps with an assist from his "chief A&R executive," set up an audition. Patsy noted that the Four-Star president was impressed: "He thought Sam's chances were very promising and that he has a good voice."

The following week Patsy was Bob Crosby's special guest on his Los Angeles TV variety show. Then, wearing one of her western costumes and singing "Walkin' After Midnight," she filmed the syndicated TV show "Western Ranch Party," hosted by Tex Ritter. Then, with Donn Hecht and Alan Block, she did "Town Hall Party," which was telecast throughout the area. Patsy rather stunned Hecht when she informed him that she was getting her "comeuppance" for tearing down the fence between country and pop—that, as a country singer, she felt like a whore singing pop. It seemed she was the darling of the West Coast, too. Even Hollywood beckoned. Patsy was contacted by a film studio and asked if she'd do a screen test. She was enthusiastic, but nothing came of the offer.

Patsy Cline loved her fans and attracted all manner of them. At the motel where she was staying, owners Charlotte White and Mary Lu Jeans were so enthralled with Patsy's music, they wrote a song, "A Stranger in My Arms," which Patsy loved. It didn't have music, so they asked her if she would compose a tune. She took the song back to Winchester and, for the first time in her life, composed

2. Had she forgotten her 1955 appearance?

music. She sent the finished product to McCall and *told* him she was going to record it at her next session for her first album.

By the end of her first week home, Patsy was on the road again. In Des Moines, she headlined at the City Auditorium with Webb Pierce and, the same weekend, did two local TV record hops.

Because of "Walkin' After Midnight," Patsy enjoyed all sorts of media exposure. She was booked to do "The Alan Freed Show" on radio and TV and took Dale Turner along to New York. "Freed was the radio kingpin and leading entrepreneur of rock 'n' roll, so I wasn't sure Patsy'd go over," Dale explained. "But his rock background didn't bother Patsy. The show was well staged, and Patsy did whatever they told her. She wasn't the least bit scared. She just threw it at 'em, without benefit of much rehearsal. Patty was great on record, but onstage with an audience, she seemed to explode."

The crowning event was to be April 7, when she was to appear live on CBS's "The Ed Sullivan Show," then one of the top-rated programs in the nation and Sunday night's most popular fare. However, difficulties arose because of the exclusive contract Patsy had signed with Godfrey. She canceled the engagement "for the time being on the advice of William McCall, president of Four-Star Records and Sales, which holds my [recording] contract." The *Winchester Evening Star* reported, "She hopes to get everything ironed out after Arthur Godfrey returns from Africa. He has been advising her on her career and, as far as Patsy is concerned, he is boss."

Suddenly, with the incredible sales of "Walkin' After Midnight," there was a cover recording, as often happened with a major hit. Disc jockeys everywhere were inundated with Calvin Coolidge's rendition and received calls from the label's irate promotion director wanting to know why they weren't programming it.

"This is a hot record," he'd say, "the first male version." The deejays responded that the record was terrible. "Oh, you think so, huh?" he replied. A typical answer was, "It's nothing like Patsy Cline's record." The promotion man would counter, "That goes to show how much you know. Take that record and speed it up and we'll see about that!"

The prankster was none other than Bill McCall, who slowed Patsy's version to 33⅓ rpm, then pressed a 45 rpm single.

On March 28, Gerald was granted his divorce from Virginia P. Hensley Cline. About the same time, Patsy had a competitor for Charlie's affection—Uncle Sam. She was in Nashville staying with June Carter of the A.P. Carter family when Charlie phoned her with news of his being drafted.

Charlie did his army basic at Fort Benning, Georgia. On a weekend furlough, he asked Patsy to marry him. Her famous reply was: "I don't know. I ain't seen the ring yet!" She was, in fact, elated. She told her mother, "It's time I put my personal life in order. I'm all set to make married life compatible with my career goals." The blissful couple set a September date, but the engagement wasn't official yet. Patsy wanted it in the newspaper.

PFC Dick was transferred to Fort Bragg, North Carolina, and assigned to the First L&L (for loudspeakers and leaflets) of the Special Warfare Center attached to the Strategic Army Corps' Radio Broadcast and Leaflet Battalion. Their wartime mission would be to broadcast propaganda and drop leaflets on foreign troops. No one listened when Charlie told them, "Hell, I don't know anything about psychological warfare. I'm a Linotype operator! You guys are making a big mistake."

"I found I could do it as well as anything," he observed, "and, once you're assigned something, you learn you might as well adapt because to do otherwise meant nothing but miles of red tape."

Lawrence Van Gelder, a newswriter and editor on cultural affairs at *The New York Times,* was stationed with Charlie. "I was a native New Yorker, so the South was a new experience. Charlie came into our unit and right away hit it off with everyone. With no imminent threats to world peace, there wasn't much to do, so we appreciated his humor. If he wasn't around, the days were boring. Charlie was a good ole boy. He did his work but liked to have a good time and enjoyed a drink. He introduced me to more kinds of southern bourbon than I knew existed."

Patsy returned to the "Jamboree" in May, but it was a short-lived honeymoon. She caused quite a stir, appearing on the WSM-Grand Ole Opry audition for the proposed CBS morning show. Gay and Dean considered it a double-cross. Any record of what actually transpired has been lost.

Gay and Dean won the network spot. "I credited that strictly to the ignorance of the CBS brass," Dean said, laughing. "They didn't know Eddy Arnold from Ernest Tubb and, when they sat down, they said, 'We'll take this one—you know, the one with the big ears and toothy smile.' The bargain-basement brand ended up on the top shelf." The network went forward with plans to add "The Jimmy Dean Show" to their morning lineup, but protected itself with an out clause.

"This was a whole new ballgame," Gay commented. "A new show, a new format. They worried about projecting a hayseed image and doing a daily live variety program from Washington. Their geniuses came down from New York in hordes to help get us ready.

"It was an invading army. Everywhere you turned, someone was looking over your shoulder. And, sorry to say, when I was counting on her the most, Patsy let us down. I knew Jimmy'd appeal to CBS, but Patsy was my bright hope, my insurance. I knew I had a magic combination. She hardly impressed the powers that be. Their headhunters searched every closet for skeletons and Patsy gave them reports full."

Rehearsals were at 7:00 A.M. Patsy was chronically late and, according to Gay and others, "showed up with liquor on her breath." She wasn't her usual exuberant self on camera, Gay reported, and the consequences were glaring. There were occasions when Patsy, now in great demand on the tour circuit, simply didn't show.

"In spite of her potential," Gay said, "CBS didn't want to muck around. 'If she can't be on time now,' they kept saying, 'what the hell's going to happen when we go on the air?' An ultimatum came down. Either Patsy would be on time or she'd have to go. And she went."

"The Jimmy Dean Show" premiered on April 8 and broadcast live Monday through Friday at 7:00 A.M. without Patsy Cline. It was the first network show, other than news specials, to originate from Washington.

The *Winchester Evening Star* of Thursday, April 4, 1957, had a front-page story that was full of surprises. Under the headline "Patsy Cline Plans Recording Session in N.Y. After Tour," Lulu McDaniel reported:

> Winchester's songstress Patsy Cline is a busy girl these days. She is currently on a personal appearance tour through Georgia, South Carolina and Florida and will leave immediately after that for New York, where she will have several recording sessions.
>
> Her latest record, "Walkin' After Midnight," has already sold more than three-quarters of a million copies.
>
> While in New York, Patsy will make "Three Cigarettes in an Ashtray," backed with "Angel," to be released right away. She will also cut 12 records for an album for Decca.
>
> The singer left Sunday on the personal appearance tour with Ferlin Husky and Faron Young, both of the Grand Ole Opry. Their itinerary included Pensacola, Fla.; Swainsboro, Ga.; Macon, Ga.; Augusta, Ga.; and Columbia, S.C.

The article went on to officially announce Patsy's engagement to Charlie and gave details of her background and climb to stardom. In mentioning her extended appearances on the Godfrey morning show, it was noted that Patsy "wouldn't be back on Arthur Godfrey for several weeks." McDaniel reported that mail had been pouring into Patsy's fan club in Telford, Tennessee, and that Patsy had been told by Decca's Paul Cohen that she "was outselling The Platters, Jerry Lee Lewis, and Bill Haley and the Comets."

Contained in the piece was a paragraph with statements Patsy would soon very much regret making:

> Patsy says she has an advantage by being under contract to Four-Star, which takes the songs put out by Decca, puts four on a record, then sends them to all the radio stations and out of the way places Decca would never reach.

The story reported that Patsy's salary had increased from the ten dollars a night she was once paid by Bill Peer to approximately a thousand dollars weekly for her Godfrey appearances. Patsy explained that she was going to "stick with western and semi-popular music," but, except on smaller shows, discontinue "wearing her fancy western duds."

The feature was illustrated with two large photos of Patsy at home, reclining in front of a fireplace, autographing pictures and answering the phone, which "these days," she claimed, took up the better part of her time.

On April 24 and 25, with Patsy in New York to do a Godfrey appearance, McCall took her into the studio with Paul Cohen. Things would be done "his way." Gone were Owen Bradley and the Nashville musicians. Godfrey regulars the Anita Kerr Singers provided backup, almost drowning Patsy out. And, in a hint of things to come, there was an innovative first for a female country singer: She was decountry-fied and steeped in hollow pop arrangements.

Patsy evidently didn't fight the decision. She was in top vocal condition and, on the uptempo numbers, belted more than energetically. Among the songs—"Today, Tomorrow and Forever"; "Fingerprints," which Donn Hecht cowrote; "Try Again"; "Then You'll Know"; "Three Cigarettes (in an Ashtray)," cowritten by Eddie Miller; "Too Many Secrets," which boasted a full brass section; "A Stranger in My Arms" and another song she'd co-written, "Don't Ever Leave Me Again"[3]—there are some fine ones. "Angel," the song mentioned in the *Star* article, wasn't recorded.

The major problem this time wasn't in the material but in the vacillation between a Hit Parade and country/rockabilly sound. "Try Again" and "Fingerprints" are lyrically quite lovely; and the uptempo "Too Many Secrets" is a romp.

DON'T EVER LEAVE ME AGAIN
by Lillian Clarborne, Virginia Hensley and James Crawford (© 1957, Four-Star Music; copyright renewed by Acuff-Rose Music, Inc.; all rights reserved; used by permission)

...I miss your loving, your kisses, too;
Ain't nothing on earth
I wouldn't do for you.
And I cried, "Baby, oh, baby,
Don't ever leave me again"...

Baby, you know I want you so,
Tell me that you're mine
Till the end of time.
And I cried, "Baby, oh, baby,
Don't ever leave me again."

"Don't Ever Leave Me Again," an uptempo ballad, sizzles with a twangy guitar and a honky tonk piano. Patsy's sultry voice, unencumbered by background vocals, ranges from her growl yodel to a smoky saloon quality à la Mae West or Sophie Tucker.

When Bradley accidentally received the New York tapes in the mail, he became livid and demanded an explanation of Cohen. He was told the session transpired

---

3. The only known releases on which Patsy contributed music under the name Virginia Hensley. Virginia Hensley is also listed in the credits of Four-Star writer Barbara Vaughn's 1956 "Wicked Love," on which Patsy may have cut a demo.

because of extreme pressure and dissatisfaction from McCall. In the future, he was assured, Patsy Cline would record in Nashville under his auspices.

☆

Patsy began making regular appearances on the Don Owens music variety TV show in Washington and Richmond's "Old Dominion Barn Dance." She maintained her friendship with Winchester disc jockey and bandleader Joltin' Jim McCoy, for whom she had first sung as a child, and he frequently put together shows headlining her.

When he could, Charlie commuted the 350 miles to Winchester to be with Patsy. Free again on most Saturday nights, Patsy paid a surprise visit one weekend with him to the Brunswick Moose Lodge. It was a reunion of sorts. Besides Bill on this particular night, Gerald was present with his fiancé, Geraldine Hottle.

"I saw all the gang," Fay said, laughing, "and held my breath. But Pat and Charlie were cordial to everyone. Bill even seemed happy to see Pat and asked her to sing. I don't think it was a matter of his wanting her back, just that the audience wanted to hear Pat. I thought he was pretty big about not letting his feelings show. That Gerald was just as happy-go-lucky as always. It seemed like another experience to chalk up."

Patsy sang "Walkin' After Midnight," then hushed the crowd. "Thank you all very much," she said. "It all started right here and I'd rather be right here singing for you than running all over the place doing this TV show and that one."

Joseph Shrewbridge, Peer's new fiddle player, recollected, "Some people made some loud and rude comments, things like, 'You don't expect us to believe that, do you, Patsy?' And a couple of ladies booed. Other times when Patsy would show up, I don't think Bill was that thrilled to see her, but he asked her onstage because the folks at the Lodge bugged him.

"When I heard Patsy sing live, I didn't feel she had a real smooth voice, but she could take a tune and keep it moving. We might be dragging along and Patsy'd come up and set everything on fire. She'd turn and say, 'Now, you got it, dogies. That's it! Keep it going.'

"What made Patsy stand out was the way she dressed. The things she wore—tight-fitting dresses, dangly earrings, and those spike heels—were the type a loose woman'd wear. And the way she painted her lips red! A lot of men and women thought she was sexy."

☆

The men sold the records, had the reputations, and drew the crowds. But there were popular female performers. Kitty Wells's 1952 hit "It Wasn't God Who Made Honky-Tonk Angels," a slap at male attitudes of the day, allowed her to emerge from the act with her husband, Johnny Wright, on the Johnny and Jack (Anglin) Show. She signed with Decca and soon became the reigning Queen of Country Music.

There were others: Barbara Allen; yodeler Rosalie Allen; Charline Arthur; Molly Bee of TV's "Pinky Lee Show"; Pearl Butler, who sang with husband Carl; Judy Canova, the movies' "Wabash Cannonball"; Martha Lou Carson, perhaps the first Queen of Country Music; Maybelle Carter of the A.P. Carter family; Wilma Lee

Cooper, who performed with husband Stoney; Texas Daisy; Skeeter Davis, who emerged solo from the Davis Sisters; Cousin Emmy; Connie Hall; Goldie Hill; Wanda Jackson, who toured with Hank Thompson and Elvis; Norma Jean, who teamed with Porter Wagoner; Judy Lynn, a Miss Idaho and Miss America runner-up; Rose Maddox, vocalist in her brothers' hillbilly band; Rose Lee Maphis, singing with husband Joe; Louise Massey; Patsy Montana, the first country female singer with a million-seller, still performing in 1992 at age seventy-three; Molly O'Day; Texas Ruby Owen, wife of fiddler Curley Fox; Bonnie Owens, Buck's first wife and a yodeler; Linda Parker; Cindy Walker; Chickie Williams; Lulu Belle Wiseman, a duo with husband Scotty; Del Wood, the pianist whose recordings, such as "Down Yonder," were popular with Opry audiences but sold MOR; and Marion Worth.

They were rarely record stars, however, or had their names emblazoned on posters for touring shows. For the most part, these women were Opry, Louisiana Hayride, Ozark Jubilee, or regional favorites.

Del Wood asserted, "The gals were window dressing to keep the men on the edge of their seats. Patsy was the first to make them do more than breathe hot and heavy. Some of the male stars who put together the package shows had other things in mind. They'd audition anything in skirts. If they liked how you harmonized their body, quick as a wink you were at a mike. It wasn't everyone, but there were plenty."

Patsy Cline, because of her stardom and pop crossover, changed the entire perception of women in country music.

She didn't have to beg for a slot in the Grand Feature Parade of the Apple Blossom Festival on Friday, May 3. She was a star and they begged her. In honor of her national fame as a TV and recording star, the Lion's Club, which organized the parade, provided a brand-new convertible for "Winchester's singing gal." After the parade, Patsy grabbed her suitcases and headed for the airport. The next night she was headlining another big-paying one-nighter, a sold-out concert under the baton of popular bandleader Tony Pastor in Dubuque, Iowa. She noted in her diary: "Plane ticket $120 ... [got] paid $700."

On her return, Patsy attempted to secure a loan from a local bank to buy a car, but was turned down. Her friend Perry Painter, who'd gone from selling cars at Schutte Ford to becoming "a big-time operator" with his own used-car company on Valley Avenue, arranged direct financing for a late-model Cadillac.

On May 15, she was in Washington, where her chart success brought radio work singing on a series of commercials. Eight days later, Owen Bradley had Patsy back in his studio. Paul Cohen's boast to McCall that Nashville had the finest musicians was the truth. These men, some poorly educated, lived their music and knew every element through experience. Singers recorded live with the musicians, as opposed to today, when musical tracks are laid and the singer comes in to "track" vocals into an isolated microphone. With singer, producer, and musicians together, a take could be accomplished in thirty to forty-five minutes. Usually it required six to eight takes to get it right—especially if things became heated between "the Cline" and Bradley.

Patsy was a quick study and always came to work prepared. But, as in everything else, she had a mind of her own. Since she had good instincts, Bradley listened when he felt Patsy was right but had no problem telling her when he felt she was wrong.

"Patsy was the high-strung type," Bradley declared, "constantly on guard and ready to show you who was boss. She was, of course! To hear her tell it, anyway. You wouldn't have to tell Patsy anything about this women's lib business. She could've taught them a thing or two.

"No matter what I'd do, I couldn't please her. She'd start in, 'Owen, I want to do it this way.' And I'd say no. Nothing would stop her. She was always trying to get her way. It was 'Owen, honey,' then 'Owen, please,' and when she got desperate it was 'Hoss, damn it!' But I had the same reply. I kidded her that she was responsible for my first gray hairs. Every once in a while, I'd try and keep her happy by saying maybe. I never showed weakness. That would've been all she needed. Finally, Patsy'd listen. I soon discovered, I had to place myself firmly in control or she'd take right over."

Bass fiddler Lightnin' Chance found that when it came to producing Patsy, Bradley was "one smart cookie." "We musicians often were amazed at Owen's knack of keeping Patsy in tow. Sometimes she'd want to yodel and he wouldn't hear of it. Patsy'd slip it in occasionally, for no other reason than to say to herself, 'My ass! Owen's not controlling me.' It was a cat and mouse game, and Owen ended up being top cat. When she gave him a hard time, he stood up pretty well. And he had this unique ability of doing it tactfully—until it got right down to the nitty gritty. Then he let Patsy or whomever know who wore the pants.

"Patsy was a hell of an artist. I liked her, sometimes in spite of herself. She was such a dynamic personality, you never tended to harp on her idiosyncrasies. Like her smoking, language, and hot temper."

Trudy Stamper, then WSM-Grand Ole Opry public relations director, and a long-time friend of Patsy's, said, "From the female viewpoint, Patsy didn't mind being pushed, but she wouldn't let you step on her. When things went against her, she didn't take it lying down. Her defense mechanisms shot into play."

Don Helms, Hank Williams's steel guitarist, who played on many of Patsy's sessions, asserted, "Patsy was picky about what she wanted. She had her ideas about tempo and arrangements. Patsy could be stubborn, especially when she saw something a certain way. She was on the I-know-what-I-want side, which I respected. It might be embarrassing, but she was usually right.

"She and Owen had friendly disagreements. I never remember the situation between them getting belligerent. But she'd stop right in the middle of everything and say, 'What's this? What's he doing? Y'all wait a goddamn minute while I have a little discussion with Mr. Bradley!' It was never anything that couldn't be ironed out."

Neither Bradley nor the sidemen had had a woman artist tell them what she wanted and how to play.

Helms told the Country Music Foundation's John Rumble: "Patsy'd say, 'Give me a C chord and let me show you how this goes.' If she had a demo, she'd play enough to give me an idea of the chord change. Then she'd sing so we could hear her phrasing. Owen was very knowledgeable and a very good musician. He'd sit down at the piano and say, 'This is what we're trying to do. This is the way it goes.'

"Patsy'd sing some and he'd play some and say, 'I think it oughta be about this tempo. Grady [Martin, electric guitar and fiddle], what do you think?' And he'd say, 'Well, I don't know. Tommy [Jackson], what do you think about a fiddle intro on this?' Grady knew how to get what Owen wanted out of the musicians."

When Bradley was ready, he'd give the command. "Okay, let's take one. Let's see if we can get lucky." Then they'd run through a number as many times as required until they got it right.

At 9:30 A.M. May 23 Patsy began recording six tunes. The material, as was often the case, reflected the turmoil and joy rampant in her life. They started with a remake of the unreleased "I Don't Wanta," then cut new songs "Ain't No Wheels on This Ship," "That Wonderful Someone," "I Can't Forget You," "Hungry For Love" and "(Write Me) In Care of the Blues," the last two by Eddie Miller with an "assist" from W. S. Stevenson. In a nod to New York, Bradley brought in the Anita Kerr Singers to provide backup vocals.

Immediately after the session, Patsy returned to Winchester to celebrate Charlie's twenty-first birthday. The celebration ended on a low note, as Patsy saw him off to Fort Bragg. Mrs. Hensley recalls she and Patsy spending the evening sewing new cowgirl costumes. Patsy also packed her bags again.

On the morning of May 25, she stacked the trunk of her dream car, a big, white, albeit used, Cadillac. She and a companion left on a personal appearance tour. Patsy was still riding high with "Walkin' After Midnight" and, on May 27, Decca released a 45 rpm of "Today, Tomorrow and Forever" with "Try Again" on the flip side. The new record was heralded with a full-page ad in *Billboard.*

On the tour, Patsy shared billing with Brenda Lee and Porter Wagoner. The stars trooped from city auditorium to high school auditorium in a cavalcade of cars, usually Cadillacs and Chryslers, a station wagon for the band, and a trailer for instruments and equipment.

During the tour, according to lanky blond singer Porter Wagoner, roots for another long and endearing friendship were laid. "You might say we were lonely and Patsy and I had a brief road fling."

"I was almost thirteen," Brenda Lee reminisced. "I'd been signed to Decca by Paul Cohen when I was nine. I had records, but this was before I had any big ones. We had done a show in this tiny Texas town somewhere between Amarillo and Lubbock. I don't remember who else was on the bill, and it's best that I don't.

"People in the business back then tended to take advantage of you. I was a kid and didn't have a manager. It was just Mama and me. That night I didn't get paid. The promoter skipped. That was a common thing. The performers who went to the front before the show got paid. The ones who didn't know better got left out.

"We were left stranded without even a dime to call home. Patsy heard from someone what happened and took me by the hand and scolded, 'Don't you ever let this happen again!'

"Mama told Patsy we were depending on the money to get to the next town. Patsy came to the rescue. She fed us and put us in the car with her mother Hilda. It was a wonderful gesture that drew me to her. In spite of the differences in our age, we became fast and very close friends."

On the road, as the mothers slept in the back, the stars in the front seat talked a blue streak.

"You make sure you get your money before the show and in cash, no matter what the promoter's excuses are. You tell him, no money, no show, you hear?"

"Okay, Patsy. Sure thing. We sure do appreciate you doing this."

"Ain't nothing."

"You could have left us stranded, considering—"

"Considering what?"

"That you don't like me."

"Who told you I don't like you?"

"The Opry gals said you were fuming mad about me being on so much."

"That was politics! Red Foley brought you from the Ozark Junior Jubilee to the Opry and when you moved to Nashville last year, he pulled strings to have you on every week. There wasn't room for the rest of us. We gals got to stick together. This business's big enough for everybody."

"I'm sure happy about your record."

"Well, thanks, but damn it, it ain't doing me no good."

"What do you mean, Patsy?"

"It's a big hit for everybody but me."

"Gosh, what are you talking about? You got a record on the charts. Decca's always been honest with me—"

"Brenda, Four-Star's making a bundle on the publishing rights and leasing 'Walkin' After Midnight' to Decca, who's wiping up with the sales. So far, I ain't got nothing but excuses. It's that damn McCall! He's keeping me under his thumb and won't let me record anything I want."

"Well, now you have a new record."

"It'll be the same. That bastard!"

Patsy rode in the Warrenton, Virginia, Fourth of July parade wearing one of her sexy "New York originals," a strapless, sequined cocktail dress with a sash made of yards of tulle. The banner on her convertible had the legend: "Walkin' After Midnight ... Patsy Cline ... Decca Recording Artist & T.V. Star ... A Winner All the Way!"

Melody Boys musician Roy Deyton saw Patsy dressed in one of her colorful cowgirl outfits that weekend at the Warrenton park where she'd won the country music championship three years before and had since returned annually for an appearance.

"Patsy and I talked about my marriage and her relationship with Charlie. I asked how things were now that she had a hit record and she told me, 'Financially, they're bleak. I haven't made any money to speak of from the record. Not many royalties and lots of deductions.' Then she went into a tirade about McCall and how he was cheating her."

Two weeks later, the Wilburn Brothers and Don Helms, now guitarist in their band, played Watermelon Park near Berryville, Virginia. "Patsy and Charlie came to the show and visited backstage," recalled Teddy Wilburn. "She was upset we hadn't called her."

"Y'all know I been cooking all day," admonished Patsy. "Supper'll be on the table as soon as we get there."

"You don't have to bribe us to sing a number on the show," joked Doyle.

Patsy lit into him. "Y'all better take me serious! Charlie'll tell you, I've been cooking since early morning and y'all are coming to eat."

"Honey, it would be nice," explained Doyle, "but we've already checked into the motel. And tomorrow morning we leave for Pennsylvania."

"Well, you can just check out of that damn motel. You don't seem to understand. I've got this big ham in the oven and I've made my famous mashed potatoes. You can't let it go to waste."

"Teddy, why are we standing here arguing with her?" said Doyle, shaking his head. "We ought to know better. Ain't nothing gonna do her till we check out of the motel and follow her home."

"Goddamn right, Hoss!"

"Okay. You win!"

On the show Patsy did "Walkin' After Midnight," and the musicians gathered their belongings and drove to Winchester. After supper, they sat up into the wee hours talking shop. Teddy told Patsy about a song, "Dakota Lil," he'd written but never recorded. It was about an outlaw and done from a female viewpoint. She wanted to hear it, so Teddy sang it.

> I wore my guns so proudly,
> I'd kill for just a thrill.
> No man could ever back me down,
> Not me, Dakota Lil...
>
> I wore my guns so proudly,
> No more I ever will.
> Though I must die no one will
> Ever forget the name Dakota Lil.[4]

Patsy loved "Dakota Lil" and had Teddy sing it over and over. "I've got to record it! Get me the lead sheet as soon as you can." According to Doyle, Patsy probably thought she could yodel on the song. "On her stage shows, Patsy'd tear the house down when she yodeled, but doing it live and putting it in a record groove are two different things. That little hiccup growl that she loved to do drove Owen up the wall. He didn't think Patsy had a country voice. He considered her pop. She had an unusual voice, but it wasn't as sterile as most pop voices. When she sang, I heard heart, soul, and tremendous feeling. To me she was country. She was a country girl, country onstage and country at heart."

She took "Dakota Lil" to Owen Bradley and was set to do it when McCall intervened. "You know if it isn't a Four-Star copyright," he told Bradley, "she can't do it." Patsy broke down and cried when she heard the news.

Decca released her first album, titled simply *Patsy Cline,* on August 5. There were twelve tracks, including "Walkin' After Midnight." Patsy's second EP was released the same day. The covers of both packages show a bobbysoxer Patsy Cline in a colorful sweater and white blouse.

4. Used by permission of Teddy Wilburn, Sure-Fire Music, Inc.

Patsy appeared with Red Foley at the August 10 Ozark Jubilee, broadcast as "Country Music Jubilee" on ABC Sunday nights. She sang "Three Cigarettes (in an Ashtray)," which she announced was the single (backed with "A Stranger in My Arms") from her new album.

Decca's full-page *Billboard* ad read: "The 'Walkin' After Midnight' Gal has 2 New Smash Songs!"

The deejays didn't buy the hype, and the public didn't respond.

Four days later in Winchester, it was a time for celebration. "For Patsy's twenty-fifth birthday, September 8, the weekend before their wedding, we were in high spirits and partied at the Moose Club," said Dale Turner. "Between the birthday and nuptial toasts, I got a taste of the games success plays. Patsy was the home town girl but a star. Her friends kept asking her to sing. She got furious and said, 'You'd think they'd leave me alone and let me have some fun.' This was an invasion of her privacy.

"I tried to calm down Patsy, saying it wasn't worth getting angry over. I told her, 'When you're well known you don't have any privacy. That's the price you have to pay.' When Bill Peer called Patsy onstage that night, she went but not without telling him and the audience off."

On Sunday afternoon, September 15, fifty friends and family members gathered at 720 South Kent Street, the large brick house Patsy was renting for her family. Mrs. Hensley decorated the living room elegantly for the occasion. A minister friend officiated at the wedding.

Patsy wore a pink two-piece knit suit, heels with a paisley print, pearl earrings, a wide inverted bowl hat with sheaves of ostrich feathers, and a large orchid corsage. Charlie had on a beige suit with a colorful tie and suede shoes. He chain-smoked before and after the brief ceremony.

Rice was strewn everywhere. Mrs. Hensley followed the couple with a broom, sweeping up. Late that afternoon, after a quick change of clothes, a reception was held at the crepe paper- and gladioli-bedecked Mountain Side Inn out on Highway 50 near North Mountain, Virginia. Patsy, sporting her trademark dangling earrings, changed into a black-and-white taffeta cocktail dress pinned with her corsage. Charlie wore his suitcoat jacket with black slacks.

Under a sign proclaiming "Welcome, Patsy, 'Here['s] to the Star that likes to Shine—Winchester['s] Own Patsy Cline," the couple posed for the traditional picture of the bride feeding the groom cake. Patsy and Charlie waltzed alongside another homemade sign that read "Welcome Patsy and Charlie. Sept. 15."

With Patsy working and Charlie at Fort Bragg, there was no honeymoon.

There were other newlyweds back in the Brunswick Triangle. Gerald took Geraldine Hottle for his third wife.

"Gerry was what Gerald always tried to be and never could achieve," said Nevin Cline. "She had looks and class. She was somebody. The only problem was that she went into the marriage with a big misconception. She thought Gerald had money. He didn't. She didn't find out until after the wedding. The jewelry store called and demanded immediate payment for her engagement and wedding rings.

"She got so angry, Gerry got all of Gerald's clothes and threw them out the windows and front door. And when he got home that night, she threw him out, too! I know, because he called me to come and pick him up."

Geraldine eventually divorced Gerald, and he married yet again.

A few days after her marriage, Patsy was in New York to appear on "Arthur Godfrey and Friends." During the afternoon rehearsal, Godfrey passed through the studio and stopped to speak.

"Hello, you pretty thing!"

"Oh, Mr. Godfrey. How are you?"

"Fine. Just fine. Hey, I just heard you got married."

"Well, yes, sir, I did."

"Are you happy?"

"I sure am! Just as happy as if I had good sense."

It was another new beginning for Patsy—one filled with career highs, career lows, and sadness. Whenever she was asked if she was happy, she said her marriage to Charlie was "made in heaven." But it was full of hell.

"LOVE, LOVE, LOVE ME, HONEY, DO"

JEAN SHEPARD: "Patsy, you're not gonna put that on. You can't in your condition!"

PATSY CLINE: "I need you to help me."

JEAN SHEPARD: "I'm sorry, Patsy. I just can't. You'll kill that baby."

PATSY CLINE: "I don't give a goddamn!"

*P*atsy had stardom but couldn't capitalize on it. It wasn't as if all the forces in her life were conspiring against it. She was in the studio, on TV, and on the road helping to beat the drums. "To be near my man," Patsy moved to Fayetteville, North Carolina, where she and Charlie rented a house on Pool Drive.

While Charlie became enmeshed in the secrets of the First L & L, Patsy uncrated wedding gifts, bought furniture and drapery, and busied herself decorating. She told her mother and friends she was "taking this marriage seriously, putting supper on the table like a good wife, making friends with the neighbors, and working on having a healthy baby instead of hit records." Still, she commuted to Nashville and road appearances.

"Country Song Roundup" had Patsy on its list of New Faces of '57, but Patsy wasn't feeling too inspired about what was happening in the studio. On November 13 she arrived in Nashville for the WSM Birthday Celebration and D.J. Convention to hype her new single, to be officially released on the eighteenth, of "Then You'll Know" with the new version of "I Don't Wanta" from the May sessions. That Friday, Lee Burrows ran into Patsy at the Andrew Jackson Hotel. She had a handsome soldier on her arm.

"Hello, Patsy!"

"Lee, good to see you!"

"How're you doing?"

"I'm fine. Doing great! In fact, I'm married. Lee, this is my husband Charlie."

"Congratulations, Patsy. It's nice to meet you, Charlie."

Lee didn't seem too enthusiastic, and Patsy gave her a look. "I was disappointed, and, knowing Patsy, she wanted a good reaction. Maybe it was the stigma of a man in uniform. If Gerald looked like her uncle, it was altogether different with Charlie. He looked like a kid in his uniform. Well, they were kids, really."

Patsy told Lee, "I'm really in love this time. It's the real thing!"

"I'm happy for you," Lee enthused, "and wish you well."

Recalled Del Wood, "When I met Charlie at the Opry that weekend, I wondered if ole Patsy had a bag over her head. I couldn't stand him. I don't know what on earth attracted her to him. Well, from the way Patsy carried on, maybe I do. But I thought, 'What else do they have in common? They come from two different worlds.' I knew if he was in the service, he couldn't afford to keep Patsy in the style she'd become accustomed to.

"They really seemed mad about each other, and love is love. If it's blind, we don't know it till later. However, I have to say that the more I hung around Charlie, the more I liked him."

On Friday night, dressed in a tight-fitting, sleeveless silk cocktail dress, Patsy was presented with *Billboard*'s Most Promising Country & Western Female Artist award and *Music Vendor* magazine's award for Greatest Achievement in Records in 1957 for "Walkin' After Midnight." Patsy was presented with trade magazine awards on December 5 by Red Foley during the telecast of "Jubilee U.S.A." in Springfield, Missouri.

She was riding a crest, except in the release of record product. Decca did nothing to promote the new single, and the deejays made no effort to play it. McCall's material, once more, proved to be wrong. After the massive success and sales of "Walkin' After Midnight," Patsy Cline was cold. She had an idea that she hoped would make her hot. She was a major recording and TV star, so why not have a manager in charge of her career?

Back home in Fayetteville, the Dicks had a delightful early Christmas present. Patsy got one of her wishes. At the doctor's for a routine physical, she discovered she was pregnant. She set about making baby clothes and becoming the best "mom-to-be in the whole world."

According to colleagues, her pregnancy exposed the two sides of Patsy. "She was happy to be having a baby," informed a male entertainer she was to work with extensively, "especially after her miscarriage while married to Gerald. And at the same time, Patsy was concerned how, just as she was gaining ground professionally, having a baby might affect her career.

"Patsy talked about a lot of things, but that was her way of rambling on and hoping you'd help her find the answer she was looking for. When she saw how excited Charlie was about the baby, she put all other thoughts out of her mind. Suddenly, where she'd been climbing the ladder to stardom, Patsy switched horses and became devoted to motherhood. That was Patsy. Just when you thought you figured her out, she'd do a full reverse."

As Dale Turner found out, "After Patsy married, I didn't want to lose touch. We spoke on the phone and corresponded. She wasn't having it easy. She asked, 'How long does it take to see a few bucks from a hit?' and I told her not to hold her breath.

"Bill McCall figured Patsy owed him since her hit gave her the opportunity to go on the road. She tried to get work in North Carolina. In the D.C. area, we were stars on the 'Jamboree,' but, where she was, no one had even seen it.

"As soon as she was pregnant, Patsy threw me a surprise. She talked about retiring. I laughed. This was not the Patsy I knew. But she sounded serious."

On December 13, Patsy and Charlie drove to Nashville, where McCall and Cohen, searching for that elusive but all-important follow-up hit, had her record another batch of Four-Star songs. There was traditional country: Hal and Ginger Wallis's standout "Walking Dream," "Stop the World (and Let Me Off)," and "If I Could See the World (Through the Eyes of a Child)," a lovely if inappropriate tune for a hoped-for hit which Patsy may have been attracted to because of impending motherhood. The "sure thing" at this session was "Cry Not for Me," cowritten by Donn Hecht.

That song and "Walking Dream" marked the first time since "Walkin' After Midnight" Owen Bradley, beset with constant requests from McCall and Decca executives, went for a pop sound. The Anita Kerr Singers, with their choruses of "bop, bop, bop" seem to be showcased equally on the former. But, in the mishmash of material, as Patsy once quipped, "nothing flew out of the coop." She was straddling the fence, with one side pushing her toward pop and her feelings leaning toward country.

"I was experimenting," Bradley said. "We'd try anything that would stick."

Thank God for the Grand Ole Opry. The money was a pittance, but considered worth what you had to give up because of the WSM and NBC Radio broadcasts. With a potentially vast audience, maybe someone who heard Patsy would go out and buy her records. When she appeared Saturday, January 11, 1958, Jean Shepard had a memorable meeting with Decca's expectant songstress that night in the ladies' dressing room. Patsy was stomping, raving mad and cursing as Jean entered.

"What's the matter, kid?"

"Goddamn it, Jeanie! I'm pregnant."

"Honey, that's great. I'm thrilled for you. Is this your first?"

"Yeah. And you know what, it may be my last!"

"What are you so upset about? I think it's wonderful."

"Wonderful? It's horrible, damnit!"

"You've gotta be kidding, Patsy. Everything's going great guns for you."

"Yeah. Here I am just coming off a big record and I go and get knocked up! I won't be able to go on the road or do TV. It's gonna really tie me down."

"Frothing at the mouth ain't gonna help any. It's done. If you'd behaved yourself and done what you were supposed to do, things like this wouldn't happen. But, honey, wait. You'll see. Everything's gonna be all right."

"Everything's gonna be awful!"

"Oh, you'll change your mind."

"No, I won't!"

At another gabfest in the ladies' room, Patsy told Del Wood about her retirement plans. "It wasn't like Patsy to be talking of quitting. Her decision was ironic because when she was married to Gerald he'd have given anything if she quit the business."

"Heck, hon, women have had babies and lived to sing again!" Del informed. "What you need to do is move to Nashville, where you can see and be seen. In this town, it's out of sight and out of mind."

"Del, it's different now. I was so consumed with singing then, I didn't care whether I made a living or not. It was something I had to do. But now I have the recognition and I want the money that goes along with it. You know, it's pretty damn frustrating when you have a hit record and don't make any damn money from it. And, try as I might, for the life of me I can't come up with another hit."

"You got a few good years left, girl! Whatever you do, don't throw in the towel."

Patsy's new album was out and dying a quick death. The next day she left for a five-day engagement on "Arthur Godfrey Time" in New York, where she and Godfrey plugged her debut set.

Anyone who'd been in touch with Patsy or heard her talking must have registered surprise at the announcement a few days later in the magazine *Music Reporter*. Xavier X. Cosse was married to and manager of Martha Lou Carson, who'd gone from the Renfro Valley Barn Dance in Kentucky to stardom on the Opry and RCA Records. Under Cosse, she had left gospel music behind and was "experimenting with city sounds," playing prominent supper clubs. Cosse was opening an office in Nashville to expand his client list, and the newest addition to his roster would be Patsy Cline.

Though the news item was small, Randy Hughes saw it.

According to Charlie, "Patsy should have been a wealthy woman from the way everything was going as a result of 'Walkin' After Midnight.' Had she been signed directly to Decca, Patsy wouldn't have a financial worry in the world. It was a disgrace the way she was taken advantage of by McCall. He had her coming and going.

"Patsy got the short end because McCall deducted every conceivable expense, such as her trip to California, hotels, meals, and phone calls, from her royalty pool. She was left with virtually nothing. To make matters worse, he controlled everything she did in the studio.

"The TV shows Patsy did paid very little back then. And she made damn little for her road dates. God, if anybody worked to earn a living, Patsy certainly did. She never stopped. I used to wonder where on earth she found the strength. She had sheer determination."

Owen Bradley related, "Patsy would often come to me and cry about the selection of songs McCall was forcing on us. She used to get so down and depressed. She'd ask me, 'Hoss, can't you do something? I feel like a prisoner.' I tried, but with her Four-Star contract, there was nothing we could do. I kept talking with

Paul [Cohen] about signing her direct to the label, which he wanted to do all along, when her Four-Star deal expired."

The January 13 release of "Stop the World (and Let Me Off)" backed with "Walking Dream" did nothing to alleviate Patsy's losing streak.

McCall and Cohen were determined to strike gold. Six songs were recorded February 13: "Let the Teardrops Fall," "Never No More," the very poignant but badly mistitled "If I Could Stay Asleep," "Just Out of Reach," "I Can See an Angel" and a pop remake of "Come On In," the first time Bradley added brass on a session with Patsy. There was nothing exciting, except for her infectious "theme song":

COME ON IN (AND MAKE YOURSELF AT HOME)
by V.F. Stewart (© 1955, Four-Star Music Company, copyright renewed by Acuff-Rose Music, Inc.; all rights reserved; used by permission)

Come on in
And sit right down,
And make yourself at home.
If I had one wish I wish I could
Go back to my old neighborhood,
Where the good folks, they all love you as their own.

Then I'd go over to my neighbor's house,
Knock on the door and they'd all sing out
"Come on in and sit right down,
And make yourself at home."

I'd sing their praises long and loud,
'Cause they're all my folks and I'm mighty proud
Of the little old town
Back home where I was born.

I wish that I could hear them say
In the good old-fashioned friendly way,
"Come on in and sit right down,
And make yourself at home."

Well, they don't lock their doors at night,
'Cause they all know they're doing right,
And the good Lord's bound
To have them for His own.

If I'd go back
To hear them pray
In the little pine church, they all would say,
"Come on in

And set right down
And make yourself at home."

Then it was back to Fayetteville to get to Springfield, Missouri, where on the twenty-second Patsy was Red Foley's guest star on the Ozark Jubilee, which was telecast the next night on ABC.

In early May, "Winchester's singing gal" returned home for the Apple Blossom Festival Parade. Arriving two days before the event, Patsy met with Lion's Club officers to have a convertible assigned. When she was told she was too late, that all the spots in the parade were filled, she grew fuming mad.

That night she ran into thirty-nine-year-old Charlie Armel (cousin to bandleader Bud Armel of the Kountry Krackers), a friend who worked as a salesman at Winchester's Kern Motors on South Loudoun. Armel was also, according to a musician, a "half-assed" guitarist, and sometime flagman at the speedway. Henry Kern, who owned the Edsel/Studebaker dealership with his brother Richard, said, "Charlie was someone who liked to help everyone, and he adored Patsy."

The next morning, Armel came into Kern's office, all excited. "Mr. Kern, we gotta help Patsy. She's in a jam. Those Lion's Club guys won't let her have a slot in the parade. Would you loan me the black Edsel convertible?"

Kern, like other Winchester car dealers, furnished parade cars to the Lion's Club, and there was one that hadn't been spoken for.

"I'll drive it," said Armel, "and take good care. I'll be fully responsible."

"Why do you want to do this, Charlie?" asked Kern.

"Well, you know how it is with Patsy. She's always struggling and this goddamn town's never given her her due. I think we oughta make 'em stand up and take notice."

Armel decorated the car himself and made a big sign: "Winchester's Own Home-Grown Star, Miss Patsy Cline—TV & Decca Records Star." With whatever clout he had, he drove the car to the start of the parade route on Saturday afternoon and somehow snuck into the lineup and, reported Kern, "took off as big as you please."

All along the route, Patsy received more recognition and applause than the celebrity grand marshal. The Lion's Club wasn't pleased and swore this would be Patsy's last parade appearance.

The following weekend in Nashville at the Opry, Jean Shepard again saw Patsy, now past her fifth month, as she rushed into the backstage ladies' room waving a corset.

"Jeanie, give me a hand!"

"Patsy, you're not gonna put that on," Jean said. "You can't in your condition!"

"Yes, I can. I need you to help me."

"I'm sorry, Patsy. I just can't. You'll kill that baby."

"I don't give a goddamn!"

Patsy slammed the corset on the basin counter. "I can't go out there and sing looking like this. Jeanie, I look awful!"

"No, Patsy. You don't know what you're doing."

Patsy opened the door and yelled, "Get in here, Essie!"

The beloved black woman who was a veteran backstage helper to the women performers said, "What you want, Miss Patsy?"

She handed Essie the corset. "Here. Make it as tight as you can."

"Oh, no, Miss Patsy. I can't do that!"

"Goddamn it, Essie. Do as I tell you!"

"Yes, ma'am. Yes, ma'am. But—"

"No buts, just do it!"

Jean looked on in disbelief. "Patsy, you're out of your mind."

"I know what I'm doing," she replied. "I don't do anything halfway. Halfway is half-assed, and that ain't for me."

Late that spring, at the Gaithersburg, Maryland, Agricultural Exposition, where Patsy was headlining the show, Roy Deyton saw her and met Charlie for the first time. He didn't like what he saw.

"Charlie, you remember Roy from Bill's band," Patsy said.

"I don't want to hear about Bill Peer."

"Patsy, maybe we oughta sit down and get a bite to eat," Roy advised.

Charlie, leaning on Patsy, stumbled to a table off the dance floor in the covered hall. Patsy and Roy ordered food. Charlie had another drink.

"Charlie, it's almost showtime. Why don't you stay here while I go—"

"I don't want you to go up on that stage!"

"But, honey, we're here and I've gotta or I don't get paid."

"Don't worry about that, goddamnit! I can support you. I don't want you in this business. You ought to be home like other wives."

"Charlie, calm down. You're embarrassing me." As she stood to leave, he grabbed her.

"I told you I don't want you to sing! Didn't you hear me?"

"Yeah, I heard you. Everybody heard you. Even the goddamn cows heard you. But I'm going!"

Charlie shot up. Patsy pulled away from him.

"I'm your husband, and you'll do what I say!"

"Charlie, you must be confusing me with someone who gives a good goddamn about what you say!"

He picked up his drink and poured it over her.

"I hope to hell you don't think that's gonna stop me! Like I told you, I'm singing!"

Patsy changed and went onstage. Charlie, mumbling, excused himself and headed for the rest room. Deyton saw him stagger off, but into the ladies' room, where loud squeals erupted.

Jean Shepard sighed with relief when she heard that on August 25, Patsy delivered her "bundle of joy." She had gone from Fayetteville to Winchester, to her mother's house. When Patsy went into labor, Charlie was able to get emergency leave and sped home to be by her side.

Patsy became the epitome of a doting mother. "Her entire life seemed transformed," Mrs. Hensley said. "Everything centered around Julie. She loved all the things associated with motherhood, feeding the baby, singing to her, changing her diapers. Even I was surprised."

Patsy wrote Brenda Lee:

> We have decided on the name Julia Simadore.[1] I think it's a wonderful name for an absolutely beautiful, precious baby. I am so proud I could shout her name from the rooftops. I had some rough going near the end, but when I hold my Julie I can forget everything. All I have to do is gaze upon her gorgeous face.
>
> You know I don't miss the rat race a bit. Well, maybe, a little! But I got a whole new career and my show now. Ever since I gave up smoking, I've gained so much weight that I got to do something. I'm on a strict diet.
>
> Well, I'll catch you later. Write and tell me your news.

A week later, Charlie returned to Fort Bragg, but when Patsy decided to remain with Julie at her mother's, he gave up the house on Pool Drive and moved on base.

It didn't take long for the constant drone of "changing diapers and powdering the baby's behind" to get to Patsy. "Sitting around the house playing the wife and mother is starting to drive me crazy. I've gotta get out. I've gotta sing." Charlie had hoped the baby would get show business out of Patsy's blood. Though he admitted he wasn't taking home a terrific salary on a soldier's pay, he thought of himself as the breadwinner and it hurt him to see Patsy having to work. But, as Patsy saw it, they were broke. Even if her recording career had hit a dead end, touring and the occasional one-nighters would bring her the type of big money Charlie could never earn.

Owen Bradley, who became head of country A&R for Decca in 1958 when Paul Cohen began devoting all his time to developing the company's Coral label, never lost faith in Patsy's potential. He wanted to sign her to Decca, but the idea was quickly shot down by Sidney Goldberg, vice-president of sales, who pointed out the disastrous downhill trend after the high of "Walkin' After Midnight." After one big record, Patsy showed no staying power and hadn't identified with the public.

As evidence of the quandary Decca executives were in regarding what Patsy Cline product to put out and how to promote it, they released "Dear God" and "He Will Do for You," two quasi-spirituals recorded December 15, 1956. Maybe it was in the spirit of Christmas. Great thought must have preceded the selection of singles, but more than a few mystifying decisions were made. With blunders such as this, it's amazing Patsy Cline had any career at all.

1. Though Patsy claimed the unusual middle name was Delilah's sister's name from the Bible, she actually fell in love with it when she saw Cecil B. DeMille's 1949 film *Samson and Delilah*, starring Hedy Lamarr and Victor Mature, one of her idols. However, the name assigned Angela Lansbury as the villainess' sister was Semadar.

Bradley felt Decca was as boxed in as Patsy. On January 8 and 9, 1959, for the first time in almost a year, he had Patsy in the Decca studio recording. Ever the innovator, he had installed stereo equipment. These were Patsy's first such sessions; though recording techniques had drastically changed, Patsy and other artists still recorded live with the studio musicians.

The sessions marked the first time Bradley used the Jordanaires, a gospel quartet who'd been providing backup for Elvis, as backup for Patsy. There was above-average Four-Star material: "I'm Moving Along," "I'm Blue Again," "Love, Love, Love Me, Honey, Do," "Gotta Lot of Rhythm in My Soul" and "Yes, I Understand." The session musicians included Floyd Kramer on piano, and Hank "Sugarfoot" Garland and Grady Martin on electric guitar. On "Yes, I Understand," in the style of Patti Page's "Tennessee Waltz," Patsy overdubbed the harmony.

Gordon Stoker, leader of the Jordanaires, has insightful memories of Patsy.

"We began working with Patsy on those January 1959 sessions. A lot of people took Patsy to be unfriendly, which we certainly found out about right away. She didn't want us, and, after a few minutes, we didn't want to be there. She yelled at Owen, 'I've never had anything like this! I don't want four guys singing and covering me up.' We stood there redfaced and didn't know what to do. Owen gave a sign to take a break. And we'd just gotten there! He took Miss Cline aside and they had a powwow, and we could see the smoke signals rising.

"When she returned, it was, 'Hello, guys, I'm Patsy.' We introduced ourselves and she said it was nice to meet us after all she'd heard. We said how pleased we were to be working with her. It might have been Neal [Matthews] or Hoyt [Hawkins], but one of them said, 'And we've heard a lot about you, too!' There we were, all smiles and laughing. She apologized, as she put it, for acting like a horse's ass. And, I think it was—well, I won't say. But someone commented, 'And a nice one it is, too.'

"She raised her voice to us more than once, but it was just the artist bubbling over. Patsy could be cold to those she didn't know. However, that was rare. She had a lot of respect for those who worked with her, and we had great respect for her. In fact, we got to love her like a sister—and sometimes that's the way we had to treat her.

"Wally Fowler opened the door for Patsy. Ole Wally had a reputation for doing all sorts of promotion, and Patsy got his number fast. She said he had his eye on her, but she taught him how to blink. He wasn't alone. Others had ideas, but Patsy knew how to take care of herself. She was hard and strict with herself and knew the ropes. She'd been up and down them enough. Patsy could be rough, then turn the charm on.

"She was the sweetest person in the world if you played your side of the cards right. But, brother, she'd fix you fast if you didn't. She'd love you to death if you did something for her, but God forbid if you turned on her. I liked her because she was brutally frank. If you messed with her, she'd strike like a snake. She'd look you right in the eye and say, 'Don't you ever cross my path again, you son of a bitch!'

"I was impressed with her professionalism in the studio. During the sessions she was all business. Patsy could do everything but read music, but that never bothered her. She could sing anything from hillbilly to standards and semiclassical. She could do anything she set her head to.

"You only had to give her a melody once and she'd sing it. Usually, we'd work up the tune with her and do it in one take. How she could turn it on! She gave me goose bumps. She didn't know the impact she had. Patsy had something and didn't know what. It was just a God-given gift. Many people say Patsy was conceited, but she was humble. I'd say, 'What a great job!' She'd answer, 'You really think I did it good?' And we'd say, 'Yeah! Are you kidding?' She was a perfectionist but didn't realize it. She simply wanted to make it the best she could.

"Patsy was sensitive. If you were talking and happened to look her way, she'd haul over and ask, 'Hey, you guys talking about me?' We'd say, 'No. We were talking about the news.' Then she'd snap, 'Oh, no, you weren't! What did I do wrong?'

"Patsy always knew what she wanted, which led to problems with Owen. He kept Patsy in check, or when he thought the moment right, he'd get her mad. He knew her capabilities. He also knew what would and wouldn't sell. Owen was good to her and good with her. He knew what she needed to do the job. Unlike many A&R men, he had great musical ability.

"We'd work everything out with Owen and rehearse. Patsy'd tell us, 'Hey, I want you guys singing here and I want you to hum with me here. I want you to go ooh, ah, ooh, ooh here and ah, ooh, ooh, ah here.' Then Owen would come in and say, 'What are you doing, young lady?' They'd get into it. He'd station himself between us and Patsy and just go to town laying it off on her. And she'd lay it right back. It was so much, so fast, I can't remember exactly what but it could get dicey. 'Young lady, you're gonna do this my way,' Bradley would say. 'Oh, no, I'm not,' she'd protest. 'Don't you forget I'm the one driving this here wagon!' he'd say. And she'd yell back, 'Don't you forget who's your best passenger!'"

Then they'd burst out laughing, and the remarks were forgotten. "Patsy was quick, but I don't know who was fastest," Stoker noted. "I don't think Patsy ever got the best of Owen. She might have thought she did a couple of times, but he just didn't let on that maybe she was right and he let her do something her way. He knew how to keep Patsy in line."

Stoker asserted that, from time to time, Patsy brought personal problems into the studio. "All of us cared about Patsy and vice versa. We helped and encouraged her when she'd be a little bit down because of Charlie. They'd have fights and she'd come in bruised or with a black eye. We never asked questions and she'd never say directly what happened. She'd just say, 'Me and Charlie had a row.' We'd ask, 'He didn't hit you, did he?' And she'd reply, 'Well, somebody did!' They'd be fighting like cats and dogs one minute, then kissing the next.

"Patsy would confide in Ray Walker, our bass singer. He was a pretty handsome guy. She was genuinely fond of him. Ray was married, with a family and was a strict, religious person. He didn't fool around, but, at the same time, he was fascinated by Patsy and she was crazy about him. They talked and shared."

The weekend of her first session with the Jordanaires, Patsy ran into Teddy Wilburn at WSM Radio at Seventh and National Streets, where she was performing on the Opry broadcast called "Friday Night Frolics."

"Patsy finished her session at five that afternoon," Teddy recalled, "and had acetates she wanted me to hear. There wasn't time that night, but Saturday, after the regular Opry at the Ryman Auditorium, Doyle and I were hosting Ernest Tubb's 'Mid-Nite Jamboree' at his record shop. Patsy came up to me with her acetates and snapped, 'Well, Hoss, I mean business. When are you gonna listen?' I advised we'd do it after the show. She said, 'If you don't find any excuses!' I told her, 'Hey, Patsy, we'll do it!'

"After the broadcast, when everyone had left and the store was all but empty, we listened to her songs on an audition turntable. She and I discussed each one and her feelings about it. She wasn't happy with a couple of takes. I told her I didn't know how she could have done them better. She smiled. That was the assurance she was looking for.

"It became a habit after that. She'd always want me to listen, even if it meant playing something over the phone. At times, she'd be crying and would say she was in trouble. Trouble to Patsy meant she was in a situation and didn't know what to do. Speaking to me helped. I didn't beat around the bush."

In February, Charlie was "costed out," or honorably discharged, a month early. He and Patsy rented a tiny house on Valley Mill Road out Route 7, a mile outside Berryville. He went back to work at the *Winchester Star,* but, as often as possible, he'd commute to dates and Nashville with Patsy.

Two singles resulted from the January sessions. On February 23 Decca backed "Yes, I Understand" with "Cry Not for Me," recorded in December 1957. There was no response. According to Donn Hecht, McCall got wind that "Patsy was running helter skelter with her shopping basket" looking for another label. As a result, McCall did nothing to promote the release. Trying to cover himself, in case he lost Patsy, McCall had her do two Four-Star demo sessions. In March, Patsy guested on the Opry twice and, on Saturday, April 4, promoted her latest release on the Ozark Jubilee, telecast Sundays now on ABC as "Jubilee, U.S.A."

If Patsy's fortunes weren't on solid ground, the news from her doctor didn't help. She was pregnant. Julie was not quite nine months. Patsy later told Del that Charlie wasn't exactly thrilled with the news. "You couldn't blame him," explained Del. "They were living hand to mouth. What they didn't need was another baby, but they both knew how to prevent such things."

Her pregnancy didn't slow Patsy down; she worked twice as hard. In June, desperate for money, she spoke to Tex Ritter about her financial situation. He contacted his niece Jane Deren, associate producer of Compton, California's "Town Hall Party," on which Patsy had appeared. Mrs. Deren hurriedly booked several southern California engagements.

Driving to Nashville on July 2, Patsy arrived in Bradley's studio the next afternoon saying of the material McCall had sent, "This stuff stinks! What's he trying to do, wreck my career? I won't record this crap." Bradley couldn't help but concur. He recalled Patsy breaking down and crying. Bradley tried to calm her, but she told him she'd spent all her money to come to town to record. Now all she'd have to show for the trip was the $20 she'd receive for two appearances on the Opry. He assured her they'd come up with something.

The songs they chose were the spirituals "Just A Closer Walk With Thee" and a southern perennial from 1890, "Life's Railway To Heaven," a favorite of

Patsy's since her days at Gore Baptist Church. Like so much else before, the tracks didn't prove to be at all commercial, but, with superb backing from the Jordanaires, they were charged with emotion and the best singing Patsy had done to date.

Ten days later, with a plane ticket and small advance, Patsy flew from Washington to Los Angeles. "Patsy stayed with me and was the delight of my life that entire week," Mrs. Deren recollected. "She was always so full of pep, I couldn't help but ask, 'Patsy, honey, where do you get all that energy?' She replied, 'That's just me!' For a star, she was the most down to earth, good-natured person you've ever hoped to meet. Everyone fell in love with her."

After the TV show, Mrs. Deren and her brother took Patsy to her various dates in his car. "Near the end of the week, Patsy woke up in the middle of the night. She was pretty sick and in acute pain. She told me she was three months pregnant. I had no idea and felt horrible, having kept her so busy and running her here and there in the car. I called my doctor and he advised we rush her to Queen of Angels Hospital. When he told Patsy she had a miscarriage, I don't know who cried the most, Patsy or me. The next morning, Patsy called Charlie. He was more worried about how she was taking it. But Patsy was in good spirits. Her energy continued to be abundant. And she entertained everyone at the hospital with her sense of humor."

In spite of setbacks and disappointments, Patsy never lost her exuberance for goals. "If you want to know what country music is all about, I'll tell you," she'd say to friends and colleagues. "It's singing in clubs and sleazy joints, traveling on dusty, rutted roads and staying in motels that have seen better days. It's signing autographs and posing for pictures and doing the very best job you can. It's meaning something special to a whole bunch of strangers who you'll probably never see again but who suddenly become like family."

This was her life. There was little Patsy wouldn't do to advance her career. She played gigs usually organized by Joltin' Jim McCoy, such as local dances, taverns, drive-ins, carnivals and the Shenandoah County Fair at Mount Jackson. She was often accompanied by McCoy and his band, the Melody Playboys (not to be confused with Bill Peer's band).

Dale Turner recalls times being so bad that Patsy wrote to her frequent employer, Don Owens, in Washington, and asked him to send her money so she could come to town and do his show. He not only got her back on the show as a regular but also began booking her in the region.

Whenever Patsy complained to touring stars or the Music City establishment about not making a decent living, she kept hearing, "Why don't you move to Nashville? That's where it's at." This wasn't Charlie's wildest dream, but Patsy began a calculated campaign to make him think it was.

"If only," she said, "I could achieve membership on the Grand Ole Opry"—which meant a guarantee of so many appearances a year—or "I keep hearing I'm too far away from Nashville, so I'm just gonna have to pick up and move there." She even had a job all picked out for Charlie. She told him that with references from the *Star*, he'd easily get a job at one of Nashville's newspapers or many printing plants.

Charlie insisted he knew not to argue with his wife once she had her mind made up. If he wanted any peace, he knew what he'd have to do. It remained to find a way to finance the move.

Patsy Cline

Side Three

. . . I know about heartaches,
I know all the mistakes
that young love can make—
I've made them . . .

—"That's How a Heartache Begins" by Harlan
Howard (© 1962 Pamper Music/Sony-Tree Music
Publishing, Inc.)

"STOP, LOOK AND LISTEN"

RANDY HUGHES: "You think Patsy's pretty?"
GRANDPA JONES: "Yes, sir, I do."
RANDY HUGHES: "Do you think Patsy's got sex appeal?"
GRANDPA JONES: "She's really got it. Just like the stink
off an ole hog!"

U ncle Sam gave the Dicks an unexpected helping hand. As Charlie has reported, "the army made a big boo-boo." Patsy's allotment checks kept arriving. It was a windfall they hadn't counted on. Patsy wanted to cash the first check, but what if the army realized their foul-up? Finally, after much consternation, she ventured to the bank. She could always say they assumed the money was due them. When nothing happened, she cashed six more checks of $137 each.

With the army surely hot on their trail, what else could they do but move? It was Nashville or bust!

SUNDOWN IN NASHVILLE
by Dwayne Warrick (© 1969, Cheerleader/Mernee and Silver Sand Music; all rights reserved; used by permission)

The sign says welcome to Nashville.
From whatever road you've been down,
It seems like the first of the milestones;
For here is the city, the town.

It's a quaint old mystical city,
Where idols and legends have stood.

Port city where dreams come to harbor,
A country boy's Hollywood.

But it's lonely at sundown in Nashville;
That's when beaten souls start to weep.
Each evening at sundown in Nashville,
They sweep broken dreams off the street.

You walk down Sixteenth to Broadway;
You walk past the new Hall of Fame
And the record man with the big cigar,
He never once asked me my name.

You'll find some discarded love songs
And visions of fame on the ground;
And pieces of dreams that've been shattered.
They drift to the outskirts of town.

The façades stand in Music City, but a unique world has disappeared. The warehouses in the shadow of the Cumberland River that symbolized Nashville as the leading furniture, printing, and Bible publishing center of the Southeast are haunted by decades of ghosts.

All streets led to lower Broadway. The hub was the Ryman Auditorium, whose ancient walls were shook by the Grand Ole Opry. Stars and fans mixed at Tootsie's Orchid Lounge, Linebaugh's Cafeteria, the Ernest Tubb Record Shop, and every hillbilly palace where a guitar picker found work.

On dark side streets, in parking lots or roadside parks such as the one in which Virginia Hensley once slept, loyal fans ate waxpaper-wrapped sandwiches from home and out of store-bought canned goods. Boarding houses and greasy spoons, such as the Trailways bus station coffee shop, were filled with a tough breed of young and not-so-young struggling musicians from all points.

Patsy and Charlie arrived in late August 1959. They rented a two-story house at 213 East Marthona Drive off Old Hickory Boulevard in Madison, north of town. Just across the street, they had a famous neighbor, Hank Snow. Until their furniture arrived, they stayed at a motel and looked up old friends.

Opry star Carl Butler and his wife, Pearl, who then lived in south Nashville on Twenty-seventh Avenue, were at the top of their list. "We met Patsy a couple of times," Pearl recalled, "on the 'Town and Country Jamboree.' While Carl sang, I palled around with everyone backstage. And, one night, there she was decked out in one of the cutest cowgirl outfits I'd ever seen. Patsy came up and said, 'Hi, Pearl. I'm Patsy Cline.' It was love at first sight. Patsy had this black address book and, before we left, she took down our address. She said, 'Someday I'm gonna be coming to Nashville and I'll look y'all up.' I replied, 'Y'all be sure 'n' come see us! If you don't, we'll feel mighty hurt.'"

Those were Pearl's favorite words. She made the statement to everyone and meant it. Carl was a hillbilly singer in the truest sense. He had a loyal following and a successful recording career. Pearl, who loved to talk and cook, went everywhere he did.

WSM-Grand Ole Opry photographer and raconteur Les Leverett recalled, "It wasn't uncommon on Sundays, after church, to find almost as many cars at the Butlers. The artists discussed the road and, most of all, ate. You'd think Pearl had been in the kitchen for two days. Toward late afternoon or early evening, someone would break out their guitar and we'd sing. By then, the house was packed. A couple of times Carl leaned over and asked, 'Hey, who's that over there?' I had no idea. Neither did anyone else. It'd turn out to be some fan who came backstage after their show to whom Pearl waved, 'Y'all be sure 'n' come see us.' And they did."[1]

In October, there was a knock at the door. "Why, my God!" Pearl exclaimed. "Oh, my gosh. Carl, it's Patsy, Charlie, and their little girl! Y'all come in here out of the cold."

"You mean, you're gonna invite us in?" Patsy asked.

"Of course. Y'all can stay if y'all want. Our home is your home."

"We've been to see a lot of people who told us to look them up if we ever came to town and not a one invited us in."

"Hon, we ain't nobody but us."

"It's sure nice of you."

"You're friends, ain't you?"

The Dicks and Butlers spent the day together, talking shop, cooking, eating, and Pearl carrying on over Julie. That night, Pearl walked Patsy and Charlie to their car. Returning inside, Pearl noticed Patsy had dropped her address book. She kept it a few days, then called the motel. The Dicks had checked out. She tried to call, but they didn't have a phone.

Charlie went to work almost immediately, as a Linotype operator at the Curley Printing Company. Patsy, now that she'd done what everyone told her she had to do, was determined to hit it big again. If she couldn't do it recording Four-Star's songs, she'd hit the concert trail. After all, she was a known commodity.

Pearl saw Patsy three weeks later in the Andrew Jackson Hotel at the WSM Birthday Celebration and D.J. Convention.

"Hon, did you lose something?" she asked.

"Yes, I did."

"Well, don't worry. I found it. But y'all don't have a phone."

"That's all right, Pearl. Now that we know you and Carl, I don't need that address book anymore."

Pearl claimed, though she and Patsy weren't intimates, that welcome at their home sealed the bond between the Dicks and Butlers.

"Whenever we saw each other at the Opry," she related, "it was like old home week, exchanging stories and talking about the children. Patsy made several road

---

1. Pearl eventually joined the act. The Butlers later took in and were mentors to Dolly Parton, who was generous to them upon her success. But when hillbilly music fell from fashion and the couple knew nothing else, there were harsh times. Their furniture and antiques were auctioned for back taxes, but Pearl was still the ever-gracious hostess.

trips with us. Carl would do the driving and Patsy and me'd stretch out in the back seat and gossip. It was rough on everyone in those days, but the women had it especially bad. We'd commiserate."

"Of all the people who say they knew Patsy well," touted singer Faron Young, "I probably met her the earliest and knew her best. I knew Patsy and Charlie, their ups and all their downs. I was a friend they could count on and I was always there when she needed a shoulder to cry on."

Faron Young was born in Shreveport, where he became a member and star of the Louisiana Hayride before joining Webb Pierce's band and migrating to Nashville and the Opry. He possessed unusual vocal styling for country music and soon became dubbed the Frank Sinatra of Country. He was a consistent hitmaker with many country top-10s and, in 1957, the number one "Hello, Walls," an early Willie Nelson tune that brought him pop crossover.

With his band, the Country Deputies, Young was in constant demand on the road. His popularity led to Hollywood, where in 1958, with Ferlin Husky, he co-starred in the musical *Country Music Holiday*, which featured Zsa Zsa Gabor.

When you talk of Nashville reputations, Young's name is bound to surface. If you believe all you hear, he would be one of the most contemptible characters in show business. Nothing could be further from the truth. It's impossible not to like him, in spite of his raunchy vocabulary and bluster.

He helped establish many careers. One example: when he was asked by a local bellhop for a job, Young didn't put him off. He set an audition, and soon Roger Miller was the Deputies' drummer.

Faron says much, sometimes too much. How much can be believed or proved is another story. He makes pronouncements that more than a few in Nashville claim to be "total B.S." He has been married to his wife, Hilda, nearly thirty-five years and has four children. But to hear him carry on, you'd forget he has a certain distinction as a devoted family man.

"Faron is truthful," Miller commented. "A lot of people say he's a lot of talk and no action. But he's a lot of talk and *some* action. His heart's as big as his mouth."

When the Dicks moved to town, Patsy talked Charlie into going to see their old friend on her behalf. Faron was, as he's proclaimed many times, "hotter than hell."

"Sheriff,[2] times are tough," Charlie said. "Patsy's records aren't selling."

"Rock 'n' roll's killing us all."

"I got a job but I'm not bringing home that much. And now we got another mouth to feed."

Charlie told Young that Patsy had seen not "one red cent" from McCall and Four-Star Records, and that she was waiting out her contract "on pins and needles."

"What can I do?" Young asked.

"You've known Patsy since the 'Town and Country Jamboree.' Can't you put Patsy on some of your fair and road dates?"

2. A nickname he acquired from his country and western movie.

"Goddamn right I can do anything I want! I gotta have a girl singer, but things are bad. Will she work for the right price?"

"Oh, yeah. She just needs to be out where the public can see her."

Young paid Patsy twenty-five, then fifty dollars a night and took care of her hotel bills and most of her meals. In that era, that wasn't considered a horrible salary for women singers. Male stars commanded a great deal more.

Patsy proved an asset to Young's show. "You could've pricked Patsy a thousand times and not burst her bubble," he observed. "She was enthusiastic and the crowds reacted fantastically. I kind of took her under my wing and taught her the ropes. We did things like that. Back then, country folk were a lot tighter. I learned from Hank Williams and Carl Smith to build a song from the heart. I told Patsy sincerity was everything.

"I helped her with her stage presence. Patsy wanted to play the guitar. I told her, 'Throw that fucking thing away and get that mike and start walking with it. As long as you're moving, they're gonna watch you. If you stand still, no one's gonna pay you any mind.'

"I traveled in a Cadillac limousine and she rode with me. Only the gospel groups had buses then. Since we knew each other for years, it was natural for Patsy and me to hang out. She had a great sense of humor and we were always cracking jokes and telling dirty stories. Patsy cussed like I do, like a drunk sailor."

Soon Faron and Patsy were inseparable. In fact, according to Young, it went beyond that. "Patsy was pretty when she wanted to be. But I'll never forget Charlie telling me that the day after he met her, he went to pick her up to take her to work in Washington. He went to her house in Winchester and knocked on the door. A woman with no makeup and her hair in rollers opened the door. He told me, 'Goddamnit, Sheriff, I didn't know who the hell she was!'

"He said, 'Pardon me, ma'am, is Miss Cline in?' The woman replied, 'Goddamn it, Charlie, I am Miss Cline!'

"Even when she wasn't at her prettiest, I was attracted to her. Patsy's body made up for the rest on those occasions. She was built like a brick shithouse. When she moved, the earth shaked. I couldn't take my eyes off her body. Ah, she had a figure like an hourglass. And what an ass. She looked good. I had other motives than just her being on my show. Oh, she knew what I was thinking. There wasn't no doubt about what I was up to."

Once when Young "tried to pull something," Patsy told him off.

"Sheriff, what the fuck are you up to?"

"Yep. Right."

"No, you little mother," she said. "You can just forget about that stuff. You ain't getting into the Cline's britches! Don't you know you're messing with a married woman? Ain't we like brother and sister?"

"Okay," Young answered. "It'll be all business from now on."

Faron spoke of the qualities that endeared him to Patsy: "Patsy had magnetism but she also had a pair of balls. Her heart was bigger than she was. She'd do anything for anyone. She'd see a girl singer and just knock her out with her supportiveness. Patsy never showed jealousy.

"When Patsy first came on the Opry, Margie Bowes, who was quite a beauty from the Virginias and later married Doyle Wilburn, was on. Patsy and me were in the wings observing. At the end of Margie's song, Patsy turned and exclaimed, 'God, Sheriff, that little girl can sing!'

"Patsy was comfortable. She was never running scared. She knew the extent of her talent and figured there was room for everyone.

"She might have shocked the shit outa a few of the girl singers from small towns and religious backgrounds. One night at the Opry this new gal came to Patsy and asked, 'What do I do about so-and-so? He keeps bothering me.' She snapped, 'Tell him to go fuck himself! That'll fix him.' Everyone thought that gal was gonna faint.

"You couldn't get ahead of Patsy. If somebody farted in her direction, she'd raise her ass and fart right back. Didn't make no difference to her who you were. She'd tell you to go screw yourself in a minute."

Patsy still wasn't happy with her earnings. In November, she and Charlie went to see Faron's dapper, sophisticated manager, Hubert Long, who also had a booking agency, about securing top-drawer engagements for Patsy. Long had a knack for show business and changed the way promoters dealt with country stars. He demanded and received big money for his acts.

Long informed Patsy his hands were full and introduced her to his "right arm," thirty-two-year-old Ramsey Dorris Hughes.

"Well, howdy, Dorris!" Patsy said.

"You've got a few names I could call you," he snapped.

"Is that right? Why don't you try calling me one!"

"No, ma'am. I respect you too much. But I want you to know your reputation has preceded you."

"Is that good or bad?"

"Depends on who you talk to."

"What have you heard?"

"Plenty! But you don't look like too much to handle. And I won't bring up any stuff if you remember all my friends call me Randy."

"Okay, Hoss."

"Randy'll do fine."

She told him of her struggles with Four-Star and that she still hadn't seen a penny from the "Walkin' After Midnight" royalties.

"We'll work on some bookings, but what you need is a manager," Randy advised.

"What's that gonna do for me? And how could I pay him on what I'm earning?"

"You don't pay anything unless you earn something. And you'd be earning more. You need someone who knows how the hell this town operates, someone who'll fight for you."

"Since you're so almighty, get rid of that bastard Bill McCall. He's bleeding me dry!"

"I'll give it a shot."

Patsy and Charlie discussed the idea with Bradley, who told them a manager couldn't hurt. What did Patsy have to lose?

Patsy Cline, after winning *Arthur Godfrey's Talent Scouts* in January 1957. On the back, Patsy inscribed to *Town and Country Jamboree* star and mentor Jimmy Dean and his wife, "Thanks a million for the helping hand you have given me and God bless you both, Humbly yours, Patsy Cline." (Collection of Jimmy Dean)

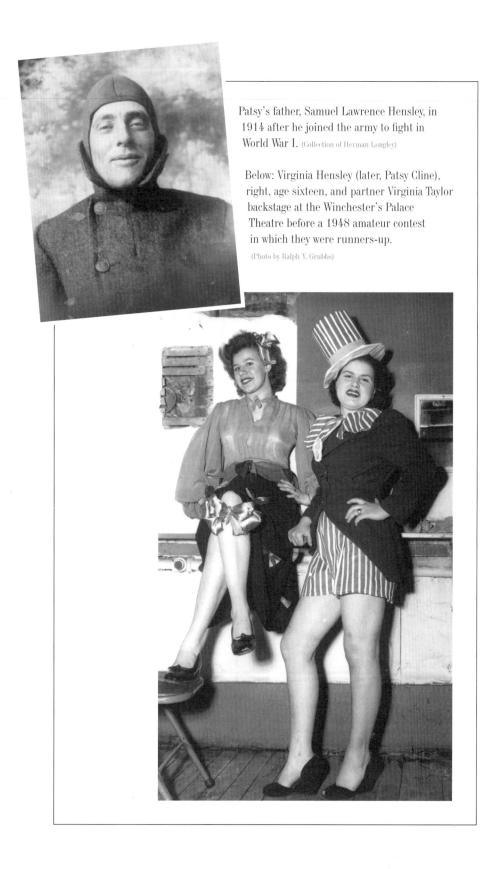

Patsy's father, Samuel Lawrence Hensley, in 1914 after he joined the army to fight in World War I. (Collection of Herman Longley)

Below: Virginia Hensley (later, Patsy Cline), right, age sixteen, and partner Virginia Taylor backstage at the Winchester's Palace Theatre before a 1948 amateur contest in which they were runners-up.

(Photo by Ralph Y. Grubbs)

Above: Patsy and Bill Peer onstage,
March 1953, at the Brunswick,
Maryland, Moose Lodge.

(Collection of Roy Deaton)

Above: Patsy and Gerald Cline
at their wedding reception,
1953. (Collection of Gina Cline)

Left: Patsy singing along to
a recording at 608 South
Kent Street, December 1956,
prior to her departure for
New York.

(Faye Crutchley/Collection of Ellis Nassour)

Above: Patsy's cowgirl look, complete with boot earrings and Western fringed gloves, 1956.
(Rush Studios, Winchester, VA)

Left: Patsy, the "Jamboree hillbilly with oomph," 1954, visits hometown radio station WINC, where she made her auspicious debut six years earlier with bandleader Joltin' Jim McCoy.
(WINC Radio Archives)

Above: Patsy riding in the 1956 Apple Blossom Festival Fireman's Parade with her sister, Sylvia Mae.
(Collection of Harold Madagan)

Patsy in 1956, wearing one of her trademark Western outfits designed and made by her mother, Hilda Hensley.
(Rush Studios, Winchester, VA)

Above left: Jimmy Dean, flanked by Patsy and
singer Dale Turner, 1955, Washington, D.C.
Capitol Arena, home of the *Town and Country
Jamboree*, a live regional telecast.

(Collection of Dale Turner Westbury)

Above right: Patsy meets
Faron Young on the *Jamboree*.

(Country Music Foundation Archives)

Above: Patsy and *Jamboree*
co-star George Hamilton IV,
age nineteen, 1956.

(Collection of George Hamilton IV)

Right: *Jamboree* stars Patsy,
Mary Klick, and Dale Turner
doing a commercial for sponsor
Gunther Beer in 1955.

(Collection of Jimmy Dean)

Opposite: The 1955 Apple
Blossom Parade, Winchester.
Patsy rides with Bill Peer (to
her immediate right) and his
Melody Boys. (Winchester *Star*)

Right: Patsy in 1956 at WINC
Radio. She played piano by ear.
(BMI Archives)

Below: Patsy poses in a win-
dowless log cabin, 1955.
(Collection of Herman Longley)

Above: Patsy and Gerald in
Nashville, 1955, for her appear-
ance on the Grand Ole Opry.
(Collection of Jenny Yontz)

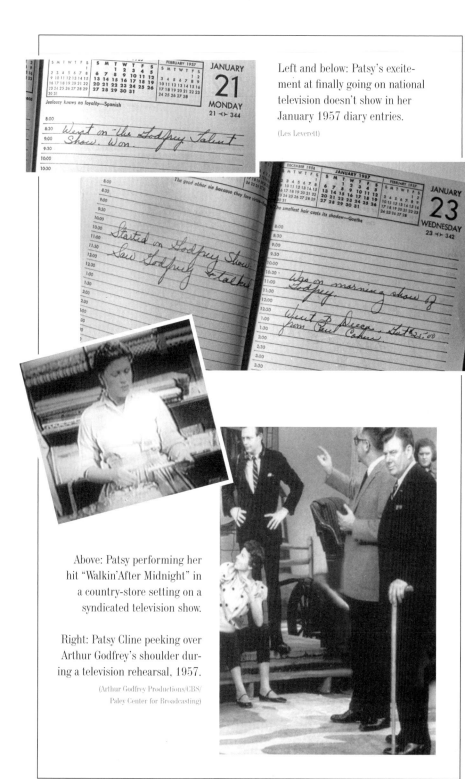

S M T W T F S — FEBRUARY 1957

JANUARY
21
MONDAY
21 → 344

Jealousy knows no loyalty—Spanish

Went on the Godfrey Talent Show. Won.

Left and below: Patsy's excitement at finally going on national television doesn't show in her January 1957 diary entries.

(Les Leverett)

DECEMBER 1956 — JANUARY 1957 — FEBRUARY 1957

JANUARY
23
WEDNESDAY
23 → 342

The good abhor sin because they love virtue

the smallest hair casts its shadow—Goethe

Started on Godfrey Show. Saw Godfrey. Talked

Was on morning show of Godfrey.

Went by Decca. Got $25.00 from Paul Cohen.

Above: Patsy performing her hit "Walkin' After Midnight" in a country-store setting on a syndicated television show.

Right: Patsy Cline peeking over Arthur Godfrey's shoulder during a television rehearsal, 1957.

(Arthur Godfrey Productions/CBS/ Paley Center for Broadcasting)

Left: Patsy Cline and Charlie Dick depart after their wedding ceremony on September 15, 1957, at 720 South Kent Street, Winchester, which Patsy rented for the occasion.

(Collection of David Grimm)

Below: Patsy and Charlie's wedding reception, 1957.

(Collection of Faye Crutchley)

Above: Patsy's early friend, the outspoken Jean Shepard (married to Hawkshaw Hawkins), a standout Opry performer.

(Ellis Nassour)

Above: Brenda Lee greets Elvis, December 1957, at the Opry, a week after her thirteenth birthday.

(Elmer Williams)

Right: Patsy at Winchester's VFW, May 1957.

(BMI Archives)

Left: A Saturday night crowd gathers for the Grand Ole Opry at Nashville's historic Ryman Auditorium, 1959.
(WSM Photo/Les Leverett)

Below: The Singing Sheriff, Faron Young, costumed by Nudie. (Country Music Foundation Archives)

Below: Opry and recording star Cowboy Copas, standing with guitar, his daughter Kathy (who would marry Randy Hughes), and musicians on WSM-TV's *Pet Milk Show*. (Collection of Burt Goldblatt)

Patsy in Nashville at Owen Bradley's barn Quonset hut studio, November 1960, for the taping of *Country Style, USA*, sponsored by the U.S. Army. With her are the Jordanaires (left to right: Neal Matthews, Gordon Stoker, Ray Walker, and Hoyt Hawkins), Jerry Byrd on steel guitar, and Hawkshaw Hawkins at piano. (Collection of Burt Goldblatt)

Producer Owen Bradley, who ran Decca Records, Nashville, at piano, with country music giant and early supporter of Patsy, Ernest Tubb. (WSM Photo/Les Leverett)

Above left: Patsy ready to hit the road on another tour as "Walkin' After Midnight" soars up the country and pop charts. (Faye Crutchley)

Above right: Dottie West, a Tennessee farm girl breaking into the business, met Patsy backstage at the Opry in April 1961. A lifelong friendship resulted. (WSM Photo/Les Leverett)

Below left: Honky tonk pianist Del Wood, an Opry regular, had numerous backstage "domestic chats" with Patsy. (Les Leverett)

Below right: Hillbilly stars and Columbia Records artists Carl and Pearl Butler were among Patsy and Charlie's earliest Nashville friends. (Les Leverett)

Left: Patsy with DJ Bill Strebeck of WMAG Radio, Forest, Mississippi, interviewing Patsy at Nashville's WSM Radio, September 1960, prior to the start of the annual Country Music Festival. (WSM Photo/Les Leverett)

Right: Rose Marie Flynt, Patsy's friend, confidante, and correspondent, summer 1960, just after Patsy found out she was pregnant. (Collection of Rose Marie Flynt)

A sign from the Nashville Country Music Festival, 1960: It's official, Patsy is signed to Decca and managed by Randy Hughes.

The Wilburn Brothers, Teddy (left) and Doyle, helped establish and guide Loretta Lynn and Patsy's careers. Teddy was often Patsy's confidante. (Ellis Nassour)

Charlie Dick, far left corner, observes Pasty being interviewed during the October 1960 Country Music Festival.

(WSM Photo/Les Leverett)

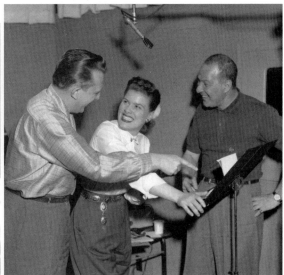

Patsy with Decca Records producer and visionary Owen Bradley (left) and New York Decca Records vice president Paul Cohen, who had faith in her potential and signed her to the label after her dismal Four-Star years.

(Country Music Foundation Archives)

Comedienne Minnie Pearl, one of the first performers Patsy was to meet in her Opry debut, was at first put off by Patsy's often unladylike ways, but they became friends.

(WSM Photo/Les Leverett)

First Decca LP, self-titled, with Four-Star songs, including "Walkin' After Midnight," August 1957

Left: Patsy in May 1961: the calm before the storm. (WSM Photo/Les Leverett)

Middle: Harlan Howard, 1965. Among his classics is "I Fall to Pieces," written with Hank Cochran. (BMI Archives)

Right: Singer Jan Howard (formerly married to songwriter Harlan Howard) in 1980. After a rocky start, she and Patsy became close friends. She made the demo of "I Fall to Pieces." (Ellis Nassour)

Aloha! Patsy departing Honolulu with (left to right) Faron Young, agent Hubert Long, and Ferlin Husky, October 1960, after headlining a USO show. She was pregnant with her second child.

(BMI Archives)

Hughes came from the middle-Tennessee town of Murfreesboro and went into the business at fifteen. He played rhythm guitar with Moon Mullican, Tennessee Ernie Ford, Ferlin Husky, and George Morgan, appearing frequently with them on the Grand Ole Opry. In 1949 he originated the first country variety television shows in Miami.

In 1955 he fell in love with Kathaloma (Kathy) Copas. The couple married in 1956, and not long after he decided to allow his musical skills to take a back seat to his financial expertise.

"Randy was working for Ferlin and making some investments," said Lightnin' Chance, now Hughes's business partner. "We were turning our stock commissions back into buying more stock. While Randy handled Ferlin, I ran the brokerage end and looked after the real estate holdings."

"When Ferlin was running hot, Hubert wanted to take over his career. He kept telling him, 'You need someone established who knows how to do things.' Ferlin realized he needed Long, but he was fiercely loyal. Finally he told him, 'If I go, you gotta take my boy.' So he did.

"Hubert took Randy and really taught him the management business. Eventually he took some of the load off him, becoming road and business manager to such stars as Ray Price, Wilma Lee and Stoney Cooper, and the Willis Brothers, not to mention his father-in-law Cowboy Copas."

Copas was a good example of how Randy's business acumen transformed a stalled career. Cowboy, along with Ernest Tubb and Hank Williams, had been a country superstar in the late 1940s, first as a performer on Cincinnati's Midwest Hayride and on King Records with such hits as "Filipino Baby," about a South Carolina sailor in World War II who falls in love with a dark-skinned girl from the Philippines; "Signed, Sealed and Delivered"; and "Honky-Tonkin'." Making a complete switch, he recorded "Tennessee Waltz," "Kentucky Waltz," and "Tennessee Moon" and earned the moniker the Hillbilly Waltz King.

He suddenly fell out of favor with fickle audiences and for almost a decade found work only on the tavern and fair circuits—until Randy stepped in. Under his guidance, Copas recorded "Alabam." Soon he was back on the charts with it, "Flattop," and a redo of "Signed, Sealed and Delivered." He was an Opry sensation.

Cowboy told everyone he owed his resurgence to Randy. Hughes's friends weren't surprised.

"Randy was one of the nicest, most straightforward guys you ever met," Husky praised. "But, above all, he was honest."

Singer Billy Walker stated, "Randy knew the business. He not only was a musician but he knew the musicians and could put together some swinging bands. What really made him stand out was this sixth sense he had about the potential of artists to become stars."

"Randy was another gamble for Patsy," Chance explained, "but he proved to be her winning bet. He was a born smoothie and, if you're going to be a manager in country music, that's the number one prerequisite. Randy went to the goal for Patsy. He didn't have much luck at first, but he tackled McCall. Randy was all for Patsy and McCall was always dipping his hands into the gravy for his share.

"Charlie told us that McCall deducted everything but the kitchen sink from Patsy's royalties. Randy and McCall were constantly at each other's throats. Randy kept harping to McCall and McCall'd harp right back. Poor Randy used to say, 'God, I wish he'd give us a break!' But I also heard how McCall would cringe at the mere mention of Randy's name."

Randy booked a dual spot on the December 12 telecast of "Jubilee, U.S.A." for Husky and Patsy. They sang solo, then dueted on "Let It Snow." The result was bagfuls of mail. That gave Hughes the idea of pairing the stars on Husky's show.

The outrageous Husky is still considered one of the consummate showmen in Nashville music history. Randy handled the singer's investments, played guitar in his band, and was his road manager. When Young didn't have work for Patsy, Husky had her touring with him. Thirty-three, he hailed from Flat River, Missouri, where he began as a disc jockey, then in the late forties established a recording career under the aliases Simon Crum and Terry Preston. He felt Ferlin Husky sounded unreal and made-up. Onstage and off, he was an eccentric. He wore foppish three-piece suits, lavender and ruffled lace evening shirts, loved gold jewelry, and smoked cigarillos. When he sang he transfixed audiences.

As Preston, he dueted with Jean Shepard on "Dear John Letter," the number one country hit of 1953, had a smash with "Gone" and later with "Wings of a Dove." He was a pioneer in syndicated country TV shows and, with Young, modern country movie musicals, which, though awful, proved to be good box office in the South and Southwest.

Women meant everything to Husky, and he had four marriages to prove it—six to date.

"During the whole time with that Four-Star bastard," Charlie reported, "Patsy only earned nine hundred dollars from 'Walkin' After Midnight' and her other recordings combined."

Donn Hecht said, "I certainly don't want to suggest that everyone's heart bleed for Bill McCall. No one loved Patsy better than me, except for Charlie, but things have been exaggerated. Those close to her never admit the staggering number of failures before and after 'Walkin' After Midnight.' Those countless sessions added up to a considerable amount over a long period. The money to pay for all that came from her royalty account.

"Patsy would do warmup sessions with the musicians to zero in on what she and Owen Bradley would shoot for in a final master session. True, Bill brought her into the studio again and again to record and contractually forced her to record Four-Star material. But the music business is a business like any other.

"Of Patsy, it's been stated that money was her biggest objective. In a way, I suppose this was true. I was in Bill's office several times when Patsy'd call collect and ask for cash advances for the rent, the car payment, her mother, you name it. They'd get into violent arguments.

"On one occasion, McCall hung up, shouting, 'She wants twenty-five hundred dollars!' He threw up his hands. 'Last week it was seven hundred. The week before, four thousand! She's a stupid, selfish girl who thinks money grows like lettuce leaves.' I remember once she told him something to the effect that she wasn't satisfied with her mother having a four-year-old car and wanted to get her a new Cadillac.

"If she wanted money, it was for some kid down the street who needed clothing for school, or a neighbor who couldn't pay a doctor's bill. I honestly believe that if Patsy had all the money in the world, she'd have divided it equally among all its people, and left herself only enough for bus fare.

"At the height of 'Walkin' After Midnight,' Patsy was in Des Moines. She was contacted by the mother of a girl who had a ticket for her show but who was rushed to the hospital for an operation. Although she was tired and ill, after the show Patsy sat on the edge of the girl's bed and spoke to her as if she'd known her all her life. She asked what her favorite song was and Patsy sang softly as the girl went into a sleep from which I'm told she never woke.

"Only once did I hear Patsy talk of wanting a luxury for herself. 'When I was little,' she told me, 'I saw a movie where this rich woman took a bath in this real fancy tub. The wallpaper looked like it was speckled with real gold. Someday, I'd like a bathroom like that.'"

Charlie recalled a time when Patsy managed a taste of revenge on McCall: "We were in Pasadena and he took us out to his garage, where he had what he called a studio. He was a helluva manipulator and wanted Patsy to do a demo. There was someone playing piano. He asked me, 'Hey, can't you play the guitar?' I replied, 'Nope. I'm no musician.' McCall turned the guitar over and asked me to beat my hand against it in rhythm with the piano. That was going to be his percussion!

"He put Patsy in front of a mike and started the tape rolling. Patsy sang but gave me a signal. I looked around to see what she was up to. She pointed toward this trash can. I got the message. I leaned over and accidentally knocked the lid to the floor. McCall was livid. He barked, 'That ruined the track. Let's do it again.' Patsy told him, 'No, Bill. I'm tired and my throat is sore.'"

Faron Young reported, "Many artists were taken advantage of by any number of crooks. McCall is probably one of the more famous. When Nashville was exploding, there were only five major labels. They weren't able to take on all the acts. It happened too quick for Nashville to absorb.

"Within a two-year period, all sorts of labels and music publishers came in. They had no morals. When Patsy and others came along, they'd do anything to get a record deal. 'Cause if you had records, you worked the road. They'd sign with anybody without thinking ahead. When you signed a contract with McCall, it was like signing everything away. Bill Peer didn't know the angles and had no one to guide him. Bill McCall screwed everybody in this town once, or tried to.

"You couldn't go to someone like McCall when you suddenly hit it big and try to renegotiate. He'd tell you in a minute, 'I got a contract.' Randy went through hell trying to deal with McCall, and all he had to show for it was premature gray hair."

It's been asked many times why Randy didn't hire a lawyer to break Patsy's contract. According to Donn Hecht, there were no loopholes. When Patsy asked for advances against unearned royalties, McCall secured them with options. Only one act ever brought a lawsuit.

"We made a demo," Teddy Wilburn recollected, "of Doyle singing Hank Thompson's hit 'Give a Little, Take a Little Love' and me doing Hank Williams'

'Long Gone Lonesome Blues.' We sent it to McCall and he released it as a commercial record."

"No permission, no contract," Doyle added, "*and* no money. We took him to court. When I was being shipped overseas during the Korean War, he called and pleaded, 'If you drop the charges, I'll get you out of the army!' I yelled, 'No way, you bastard. You're gonna pay.' And pay us he did."

☆

Patsy had a way with people when she wanted something badly enough. Once, she got what she wanted just by asking. Late in 1959, Opry stage manager Ott Devine was watching the show when Patsy came up behind him.

"Mr. Devine, I've been invited on the Opry many times," she said, "but do you think I could become a full-fledged member? That's one of the reasons I moved to town."

"Patsy," Devine declared, "if that's all you want, you're on."

"Just like that?"

"Just like that, but we'll make it official with an announcement."

Patsy's membership was prestigious to the Opry, which, in a press release based on facts Patsy provided, made much ado about her hit record and work with Husky and Young, "Town and Country Jamboree" days with Jimmy Dean, appearances on the Ozark Jubilee, "Town Hall Party," the Bob Crosby and Alan Freed TV shows and, especially, the Arthur Godfrey shows and appearances with Pat Boone and the McGuire Sisters. It closed with Patsy's philosophy as a country music singer: "I don't want to get rich, just live good!"

Patsy lent her services to many Opry-sponsored benefits. On December 21, for example, she starred with Roy Drusky and Porter Wagoner in an Elks show for the Tennessee Vocational Training School. She served ice cream, cake, and candy to over 750 underprivileged children and assisted in handing each a new dollar bill.

On January 9, 1960, Patsy was brought onstage by announcer Grant Turner and accorded regular cast membership, which meant she had to guarantee her availability two-thirds of her weekends a year. The on-air exposure would be massive, but the pay had increased only slightly, to fourteen dollars an appearance.

Marshall Louis (Grandpa) Jones, the banjo-playing comic in overalls, and Randy observed Patsy as she was accepted into Opry annals. "That gal of yours is really something," Jones proclaimed. "I'll tell you, she sure can sing. She may be ahead of her time! When she's here, she causes quite a sensation. No matter where I am when she comes in, I can't miss her."

"What do you mean, Grandpa?"

"Well, sir, I know which way she went 'cause she's got all the men running after her. They just follow that wiggle in her walk."

"You think Patsy's pretty?"

"Yes, sir, I do."

"Do you think Patsy's got sex appeal?"

"She's really got it. Just like the stink off an ole hog!"

Jones had another handle on what made Patsy tick: "She was, to say the least, one tough lady. You didn't mess with her when she'd start carrying on. I'd up and say, 'Miss Patsy!' and she'd say, 'Grandpa, you gonna try to make a damn lady out of this girl?' I knew better.

"Patsy wasn't always the model of patience, but I gave her credit where credit was due. She knew how to get things moving when they bogged down. We were at WSIX-TV for an Opry special. We got there early and, at noon, we were still going nowhere. We waited till we were blue in the face. Not wanting to say anything that'd ruffle any feathers, I went to Patsy and said, 'Well, Miss Patsy, they better hurry up 'cause I got a date in July!' She told me, 'Damn right, Grandpa. I've gotta get, too.'

"She took care of things. Patsy strutted over to whoever was in charge and raised hell. Immediately, everything fell into place and we got to work. Jimmy Dean used to preach to Patsy about the time ethic. It must have sunk in. She didn't cotton to those hurry-up-and-wait situations. I could talk more about her, but it wouldn't help to know her better. She was unique, fascinating. You really'd have had to be around her. Patsy was definitely one of a kind!"

Owen Bradley certainly subscribed to that notion. He knew what to expect. Patsy's personality was strong and she had no problem bucking him even when she knew she wouldn't get her way. In the studio, Bradley could do whatever he wanted in terms of creating music—if the artist cooperated and there was a track record of hits—but his fondness for Patsy and belief in her potential held no sway at Decca's New York headquarters.

Randy's battle with McCall had some effect. The material at Patsy's January 27, 1960, session, her first in six months, was an improvement and included a non–Four-Star song.

Charlie told the Country Music Foundation's John Rumble and Paul Kingsbury how well Patsy knew music. "When Patsy and I started going together, a record would come on the radio and she'd say who it was. Half the guys I hadn't heard of." She liked Kay Starr, Teresa Brewer, and Sophie Tucker and the country singers Goldie Hill, Wanda Jackson, Charline Arthur, and Kitty Wells and had their records in her collection. Patsy loved to listen to pop and rock 'n' roll but bragged she was nothing but a country singer.

This time, in the studio, she apparently won out over Bradley. There was no vacillation between country and pop. Much to New York's chagrin, there was nothing remotely pop. She recorded the 1949 Hank Williams million-seller "Lovesick Blues," replete with yodeling, though quite modified from the hearty way she sang it on live appearances.

The other tunes were "There He Goes," a female version of Carl Smith's 1959 hit, with lyrics by Eddie Miller; "How Can I Face Tomorrow?"; and "Crazy Dreams," with its wonderful country shuffle, courtesy of Kramer, steel guitarist Jimmy Day, from Ray Price's band, and the electric guitars of Garland and Martin (who also played fiddle). These songs were "cowritten" by W. S. Stevenson. Patsy overdubbed harmony vocals on the two latter tunes. This was to be her last session under the Four-Star contract. Considering the about-face in style, there might have been the feeling, "This is the end, so let her do whatever she wants. If it sells, it sells. If it doesn't, it doesn't."

Rock 'n' roll had thrown country into turmoil. A sophisticated Nashville sound was emerging. Though these songs, in retrospect, are quite good, they did nothing to explore Patsy's real singing potential. Nor was this the music a new generation of country fans wanted.

On March 7th, Decca released "Lovesick Blues" with "How Can I Face Tomorrow?" There were no full-page advertisements, and McCall didn't bother to send a letter to deejays. Again, neither they nor the public responded. This isn't to say Patsy didn't enjoy good record sales. In fact, an interesting phenomenon, still true, was taking shape. She had a strong following who were quite vocal in their approval of what Patsy recorded. She received huge amounts of mail; colleagues recall her going off to the side during TV specials to read and answer her mail and autograph photos with personal messages. While she appealed to die-hard country fans, she also lured an audience of urban romantics to her shows and broadcasts, such as the Ozark Jubilee, where she was frequently booked and always warmly received.

That Patsy was changing with the times was quite evident in a Jubilee ABC-TV broadcast in February: She appeared singing that most hillbilly of numbers, "Lovesick Blues," not in her traditional cowgirl outfit but in a handsome, trailblazing pants suit.

Patsy covered the spectrum, from swinging uptempo numbers to ballads of dreams and love that might have been. She was also the first country female, other than Brenda Lee, to have a teen following, which was Decca's rationale in releasing her on 45 rpm EPs. The younger set identified with her songs about loss, loneliness, and pain. She was immensely popular among GIs as well and was often featured on recruitment transcriptions. What attracted Patsy, other than the money, to these canned shows was the opportunity to sing what McCall wouldn't allow her to record, including songs at the top of the country and pop charts.

Patsy guested on the June 4 Ozark Jubilee, telecast on the fifth. She dueted with Cowboy Copas on "I'm Hog-Tied over You." The audience went wild. In a moving tribute to Hilda, Patsy sang "Mother, Mother," joined by Copas, Eddy Arnold, and June Valli.

On June 7, Patsy did "Country Style, U.S.A.," promoting her March single, and singing "one that's always been one of my favorites," "When Your House Is Not a Home" by Roger Miller. Five days later, she angered Opry executives by arriving for her Opry appearance in a clinging white western blouse accented with a kerchief around her neck, and gold lamé trousers.

"Everybody was punching the other to look," announcer Grant Turner remembered, "but you could see her coming for a country mile. I thought she looked great, but I didn't run the place. Patsy was told she couldn't go on dressed like that. She was fuming mad, but either went back home or sent someone for another outfit. When she went on that night, she was much more subdued and all the little kiddies could feel safe."

Plagued since May with minor medical flare-ups she attributed to stress, Patsy saw her doctor and got an unexpected diagnosis. She was pregnant. Good news, bad news, feeling great, or feeling poorly—nothing stopped Patsy. When she informed Charlie, she barely took the time to let the consequences of the news sink in before she was upstairs packing.

On August 1, Decca released the last of the Four-Star product, "Crazy Dreams" with "There He Goes" on the flip side.

Jo Ann and Gus Thomas visited the Dicks that weekend. She was a regional singer[3] who first met Patsy in 1958, before she married, backstage at the county fair in Rhinehold, Pennsylvania; he used to back Patsy on the "Town and Country Jamboree." In 1960, when they were living in Georgia, Charlie called and wanted to know when they were coming to visit at the Madison house. They took him up on his invitation a few weeks before Thomas was scheduled to ship out for Korea.

"Patsy and Charlie insisted we stay with them or we wouldn't be friends anymore," Jo Ann recollected. "They had friends visiting from Texas, too, so the house was full. It was really hectic. And Charlie was in a wheelchair. He'd broken his pelvic bone in an auto accident. Patsy was on the Opry Saturday night. Gus pushed Charlie into the Ryman and backstage. We were laughing like a bunch of kids.

"I went to the backstage ladies' room—also the women's dressing room—with Patsy and helped fix her hair. That night, after Patsy sang, Hank Williams, Jr., made his first appearance on the Opry."

On Sunday, Patsy was in the kitchen preparing a special dinner. She made one of her famous "everything but the kitchen sink" casseroles. "When she took the dish out of the oven," Jo Ann reported, "it fell to the floor and broke into a million pieces. Patsy stood there and cried. She said she didn't have any more food, so Gus and I went and bought a bag of groceries. They were having real financial problems. Monday, we checked into a motel, and Patsy was really hurt. We explained Gus was going overseas and we needed some time to be alone, but Patsy had a hard time believing us."

The Elvis and rockabilly trends didn't escape the notice of Bradley or RCA's Chet Atkins. They were ahead of their time and at the forefront of the new sound. Brenda Lee, still produced by Bradley, was emerging as a major pop and rock star. RCA Nashville was having a lot of success in the pop arena with the world popularity of Elvis and the smooth stylings of Eddy Arnold and Jim Reeves.

There was no shortage of creative talent. The same sidemen who played for Bradley and Atkins when they recorded Kitty Wells, Ernest Tubb, Webb Pierce, Hank Snow, and Porter Wagoner played for the producers when they recorded Patsy, Lee, Arnold, and Reeves.

An example of their versatility can be heard on the recruiting transcriptions. On September 6, five months pregnant and two days away from her twenty-eighth birthday, Patsy stunned the musicians in the studio for "Country Style, U.S.A." when she handed them sheet music for "Stupid Cupid," a teen throb hit in 1958 for Connie Francis, but they immediately rose to the occasion.

She was assisted by swinging Hank Garland, whom Patsy introduced for his own slot. "When it comes to picking a guitar, well, this fella just can't be beat." A much-subdued Garland performed an instrumental called "Josephine." Patsy performed "Crazy Dreams," accompanied by a mellow country fiddle, then ripped into Carl Smith's "Loose Talk," his 1955 country chart-topper, assisted by Garland's innovative guitar echo effects and Marvin Hughes's blues piano.

"Don't forget now," she said in closing, "we'd like to hear from you." The Governor's Island, New York, APO was inundated with letters and photo requests.

3. Later a Lebanon, Pennsylvania, WVLV Radio disc jockey.

Though Bradley and New York sales director Sidney Goldberg seriously considered signing Patsy, no decision was made. Bradley feared Patsy might switch to another label. Indeed, Patsy and Randy were shopping around. There was outside interest. Charlie recalled that at a benefit at the Carousel nightclub in Printer's Alley, Patsy asked guitarist Chet Atkins for his autograph. He wrote, "When are you coming over to RCA?"

Now "the prize" could be Decca's. The questions Bradley must have asked himself when he mulled over signing Patsy were, "Can we work together? Can I maintain control? And will she listen?" In spite of their disagreements, Patsy knew she had a producer who brought out the best in her. Either that or she listened to Randy, who respected Bradley and his instincts. Randy felt pop was the direction in which to push Patsy. With Bradley, it could happen. Right after Hughes informed him Patsy was officially free of obligation to McCall and Four-Star, Patsy herself called Bradley.

"Owen," she said, "I have a lot of faith in your talent. Together we can accomplish what I've dreamed of. I want to stay with Decca."

"Then you're on," Bradley said enthusiastically.

"Great. In that case, will Decca advance me some money against my royalties?"

"What royalties?" Bradley replied.

Patsy had been spending money she wasn't earning on furniture and clothes. The label showed their faith in her with a handsome advance. Bradley advised that the New York brass, in granting approval, had method to their madness. "The assumption was that if we were nice to Patsy, she'd be nice and record the way we saw fit." Patsy didn't see it that way: More than once, Bradley was to know how Bill McCall felt.

"THAT'S HOW A HEARTACHE BEGINS"

PATSY CLINE: "I won't do it! I hate this song!"
OWEN BRADLEY: "You said you liked it."
PATSY CLINE: "I didn't want anything slipping by me."
OWEN BRADLEY: "The song's perfect."
PATSY CLINE: "Then you record it!"

On September 10, 1960, after their appearances on the Prince Albert Smoking Tobacco portion of NBC's Opry broadcast, Patsy and Del Wood's conversation came around to husbands. Patsy told Del of a row between her and Charlie. "Since I went into my marriage with Gerald with my eyes closed, I shouldn't been at all surprised at the lack of communication between us. But my marriage to Charlie was different. He knew from the beginning what I wanted and he's been there with me all the way."

"Sweetie, you know what keeps marriages together?"

"No. What?"

"Economics—and security. Theirs! Get rid of him if he starts to mess you up!"

"I couldn't ever let Charlie go, especially since we've made it this far. I ain't no different from most people. Since I was a kid, I've gotta be constantly reassured that somebody loves me. Charlie's my security and I'm his."

The problems between the couple got worse, according to Del, not because of physical abuse or drunkenness. "They were two of the most enchanted but disillusioned lovebirds and two of the most reckless people I've ever met. But they were definitely in love in spite of themselves.

"Baby Julie, who celebrated her second birthday at the end of August, helped add a stabilizing force to the marriage. This time Patsy was hoping for a boy. She felt that force would increase by leaps and bounds with another child.

"It wasn't hard to like Charlie when he was sober. Through the years, I heard a lot of tales out of school about his beating on Patsy, but, if he did, I would imagine he'd be one dead son of a bitch. You didn't want to get Patsy riled. When she got roaring, you'd best get moving!

"We spoke of everything under the sun and Patsy never much mentioned anything like that. From what she was saying, especially during her last months of pregnancy, the problem was his neglecting her. You know, sexually. She was starved for affection.

"Charlie never appreciated what type of wife Patsy was and wanted to be. He surely didn't understand her drive to be a star. In fact, he was jealous of her success. He was a man. It wasn't the natural order of things.

"Husbands of singers and entertainers don't mind taking the benefits, but they mind the fact that it's the wife who's earning them. They love the money but don't love you enough. And money was a problem with them. They had lean times. I can remember a few times Patsy begging the Opry officials to let her on so she'd have that pittance they paid. Sometimes it was the make or break between paying the rent or phone and gas bill.

"Neither foresaw the expenses a show business career requires. You may not be earning a nickel, but you have travel, music preparation, recording, and costume expenses. Everybody told Patsy to come to Nashville to make a buck, but in reality it was only a base from which to commute to work. If you had a few good records, the country fans were loyal and you could play weekends on the road the rest of your life. And some of us have!

"Patsy hated to go off and leave that precious Julie, but the bills had to be paid. But she also hated to leave Charlie. He had a job, so he couldn't go out with Patsy. He always wanted to know why she didn't stay home and let him support her.

"Charlie used to bitch with Patsy before she'd leave, then he'd call and bitch with her on the road, usually when he was drinking, and want to know when she was coming home. He'd tell her how much he needed her and then, when she'd get home, all he'd do is bitch some more. It went on and on. She had to work not only to live but also to survive. And not always from the financial side. I've never known anyone where it meant as much to be a star.

"Patsy'd go to Timbuktu to sing and would probably pay her own expenses. She thrived on the applause. It was heaven on earth. With the money she bought furs, fancy cars, and beautiful clothes. She'd have given anything to have the kind of love at home that the public gave. She'd tell me, 'Things are gonna get better.' They were like monkeys in the zoo! At each other's throats one minute, then hopping all over each other the next. The road wasn't the problem. Or the fact that Patsy was the star. If you have a tight marriage, the road or the temptation of other men, other women, isn't going to disturb it.

"Patsy had plenty of chances to cheat. But it was her unfortunate experience, as it was mine, that anyone within her age group figured she had money to lavish on them, and anyone younger or older just wanted a place to crawl into and have someone wait on them. She had no desire to be a waitress or a wet nurse.

"One night she said something I've never forgotten. Grant was introducing her as the biggest female star of country music. She said, 'Del, I'd rather be a beloved wife than a woman bigger than life.' I've heard a lot of entertainers say you have all the loving in the world when you walk out on that stage and you feel the beat of that applause. But, hell, when you leave that stage and the spotlight goes off, that goddamn applause don't help any when you're laying in that bed being ignored. No hit record's worth that."

"Patsy and Charlie," Faron Young said, "were always at each other. At first, it was small, silly things. They'd tear into a good fight and an hour—no! fifteen minutes—later they'd be cooing.

"God forbid someone should try to take advantage of Charlie! Patsy's wrath was a thing best left unencountered. When he was on the road with us, we'd play pool. One night I beat him for about fifty dollars and he gave me a check. That thing bounced from here to kingdom come. I went to Patsy and told her, 'That son of a bitch's gonna pay me!'

"She turned on me and grabbed the check out of my hand and tore it up. She took fifty dollars out of her purse and threw it at me. She yelled, 'Here, goddamn you, go and take advantage of him again!' Then she gave it to Charlie in spades and told him, 'If you want to bet on pool games, use your own goddamn money!'"

From early in their marriage, Faron claimed, "Charlie treated Patsy like a dog. He'd get her up in front of a bunch of people and call her a no-good whore, and everything else. He was drunk, just drunk. And jealous. Once he'd see Patsy was getting attention from somebody, he'd be right on top of her and sometimes even say something to that person.

"The only time you'd see Patsy down and crying the blues was when Charlie gave her shit. She'd come in from the road with money. He'd take it and blow it, gambling at pool, shooting dice. Stuff like that. Anything. He couldn't win. But he could drink."

Charlie grew upset at Patsy's long absences—after a few drinks, friends observed, he berated her, saying such things as, "You ought to be home being a wife, instead of hauling all over singing and fooling around."

For about a year, Young "never tried to fool with Patsy"; then he began his campaign "to get her" in earnest. Witnesses reported she laughed him off.

"We did become very close," Faron said, "but all I ever got was the same ole same ole—you know, the story of what hell Charlie was putting her through—and I'd commiserate. It was depressing and not what I had in mind."

The Dicks' reputations as heavy drinkers gained considerable foothold. "The stories about Patsy are untrue," Charlie asserts. "She enjoyed a drink now and then, but she wasn't a drinker and never a drunk. We'd go to Tootsie's after the Opry and have a beer, but that was about it. We partied and had a good time, but I was the one who raised hell and did the drinking."

"As husband and wife, Patsy and Charlie, like any couple, had rocky roads," Kathy Hughes said. "Patsy leaned on Randy when anything went wrong. It was especially so when she and Charlie had problems. Randy was her soothsayer. But we were used to that, since we'd gone through the same thing with Ferlin.

"Patsy threatened to leave Charlie, but that got to sound like a broken record.

They'd go through a bad time and then would be okay again. We had calls in the dead of the morning. Patsy was upset and excited and wanted Randy to come over and help her.

"When you get calls like that—made in heated moments—you don't know what's going on because sometimes that person makes the situation worse than it is. As far as I could tell, Patsy and Charlie were in love and married. That brings lots of joys and problems."

Jean Shepard noted, "Oh, my, there had to be some love there! Patsy was no angel. That doesn't come out often. It's ole Charlie that gets it. He was no angel either, but I don't know which was the biggest burden. Maybe they both deserved each other *and* medals!

"Patsy and I got along well because, like me, she was plainspoken. She had a great sense of humor. I don't think, though some might disagree, I was quite as brassy as she was. But that was Patsy, and I liked her as she was. You either did or didn't, and vice versa. There weren't many people that met her who didn't like Patsy. She could be mean as hell, but she could be as adorable as they come.

"The same for Charlie. I love him to death, but he had and has his problems, and they mostly come in bottles. That doesn't take away from the fact that he's one helluva nice guy."

From all indications, Patsy had come full circle. It was life with Gerald all over again, only this time with booze.

Whatever Patsy and Charlie's personal dilemmas and her current financial crisis, as every friend of hers attests, Patsy was overly generous.

"Of course, this is going to sound like a mother talking," stated Mrs. Hensley, "but Patsy was never a selfish person with only her interests at heart. Her song 'Come On In' pretty well summed up her life. She was a good-hearted soul and never knew the meaning of the word no.

"As a child she'd bring friends home from school to play and insist they stay and eat supper. We had hardly enough for ourselves, but somehow I managed. Our doors were never closed. That's the type of home I believed in having and this carried over into Patsy's life."

Del Wood, remembering Patsy's constant praising of her mother as her best friend, said, "Patsy, her brother, and sister seemed to have a normal, happy home life in spite of their father's absence and Patsy working one-nighters from the time she had to quit school. Hilda wasn't an uneducated woman. She was a gifted seamstress.[1] She was also quite attractive—Patsy favored Hilda a lot. Not only in looks but also in outlook. Patsy spoke of her mom always lending a helping hand whether she knew the people or not. This must have influenced Patsy a great deal.

"Patsy's heart, home, and wallet were always open. She especially wanted to do for her mom. She regretted that while Hilda helped make her life such a good one, hers suffered having to raise Patsy, Sylvia, and Sam alone."

---

1. In 1992, at the age of seventy-five, she still plies her craft in Winchester.

Pearl Butler smiled warmly. "To put it simply, Patsy was an easy touch! If you want to talk about what a compassionate, thoughtful person Patsy was, I'll start cooking something to eat for us. Anyone in trouble or need only had to go see Patsy and she was there with a good word or helping hand. But people didn't take advantage of her. She'd know."

Brenda Lee has deeply etched memories. "Those were my formative years, and Patsy had a big influence. We had a good, close relationship. It was wonderful to be involved with someone who was unique. Most people, especially an established star, wouldn't have bothered with a youngster. But Patsy treated me as a peer. She loved all the girl singers. She was so unselfish and not the least bit envious or jealous. She didn't mind their successes. That made a good impression. A lot of Patsy rubbed off on me.

"From the time Julie was two, when Patsy and Charlie first moved to Nashville, I went to their house in Madison. It was cute but tiny. Patsy was always saying, 'One of these days, l'il sister, I'm going to have me a real house!' They found one in town and were buying it, but Patsy wanted a real dream house like the movie stars.

"Either Patsy would pick me up or Mom would take me over. I couldn't wait to get there. She was big on costume jewelry, and I used to love to play in her jewelry box and walk around in her spike heels. Patsy had things everywhere. Not strewn about. She was neat. She didn't have any room. She was a pack rat waiting for the day she'd move to bigger quarters. Patsy loved to shop! She'd get things and didn't have any place for them.

"Patsy liked being domestic. She loved cooking but wasn't the type who'd throw something together in an hour. She needed all day. She was as much a perfectionist in that as she was in everything else. I helped Patsy with Julie or in the kitchen. And we'd sing. I'd listen to Patsy, and she'd listen to me. Then we'd both sing. I'd ask her how she did this or that and vice versa. We had that little hiccup thing we called yodeling. She'd yodel up a storm. I envied her. She tried to teach me but I was a lost cause. Patsy didn't give up, though. She wanted to yodel on her records the way she did on her live shows but Owen wouldn't hear of it. Except for that one time in Texas, I never saw Patsy perform. I regret that very much."

Brenda learned other things from Patsy. "A few unusual words. I wouldn't say Patsy was rated X, but she'd come in under R! I don't mean that in a detrimental way, because Patsy was Patsy. She was honest and blunt. Patsy never had a problem saying what she thought. She didn't offend anyone when she cursed or set out to be vulgar or common. It was her mode of talking. I used to wonder who on earth in her family she took after. But it wasn't anyone. It was just Patsy!

"When I was on the road as a kid with Faron, Mel Tillis, and George Jones, they'd tell me jokes—none of which I understood. Then they'd say, 'Hey, Brenda, go tell so-and-so that.' And I'd go up to someone and do it. They'd say, 'Lord, all that coming out of a kid's mouth!' The guys were on the floor laughing. *They* thought it was funny.

"Patsy was the most generous person you'd ever want to meet. I liked her so much more because of what she did for her friends and even strangers. Because she came up struggling, she had a good heart. I loved her dearly, and when she had Julie I said, 'Patsy, if I ever have a little girl, I'm going to name her Julie because I love you so much.' She'd answer, 'Oh, you will not!' And I'd retort, 'Yes, I will. You wait and see!'"

Del summed up Patsy's giving nature: "Even when she didn't have it, she'd spend it. And not always on herself. She'd give anyone the skirt off her backside if they needed it."

The house Patsy and Charlie were buying was a small but lovely red brick house situated on a huge lot in the 5000 block of Hillhurst Drive off Dickerson Road in northeast Nashville. She had Randy keep her working in order to keep up the house payments and go on furniture and appliance shopping sprees.

One of the better-paying jobs was an October 1960 U.S.O. show for military bases in Hawaii. Packaged by Hubert Long and Randy, it headlined Faron Young and Ferlin Husky and also featured Jerry Reed. Prior to setting off for the islands, Patsy and Charlie spent a long weekend in the "Brunswick triangle." On Saturday night, to almost everyone's surprise, Patsy and Charlie paid a visit with Fay and Harry Crutchley to the Brunswick Moose Lodge. Bill Peer and the Melody Boys, as usual, played for the dancers. Although a majority of those present knew the situation between Patsy and Bill, she was a star and they wanted to hear her sing. On hand was Bill's second wife, Dolly Huffmiester, who, along with guitarist John Anderson, sang with the band.

Melody Boys Joe Shewbridge and Roy Deyton remember the occasion. "Folks kept bugging Bill about why he wasn't asking Patsy to sing," Shrewbridge said, "so he grudgingly asked. Patsy gladly accommodated, but afterward Dolly got terribly upset. She told him, 'How the hell can you invite her to sing after the way she did you? Where's your pride?'"

Deyton, who played upright bass, guitar, and fiddle, said, "Most of the band were happy to see Patsy. In spite of everything, we adored her, but none of us could blame Dolly, who was once one of Patsy's best friends. Patsy had made fools of them and Dolly didn't see why they had to be reminded of it."

"I don't see why we have to kiss her ass and say thank you!" Dolly was reported to have said.

For the trip to Hawaii, Patsy and Reed received expenses and a per diem of fifty dollars. Upon their arrival via Pan American clipper, agent Hubert Long had Faron, who was wearing shorts, and Ferlin, decked out in aloha shirts, and Patsy bathed in fragrant leis. Patsy, in her sixth month, loved the native, loose-fitting muumuus.

"Patsy had to see a hula show," Faron recalled. "We didn't hear the end of that. We did all the typical tourist things, such as sightseeing at Pearl Harbor and going to a luau. I don't think Patsy ever stopped taking pictures!"

She had her tiny Kodak with the flash attachment permanently draped around her neck, directly underneath her daily assortment of leis. During the day, she wore sunglasses and a wide-brim hat made of dried palm fronds. She was never without her two large purses—one of them, made of straw, was basket-sized. At night, she wore her famed gold lamé trenchcoat.

The main engagements were at Pearl Harbor and the Marine Corps Air Station at Kaneohe on the east side of Oahu. But there were also two nights in Honolulu at Kaiser's Dome, now part of Hilton Hawaiian Village.

"The GIs knew Patsy and wanted her autograph and their picture taken with her," Faron said. "I don't remember her ever saying no. She loved it! The only time I can remember Patsy down was one afternoon onstage. She had hundreds of those guys screaming, yelling, applauding, and foot-stomping at Kaneohe, but when she was introducing 'Walkin' After Midnight,' something happened that really depressed her. She said, 'Back when I used to play with Arthur Godfrey—' And they cracked up. They were laughing so hard they wouldn't let her finish. She came off hopping mad and told me, 'Those ignorant sons of bitches took what I said wrong!'

"I took Patsy into my arms and soothed her. 'Honey, don't think anything of it. Shit! They're a bunch of gyrenes! What did you expect? They didn't mean anything. They were just having a good time at your expense.' I went out and did my portion of the show and calmed everybody down. I asked them, 'Hey, you want to hear another number from Miss Patsy Cline?' And they went wild, and Patsy returned to the stage and sang and sang and forgot about what happened."

Upon her return to Nashville, Patsy made the rounds of the annual D.J. Convention, as the celebration was now called. Decca had made her signing official. Even with no new release since August, there were posters everywhere, stating: Welcome D.J.'s and Sincere Thanks ... Patsy Cline of Decca Records—Manager and Booker Randy Hughes. Patsy and Bradley were also selecting material for her first official Decca session, which was set for the middle of November. This was an all-important event, which had to produce a hit.

And Bradley had just the song he knew would do it.

Patsy's friendship with Roger Miller introduced her to a new breed of Nashville songwriters who were considered radical by the establishment.

"I was a musician," explained Miller, "but I wanted to write. I was unlike any other in Nashville. Patsy thought my music was unique and wonderful. Of course, I agreed with her. That made *two* of us! I was just a musician she thought was pretty amazing for some reason. She thought the same of Doug Kershaw.[2] Patsy had a self-contained show, independent of Faron's, but no band. We [the Country Deputies] played behind all the acts and I was the drummer.

"I'd been doing okay as a writer and had a couple of records that had done fair, but Patsy was a star. There was a distance between writers, musicians, and the so-called stars. Patsy wasn't like that. She loved good talent and dug all of us songwriters.

"She was a great singer, a belter. There're people who sing and those who really *sing*. Patsy was in the latter category. Everyone respected her as the best female country singer. What amazed me was she could yodel and turn right around and do pop. There was no one like her.

2. The Louisiana Cajun fiddler.

"I can just see her coming in her cowgirl outfits with red western boots and hat and standing there singing her butt off, singing her soul at you. She didn't make predictions about the future for me. But she was one of the first who appreciated what I could do.

"On those long road trips, being with Patsy in the back seat of the car was a wonderful way to while away the time. There was never a dull minute with her around. We had some good times and created a lot of wonderful memories, but Patsy and I weren't intimates. Patsy was a loner and didn't have a lot of friends. Patsy never confided in me about business or her personal life. She didn't have any problems. As far as I could see, she always seemed to know where she was going. She and Charlie had their ups and downs, but nothing that much for me to know. He could get a bit rowdy when he was drinking, but I don't know what that entailed.

"The writers and musicians hung out in the upstairs rear of Tootsie's. After a few laughs and beers, when Tootsie was about ready to throw us out, we'd get a group together, especially on Fridays and Saturdays, and go to someone's house and talk, play, and sing the night away. Patsy and Charlie'd hang out after the Opry at Tootsie's and became part of the clique.

"I was Patsy's friend because I amused her. She loved to laugh—no, howl! I was a clown. I made everyone laugh, but Patsy's laugh was the greatest. It was a raucous thing. You could hear it all over the building. Anytime anyone'd ask Patsy about Roger Miller, she'd just throw her head back and laugh. Now we didn't have anything on Patsy in the storytelling department. She could tell some dirty jokes!

"Patsy taught me a lot of slang. We were on a flight once, so it must have been to New York. She leaned into me and cracked, 'Hoss, I saw you on the tube!' I asked her, 'What the hell's a tube?' She got real smart. 'A TV, goddamnit!' I said, 'Thank you very much!'"

Jan Howard was part of another vital personal and career relationship with Patsy. She was born in West Plains, Missouri, seven months before Patsy. When she decided on a show business career, Jan headed for California, where she met songwriter and song plugger Harlan Howard.

He wrote songs and she did vocals for the demos that were circulated to artists and record producers. At thirty-two, he was riding high. His "Pick Me Up on Your Way Down"[3] was a hit for Charlie Walker.

"Harlan and I hadn't been married long when we decided Nashville was the place to be," Jan commented. "I had a single on Challenge Records and was invited on the Opry. I wasn't a fan-type person. I didn't get too excited about many singers, but I enjoyed Patsy's style.

"I was too shy to go up and say, 'Hi, I'm Jan Howard.' I was afraid she'd say, 'Jan who? So what?' The only time I'd hang around was when Patsy was on. I'd come early to see her or stay late. I'd watch her sing, then go change for my spot. Afterward, I gathered my things and went home. Some of the Opry folks were nice, some weren't.

3. Not to be confused with Patsy's 1956 recording.

"One Saturday, I came offstage as Patsy arrived. I stood in the wings to hear her. She had on her trademark fringe cowgirl outfit, hat, and white boots. When she finished, I grabbed my things and, on my way out, went into the ladies' room where we changed. There were a couple of small dressing rooms off the stage, but they were for the male artists and musicians. The girls rated last in those days. The restroom door swung open. In rushed Patsy with her hands on her hips. She was fit to be tied. I thought, 'What a time to meet her!' And then she exploded at me."

Patsy went right up to Jan and shot, "You're a conceited little son of a bitch!"

"What?" asked Jan, crushed.

"You heard me, stuck up! I've been watching you. You just go out there, do your spot, and leave without saying hello to anyone. You think you're too good to talk to other folks around here? What do you have to be conceited about?"

Jan's temper flared. "Now, you wait a minute there, lady. Let me tell you something! Before I ever moved here, from the time I heard your first record, I've been a great fan of yours. I love to hear you sing. I was only following some advice I was given."

"Advice? What kind of goddamn advice?"

"A friend told me the best way to stay out of trouble around here is to do your spot and leave. Don't hang around."

"So that's what I've been doing wrong," Patsy exclaimed.

"And that's what I should've done tonight! It would have been better, but I wanted to hear you sing. Back where I was raised, when a stranger comes to town it's the job of the people there to make that person feel at home. Except for Jean Shepard, Hawkshaw Hawkins, and Ray Price, not a damn soul here's made me feel welcome. Including you!"

"Goddamn it, now, Hoss. Hold on!"

"I'm not finished. You're all a bunch of snobby bastards. I'm sorry I stayed." Jan darted for the door.

"Whoa there, little dogie. Whoa!" Patsy grabbed her. "Slow down! Hoss, you're all right. Anybody that'll stand there and talk back to the Cline like that is all right." Patsy laughed so hard, Jan's red face cooled and she began laughing, too.

"Hi, Jan. I'm Patsy."

"I know. Nice to meet you."

"I can tell we're gonna be friends!"

They were.

"Patsy was a fantastic person," Jan reminisced. "That sounds so inane when I'm describing someone I absolutely thought the world of. I love honesty. I take people for what they are to me, not what they are to anybody else. Patsy was honest and blunt, and I admired that."

Howard and his sometime writing partner, singer Hank Cochran, twenty-four, met in California. Cochran began writing in Greenville, Mississippi. "I'd done some recording on the West Coast," he explained, "and, after we relocated to Nashville, I was trying to get it together. I wasn't having any success. There was a place called Mom Upchurch's on Boscobel Street, where us half-starving writers and musicians stayed.

"Roger Miller; Johnny Paycheck, who went under the name Donnie Young;[4]

4. One of several pseudonyms he used. His name is Donald Lytel.

George McCormick, who worked for Wilma Lee and Stoney Cooper's Clinch Mountain Clan; Shorty Lavender,[5] Ray Price's fiddler; and Darrell McCall, a Texan who played bass for Audrey Williams, Hank's first wife, stayed there. All of us were going down the up staircase. I was making fifty dollars a week, sending half to California to my wife, Shirley, and the kids and trying to live on the other half. It was possible in those days. Mom'd let us board for ten dollars a week. I was twenty-five and figured I had lots of time."

One night while Cochran was mulling over song ideas and his life's situations, a title, "I Fall to Pieces," came to mind. He called Howard, who told him to bring it over to his house the next morning.

"Hank arrived around breakfast," Howard said, "and we had coffee. He had this song going and sang it with his guitar, 'I fall to pieces, Each time I see you again.' And that was about it. I told him, 'Hey, I like that, and we started piddling around."

"We wrote it," recollected Cochran, "in one of our many down periods, and it was tinged with the right amount of, I guess you could say, hurt and despair."

There are several versions of how "I Fall to Pieces" came to the attention of Bradley and Patsy.

Jan did a demo for the writers' publisher, a small firm called Pamper Music in Goodlettsville, twenty miles north of town. The studio was a converted garage in back of the office.

"I loved the song," Jan noted, "and wanted to record it. Harlan said fine. Not long after, he was floating on cloud nine telling me how he'd pitched it to Owen Bradley at Decca, who wanted it for Brenda Lee."

Cochran explained he took the song to Bradley "after it had been turned down by a whole bunch of people."

"When Hank played it for me, I liked it right away," said Bradley. "But no one else did. Four artists had turned it down."

He felt it was unique. Jan found Bradley's intuition for a song even in demo form incredible. "He could hear simple chord structure and literally have it arranged and orchestrated in his head. He heard the end result before it was ever recorded."

Then Lee, now established in pop, rejected it, feeling it was too country. Bradley called in a handsome Atlanta crooner, Roy Drusky, with two Decca top-10 country ballads that year, to hear the demo. Drusky decided against it. "Thanks a lot, Owen," he said, "but it's not for me."

"Roy, it's perfect for your voice," the producer answered. "We can have a big hit."

"I really like it. It's a beauty, and I'm sure you're right, but a man could never sing this. It'd kill him!"

As Bradley recalls, Patsy was either nearby or within hearing distance. Drusky remembers bumping into Patsy just outside the studio. She was stretched on a couch in a plaid shirt and jeans, talking to a friend.

Bradley became quite upset with Drusky. "Well, it is a hit!" he admonished. "You don't want a hit?"

"Yeah, but it's a girl's song, Owen! You don't hear a man saying, 'I fall to pieces.' It's ridiculous."

5. Later a top Nashville agent.

"That's all right, then. I'll get somebody else to record it. And it's going to be number one."

Patsy piped up, "Hell, if it ain't a man's song I'll record it."

Drusky says that, as he left, Patsy remarked, "Drusky, that's a hit song you just let go, and I'm gonna get Owen to let me have it."

Bradley called Patsy into his office. "Come here. There's something I want you to hear."

Patsy loved it, or so she claimed. Bradley was excited that he had found who he now realized was the perfect artist for the song. They set a session date.

But, according to Cochran, "Darrell McCall told me Patsy was directly on Decca now and looking for material. He took me out to Patsy and Charlie's in Madison. We had a few drinks and I played 'I Fall to Pieces.' She said she wanted it. I don't know if she even knew what the song was. She might have said yes because of those lean years with Four-Star. Now she was free to pick and choose and had a songwriter coming to her."

"She wanted it," Bradley said, "then, funny thing, didn't like it."

"Didn't like it?" exclaimed Jan. "Let's be more definite. Patsy hated it. She told me, 'I hate that goddamn song,' knowing full well I was Harlan's wife. That didn't stop her from speaking her mind. She said, 'I'm never gonna sing that thing.' As the session approached, there were some words flying between her and Owen.

"She liked the other side of the demo, 'Lovin' in Vain' by Freddie Hart. I told her, 'Oh, no, Patsy, that one's mine!' But when I took it to Joe Johnson [Challenge Records], he wouldn't let me record it. I told Freddie, 'Don't you worry. I'm going to get you a record.' And I took it back to Patsy and told her it was hers."

Patsy left word with Bradley that she'd changed her mind and wouldn't record "I Fall to Pieces." She never told Cochran or Howard why, nor did she ask them to make revisions.

Charlie has stated, "The fact that it had been turned down by a lot of artists didn't particularly tickle Patsy. She told me, 'These people were already on major labels and had good records, and if they turned it down, why would I want it?'"

When they next met, Owen was blunt with Patsy. "New York says this is the sound the public wants. It's the type of material that brings out your best. Sidney Goldberg says you're only selling ten to fifteen thousand on each single."

"What's wrong with that? For a country female singer that's great!"

"They feel you can do better. And if this doesn't work, we can always go back."

"What the hell do they think I am, a machine? I just got rid of one Hitler, and if they think that by advancing me a little money they can make me record what they want, well, they've got another thought coming. Owen, I won't do it! I hate this song!"

"You said you liked it."

"I didn't want anything slipping by me."

"Oh, so that's your game. The song's perfect."

"Then you record it."

They went one on one until November 16 at 2:30, "when, much against her will," confirmed Cochran, Patsy, seven months pregnant, recorded "I Fall to Pieces." "She and Owen argued quite a bit, but struck a deal. Patsy'd gone wild over Freddie's song. Owen said, 'Okay, you cut "I Fall to Pieces" and I'll let you do "Lovin' in Vain."'

"Owen had ideas of his own that differed from the way we wrote the song. He knew what he was going for and kept at it until Patsy and everybody found it. The way he used the Jordanaires was wonderful. The end result is nothing like the demo we cut."

Bradley's concept wasn't necessarily Patsy's concept. "Patsy could drive me nuts," claimed the producer. "No matter what I'd do, I couldn't please her. She'd start in on me and then have Charlie bug me. She'd say, 'Owen, I want to do it this way,' or she'd send Charlie over if she was mad and not speaking, and he'd say, 'Owen, Patsy thinks it ought to be done like this.' I stuck to my guns."

The session was done the old-fashioned way, with singer and musicians together live. Patsy sat in the middle of the studio on a stool with a microphone and music stand, with the Jordanaires on her left. The group was one of the most in-demand properties in town, often doing up to three sessions a day.

In the warmup, after Bradley worked with her repeatedly, Patsy drifted into doing "I Fall to Pieces" as she felt it. But the song wasn't rockabilly or uptempo western swing. It was a poignant ballad requiring Patsy Cline the spellbinder and weaver of magic, not Patsy Cline the belter.

The Jordanaires' Ray Walker asserted that "when Patsy got to the ending, she came up on the tag an octave and started doing it faster. Right in the middle of our 'oooohs' and 'aaaahs,' we stopped. Patsy wanted to know what was wrong. I asked, 'Is that the way you're ending it?' She told me she felt safer belting the end instead of doing it as she and Owen worked it out. I said, 'Patsy, you almost had me in tears, then you just let the clowns walk in.'"

They talked it over, and on the second try a very gutsy Patsy went for the poignancy inherent in the lyrics by singing in a lower register. When the time came to roll the tape, Bradley lowered the studio lights to set a mood.

Paul Kingsbury of the Country Music Foundation analyzed the proceedings: "'I Fall to Pieces' evolved as Bradley reworked the structure, starting with the rhythm section. From the plaintive chimes of Hank Garland's [electric] guitar on the opening, the track sets a distinct mood—Garland's echo-treated guitar cascading on the chorus, the Jordanaires hovering in the background like spirits of regret, Ben Keith's steel [guitar] wafting in, Hargus "Pig" Robbins's piano showering notes like so many teardrops, all propelled by an undeniably catchy shuffle rhythm. Above it all, Patsy's voice floats, forlorn and inconsolable. It was a bravura performance by all."

Personnel included Randy playing acoustic guitar; Owen's brother Harold on six-string electric bass; Bob Moore, acoustic bass; and Doug Kirham, drums. Though Randy's playing was adequate, it wasn't considered good enough for recordings, and his mike was turned off.

The session also yielded "Shoes," cowritten by Cochran, based on an idea of Velma Smith, wife of Pamper Music's president, and "Lovin' in Vain," which gave Patsy the opportunity to cut loose "with the type of beat that's kept me eating."

There was to be a fourth tune, another of Cochran's called "Perfect Example of a Fool." When things dragged during the prerecord of "Lovin' in Vain," Hank went for a drink. When time came to work on the new song, Patsy discovered she'd left the demo at home. Cochran returned about 5:30, which was quitting time.

As they listened to the playback of "I Fall to Pieces," Bradley remembered that Patsy told him, "I think I've found out who I am and what we've been looking for."

"What do you mean?"

"We don't have to search for my identity anymore," she replied. "This is it. We're doing it right!"

As she walked away, she turned and winked, saying, "And, after all, if we don't do well, we can *always* go back to selling ten to fifteen thousand copies!"

"The day after the session, Patsy and Charlie came over to the house," Jan recalled. "We were talking as Harlan and Hawkshaw Hawkins played a hockey game. Patsy was going off Saturday to Louisville for a fair date. She and Harlan got on well. They shared the same birthday, so they considered that special. They'd been kidding around and she remarked, 'Guess I'm gonna have to start singing "I Fall to Pieces." I don't like it worth a damn, so I've never learned it. And I gotta do it this weekend.' Harlan didn't bat an eye. He didn't care what she thought, as long as she recorded it!"

There's an aspect to Patsy Cline that continues to mystify music historians. She was less than sure of her own musical instincts and uncertain whether Bradley was leading her down the right road. Patsy consistently sought peer approval.

That weekend before she set off for Kentucky, Patsy was at the WSM studios in the National Life Building on the "Friday Night Frolics." Between performances, she and Teddy Wilburn went to his office, where Patsy played an acetate of "I Fall to Pieces."

"She told me how much she hated it," Teddy commented, "and how Brenda and Roy turned it down. She insisted Owen forced it on her. When I heard it, I was surprised. I liked it. She seemed relieved. I told her, 'I have one complaint. I don't care for the guitar work. You have some great sidemen there, but I don't like it.'

"It goes to show how much I knew! The guitars were part of what made the song such a hit."

"From the songwriter's viewpoint," explained Harlan Howard, "Patsy Cline was the greatest reader of lyrics that I've ever worked with. She understood that certain lines in a song are just there to be sung. They're not emotional lines.

"Patsy had the knack to hold back on those lines, then when she got to the really juicy part of the song she'd give it everything she had. Songwriters love that because we know, in order to write a song lyric, every word in the song can't be great. You have to have lines that lead to the best part. Patsy comprehended that. She realized there was more to singing than standing at the mike and doing a song."

Through the sophistication and instincts of Owen Bradley, Patsy Cline was gaining confidence. It would just take a while longer to strike paydirt.

Christmas came and went with Patsy and Charlie still struggling. She had high hopes "Lovin' in Vain" would finally produce a hit.

On January 21—in her ninth month—Patsy made one of her required appearances on the Opry. Charlie got off work and came to the Opry, but Patsy went home alone. She had a restless night. Charlie came home at 6:00 A.M. Sunday morning and crawled into bed. Patsy woke him about an hour later and complained of intense labor pains. He said he thought it was a guise to get him up or penalize him for staying out all night. Patsy called neighbor Joyce Blair. "Blair, it's time!" announced Patsy. "Charlie won't budge. Will you take me to the hospital?"

The Blairs rushed over. In the excitement, Charlie woke, mumbled a few choice comments and went back to sleep. Mrs. Blair took Patsy to St. Thomas Hospital. As they neared the entrance, her car stalled. Attendants rushed Patsy in through Emergency and up to the maternity floor.

When Charlie got up hours later, the house was quiet. He thought it was a joke and slowly maneuvered from room to room. No one was home. Julie was with the neighbors. Patsy was about to deliver. He jumped in the car and sped to her side.

Patsy gave birth to a boy, whom the Dicks named Randolph. Everyone assumed he was named after Randy Hughes, but the name came from Patsy's half-brother. He was to be known as "little" Randy, so as not to be confused with Hughes.

Upon its release January 30, "I Fall to Pieces" had as much impact as Patsy's Four-Star material. The hit Bradley predicted didn't happen, "and don't think Patsy didn't remind me! I can honestly say that, while I never got sick of Patsy, I swear sometimes I thought she was trying to push me over the edge."

Deejays virtually ignored the song, but Hal Smith of Pamper Music had great faith in the potential of Hank Cochran and Harlan Howard. He hired promotion man Pat Nelson to work the road. His strategy was to tell country programming directors what a radical departure the song was for Patsy. To their pop counterparts, he pointed out what a radical departure it was for a country artist. According to Charlie, in spite of Nelson's efforts, it didn't happen. "It received limited play, but not the big boom you need for a hit. When everyone was about to give up, Pat stayed on the job."

On February 9, less than three weeks after Randy's birth, Patsy was in Bradley's studio filming a segment for the army's syndicated TV version of "Country Style, U.S.A." Her on-again, off-again battle with the waistline was a losing one, especially after her pregnancy. She looked bloated.

Faron Young was the guest host in a country store setting. He introduced Patsy, who sang "Walkin' After Midnight." Reported Lightnin' Chance, who played on the date, "They brought in bolts and bolts of fabric and stacked them on a countertop. Patsy had her hair pulled in a bun and was overly made up. She had on a short-sleeved white blouse and this pleated gingham dress with two wide straps running up from her waist over the shoulders. It looked like an apron. I charged up and told her, 'Well, hello! You look like you just got back from town selling eggs and milk.' And she picked up one of those bolts and whacked me in the head.

"She looked thirty pounds heavier, but it was more that dress than the fact she'd gained weight. It was all the rage to show country girls in gingham. On most of the programs, they were always bringing in bales of hay. I thought, 'Someday they'll do a country show without a hayseed image.'"

Some of the loveliest pictures taken of Patsy are outdoor shots in everyday, casual clothes, such as slacks and sweaters. Yet, as though ashamed of her assets of piercing brown eyes and soft, wavy brown hair, she often disguised her natural beauty and made herself look cheap and ugly. As her popularity crossed over to pop, she wore bordello-style dresses, horrible wigs, and gaudy costume jewelry. She was heavy-handed with cosmetics, especially her ruby red lipstick.

In March, Pat Nelson had a breakthrough when a deejay at a Columbus, Ohio, pop station began playing "I Fall to Pieces." By then Decca had written off any hope of seeing the tune become a hit. With his Columbus airplay, Nelson talked record distributors into ordering the single and fanning it across the area. His shrewdest move was getting "I Fall to Pieces" on jukeboxes. After four months, momentum built on the two levels—pop and country—Nelson had gone after. Decca saw movement and, their faith restored and much against established policy of ballyhooing product they'd considered a lost cause, began a heavy promotion campaign.

☆

On April 1, Dottie West, twenty-eight, first met Patsy Cline backstage at the Opry. She went up to her and said, "Hello, I'm Dottie West."

In her best high and mighty voice, Patsy snapped, "Oh, you are, huh?"

"Yes, and I just want to thank you for that letter you wrote me."

Patsy gave Dottie a puzzled look. "What letter, Hoss?"

"Right after I first heard 'Walkin' After Midnight' I wrote you to say what a big fan I was."

"That was 1957!"

"But I remember. I still have it! You sent back a real nice reply. You told me if I ever came to Winchester, you hoped we could meet. Well, I never got to Winchester, but here we are now both in Nashville."

"Ain't it the truth! Where're you from?"

"My husband and I just moved here from Cleveland, Ohio. But I was born outside McMinnville."

"Where's that, Hoss?"

"Oh, southeast of here, near Murfreesboro."

"Okay. I know where that is."

"I used to live here before I married."

"Well, Dottie, are you a singer?"

"I've made a couple of records, but nothing like you. My husband Bill is a guitarist and record engineer."

"Yeah?"

Dottie noted that Patsy showed a genuine interest in her career and, in a matter of minutes, they were like old friends. There are interesting similarities in their backgrounds.

Dottie was born Dorothy Marie Marsh, the eldest of ten children in a poor farm family. She loved music and played several instruments. At twelve, she made her debut on a Nashville radio show. Her budding career was cut short when her father deserted the family. Mrs. Marsh moved to town and opened a restaurant, where Dottie worked as a waitress. She managed to finish high school and went to Tennessee Tech (Polytechnic) in Cookeville, where she studied the cello. She graduated in 1952.

With Bill West, whom she met in school, she moved to Ohio. They married later that year. In Cleveland, by 1955, Dottie and Bill became regulars on the popular regional TV show "Landmark Jubilee." She made her first records in 1959 and, by 1961, was writing songs.

"Patsy invited me over to her house," Dottie recalled, "and, before you knew it, we were visiting and calling each other as soon as we'd come in off the road. I wasn't that busy, to say the least, in those days and, like everyone starting out, we were having a difficult time.

"With 'I Fall to Pieces,' Patsy was the hottest thing going. She finally had some money and she was extremely generous. No one had a heart as good as Patsy's. There was no barrier so tall that she wouldn't leap for you, no problem—financial or otherwise—she wouldn't help you solve. She didn't think only of herself. She thought nothing of buying a couple of bagfuls of groceries and dropping them off to someone in need. If kids were involved, she was especially thoughtful. She was constantly giving away clothes.

"Patsy'd have all us girl singers over. We'd have our little hen parties while the men drank. We thought of Brenda as more of a sister, but, all of a sudden, there we were looking up to her like a big star. She was so cute and tiny and, oh, what a personality! A kid, but so grown up. In many ways, thanks to Patsy!

"Patsy loved to cook. She made the greatest stuffing for pork chops, fantastic glazed and smoked country hams, and the best mashed potatoes you ever ate.

"She was very supportive. She used Bill from time to time to play steel guitar for her shows and invited me to tag along. We'd go from date to date in her car. Patsy loved fancy cars and she was so proud of her Cadillac. It was the biggest, whitest Cadillac she could find.

"Sometimes, when he could get off, Charlie'd go with us and drive, but, oh, boy, could Patsy drive that car. She was a daredevil behind the wheel. On one tour, Roy Orbison was a headliner and rode with us—once. Patsy scared the poor man to death. He was in the back seat, holding on for dear life. Every time he'd say something, Patsy'd laugh and say, 'Relax, Hoss,' and she'd go faster.

"None of us girl singers were working that much. It wasn't long before Patsy put me to work when I didn't have anything booked. I wasn't singing, but helped with her wardrobe and hair. It was an exciting time with 'I Fall to Pieces' becoming a hit. Just by watching her, I was able to learn so much. She completely reinvented me as a singer. The best advice I ever got was when she told me, 'Hoss, if you can't do it with feeling, don't do it.'"

"Patsy was the type who'd do anything for you!" Roger Miller boasted. "She didn't know the meaning of 'in harm's way.' A bunch of us musicians went into Juárez, Mexico, after a Faron Young date in El Paso. Patsy tagged along. The guys bought a little grass, then worried how they were going to get it back across the border.

"Nothing scared Patsy. She said, 'What the hell y'all worried about when you got the Cline here? Give me that stuff. I'll take care of it.' And she grabbed it and stuffed it down her bra. She was cool as a cucumber as we crossed the border. She never even held her breath!

"Patsy had a good soul and heart. She was someone you'd want in your corner. One of her great attributes was that Patsy didn't hold herself apart from the rest of the world. She was one of us."

A songwriters' clique developed that included Miller, Cochran, Johnny Paycheck by whatever name he was using at any given time, Ernest's son Justin Tubb, Wayne Walker, and Mel Tillis.

"It was a few writers and singers," related Roger, "and one or two others we let in because we liked them. Patsy and Charlie were accepted early on. They enjoyed being with us more than we enjoyed being with them! Bill was a great musician and Dottie was like Patsy's sister. Sometimes Harlan and Jan would come, but they kinda kept to themselves or ran with the Carter clan—Mother Maybelle's daughters Helen, Anita, and June (now Mrs. Johnny Cash).

"We gathered at Dottie and Bill West's house on old Highway 65 across the Cumberland River. There was no bridge so we took a ferry. Like the rest of us, they didn't have any money. It was a place to get together. There was a camaraderie you don't see today. We loved to have picnics and they had this big porch with a swing. We'd sit around sipping drinks and talking shop. Patsy, Charlie, and me were the life of the party. Dottie was taking care of her toddlers. Patsy had Julie and little Randy. The girls'd fuss about in the kitchen and go crazy over those kids. We didn't have nothing, but had so much.

"Dottie was famous for her magazine clippings. She'd cut pictures out of *House Beautiful* and say, 'Someday when I have money, I want a house like this. No, this. No! This.' I looked at the scrapbook she'd compiled and said, 'Honey, make up your mind or you're gonna be an architect's nightmare.' Patsy chimed in, 'Or mother lode!'"

"If members of the clique were missing," Dottie explained, "it was because they'd stayed too late into the morning at Tootsie's. That was the hangout, especially after the '[Friday Night] Frolics' and the Opry. The Ryman wasn't air-conditioned and, especially in the summer, most of us couldn't get out the back door and across the alley into Tootsie's second-floor room fast enough—Patsy, Charlie, Bill, me, and the clique.

"We'd be quenching for something cool to drink. As soon as Tootsie saw us, she'd send our orders over. She knew what everybody drank. It was nothing more than a roadhouse, but it was like a second home. The tables had red-and-white checkered tablecloths and tin ashtrays and napkin holders. The walls were covered with hundreds and hundreds of autographs. We loved to go there, if for no other reason than to have Maggie's hamburgers and chili. With Tootsie keeping IOUs, we could have a good time no matter who was working and who wasn't. Even though we might be appearing on the Opry, no one was making big money.

"Patsy loved to laugh and, to be frank, she enjoyed the stardom and adulation. Everyone enjoyed Patsy, but it would have been impossible to take the spotlight away even in a roomful of people. She had that certain something.

"Tootsie, another lady you didn't mess with, had more IOUs on Charlie than anybody. When Tootsie was ready to close, she'd holler 'Closing time!' If the guys who'd had too much to drink didn't budge, she'd go around and jab them right in the rear with a hat pin. They'd rear up, yelling 'Good night, Miss Tootsie!' I bet Tootsie used that pin on Charlie more than anyone. When he'd say he enjoyed a beer now and then, I'd razz him, 'Yeah, and you have the wounds to prove it.'

"On the road and off, Patsy and me did everything together. I was her friend and probably greatest fan. I couldn't watch her perform enough. We both were in awe of the business, but Patsy didn't think of herself as a trailblazer. She was making it the hard way. Even if she'd taken the time to stop and reflect, that fact wouldn't have hit her. She was too busy doing it.

"When we stood waiting to go on at the Opry, she talked about that spot behind the microphone and the legends that stood there—Hank Williams, Red Foley, Roy Acuff, Ernest Tubb, Tex Ritter, Mother Maybelle, Minnie Pearl. I added Patsy's name. I was so proud of Patsy and told her many times. Once was in Tootsie's. It was just the two of us scooping down Maggie's chili. 'I Fall to Pieces' came on the jukebox. It was beginning to look like it had staying power and would make it big-time.

"Unlike me, Patsy enjoyed hearing her voice. I used to get such a kick out of that. There we were listening and I took Patsy's hand and told her, 'I'm sure rooting for you!' She thanked me and replied, 'So am I, Hoss! But good God, Dottie, I came so close once before, then nothing. This time it's gonna happen. I can taste it!'"

By 1961 it was the best of times for Patsy. She had her son and two hits. Even in the best of times, however, Patsy and Charlie's marriage was plagued with drama.

In April 1961 Patsy had a premonition of death, which she would relate having again and again to Dottie, June Carter, and others. On Delta airline stationery she wrote a will "To Whom It May Concern," making known her wishes for her children's care and education; to whom she'd leave her money, clothing, jewelry, and furniture—all inventoried in detail; and how and where she wished "to be put away." She went so far as to have the will witnessed. She then stashed it away, later informing her mother of its existence.

Patsy's will made plain that, although she expected Charlie to be in her life, he would not be enriched by her success. He'd get only whatever car she was driving at the time.

In letters to Rose Marie Flynt, an aspiring Maryland singer she'd known since 1959, Patsy described in intimate detail Charlie's spending, thoughtlessness, and verbal and physical abusiveness. Often, she was in divorce mode, complaining of his drinking and leaving her alone while he stayed out until the wee hours.

"I'm sick of his shit," she wrote in spring 1961. "If these 2 kids weren't here I would never have come home." Then, in the next breath, she discussed plans for the Opry to be broadcast nationally, her hopes for "I Fall to Pieces," and an upcoming appearance on Don McNeill's *Breakfast Club* radio show.

In happiness or drowning in the blues, Patsy Cline was totally unpredictable.

"(WRITE ME) IN CARE OF THE BLUES"

BILLY WALKER: "Let's bow our heads and pray. Patsy?"

PATSY CLINE: "I'm in traction. You go ahead."

BILLY WALKER: "Lord, we want to thank You for sparing this woman's life. Watch over her through the healing process."

PATSY CLINE: "And, Lord, please let 'em get some meat in this damn hospital. That's enough praying for today. Amen!"

$\mathcal{O}$n the April 3 issue of *Billboard*, "I Fall to Pieces" entered the country charts and began its ascent. Jordanaire Ray Walker remembers what happened a day later. "Patsy came running down the stairs in [Decca's] Studio B, squealing, 'They say I got a hit on my hands! They'll never get my car now, Hoss! I'm paying cash.'" She had come to Owen Bradley crying that the finance company was on the way to repossess her car, and that she was about to lose her refrigerator. The results of Nelson's dedication so heartened Bradley that he gave Patsy an advance large enough to cover her immediate needs and then some.

"After we had a hit, Patsy and Charlie came by the studio," said Bradley. "It was still hard to believe we'd really done it right and the public accepted 'I Fall to Pieces.' Patsy had what eluded her for four years and I was feeling pretty pleased. I told them, 'I hope now y'all will leave me alone for a while!' And we had a good laugh."

Jan Howard recalled, "Harlan was reading *Billboard* and yelled, 'Hot damn!'

I said, 'What?' He got excited because 'I Fall to Pieces' was starting to climb the charts. He smiled, 'You know something, honey. I bet Patsy'll start liking it now!'"

"I don't think she ever did like it," Bradley pointed out, "until it became a hit!"

An unprecedented first for a female country artist occurred when Patsy cracked the *Billboard* pop charts in 1957. It was more than anyone—Bradley, Howard, Cochran, the Decca New York executives, Randy, and, especially, Patsy—expected when it happened a second time with "I Fall to Pieces." With her pop recognition from and total sales of 750,000 copies of "Walkin' After Midnight" and now "I Fall to Pieces," Patsy could hold her own with any country male superstar.

The fan magazines took note. *Country Song Roundup* was an early supporter, running a long article on her transformation of the way the women singers of the day dressed. The article noted:

> The ensembles she wears on-stage depend on the occasion and location. She has something in her wardrobe to answer every requirement—fringed costumes, full-skirted dresses with tight bodice, formal-type wear, skirts and blouses. Slacks and blouses answer most of her at-home requirements, and one of her major concerns always is that everything must have that "just pressed" look.
>
> In the make-up department Patsy perhaps does more with lipstick than any other cosmetic. She limits her use of rouge, powder and eye make-up, because she has a very lovely complexion and looks always as though she's just come back from a morning walk in the cool, spring air. She accentuates this look by applying her lipstick brightly and liberally, and makes certain it remains that way with frequent retouches. . . . Shoes are one of her weaknesses, and there she goes overboard, possessing the kind with straps, without, backless, high heels, low heels and any other types that appear as the current fashion.

Patsy was in WSM Studio B on May 10 recording a show for that week's "Friday Night Frolics." She sang "I Fall to Pieces" and "Lovin' in Vain." Sonny James was her coheadliner. After the show, Charlie met her and they stopped at Tootsie's for a drink, then Patsy went home to pack. Thanks to the success of "I Fall to Pieces," Decca was finally sending her on a promotional tour—alone.

Louise Seger, a transplanted Mississippian in Houston, called KIKK radio throughout the day from home and her job to request Patsy Cline records. In early May, while she was speaking to deejay Hal Harris, she learned that Patsy would be playing the Esquire Ballroom. She spread the news and gathered together a group of friends, all dressed in western clothes, for the appearance at the gigantic barnlike club on Hempstead Highway. Louise had insisted they arrive early, and they did. In fact, they were the first. While enjoying her beer, Louise looked up.

"I saw this girl looking over the place. I thought she was Patsy's agent. The only time I'd seen Patsy was four years ago on Godfrey. Then something went *ding, ding, ding!*" Patsy took a seat three tables over from Louise, who was about to burst. She told her friends, "I'm going over there." All eyes were on her as she walked slowly to the other table.

"Excuse me. Miss Cline?"

"Yes," Patsy said, smiling.

"I just wanted you to know how much I admire your music. I have 'I Fall to Pieces' played for me four or five times every day."

Patsy thanked her and Louise introduced herself and asked Patsy to join her group. Everyone was drinking and talking, but Patsy kept looking around the club. "This is a mighty damn big place, isn't it?"

"Yes, ma'am," answered Louise, "but, boy, it's gonna be packed."

"I only hope I can about half fill it."

"Half ain't the word, ma'am. You're gonna fill it."

"I'm worried about the band. I don't know any of the musicians and I wonder if they know my music. Do you?"

"Yes, ma'am, every beat."

"Would you do me a favor and, during the show, watch the drummer so he won't rush me? He's the one who can really mess me up. But if you know the tempo, you can let him know when he's going too fast."

Louise happily complied, during both shows. Around midnight, after Patsy signed autographs and posed for photos, Louise heard Patsy calling a taxi to return to the Montague Hotel. "No, you'll go with us. We'll go to my house so you can have something to eat."

Patsy collected her money and piled into Louise's Pontiac with the others. At the house, Patsy put on an apron and helped in the kitchen. After they ate and the others departed, Patsy and Louise sat at the kitchen table and talked about "broken hearts, husband problems, children problems, loves lost, loves won. We sounded like two people writing country songs!"

Patsy said that after many setbacks everything she had dreamed of was happening. "I wanted stardom, and, this time, it looks like I hit paydirt. I've got the two most wonderful babies in the world, but the thing I want more than anything is for things to work between Charlie and me. I'll stay as long as I can for no other reason than the children. I'd love to leave, but I don't have the guts. Since the baby, it's been pretty awful." She described their fights. "Lots of times he bruised me so bad I had to work all covered with makeup to hide a black eye. I get so mad I'd like to throw one of those iron skillets at him. I'll go to pick up something else and then I'll think, 'Oh, no. I just bought that.'"

They traded stories until almost 4:00 A.M. Saturday.

"It's been real nice, Louise, but I better be getting to the hotel. I have an eight o'clock flight to Dallas."

"Why don't you stay here? It makes sense. If you don't mind getting up a little early, there's a deejay friend who'd love to interview you."

"Okay. Sure!"

Louise called Hal Harris at home. His wife answered and told him it was some crazy fan who had Patsy Cline at her house.

"Oh, God," he mumbled, "Louise's drunk!" He picked up the phone. "Louise, do you know what time it is?"

"I had to reach you before you left for the station. I've got Patsy Cline at the house."

"And I've got Marilyn Monroe in bed. Now, honey, you sleep it off and I'll play 'I Fall to Pieces' for you in the morning."

Louise couldn't convince him of her coup. She set the alarm. When it went off at 5:30, Louise called KIKK. Harris had just arrived. "Hal, what's the oldest Patsy Cline record you've got?"

"Hell, I don't know. I'll look and see."

"Get an old one and play it next."

She crept into the room where Patsy was sleeping and plugged the radio in. When Harris began to spin "Hidin' Out," one of Patsy's first releases, Louise turned up the volume. Patsy shot straight up.

"My God! What the hell's going on? Who's that?"

"Don't you know?"

"No, but she sure is loud."

"That's you, you fool!"

"When did I ever record that?"

"I don't know, but Hal found it. Hurry. We've gotta go downtown, get you packed, stop by KIKK, and get you to the airport."

They sped to the Montague. Patsy changed as Louise threw her belongings into suitcases.

"Louise, pack everything carefully!"

"Sure thing. Don't worry," she replied, surveying a room that, it appeared, a hurricane had wrecked.

Patsy came out of the bathroom in red western slacks, a white satin western blouse, and yellow squaw boots. Patsy checked out and they headed out the Gulf Freeway to KIKK in Pasadena. They entered through the back door and meandered through the station until they found Harris's control room. He was dressed in old Bermuda shorts, a blue wool sweater that had been washed and dried one too many times, and tennis shoes that had holes cut over the toe area. He wasn't wearing socks, hadn't shaved or combed his hair.

Louise tapped on the window. Harris turned, did a double take, sat staring at Patsy and Louise, then jumped up and opened the door. He was speechless. "Hal Harris, I'd like you to meet Miss Patsy Cline. Patsy, this is the man who plays your music for me."

Louise reported, "Hal fell through his asshole and hung himself!"

Harris ran around in circles, grabbing records, jumping to the microphone to do his patter. Finally, he announced, "Ladies and gentlemen, I'm going to play a record by a young lady who was in town last night. And I have a big surprise for you. She's right here in the studio, so stay tuned. Here's Patsy Cline singing 'I Fall to Pieces,' which I'm sending out for Patsy's biggest local fan, Miss Louise Seger."

After he started the record spinning, Harris talked to Patsy, getting some statistics. Then they did a fifteen-minute interview. By 7:00 Louise had Patsy on her way to the airport.

Patsy gave up a lucrative one-nighter on May 27 to be on the radio network portion of the Opry. "She wasn't too pleased," said Grandpa Jones. "Patsy was doing her pacing bit and just a-fussing so I asked what was wrong."

"Grandpa," Patsy complained, "I wanted to be a member of the Opry, but I didn't know it was gonna wreck my career!"

"What do you mean, gal?"

"I gave up a thousand dollars to be here to do one song for twenty bucks!"

"Honey, you can't look at it that way. This is a national broadcast. Your song's gonna be heard by thousands."

"Grandpa, don't go trying to talk sense to this ole gal! I got four mouths to feed."

"I know. I know. But the Opry'll always be here for that rainy day. You gotta learn to look at the broad picture and not what you have to put on the table tonight."

Louise never expected to hear from Patsy. But less than three weeks after her visit, Louise received the first in a series of intensely personal letters from Patsy.

May 29, 1961

Dear Louise & All,

Wanted to take time out to write a line or two to thank you folks for the nice way you treated this ole country gal while I was there. I sure do appreciate all you done, because if you hadn't been so nice I wouldn't have been able to go to the radio station. My sincere thanks and hope I can be as nice to you all sometime. Tell Hal "hello" for me.

Hope this finds you well and things going great. As for me, the kids and myself are fine and hell is still a poppin' of course. Ha. Don't know how much longer I can stand this way of living, but the little ones always come first with me. Till then I'll grin and bear it. Ha.

Now for the really big news. Well I'm nearly up on the moon and don't need a rocket. My record sold 10,000 in Detroit last week alone and is hitting all pop charts. It's #1 on both pop stations here in Nash. & is the #1 seller at Decca and is already being put in 3 albums[1] right away of different artists. I do the 5 Star Jubilee[2] on July 7th, and it's in color. Swingin' huh? I think I told you I'm getting things in shape for the Dick Clark [show] but don't know the date yet. But I'll let you know.

I'm going home next Tuesday and while there, they are proclaiming a Patsy Cline Day in my home town. Ain't that a kick in the head? I wish

1. Special-product albums, such as *Ernest Tubb's Mid-Nite Jamboree.*
2. Carried briefly Friday nights by NBC while ABC decided on renewal of "Jubilee, U.S.A." The program featured rotating hosts: Tex Ritter, Jimmy Wakely, Carl Smith, Snooky Lanson, and Rex Allen.

they would just left it like it was, but I do appreciate the noise they are kicking up. So I guess I'll have to do what *they* want that day. The mayor is gonna be there and recognize me and so on. Any way, it sure is a good feeling. I can't really believe it.

Guess I'd better close and get busy with this ironing I've got here.

Be sure and kiss the boy [Louise's son] for me. He sure is a doll and tell the couple that was there that night "hello" and I hope I didn't bore them with my troubles, and I think they are wonderful folks. I still want all of you to come down to see us and the Opry. So write soon and thanks again. (Dallas was a swingin' date.)

Hope to see you again soon.

Love & Luck,
Patsy Cline & Family

The best marriages are born of compromise. Enhancing one aspect often means sacrificing another. Neither Patsy nor Charlie would compromise, and only Patsy made the sacrifices.

Those who knew the Dicks well pinpoint this period as the time the problems became insurmountable. Though proud of her accomplishments, Charlie found Patsy's stardom was a blow to his pride.

"No matter how their day started," Ralph Emery, then a WSM disc jockey and Opry announcer, said, "it seemed it would end in some argument in which they'd accuse each other of all kinds of things—usually because of Patsy's insecurities and Charlie's drunken jealousy."

"What really bothered Charlie," Faron Young asserted, "especially if he was drinking, was when someone called him 'Mr. Cline' or introduced him as 'Patsy Cline's husband.' That's a natural ego thing to piss you off. Whether you're the husband or wife, when you have somebody in the business, you have to accept being relegated to the background."

Young described the two sides of Charlie. "Sober, I love him. He tried to do a lot for Patsy. He loved her and them kids. He had a job at the newspaper printing plant but worked like the dickens for Patsy. He'd go around to the record companies and call and write the deejays.

"But, hot damn, if he's drunk and I see him coming, I'll cross the street to get away from him. He gets so damn belligerent. Charlie would beat Patsy around and chew her out something terrible. He was just a Jekyll and a damn Hyde!"

Young related an incident that occurred at the Dicks'. "Charlie borrowed a car from one of my guitar players and went after some whiskey. Would you believe he hit a bridge and demolished the car? Didn't hurt him! The car wasn't worth more than eight or nine hundred dollars, but it was all that guitar player owned. He had no insurance and Charlie never paid him a nickel. I don't know if Patsy took care of it in the end. I only remember the car being towed to the junkyard.

"With Patsy's stardom, her lot improved. She'd gotten to where I was paying her three hundred dollars a day. I couldn't keep her much longer—couldn't afford to pay her. All I needed was a one- to two-hundred-dollar-a-day girl singer. After 'I Fall to Pieces,' Patsy was ready to go on her own. The tide had turned."

Patsy Cline was the reigning Queen of Country Music and crossing over to strong pop airplay. Randy had countless offers. On Patsy's return from Texas, she stunned him with the news that she was taking time off. She flew home with the children to be honored with Patsy Cline Day and to attend her sister's graduation. Not finishing high school was something Patsy regretted, and she was proud of Sylvia Mae, or Sis, as she preferred to call her, who'd always been a favorite.

Randy wasn't quite so taken aback when he learned Patsy'd be working, too. As it turned out, it was for one night only and little money.

Melody Boy John Anderson observed, "Patsy gave Winchester hell through the years for not honoring its home town girl's accomplishments. She'd told me about wanting to be in the Apple Blossom Festival Parade, but that officials hadn't asked her again. She had a chip on her shoulder about Winchester's attitude toward her growing up on the other side of the tracks, South Kent Street. Now Patsy was a star and she was enjoying every moment of it."

At the Winchester Country Club, the mayor presided over a dinner in Patsy's honor. Various speakers sang her praises. One of these was said to have been WINC Radio station manager Philip Whitney, who in years past irritated Patsy when he said that little Virginia Hensley who came to Joltin' Jim McCoy's show wasn't quite ready for stardom but later worked hard to achieve it.

The story of that occasion has circulated and become exaggerated with age. One attendee said, "That night everyone went on about how proud Winchester was to have Patsy Cline as a native. When it came time for Patsy to respond, there was a loud round of applause. No one was prepared for what followed. Patsy, who was all dolled up, surveyed the audience and after a long pause exclaimed, 'I'll tell you sons of bitches this dinner ain't enough! It's all very nice for you to recognize me now that I've made it, but where were you when my family needed your help? Where were you when I needed your recognition? Nowhere to be found. In fact, you laughed at me behind my back. Well, you can all go to hell!' And Patsy, not forgetting her key to the city, stormed out."

Claude B. Smalts, Jr., mayor at the time, and Whitney, had no recollection even of such an event. Smalts, a local florist and a long-time family friend, couldn't remember ever giving Patsy the key to the city.

"She certainly deserved it," he said, "and, as far as I was concerned, she always had it. Now, about her response at that dinner, Patsy surely might have been thinking such thoughts, and with good reason, but she'd never have acted in such a fashion—especially if her mother was present. I am sure she couldn't have been more gracious."

Whitney concurred. "Patsy could be as feisty as she wanted to be, but she knew the time and place."

On June 9 "Winchester's Only Patsy Cline" appeared live at the Winchester Drive-In Theatre on Route 11. It was a bumper-to-bumper crowd with an admission of seventy-five cents. After the double feature, Patsy was introduced by Joltin' Jim McCoy. She sang, accompanied by McCoy and his Melody Playboys; the highlight was her smash hit. A huge ovation was marred by a loud chorus of boos. "The mildew of envy permeated everywhere," McCoy recollected. "As in every town, you'll find jealousy. Winchester was no different. There were a lot of folks, sorry to say, who couldn't accept a home town girl making it big. It was sad. Patsy never forgot her roots. Even when times were tough, she never asked for more than her expenses just so she could come home and visit her family."

"The booing was from a bunch of ridiculous women," insisted Fay Crutchley. "Pat had been the center of a lot of things that had happened in the area. It had gotten around about her. There'd been quite a few men in her life, and there were more than a few local gals who didn't care one bit for Pat. It was jealousy."

Less than two weeks after receiving Patsy's letter, Louise was driving to work. It was a humid Texas morning. She had her windows open and the radio tuned to KIKK, listening for Hal Harris to play "I Fall to Pieces." Instead, a news bulletin came on. Louise heard the words but in the wind and traffic noise couldn't comprehend what they were. She pulled off the road. She'd heard correctly. Patsy Cline had been critically injured and was near death.

After a week at home, Patsy brought everyone to Nashville to see their new house on Hillhurst Drive. As a graduation present, Patsy planned on taking her sister and family to the Opry. Patsy, the babies, Sylvia Mae, her brother Sam, and Mrs. Hensley left Winchester early Tuesday, June 13, 1961, in Mrs. Hensley's Cadillac. They arrived late in the evening.

On Wednesday afternoon, Sam drove himself and Patsy to Madison Square Shopping Center in Madison, where Patsy bought her mother material to make her some dresses. At about 4:30, Patsy saw a rainstorm brewing, and they headed home, driving along Hills Lane, a section of Old Hickory Boulevard. Five blocks from where Patsy pointed out to Sam her former house, tragedy struck. According to Patsy's watch, it was exactly 4:43 P.M. In her June 23 letter to Louise, Patsy wrote:

> . . . We came on top a bridge and then the road drop[ped] in a valley like
> about a block long then the road went up another little hill. Coming toward
> us [in the other lane] were two cars and a woman [in the second car]
> tried to pass the car in front of her. There wasn't enough passing room
> in this little valley. It was marked with a double yellow line all the way
> but she gunned her car and tried to get around, then hit us head on. No
> way at all getting out of it for us. I went through the windshield and back.
> I've cut my face.

She did a sketch of her face and the area from her head, just above the hairline, across her forehead to her left and right eyebrows and nose where she was badly lacerated.

> Yes, it missed my eyes by 1/4 in. My right hip was knocked out of its
> whole socket and ligaments are pulled and [my] right wrist fractured.
> Brother had a hole punched in the chest big as a dime, about 3 in. deep,

with a few cuts & bruises. The woman in the other car broke all her teeth & jaw bone and cut her lips and chin. It killed her cousin & cousin's little boy . . .

Dottie West was at home listening to the radio. "I just couldn't believe what I was hearing. The accident occurred at Hills Lane and Gibson Road in front of Madison High School, which wasn't far from where Bill and I were living. I was a mess. My hair was in curlers and I didn't have on any makeup. But I dropped everything and jumped in the car and drove like crazy to the site.

"What I saw showed me a lot—not that I needed any proof—about the real Patsy. I pushed through to where Patsy was. As soon as she saw me, she made a joke about my curlers.

"Patsy was still laying on the side of the road. I got real angry that they'd left her there. She'd cut an artery and was a bloody mess. Then I was told that, as bad off as she was, Patsy was more concerned about her brother and the others. She insisted that the ambulance drivers take them to the hospital first.

"I went in the ambulance with her to Madison Hospital. On the way I picked the glass out of her hair that she got when she was thrown through the windshield. It was amazing she was alive. I tried not to look at her because I didn't want her to see me crying. She'd look at me and say, 'Oh, Hoss.' She made jokes all the way. There I was crying and laughing at the same time. I marveled at her strength. I thought, 'My God! This lady's absolutely amazing!'"

Mrs. Hensley stayed with her grandchildren, while Charlie, Dottie, and close friends kept vigil at the hospital.

Mrs. Ruby Nell Angell, thirty-two, was declared dead on arrival with fatal injuries to her head. She was riding in the car driven by her cousin, Mrs. Harold Clark, twenty-two, who was admitted with numerous cuts and bruises but listed in fair condition. Mrs. Angell's son, Jimmy, six, was listed in critical condition with injuries to his chest. He died shortly thereafter.

Dr. Hillis Evans, the attending physician, told Charlie that Patsy's injuries were so serious and life-threatening, it looked hopeless. As she was prepared for surgery, Patsy witnessed Mrs. Angell die. All through the long operation, Patsy's prognosis was touch and go. Dr. Evans expected her to live only a few hours.

In a touching gesture of concern for their colleague, several hundred members of the Grand Ole Opry gathered en masse outside Madison Hospital immediately following the surgery. Patsy later extolled the fact that at least half of them stayed to keep watch from 7:00 P.M. to 2:00 A.M.

"They can't believe she's alive," Charlie said over and over. The next day, he wasn't optimistic. "The surgery went okay, but it don't look good," he told Dottie. She and close friends, such as the Dicks' neighbors the Blairs, tried to build Charlie's faith. "Patsy needs you now more than ever," Dottie advised. "Don't give up. You know she's a fighter."

That evening, as she lay in drug-induced semi-consciousness to relieve her pain, Charlie and Joyce Blair were startled when Patsy called out, "Charlie!"

"I'm right here, honey." He and Mrs. Blair rushed to the bed.

"Jesus was here, Charlie. Don't worry. He took my hand and told me, 'No, not now. I have other things for you to do.'"

"Okay, honey. Okay."

Patsy drifted off.

"God, Joyce, I don't want to lose her."

"Charlie, you heard Patsy. We have hope! You know Patsy and God are never wrong!"

On Friday, Charlie informed reporters Patsy was off the critical list. "She's improving. Patsy's got an awful bad cut on her forehead and one hip was dislocated. But she's conscious and talks okay. The doctors say it's going to take a lot of rest and time, but we think she'll be all right."

Dr. Evans described Patsy's condition as "fair." Charlie relayed that Patsy's brother was already able to sit up and get in a wheelchair.

Flowers, telegrams, cards, and letters arrived from industry executives, the Opry, recording artists, deejays, and fans. The hospital switchboard was inundated with calls day and night. Attempting to get through were Winchester's Joltin' Jim McCoy and Patsy's friends Fay Crutchley and Louise Seger.

"We appreciate everybody thinking of us," Charlie told the press, "but the hospital's not equipped to handle so many calls, and it's slowing down other business." He explained that, on doctors' orders, Patsy was to have no visitors outside of the immediate family. He was now employed by the Nashville Printing Corporation (the *Nashville Tennessean* and *Nashville Banner*) but was able to take time off to be at Patsy's bedside.

Saturday night at the Opry, announcer Grant Turner apprised the audience of Patsy's weak condition and asked for their prayers. The Opry ended at 11:15, and the stars and fans would pass through Tootsie's Orchid Lounge, then cross Broadway to the Ernest Tubb Record Shop for the "Mid-Nite Jamboree." "Just a little before midnight," remembered Ernest Tubb, "this young couple came in. The husband approached me with his wife, this tiny little thing named Loretta Lynn. Mooney said they'd just moved from Indiana. We'd met at the Opry. Loretta, along with Jan Howard, Margie Bowes, and Connie Hall, had been named Most Promising Girl Singer at the 1960 Convention. He wanted to know if Loretta could sing her new single. It was on Zero Records, a small Canadian label nobody'd ever heard of. He and Loretta'd been driving from city to city across the country trying to get deejays to play it. So I put Loretta on.

"Before the show, we talked. She was a big fan of Patsy's and asked about the car wreck. God bless her, Loretta was real upset. I tried to calm her down, 'Now, Loretta, honey, don't you cry. Patsy's hanging on. She's a trouper!' She told me she wanted to let Patsy know how she felt and had an idea. I thought it sounded real nice and agreed."

Tubb introduced Loretta, who sang "I'm a Honky Tonk Girl," which she'd written. At the end, she said, "Friends, I'd like to do something special for someone I admire a great deal. This is the hit song by Miss Patsy Cline that's a way up there on the charts. I guess y'all know she's over there in Madison in the hospital 'cause she's been in a real bad car wreck. So I want to dedicate this to her. Patsy, if you're a listening, this song's for you, 'I Fall to Pieces.' I hope you get well real soon!"

Loretta later explained that before stepping to the microphone, she took an issue of *Country Song Roundup*, a magazine that printed lyrics to country hits. "I loved 'I Fall to Pieces,' but I didn't know it by heart. When it came to my turn, I did my song. Then I had Mooney hold up the lyrics to Patsy's song and I read the words as the band played."

At the hospital, Patsy was listening. Charlie sneaked in a radio so Patsy could hear the Opry. They stayed tuned for the "Mid-Nite Jamboree."

"Well, I'll be damned," exclaimed Patsy. "Can you believe that. She sang my song and dedicated it to me. That's pretty nice of that gal. Charlie, go down to the record store and thank her and tell her I want to meet her."

When Charlie arrived, he looked for Loretta amid all the well-wishers. "I saw this skinny girl in western clothes and went up to her.

"Are you Loretta Lynn?"

"Yes, sir, I sure am. Who are you?"

"I'm Charlie Dick. It's nice to meet you."

Loretta smiled and replied, "Well, it's sure nice to meet you!"

There was a pause and Charlie suddenly realized that his last name wouldn't mean anything to Loretta. He quickly added, "I'm Charlie Dick, Patsy Cline's husband. She sent me to thank you."

Charlie recollected, "Loretta threw her arms around me and nearly hugged me to death. Then she hollered out to her husband."

"Doo!" called Loretta, "this is Patsy Cline's husband, Charlie Dick. She sent him down here to thank me for singing her song on the broadcast."

Mooney came over and they shook hands.

"Loretta, Patsy really enjoyed what you did and she wants to meet you."

"Oh, my goodness, honey. I just can't believe it. Patsy heard me on the radio and wants to meet me!"

Charlie related that Loretta nearly had a fit. He spoke to them a while and found them to be an interesting, hard-working, struggling couple.

"He introduced himself as Mooney," said Charlie, "but Loretta kept calling him Doo and Dolittle. I wanted to ask what it meant, but didn't have the nerve." He found out later that his real name is Oliver and that Mooney was a throwback to Lynn's moonshining days in the Kentucky hills, and his less familiar nickname was what Loretta liked to call him because he did so little.

"It was after one in the morning," observed Charlie, "and the hospital was strict on the rules. Also, it was quite a distance from downtown. I asked Loretta and Mooney what they were doing in the afternoon and made arrangements to take them to see Patsy."

Loretta discussed meeting Patsy: "Charlie took us up to the fourth floor and showed us in. The room was all bright and cheery. There were flowers all over the place. I remember thinking 'My goodness, all the florists in this here town must be sold out.' Patsy was all in bandages. Her face was bandaged up from up around her eyes to her hairline. Her leg was in a cast hanging from a pulley. It was just pitiful. I said, 'Hello, Patsy. I'm Loretta Lynn.' I was looking at her and trying to talk, but I could hardly keep from crying. I thanked her for her thoughtfulness in inviting Doo and I to see her. She thanked me for my thoughtfulness.

"Patsy quipped, 'Hey, we sound like a love duet!' As bad off as she was, she made jokes and asked about my career. We talked a good while and became close friends right away. That's the way it was with Patsy. We were cut from the same cloth."

"Patsy and Loretta got on famously," Charlie said. "They were talking a mile a minute. Patsy was bandaged up pretty good, but that didn't stop her from chattering away and laughing up a storm. They talked about how hard it was for a girl singing in country music and traded stories back and forth about the politics of the Opry.

"Mooney and I went out in the corridor and talked. He said what a hard time they'd been having, but that things were starting to look good now that Loretta had a hit. She'd been on the Opry several times and met the Wilburn Brothers, who took her to Owen Bradley at Decca. I told him Patsy's situation only recently started looking up with 'I Fall to Pieces.' We discussed how it was having a wife who was in the business and working the road.

"They'd resettled from Butcher's Hollow, Kentucky, to Custer, Washington, and now to Indiana. They'd been coming and going to and from Nashville since Loretta first sang on the Opry and finally were sharing a house with a friend. Mooney was trying to find work as an automobile body repairman. I suggested we ought to get together sometime and have a few beers. He was for that. It was the beginning of a long and loyal friendship. Although Loretta wasn't a drinker, Mooney enjoyed partying and they became regulars in the clique."

"Patsy relished her success so because she came up rough," said Loretta, "sort of jerked by the hair. The first time I heard her was on the radio when I was living in the state of Washington. She had 'Walkin' After Midnight' out and had just got married to Charlie. I was a fan, so meeting her the day after the 'Mid-Nite Jamboree' was a thrill."

Patsy Cline and Loretta Lynn may actually have met not long after Loretta's October 1960 Opry debut. When she first appeared, Loretta was advised to dress nicely and to wear high heels. "But," Loretta recollected, "I didn't have a nice dress and I had to wear low-heeled boots." The girl singers in the dressing room referred to Loretta as a "country bumpkin." It's alleged that Patsy was present.

The women "ganged up on the side [in the wings] to watch the new competition." Loretta sang her new single, "I'm a Honky Tonky Girl" and brought the house to its feet with cheering and applause. Opry manager Ott Devine was so impressed he invited her back the following week. She had been voted Most Promising Girl Singer by the country deejays. When this was announced, Patsy is said to have blurted out, "Most promising what?" and the rest of the women laughed.

"Oh, we were just being nice and nasty," one participant insisted, "and Patsy was right in there with us."

In her autobiography *Coal Miner's Daughter,* Loretta wrote that Patsy "was like Hank Williams, the way she got this throb in her voice and really touched people's emotions." She recollected that career and marital problems brought her and Patsy closer and closer. But more than a few people in Nashville claim Patsy and Loretta weren't that close; others dispute this.

Jean Shepard said bluntly, "Loretta made a lot of statements in her book that don't hold water. Patsy was a loner, which made a lot of people think she was conceited, which she wasn't. But Patsy had no super close friends. She and I were having babies about the same time and talking about motherhood and all. But I'd never say we were bosom buddies."

"When Loretta first came to town," recalled songwriter Lee Burrows, "she was brought to a dress shop by Vivian Keith, who worked with [agent] Hubert Long and the Wilburn Brothers. She told the manager, 'Loretta doesn't have anything. Can you do anything?' She gave her two dresses. When Patsy got wind of this, she called Loretta over and gave her a bunch of clothes."

Dottie noted, "Loretta spent time with Patsy at home. Sometimes, after the 'Friday Night Frolics' and the Opry, Loretta and Mooney were with us at Tootsie's. And not everyone was welcome in that group. But Loretta didn't drink anything stronger than a Coke. Whether Loretta was Patsy's closest buddy, I don't know. Does it matter? Patsy enjoyed playing the role of mother hen."

"There were so many wonderful things about Patsy," said Loretta. "I'll say this and let it rest. She was *my* closest friend. She was the one person, other than my husband, I could turn to in a crisis. What stands out in my mind most about her is that she was my pal even in jams. There was a lot of resentment when I first came to town. There were a lot of girl singers trying to get to the top then. Somebody'd get a little jealous and I'd speak when I'd have been better off keeping my mouth shut. But Patsy was strong-willed and always taking up for me. If it hadn't been for her, I don't think I would have lasted."

Teddy Wilburn was associated with Loretta from the beginning. He, Doyle, and their brothers Lester and Leslie managed and booked her, in addition to publishing her songs. She was featured on their live and TV shows, and not, as depicted in the film *Coal Miner's Daughter*, on any Patsy Cline show. In fact, she and Patsy never sang together onstage. Much misinformation about Patsy and Loretta's careers came about due to the dramatic license taken when the Wilburns, because of a contractual dispute with Loretta and disagreements over the script, refused permission to be portrayed. Many things the Wilburns did for Loretta were attributed to Patsy.

"I know most of Loretta's association with Patsy," Teddy claimed. "What made the illuminous bond between them was when the girl singers got up in arms over Doyle getting Loretta so many Opry guest shots. There were about eighteen in a row, probably more than any artist in history. The girls who stood idly by waiting for their opportunity planned a meeting to put a stop to it. There were only a few regular female singers—Kitty Wells, Jean Shepard, Doyle Wilburn's [then] wife Margie Bowes, Skeeter Davis, and Patsy. Others, such as June Webb, who sang with Roy Acuff, worked with groups but weren't presented in a solo spot. Those with recording contracts, like Skeeter, Dottie, Jan, and Loretta, vied for guest spots, especially on weekends when the star girls worked the road. Ott Devine, the Opry general manager, would pull from the list.

"They got together, supposedly at Dottie's, and planned to go to Ott and say if Loretta's spots continued, they wouldn't be available when they were needed. Doyle met with Ott and Loretta was quickly made a regular member."

Loretta charged, "Different girls started calling and saying I ought to return to the West Coast. One asked who I was sleeping with to get on the Opry so fast. It hurt so much I cried day and night. Mooney said, 'If you don't quit crying, I'm gonna take you back to the West Coast and forget it.' The girls called a party and invited Patsy. They didn't know me and Patsy was friends. There was about six of them, younger ones just coming up. I'm not saying who they were. Kitty Wells wasn't one. She's too good a person to do that. Patsy called and told me to get my hair done. She bought me a new outfit and made me go."

When they arrived, Loretta said, there were Cadillacs all around the house. "We went in there, and they didn't say a word. That ended their plan. Patsy put the stamp of approval on me, and I never had any problems again. They're all my friends now."

"I'm a very straightforward person," stated Jean, "and what I'm going to say contradicts Loretta. She heaped a lot of crap in that book of hers. I won't lie. I don't know where she or that meeting was. My feelings are hurt because *I* wasn't invited! I don't know a thing about it, and I was one of the successful girl singers on the Opry. None of the girls—Dottie, Jan, Skeeter, Pearl, Goldie [Hill]—know a thing about it. This has been embarrassing. A fan came up to me and asked, 'Jeanie, is it true all you women singers tried to keep Loretta off the Opry?' I asked, 'What are you talking about?' And she told me and I replied, 'You've got to be kidding!'"

"Who of the women had time for that kind of garbage?" Del Wood said. "We were on the road an average of three weeks out of five. All the singers were individuals with unique styles. Nobody sang like Kitty and nobody sang like Jeanie. Nobody could sing like Patsy and no one wanted to sing like Skeeter. There I go trying to be funny again. Patsy had lots of friends, but few intimates. When you get to know someone backstage, you feel you know them to a certain extent but don't call them your closest friend."

Dottie defended herself: "Rumor has it that the famous meeting was not only instigated by me but was also held at my house. If any such meeting took place, it *didn't* take place at my house, nor was I invited. Jeanie told me it was in Loretta's book and I said, 'Oh, my goodness, that's terrible!' Jeanie said, 'It was supposed to have been at your house.' I yelled, 'What?' She asked, 'Don't you know about it?' and I replied, 'No.' She said, 'Neither does anybody else.' Sorry to say, it's legend now. It's not in my heart to do that kind of thing."

Jean suggested asking Charlie. "He's a truthful person. If something took place, even if it made him look bad, he'll tell you."

Charlie declaimed knowledge of a meeting. "I worked nights then. I wouldn't have known unless Patsy told me, and she wouldn't since I wasn't big on gossip. I heard about it from Loretta. If she said it happened, it happened. I asked Loretta where it took place and she won't tell me."

Regarding the meeting and recriminations, Loretta stated: "I don't remember no formal meeting at anyone's house. I got a call from a man—I won't say who he was—who told me what the girl singers were planning. I didn't give names in my book and, if I was gonna tell, I would've said it then. It was a jealousy thing. But do you know any singer who comes to town and doesn't have the same thing happen? It weren't no big deal. Who made it a big deal? It's all blown out of proportion."

Loretta's reminiscences with Loudilla Johnson, co-president of the Loretta Lynn Fan Club, about her friend are poignant: "Patsy was my best buddy. She gave me clothes 'cause I didn't have anything. Many times when she bought something, she'd buy me the same thing. I still have the dresses in my closet. Patsy gave me rhinestones. I thought they were diamonds. She gave me a pair of panties I wore for three years. She used to kid me that they were holier than I was. She always seemed disappointed I didn't drink and carry on.

"Patsy was a star, but she promoted me with the radio stations. When I wasn't making any money, she offered to pay me just to go out on the road with her to keep her company. She was never a phony. Some people found her harsh 'cause she'd say what she thought. Patsy'd do anything in the world to help you if she liked you. She'd known hard times, and I saw her go from nothing to the top. I knew her when she was having it rough and when she had everything. The things I remember most are little everyday things. We'd talk, sharing our happy and sad times. We shopped. She taught me how to get the best for my money.

"She was a real pretty girl, much prettier than any of her pictures. Patsy loved pretty things in her home and beautiful clothes. She liked to embroider. It kept her from being nervous, especially after the accident. Patsy was a great cook. She enjoyed cooking shrimp and would invite me and Mooney for supper. She loved rabbit and Mooney'd go hunting and bring some home. Then Patsy'd come to our place and we'd eat together. And, like me, she loved bologna. More than anything, Patsy loved her babies. The thing she hated most about the road was leaving those young'uns. We had that in common. Patsy gave me pointers on how to start and end my shows. She said, 'Give it a lot at the end.' I liked the way she opened her shows with 'Come On In.' Right away, it made the audience feel close to her."

Patsy was amused in the hospital one evening while listening to her radio. Before spinning her record, a Nashville disc jockey intoned, "Here's a gal who did just what her song says to make it a hit! Here's Patsy Cline singing 'I Fall to Pieces.' Patsy, you didn't have to go that far! We love you. Keep those cards and letters coming to Patsy in Madison Hospital."

"Mail by the sackfuls arrived," noted Dr. Evans. "Patsy was overjoyed. She kept saying, 'Ain't it wonderful that so many care. I've got to send thank-you notes and I'm gonna answer every single one of them letters.'"

In little more than a week after her surgery, Patsy proved true to her word. The nurses were constantly stopping by the post office for stamps and putting her letters in the mail. On June 23 she wrote Louise:

> I was sure glad to get your two cards and letters [that] came with them and even tho I'm in bed and in traction, I hope you'll be able to read this.
>
> Honestly, I've gotten so many calls, telegrams, cards & letters that I'm just stunned. I didn't know there was so many people in this world that knew of me, but it sure gives me faith and a wonderful feeling to know how many fans & friends are wanting me well again. . . .

Patsy described the accident, then wrote:

> Of course, they don't have insurance but John does. Three different kinds

that will pay everything. So I hope to get 35 to 40,000 out of it. Plastic surgery will have to be done on me in 3 mos.

I don't think I'll *ever* be able to ride in a car again. I just thank God above that I can see *perfect* and my *babies* weren't with me. Dr. says I'll be home in 12 days and singing by [the] end of 2 mos. I cut an artery and I lost lots of blood. They thought I was gone twice during the sewing up & have give me 3 pts. of blood. That's the story gal.

Hope all is well with you all. Thanks so much for the cards & tell all in Houston hello and KIKK. I must close. My eyes get tired so quick. Write me.

Love Always, Patsy Cline

P.S. I think someone said you called to the hospital. Thanks so very much gal. They won't let me have a phone or too many people in yet. But I am out of pain now. Already got some stitches out 3 days ago. I've got black eyes & [am] black & blue places all over.

As a result of her accident and near death, extraordinary changes came about in Patsy's persona. She virtually became a new woman. When she'd complain about her aches, bruises, and assorted injuries, she'd add, "But, as the Lord knows, there're no gains without pains."

She told her mother, "You don't appreciate home till you leave it and, let me tell you, you can't appreciate life till you've almost left it. Some people hope and die with their song still in them. Oh, how I want to sing. But the pain's so unbearable sometimes I thank God when I go to sleep. And when I can't, I still thank Him that I'm alive to be awake. This ole gal used to think happiness resulted when my earnings matched my yearnings. Not anymore!"

Singer Billy Walker lived in Madison and stopped by the hospital regularly. Raised on a ranch, he started singing as a child. He was managed by Randy, and occasionally he and Patsy worked together. "Patsy had a unique personality and we got to be close. But we weren't too friendly right off the bat. She kind of had an overzealous spirit. Some wives, especially my [then] wife Boots [Sylvia Dean], didn't take to that, so I kept my distance. Patsy was misunderstood; she wasn't after the husbands, she wanted to be one of the guys. I was embarrassed by her language, but that only egged her on. She got the biggest kick out of that. The easiest way to spot a lonely person is in a crowd. That was true of her. When Patsy was accepted as a member of the Opry, I got to know her more serious side.

"Boots and I visited, but we also did a lot of praying. We'd stand around the bed and hold hands with Patsy and pray together. Sometimes Charlie'd be there and sometimes he wouldn't. What I admired most about her was Patsy's amazing faith and courage. Regardless of how desperate her situation got or how low she'd feel about what happened, she always had a cheery outlook and a joke to tell. She hadn't been a particularly religious person but the accident brought Patsy a real depth of the Lord."

The Reverend Jay Alford of the Madison First Assembly Church of God visited Patsy on his hospital rounds. "She talked about how much singing in her church choir as a child with her mother had meant to her," Walker said, "and how she felt at times because business pressures didn't give her the time to be religious. She said, 'Deep down in my heart, I know I want to please God.'

"One morning after we had prayed, Patsy took my hand and said, 'Billy, I want to leave here and live a little bit better life than I've been living. I wish the demands of the business didn't put so much pressure on me. More than anything, I'm fighting to keep my marriage together and make it work for the sake of my babies.'"

Patsy broke down and cried, "You don't know how much it would mean if I could have a decent home life."

Walker took Patsy's hand. "Okay, Patsy, let's ask God for His help. Let's bow our heads and pray." There was silence. "Patsy?"

"I'm in traction. You go ahead."

Billy led and she followed, "Lord, help me to remember that nothing is going to happen to me today that You and I together can't handle. We want to thank You for breathing strength into this woman's body. We ask that You watch over and nourish her through the healing process. Give a special blessing to her wonderful family so that, together, they might find the peace and happiness they deserve."

He asked if there was anything Patsy wished to add.

"Dear God," Patsy beseeched, "I been lying and forgetting the faith I have. I know I'm not worthy, but I need You so. Help me turn back on the right path if it's not too late. And, Lord, please let these Seventh Day Adventists get some meat in this damn hospital. I'm tired of eating all this grain! That's enough praying for today. Amen!"

Ann Tant met Patsy in 1959 while she was talent coordinator of the Dixie Jubilee. "This was an Atlanta-based Grand Ole Opry–type show performed in an auditorium in East Point. The local talent included Jack Greene, Joe South, Ray Stevens, and Jerry Reed, with a continuous round of visiting guests. It was broadcast Saturday nights over the radio.

"I was a huge fan of Pat's and booked her as often as possible. She and Charlie'd drive down in their big white Cadillac. Pat loved to laugh and all of us enjoyed a good time, so there was never a dull moment.

"Paul Strickland, a Jubilee producer, adored Pat. He ran a novelty item company called S&M Sales. Pat used to kid him something terrible about the name. One night he gave her this cigarette lighter emblazoned with the Confederate flag that was also a music box that played 'Dixie.' It became one of her treasured possessions. How she loved to go up to some unsuspecting soul and light their cigarette. She couldn't wait to watch them jump!"

When Ann relocated to Nashville in 1961 to work for Mercury Records, the Dicks were the first persons she contacted. It wasn't long before she was part of the clique.

"After the Opry and half the nights during the week, we'd stroll into Tootsie's. She was a wonderful lady with great gusto and a heart as big as all outdoors. Tootsie kept us together. She kept IOUs on half of us. When Roger Miller made it big, he gave Tootsie this huge freezer for all his IOUs. She busted out crying. We didn't go in there just to drink. Tootsie had a great cook named Maggie who made the best damned red beans and cornbread. During the week we'd sit downstairs, right up front, but weekends, when the upstairs artists' lounge was open, we'd be there hanging out. Often the party'd carry over to Sunday."

What amazed Ann was that, even in greatest adversity, Patsy's sense of humor never failed her. "Pat meant so much to me and now I felt she needed me to rally around. Bad as I wanted to see her, I wasn't looking forward to seeing her in that condition. Since I'm more than a bit squeamish, I hated hospitals. It took all the strength I could muster to go into her room. I didn't get too close. I could see more than I wanted. Her head was all bandaged and she had black eyes.

"I spoke softly from across the room, but Pat said, 'Hoss, come over here so I can talk to you without yelling.' I had to push myself. The closer I got the worse she looked. Pat was truly blessed to survive that wreck. She was covered with scars and bruises. I got sick and fainted dead away. When they brought me to, I put my head down and threw up."

After everything was cleaned up, Patsy laughed, "You got some nerve coming to the hospital to do this!"

"Yeah, I know. Isn't this awful? I come to cheer you up and go and pass out."

"And vomit all over my clean floor!"

Patsy wanted to know all the gossip. The women talked fast and furious. At one point Patsy caught Ann staring. "If I look bad through your eyes, Hoss, you oughta see me through mine! Ain't enough makeup in the world to make people stand looking at me."

"Oh, Pat!"

"It'll take some fancy stitching to make me all beautiful again. Well, there's one thing I'm glad of."

"What's that?"

"I had the good sense to have my pictures taken before this. Now I can look at the pictures and then look into the mirror. It'll be just like the story of the beauty and the beast!"

On June 27, more of Patsy's stitches were removed and reconstructive surgery was begun on her forehead. Patsy wrote to WSM's Trudy Stamper on July 3:

> ... If you can't read this letter, blame it on this splint they've got my wrist in. ... I'm doing lots better and my operation last Tuesday week was a great step forward and the Dr. says after three mos. more, after this heals up and I recover good I'll go back for another operation to have these scars cut out & pulled together again. I'll be good as new then.
>
> But I'll be back to singing in between [the] time now & that operation even with the scars. [A] little make up should make me presentable enough to stand me. ...
>
> I'll be cutting an album of some of my songs and some standards as soon as I can stand up. I've got to cut a single, too, because there's not a song in the can at all.
>
> Well I'll close and turn up again for another needle. If someone poured water in me, I'd look like a flower sprinkler from all the needles I've gotten. ...
>
> Love, Patsy Cline

P.S. My thanks to [bluegrass artist] Ira Louvin who had all the [Opry] artists sign two pages of autographs to me last Sat. nite. I'll always keep it. Sure made me feel great.

Joltin' Jim McCoy in Winchester received this letter from Patsy, dated July 7:

> I would have wrote to you all before this but I am now getting back to my self again. . . . John stayed here 2 weeks & went home. . . . I'm improving real good. The 4th they let me up in a wheelchair by someone lifting my body up. I'll be on crutches a month after I leave the hospital the Dr. says. I'm still a very lucky girl. Lucky to be alive, be able to see, and that my babies were not in the car. . . .
>
> I'm writing this & the details [of the accident] 'cause everyone has been so mis-informed, and I wanted to straighten everyone out. It was entirely the other woman's fault & we have witnesses to prove it and pictures. . . .[3]
>
> I lost so much blood they wondered about me twice. But they can't keep this ole Va. gal down. Mom is still here with me and said tell you "hello" and she misses Winc[hester]. Ha . . .
>
> You all be good & keep up the good job you are doing for us country gals & boys. . . .

The July issue of the Patsy Cline Fan Club newsletter retold the story of the automobile accident and carried a long open letter from Patsy describing details of the initial and follow-up surgery but ended with Patsy optimistically looking forward to her second album and recording again.

Mrs. Hensley explained, "You couldn't hold Patsy still. All the time she was in the hospital, she spoke of nothing else but the day she could get up and sing again. She was going to have to manage on crutches, but that didn't bother her. That's probably the first time I realized how important her career was to her."

Dottie West concurred. "Patsy was ready and raring to go. If they had brought a microphone to her room—and Patsy wanted them to at one point—she would have done a song from that bed."

Ernest Tubb was surprised by Patsy's zest. "She was itching to get to work. She asked if the Opry was ready to have her back and I told her how much we missed her."

Patsy said, "Well, tell them I'm coming. They'll have to put a ramp out in the alley so Charlie can wheel me onstage."

Gossip and a scene in the *Coal Miner's Daughter* film have contributed to the rumor that Patsy had Charlie and friends sneak her bottles of beer. "That couldn't have happened," Dottie declared. "The hospital was run by the Seventh Day Adventists, who were extremely strict. About the only thing Patsy wanted sneaked in was some down-home cooking. She didn't care for the food at all. Patsy was having soybeans for breakfast, lunch, and supper. She hated it!"

3. The police report put full blame on young Mrs. Clark.

On one visit, Patsy told Tubb, "I sure hope you brought me some red beans and cornbread!"

"Hon," he replied, "if I'd known you was hungry, I'd have gotten Maggie [at Tootsie's] to fix you up something."

"I don't want to hear about it," she moaned. "That's how hungry I am!"

"I Fall to Pieces" was gradually making it up the *Billboard* country and pop charts, week after week, rung by rung. Decca was amazed by the staying power of the song in the pop arena and sales continued to build from market to market, starting in the South and Southeast, then through the West and Midwest.

"Sales were zooming," pronounced Owen Bradley. "We were having our cake and eating it, too. 'I Fall to Pieces' was a smash everywhere in the nation, with one glaring exception, New York City. Decca headquarters had the pop sound they wanted from Patsy and yet couldn't bring it in on their home ground. After that, [vice president of sales] Sidney Goldberg didn't have much to say. They pretty much left us alone."

Soon Patsy was in a wheelchair, and Charlie was taking her down to the tree-filled hospital lawn, where they'd have lunch and often feed the squirrels before he went to work. Dr. Evans released Patsy on July 17, and she came home to Hillhurst Drive. She was far from recovered, as she informed Louise Seger in a letter dated July 20:

> Being as I have nothing to do but sit and lay around, thought I'd let you know the latest news which the Dr. told me just three days before I came home. ... [It] was real great to learn that I'll be on crutches for the next 5 to 6 *mos.* Can't put this leg on the floor for 3 mos. but I'll be singing *anyway*. Randy (my manager) says he will tell the people who want me [he will] not work me over 6 days at a time. And the Dr. said also that for the next 2 mos. I'll have to have someone with me on all trips. That's just great!
>
> I know Charlie won't be able to go with me on all of them but I don't know who else will & can go. Any way what that Dr. don't know won't hurt him. ... I'm gonna cut an album & 2 singles the first 2 wks. of Aug. How about that 'I Fall to Pieces'? No. 1 in 3 trade magazines and one more to go.
>
> If it stays in the pop charts 2 weeks in the Top 20, I'll get to go to N.Y. to receive a *pop award* on it. Ain't that a kick in the head? Wee-ee-ee! I still can't hardly believe it's No. 1. Louise, I look at it and I cry I'm so tickled. I know I'll get 3 or 4 country awards in Nov. here at the convention. Sure will be great.
>
> Well, I guess I'd best close and get to sleep. I get tired real easy and I can't write half anyway 'cause of this write [sic] arm in the splint. ...
>
> I go back in 3 wks. for the plastic surgem [sic] to see what's got to be done and then in 3 mos. I go back to the hospital for the surgery. Sure hate that. Write soon. I go to Tulsa and Enid, Ok. the 29th and 30th

of this month. Ha. Wish me luck. They say I won't make it but I'm gonna show them. Will be with [steel guitarist] Leon McAuliff.

"I've never had a song that was a hit as long as 'I Fall to Pieces,'" Harland Howard pointed out. "We were number one on many radio stations, and the first trade number one was April ninth, but it didn't hit *Billboard*'s number one till August seventh. It remained on their charts for thirty-nine weeks. This was the song that put me on the map and established Patsy as a real force in the business.

"Patsy wanted to see Hank and me. She had two sterling-silver bracelets, which were the rage then, engraved to us with the words 'Thanks for the hit.' I thought, 'Wow! Singers give writers presents when they write them a hit.' But that was Patsy 'cause it's the only gift I ever got."

Loretta Lynn remembers the week of August 7, when she came to visit Patsy.

"I finally did it, Hoss," she exclaimed. "I got me a number one! Ain't that incredible? A number one!" Loretta told her how thrilled she was for her. Patsy grabbed her hand and said, "Oh, I never want to record again! I just want to enjoy this one song forever."

"GOTTA LOT OF RHYTHM IN MY SOUL"

FARON YOUNG: "Some people will do anything to get applause!"

PATSY CLINE: "It's talent and guts they're applauding!"

FARON YOUNG: "They can't help it when you go out there with those sympathy sticks!"

PATSY CLINE: "You jealous son of a bitch! You take 'em and you go out there."

FARON YOUNG: "I wouldn't want to deprive you."

As Harlan Howard predicted, Patsy didn't hate "I Fall to Pieces" so much when it reached number one in the trades and on the top country radio stations. When "I Fall to Pieces" reached the *Billboard* pop charts top-40, Randy placed an ad in the magazine that read: "I have tried and I have tried but I haven't yet found a way to thank so many wonderful people for so much. God bless you all. Gratefully, Patsy Cline." Patsy proved a country solo woman could actually sell records and get them not only on the country charts but also high on the pop charts. She was acclaimed one of the nation's leading recording artists, ranked in popularity among such popular stars as Jimmy Darren, LeRoy Van Dyke, and Bobby Vee.

She returned to the Opry on July 22. The late Grant Turner, the Opry announcer, recalled the night when Charlie brought Patsy onstage in a wheelchair. "She got a standing ovation and didn't even sing. I lowered the mike so she could speak into it from the wheelchair. She couldn't believe the outpouring of love from the audience and tears just poured down her face. She quieted the crowd and said,

'I want y'all to know that I'm recovering, and soon I'll be back and I'll be singing. I thank you for your support and the hundreds of your cards and letters. God bless you!'"

Since she'd soon be on her feet, Owen Bradley, also in an effort to give her something to look forward to, set about finding material for her next recording session. The pressure was on for Patsy and Bradley to produce a followup smash.

Patsy dropped by Bradley's office one afternoon and they reminisced. "Well, we finally did it!" Patsy said. When she began fumbling for words, he knew she wanted to get something off her chest. "Owen, I have to tell you the truth. I still don't care for 'Pieces.' It's the B-side I like."

"If this is true confessions time," he said, "I'll level with you if you promise not to throw anything at me."

"Let's have it, Hoss."

"After we started working with it, I really didn't like it either!"

The Nashville-based songwriters, whether they were successful or struggling, were special to Patsy. They were a funny lot, always eager to entertain with jokes and crazy stories; they'd do anything to please her.

"It wasn't like we were writers and she was just a singer we wanted to get to," Harlan Howard said. "There was a bond. It was dog-eat-dog among us as we tried to give her the best songs we had. She was quite demanding. Patsy wouldn't settle for just any ole song. It had to be your best shot. That might have had a lot to do with her long dry spell with Four-Star. Now she could record what she wanted—well, with Owen's consent—and she went at it with a vengeance."

Dottie West remembered the heated competition to come up with hits for Patsy. "Sometimes Patsy would have songwriters breathing down her neck. I was at Patsy and Charlie's house in Madison a few times when Hank came over after finishing something he thought was right for Patsy. He'd run in and throw his arms around her and insist, 'Hoss, forget those others. I've done it! I've done it *again*! I've written you a smash.'

"They'd go upstairs and downstairs, as he'd tell her about the new song. Hank would follow her with his guitar as she cleaned the house or cooked, the whole time telling Patsy, 'It's a great one! One of the best I've ever written.' She'd say, 'Come on, Hoss, cut the B.S. and let's hear the damn thing.'"

Billy Walker described an incident with another writer. "In late 1960, when I decided to relocate in Nashville full-time, Willie Nelson came too and lived with me for three months. I knew Willie from home and had recorded one of his songs. In Nashville, he wrote a song especially for me, 'Funny How Time Slips Away.'" Patsy heard the demo and decided she was going to record it.

"Now, you just wait a minute," Billy scolded her. "It's mine. I'm gonna cut this one myself. Get that into your head!"

"Oh, come on, Hoss," Patsy pleaded. "Let me have it!"

"Naw."

"Now, don't y'all fight over it," Willie interjected. "I got more where that came from. How about we give Miss Patsy the song you just cut the demo on?"

"Great! Patsy, it's over at Starday Records. I'll get it for you. You're gonna love it!"

"All right," she relented, "but I'd rather have this one."

"You ain't gonna. And that's final!"

Billy had tried to get Starday "and just about everybody else in town" to give Willie a house contract as songwriter, which would have meant a weekly retainer of fifty dollars. Walker explained that Willie didn't care so much about the money, he just wanted to get into the business. Suddenly at twenty-seven, thanks to Faron Young's recording of "Four Walls," which was a country number one hit and got as high as number 12 on *Billboard*'s pop chart, Willie was hot.

This wasn't outlaw Willie with the bandanna and scruffy beard but the clean-cut, neatly combed, short-haired Willie in trendy sharkskin suits and thin ties. He had a song "sitting around gathering dust" that he thought was good. He gave it to Billy, who cut a demo with only his guitar as instrumental. The song had been circulating endlessly from label to label and producer to producer with no results. Billy retrieved it and brought it out to Patsy. When she played it, she hated it.

"I might have been partly responsible for Patsy's attitude on that song," admitted Charlie. "On my way to work one afternoon, I stopped in Tootsie's for a drink. I was introduced to Willie Nelson. We hit it off, and when he found out I was Patsy's husband, he gave me a demo for her to listen to. Late that night when I got home and had a little bit more to drink, I put his song on the hi-fi and played it over and over."

Nelson's writing style was starkly unique for the period. Charlie was swept away by the song's honky tonk mellowness and the way Willie phrased the lyrics ahead of and behind the belt, with Walker's voice occasionally breaking. On the demo, the way Nelson conceived the piece, it was a "talker."

Patsy came in the room on crutches. "Could you please turn that damn thing down?" Charlie did, but continued to play it.

"Ain't you sick of hearing that yet?"

"No, ma'am!"

"Well, I am!" Charlie let it play again. "Honey, are you gonna play the damn thing all night? What's the name of it, anyway?"

"'Crazy.'"

"And it sure is."

"It's the song Willie gave me for you."

"Well, I don't want anything to do with it."

Patsy, still upset at losing "Funny How Time Slips Away," later put the Billy Walker demo of Willie's song on the record player. She screamed, "Holy shit! It's that damn record!"

"What are you talking about?"

"It's that record you nearly wore out! I can't believe Billy thought I'd like it. Wait till I get my hands on him! I hate it!"

"But, honey, it's a great song!"

"Then *you* record it!"

☆

Patsy never stopped surprising Charlie with her musical abilities. The couple had gotten nice and cozy in the living room, when "I Love You So Much, It Hurts," the Floyd Tillman standard from the late 1940s, came on the radio.

"Honey," Charlie remarked nonchalantly, "why don't you sing that in your act?"

"Well, maybe I will." She got up and went to the piano. He named a chord for her. "You know I don't know chords, but let me give you a little by ear."

She played the song and stopped after hitting a particular note. "This key? Is that the chord you want?"

"No, a woman can't sing that note. It's too low."

Patsy got her dander up. "Oh, is that right? Well, let me try."

And she did it. "Probably just to spite me!" Charlie asserted.

He explained that at home, Patsy had her songs and he had his; in the studio, Patsy had hers and Owen Bradley his. "Their ideas didn't always mesh," Charlie stated. "They could be immovable objects. In the end, they'd give a little to get the job done. And you know what? They were never that far apart to begin with."

"Maybe," said Bradley, laughing, "but that wasn't the case with 'Crazy.' Patsy didn't like it and was absolutely determined not to record it. 'Crazy' was early Willie Nelson, but I thought him to be a good writer from the time his material started making the rounds. I was terribly impressed with 'Crazy.'

"Patsy thought it was terrible, period. I told her over and over again how much I liked it. I thought maybe the more she heard it, the more she might like it. Wrong.

"I'd put it on and say, 'See what I mean?' She'd reply, 'I don't care what you say. I don't like it and I ain't gonna record it. And that's that.' She was quite emphatic, but I had a little talk with her and smoothed her feathers. I told her we were going to do it. And that was that."

Bradley set August 17, just over two months since Patsy's near-fatal automobile crash, for her triumphant return to the studio.

On August 13, a special transcript session of "Country Music Time" was set, with Patsy as guest star. Charlie wheeled her into Bradley's studio and with great fanfare Sergant Tom Shaw expressed delight that Patsy was back. She sang the 1927 Harry Woods classic "Side by Side," also a 1953 top-5 pop hit for Kay Starr, one of Patsy's idols. She announced she'd be recording it for her new album.

The following day, Decca released Patsy's first 45 rpm EP in four years. It contained "I Fall to Pieces," "Lovin' in Vain," "Lovesick Blues," and "There He Goes."

"The night before the 'Crazy' session," Charlie said, "Patsy complained about the song again. 'Well,' I interrupted her, 'if you don't like talking it, why the hell don't you just sing it all the way through?' She liked that idea, and, when she discussed it with Owen, so did he."

Three recording sessions, designed to come up with enough new material for a second album, were planned. The dates marked Patsy's single most productive time in the studio. The potential songs poured in. Patsy and Bradley had an array of excellent material to select from.

Patsy and Bradley had whetted New York headquarters' appetite with "I Fall to Pieces." Now they were banking on another smash, only this time they wanted something stunningly sophisticated. Bradley had shown he was adept at handling pop arrangements with his string-heavy session with Brenda Lee on "I'm Sorry," which skyrocketed into *Billboard*'s number one pop position. For Patsy's session he now brought in Bill McElhiney, the trumpeter from his dance band, to do the string arrangements.

On the seventeenth, Patsy hobbled in on crutches to a rousing welcome from the veteran sidemen from her sessions. She laid her crutches against the wall and propped herself against a stool at the microphone for the warmup. They started with "True Love," by Cole Porter. The tune was sung by Bing Crosby with a slight assist from Grace Kelly in the 1956 musical film hit *High Society.* On her track, the violin introduces Patsy's low-key vocal. She even had the audacity to mimic Decca's multimillion-selling superstar by humming on the same verse where Crosby crooned. When you hear Patsy's rendition, it's impossible to reconcile the simple beauty she manages with her crass, brassy tomboyish personality.

Bradley's production marked a milestone in country music. "That's when I began letting the strings creep in. It wasn't intentional. We just thought it sounded nice.

"Patsy liked a big, full sound and didn't care if that meant a lush string arrangement. We walked a fine line between country and pop—pretty far ahead of the way things were being done."

On the Bob Wills classic "San Antonio Rose," Patsy did a down-home vocal, with yodeling as the only essential missing element. It's one time Bradley should have rethought his policy.

There was a remake of "A Poor Man's Roses (or a Rich Man's Gold)," which Patsy had sung on her second "Arthur Godfrey's Talent Scouts" appearance. It was a personal favorite of hers. She wanted to record it anew in stereo.

According to Dottie West, everything ran smoothly until "Crazy." "She tried it again and again, but it wasn't working. Owen tried to help her. After about two hours, which was a lot for Patsy, they were ready to give up. But Patsy pleaded, 'Owen, let me try it one more time!'"

"The problems were physical," Bradley noted. "Usually Patsy got things right away. We recorded her live on three tracks and didn't even have to overdub. She'd be so prepared, one take was all we'd need. Of course, afterward, she wouldn't be satisfied and would tell me, 'Owen, let's try it one more time.' I'd gotten used to that and would simply tell her, 'No, Patsy. Really it's fine, honey.' She'd counter with 'But I'd like to—' and I'd tell her again, 'No, Patsy.'

"Everything about the way Patsy was doing 'Crazy' was great. I could see it would be one of her best recordings. She picked up on the emotion of the lyrics and put herself into the story of a tune. But that day something was bothering her."

Bradley finally asked, "Hon, what's wrong?"

"I'm having a difficult time on the high notes. They keep hitting my ribs. I'm still healing and it hurts like hell."

"Why don't you take it easy? We'll do the track without you. You know, just lay down the music. You can come in when things are better and dub the vocal."

She concurred, but, thinking Bradley would let her have her way on something she desired desperately, she asked to do another song.

"Patsy called me at our Sure-Fire offices across the street from the studio," explained Teddy Wilburn. "She said there'd been a last-minute snag and they needed an extra song. She asked for the lyrics to a song we recently recorded, a cover of the Gogi Grant hit 'The Wayward Wind.' Patsy played both versions over and over at home.

"I found the lead sheets and ran across to the studio. While I was there, Patsy and Owen went over the song once and talked it over with the musicians. Then went right ahead and did it, just like that."

Patsy's vocal is enchanting in its casualness. She creates a lilting mood as she almost whispers the lyrics and beautifully extenuates the high notes without getting anywhere near her potential.

The following Monday Patsy cut the vocal to "Crazy" in one take. "And that's the record you hear," Bradley marveled. "It was the height of her career and, perhaps, one of the best tracks we ever made."

Bradley's concept for "Crazy," though a complete departure from Nelson's demo arrangement, is simple, smooth, and electrifying. Floyd Cramer's piano and the first strains of the Jordanaires' "doo, doo, doos" give way to Harold Bradley's laid-back electric bass, as Murrey "Buddy" Harman's percussion brush segues into Patsy's phrasing of Nelson's lyrics. The rhythm section—Grady Martin, electric guitar; Walter Hayes, steel guitar; Bob Moore's bass; and Randy Hughes, guitar—makes it high-tech torch all the way. But Patsy weaves the real magic. On lines such as "Worry / Why do I let myself worry? / Wond'rin' what in the world did I do?" and "Thinking that my love could hold you," Patsy sings like she's playing them on a violin. When she takes the liberty of adding "Ooohhh" before the word "Crazy" in Nelson's last verse, it's one of the sexiest moments in recording history.

Three days later, Patsy returned for two intense days. On the twenty-fourth she recorded "Who Can I Count On?"; the uptempo, rockabilly "Seven Lonely Days"; the song she'd recently heard on the radio, Floyd Tillman's "I Love You So Much, It Hurts," which was born again in Patsy's scorching torch rendition; "Foolin' 'Round" by Harlan Howard and Buck Owens; and a wise selection from the early 1930s, George Brown and Peter DeRose's standard "Have You Ever Been Lonely (Have You Ever Been Blue)?"

On the twenty-fifth, Patsy started with "South of the Border (Down Mexico Way)," which she had listened to her half-sister Tempie Glenn play in her youth. This time around, Hargus "Pig" Robbins handled the keyboard. Mrs. Hensley noted that there was something about the song that fascinated Patsy. Obviously she never forgot it. On the session, as she relaxed and didn't strain for histrionics, Patsy sang it as an echo of her childhood.

The artist and producer did a stereo remake of "Walkin' After Midnight" to use for Patsy's forthcoming album. Not only did they want to avoid having to lease the Four-Star master recording, but they wanted to try something fresh and different.

The other songs were "Strange," co-written by Mel Tillis, and "You're Stronger Than Me," co-written by Hank Cochran.

Patsy and Bradley disagreed over recording "You're Stronger Than Me." Cochran, always in the studio when one of his tunes was done, reported that though Patsy liked it, Bradley wasn't thrilled. "Patsy came through with flying colors," Hank said. "I was not only her friend, but she really loved the song. She insisted they do it." Bradley, a big fan of Cochran's, may have found it too similar to "I Fall to Pieces."

Harlan Howard tells a story about how "Foolin' 'Round" got recorded that points up how Bradley knew which of Patsy's buttons to push. "Buck had a number one with it on Capitol and Kay Starr made some pop noise with it. One afternoon, when Owen and Patsy were looking for material to fill out the session, he was looking through the *Billboard* charts and saw the song was still listed."

"Can you do 'Foolin' 'Round'?" Bradley asked Patsy.

"No. It's a man's song."

Bradley, maybe to remind her of Roy Drusky's reaction to "I Fall to Pieces," repeated, "Patsy, can you do this song?"

"Yeah. Sure I can!" she snapped.

The unique treatment they gave "Foolin' 'Round" is, if nothing else, exotic. It runs the spectrum from rockabilly to a quasi-rhumba beat.

That night Patsy didn't stay for the playback party. She was in a rush to finish so she could hurry home. She had friends and their children coming over to celebrate Julie's third birthday.

Lightnin' Chance observed, "Owen kept Patsy selling records by keepin' her mad. That bitterness came out in her voice inflections, and inflections get picked up by a mike. Patsy was terribly moody. I often told Randy, 'Man, I wouldn't put up with her for thirty seconds. That's the meanest witch I ever saw!' None of us envied Owen or Charlie."

"Patsy could be mean to Charlie when he was at the sessions. I didn't know whether she liked having him there or not, but he was there, and if he was there it must have meant Patsy wanted him there. If she got upset, she'd say things that were a little out of context of the situation. But he usually let them roll right off. Since I loved Patsy as a showman, I formed a mental block against a lot of things that transpired.

"If she really got going when we worked together, I'd bug her by telling her off. I'd say, 'You mean bitch, how the hell can you do that?' She'd scowl at me and after a while she'd sidle up and say, 'Why the hell don't you let me be mad when I want to?'"

In retrospect, given her vocal qualities and range, it's hard to imagine Owen Bradley being doubtful of the direction in which he was taking Patsy. Teddy Wilburn reveals another side of the producer. "A few days after the last August session," Teddy recollected, "Owen phoned and talked about what he, Patsy, and the musicians had accomplished. He sounded concerned, which wasn't like him. I knew he had added strings to the session, and he seemed to be second-guessing himself."

Bradley sought a favor. "Teddy, I want you to hear what I've just done on Patsy's tracks."

Wilburn met the producer at the studio, where Bradley put on the session tapes.

"Owen, I don't know what you're so concerned about," Teddy said. "The session is pretty evenly balanced between traditional country and the new sound."

"Wait. Let me put on 'Crazy.'"

He ran the tape. Bradley shut off the recorder very solemnly. "I want to know, do you think I've gone too far away from country?"

"No. I don't think so. Patsy's had a couple of really fine records. It's not like she's just got one hit behind her. She's made her mark with each of her big sellers in country and pop. She's crossed over. It's what her audience wants. She's not the Wilburn Brothers! Not to worry."

Bradley thanked Wilburn, turned the lights out, and locked the studio. There was no turning back now.

Amazingly, Patsy hit the road. Charlie took an extended leave from his job to be at her side. Their lives had changed drastically. Patsy, in her weakened and bruised condition, was dependent on Charlie as never before, and on her career to pay the ever-mounting hospital bills as lawyers wrangled over the insurance payment. As a result of the accident, Patsy was on edge and often in great pain.

Though Charlie has more than his share of detractors, even among friends, when Patsy needed him he was there. He may not have liked it, but she only had to ask. That, however, didn't mean they were always cordial to one another.

On September 8, Patsy and Charlie celebrated her twenty-ninth birthday. One of her presents was the money rolling in from "I Fall to Pieces," which was still selling well. The *Billboard* issue of Tuesday, September 12, had the song in its highest slot yet, the number 12 position on the pop chart. That was three notches above Elvis's "Little Sister" and four above Roy Orbison's "Crying."

Patsy returned to the Opry to sing on September 16. She arrived in a wheelchair, since her leg was still in a cast. Charlie pushed her up the ramp into the back entrance to the Ryman Auditorium. He helped her onto her crutches, and she made her way to the wings, took a seat, and held court. She was engulfed by well-wishers.

"Considering what happened, Patsy had a marvelous attitude," remarked Gordon Stoker of the Jordanaires. "She may have been hurting on the inside, but she was all smiles. The only thing that seemed to concern her were the scars on her forehead. She tried her best to cover them with a lot of makeup, but they were still quite visible.

"She told me the surgery and all was a lot to pull through. Seeing her, I couldn't begin to understand. I could only imagine the inner strength she mustered to get back on her feet. It was a miracle. When we talked privately, Patsy said she wasn't looking forward to plastic surgery, but felt it was a career necessity. She didn't even bring anything about her accident up unless you asked, and then only to trusted friends. She wasn't looking for sympathy."

Grant Turner gave her quite a welcome. As Patsy hobbled to the microphone with her crutches, her appearance was met with pandemonium. She'd already started crying. Charlie, Pearl Butler, and Jan Howard helped her wipe away the tears. She sang "How Can I Face Tomorrow" and received a standing ovation. She sang "Lovesick Blues" and received another. She hobbled offstage. The cheering didn't stop. The audience wouldn't quit until Patsy sang "I Fall to Pieces." She brought the house down and waved good-bye, then hobbled off into Faron Young's arms.

"Some people will do anything to get applause!" Young razzed.

The emotion of the moment overtook Patsy and she exploded, "No, Sheriff, it's talent and guts they're applauding!"

"Well, goddamnit, who wouldn't? They can't help it when you go out there with those sympathy sticks!"

"Why, you jealous son of a bitch! Here, you take 'em and you go out there with 'em."

"Oh, no, honey. I wouldn't want to deprive you. Hark, your public is demanding you."

Patsy went out for another bow and, as she exited offstage, she swung one of her crutches at Young.

"Goddamnit, Patsy. Can't you take a joke? Shit! I was just kidding around."

Charlie got between them. Young kidded Patsy later that it was a close shave, and that Charlie saved his life.

Pearl Butler had no doubt Young was having fun. "He loved Patsy too much to be jealous. She was on edge and got a bit upset. They hugged after things cooled and it was forgotten. After that it became a standing joke and Jan [Howard], Jeanie [Shepard], Dottie, me and some of the other girl singers would ask Patsy if we could use her 'sympathy sticks' for one number, so we'd get a standing ovation."

Decca released the "Crazy" single, with "Who Can I Count On?" as the flip, on October 16. Five days later, Patsy, in her first appearance without crutches since the accident, introduced the song on the Opry.

"'Crazy' is my favorite Patsy Cline song," Loretta declared. "When Patsy did it on the Opry, she got three standing ovations. When she left the stage, Patsy was so moved she was crying. She took my hand and said, 'Girl, I guess that's gonna be my song.'"

In the October 31 issue of *Billboard*, Patsy was named Favorite Female Vocalist in the country deejay poll for "I Fall to Pieces." It was the first time Kitty Wells wasn't given the honor in nine years. Bradley was chosen Country and Western Man of the Year while Harlan Howard was picked as Favorite Songwriter (for that year's body of work). Patsy was thrilled for Loretta, who was named Most Promising Country Female Artist.

During the WSM Country Music Festival, or D.J. Convention, that began November 2, Patsy was named *Cashbox*'s Most Programmed Female Vocalist and *Music Vendor*'s Female Vocalist of the Year along with four other awards. "This is my second record hit now," she said at the ceremony, "and I never thought I'd be able to get the first one, let alone the second one. Thanks to all you nice folks, you've made my 'I Fall to Pieces' number one."

Songwriter Justin Tubb recalled, "During the D.J. Convention, I was driving down Broad Street to Tootsie's. I met Patsy and Charlie coming the other way. We stopped right in the middle of the street. She was riding high and happy as all get out."

Patsy got out the passenger side and yelled, "Hoss, follow us to the hotel. Decca's got us fixed up for the night. *And* bring your guitar. I wanna hear that song."

Tubb had written "Imagine That" and had sung a few lines to Patsy previously.

"That's it?" she wanted to know. "Where's the rest? I wanna hear the whole thing."

"Hon, I don't have time right now," Tubb replied.

But, that night, Patsy had him captive, and he played the song for her, Charlie, and their friends. "I don't know how many times I sang it," he laughed. "She got so excited. She felt like I did about it when I wrote it. When you give up a song you've written, it's kinda like giving up a baby for adoption. You know the artist will love it as much as you and take good care of it. So you let it go, knowing your song's in good hands."

On November 13, "Crazy" entered the *Billboard* country chart, followed the next week with its debut on their pop chart. A week later, Patsy's second album, *Patsy Cline Showcase,* was released, with the Jordanaires receiving featured billing. The twelve tunes also included "I Fall to Pieces," and the songs recorded at the August sessions. The three missing—"Strange," "Who Can I Count On," and "You're Stronger Than Me"—were to be released as B-sides of singles.

"Crazy" wasn't lagging behind, trying to find acceptance, as happened with "I Fall to Pieces." It was skyrocketing up the other trade magazines and country radio charts and making strides in the pop arena. Most impressive was public response. Patsy Cline became the rage.

Patsy Cline

Side Four

. . .'Cause if you weren't
there to share my love,
Who cares if the sky
should fall?
For anyone can see
How much you mean to me.
You're my life, my love,
my very all . . .

—"Today, Tomorrow and Forever" by M.G. and
W. Burkes (© 1955, Four-Star Music Company;
Acuff-Rose Music, Inc.)

"IMAGINE THAT"

HANK COCHRAN: "I found it. I got a hit for you!"
PATSY CLINE: "Get your ass over here with it!"
HANK COCHRAN: "I'm on my way!"
PATSY CLINE: "This better be good!"

*P*atsy was invited to appear on the Grand Ole Opry at New York's Carnegie Hall, the first full-fledged country production at that cultural bastion of classical music. Among the forty performers were Minnie Pearl; Faron Young; Jim Reeves, the male pop crossover champion; Marty Robbins; Bill Monroe, the Father of Bluegrass; and Grandpa Jones.

Country music in New York was a novelty, though star "spectaculars" played Madison Square Garden annually. But if the event on November 29 wasn't enough in itself to become a cause célèbre among transplanted Tennesseans and southerners, the controversial and smug Dorothy Kilgallen made it one. The *Journal-American* columnist, who wrote the syndicated "Voice of Broadway" and was featured with Arlene Francis and Steve Allen as a panelist on CBS's *What's My Line?*, made cheap shots almost daily at the coming of the "Carnegie Hallbillies."

Onstage in Winston-Salem, North Carolina, on November 25, Patsy had a few words for Kilgallen or, as she called her, "Miss Dorothy, the Wicked Witch of the East." "We're gonna be in high cotton next week—Carnegie Hall in New York City. That ole Dorothy Kilgallen in the *New York Times* [Patsy got the newspapers confused] wrote 'everybody should get out of town because the hillbillies are coming!' At least we ain't standing on New York street corners with itty-bitty cans in our hands collecting coins to keep up the opera and symphonies." [The show was a benefit for the pension fund of the Musicians Aid Society.] Miss Dorothy called us Nashville performers 'the gang from the Grand Ole Opry—hicks in the sticks.' And if I have the pleasure of seeing that wicked witch, I'll tell her how proud I am to be a hick from the sticks!"

Kilgallen was one of the most powerful and reviled reporters of the time. A sentence in her column could make or break reputations. She was addicted to music—except country, which she despised.

WSM's Trudy Stamper wrote in a newsletter: "At first it looked as if just everybody and everything was against us. New York folks who were supposed to know said, 'Nobody will come! We'd just make fools of ourselves.' One of the wheels called the Thursday before our Wednesday date and said he'd heard we'd called it all off. You can imagine what Mother told him! Anyway, we were scared. Ott Devine, the manager of the Grand Ole Opry, and Bob Cooper, the WSM general manager, and me—we couldn't sleep, eat—are completely minus of fingernails—thought seriously about slitting our throats. We had practically no advance ticket sale. Thought maybe nobody would come."

What no one counted on were the fans of Patsy Cline.

Phil Sullivan reported from New York for the November 29 morning edition of the Nashville *Tennessean*: "Several extra clerks were put on at the hall yesterday to take reservations and answer questions from callers. The 2,700-seat hall was half-reserved last night, but for every reservation made there were ten calls asking for information, according to Nat Posnich, treasurer of the hall.

"'We'll come within an ace of selling out,' he said. 'This is an entirely different type of crowd from what we have been accustomed to. These people don't ordinarily make reservations. They just call up for information, then hang up and show up for the program.'"

On her turf, the hillbillies outfoxed the Wicked Witch of the East. Trudy Stamper's "small-town public relations sense" helped provide the last-minute rush. Somehow she got Jack Benny to come to Carnegie Hall on Monday and stand in line as if to buy a ticket. While all the photographers clicked away, Benny quipped, "I should be buying a plane ticket to Nashville. I'm paying seven-fifty here for what would cost me one-fifty there!" The photo appeared in all the papers the following day, even the *Journal-American.*

Almost all of the stars, including the Jordanaires, Ben Smathers and the Stony Mountain Cloggers, and fiddler Tommy Jackson arrived via a chartered TWA aircraft dubbed "Grand Ole Opry Liner." There were two exceptions: Minnie Pearl, whose husband, a commercial pilot, flew her up Sunday in order to appear on the "To-night" and "Today" shows; and Marty Robbins, who took the train because of his fear of flying.

Cousin Minnie was at LaGuardia Airport on Tuesday to welcome the Opry plane and to pose for WSM–Grand Ole Opry photographer Les Leverett on the stairway ramp of the plane with Grandpa Jones, Bill Monroe, Jim Reeves, Faron Young, and Patsy. That afternoon the Opry stars gathered at City Hall to receive a gold key to the city from Robert W. Watt, director of commerce, standing in for Mayor Robert Wagner. After a brief ceremony, the stars moved outside to the steps of the historic lower Manhattan site for more pictures. A lavish press party followed at Carnegie Hall. The gilded bar of the hall was a mob scene of pushing, shoving photographers and reporters from the local and Tennessee press, wire services, WSM, and industry trades. Patsy was riding high in the country and pop charts.

Everyone wanted her picture and an interview. Trudy Stamper attempted to introduce Patsy to important writers and executives but could hardly reach her.

Patsy made an early getaway to the Barbizon Plaza Hotel at Central Park South, where she spent time with her mother, whom she'd flown up.

The Carnegie Hall program stated: "Over seven million people have traveled to Nashville to see WSM's live Saturday night radio show, Tennessee's largest tourist attraction. Someone has said, 'More people go to more trouble to see the Grand Ole Opry than any other show in the world.'"

Upon arrival for the sound check, Patsy and Randy and Grandpa Jones and his wife, Ramona, were awed by the great four-decked auditorium, which had recently been redecorated in white and lively reds. "This is the prettiest hall I've ever been in," Patsy exclaimed. Playing Carnegie Hall was a moving experience for her. She and Randy toured the backstage area extensively.

Patsy described her feelings to Dottie: "As I walked to the stage up this flight of stairs, all I could think of when I touched the railing was of all the famous, fantastic people—singers and musicians of all kinds—who had walked up those stairs to the stage. I got a rush when I walked on to this cheering mob. I could feel the good vibes as I moved to the microphone. The acoustics are so good, you don't need a mike! You can just stand there and be heard even way up yonder in the last row of the uppermost balcony. They call it the gods 'cause that's how high it is!"

She wore a black-and-gold brocade cocktail dress pinned with a huge white orchid. Randy stepped into the house band that night to play guitar on Patsy's segment.

Bobby Sikes, a guitarist and backup singer with Robbins, observed, "She just about blew the end of the building out when she sang. For Patsy, especially, life was to be enjoyed. She was vibrant, bouncy. She took life with a grain of salt and it came over in her performance. The musicians have to get most singers cooking and driving, but with Patsy it was the opposite. She cooked and drove the band. You felt like playing up a storm when she was in the studio or onstage with you. That's the way it was that night.

"Nothing scared Patsy and, onstage, she was willing to try anything once. That night was a success. From looking, there was no way you could tell all those folks were hillbillies! They'd turned away hundreds and people were hanging from the rafters. They stood in their seats and filled the aisles, yelling and screaming for more."

A writer interviewing Patsy was so impressed, he raved: "Patsy Cline comes over like Ava Gardner, Marilyn Monroe, and Gina Lollobrigida all rolled up in one!"

Like back home, fans in everyday bargain-basement clothes and western wear freely roamed up to the stage to take flash pictures. Bill Monroe, cutting an imposing figure in his snow-white twelve-gallon hat, raved about the audience, "They're amazing, ain't they? You get a cross-section of people here that I don't think you'd find anywhere else in any kind of music. There're people from Japan, Europe, country folks, tarheels, rednecks, college graduates, doctors, lawyers. And yet they all mix without friction. It goes back to the music. What we do—bluegrass—is honest music. It feels good to play and it feels good to listen to."

Phil Sullivan critiqued the evening: "For one who knew Carnegie Hall only through reading of the great princely affairs that have gone on there, it was novel to see tattooed snakes moving down the halls on bare arms. It was that kind of crowd. Leather jackets mingled with mink stoles and clerical vestments."

New York Times reviewer Robert Shelton wrote: "It was an unusual sort of opera. . . . Its musical score was very much in the American idiom; its libretto was casual and folksy. Most of the recitatives were delivered by a radio announcer and there wasn't a coloratura or a basso in the house."

"They did come . . . they heard . . . they loved it. . . . Nashville conquered New York," wrote Trudy Stamper in her newsletter. "The hipsters in New York knew that the Grand Ole Opry is the Big Time, and with the Good Lord willing, we'll go on forever."

After the show, the stars, musicians, and dancers quickly returned to the hotel to get their bags. At 2:00 A.M. they boarded a bus for LaGuardia Airport and, at approximately 3:30, departed for Nashville. "It was quite a night," Sikes reported, "so coming back we broke out the booze. There was enough energy on that plane to provide the fuel to fly us home. It was a real high. Everybody was having a big time. Roger Miller [still one of Young's Country Deputies] ran up and down the aisle mugging it up just like J. Fred Muggs, the 'Today' chimpanzee. Faron was flying the plane! That was reason enough to have a stiff drink."

Young explained, "I had a pilot's license for my Piper Cub, but this was a big four-motor job. It was a festive mood and Captain Sam Lucky and I had gotten to know each other pretty well. He ran me up to the cockpit and let me have a look-see. I sat in the copilot's seat and as I discussed the controls, Captain Lucky said, 'Sheriff, you want to take over?' Well, I guess I could've gone through the roof. I was like a child with a new toy. It was only for a few minutes, and under Captain Lucky's watchful eye. But, from what I heard, you woulda thought once I took over the crew had to prepare everyone for a crash landing!"

Charlie was tending shop in Nashville. Patsy and Randy sat together. A popular and still prominent Nashville reporter who was on the scene commented that artist and manager "were so lovey-dovey, all snuggled up, that no one had to wonder about their relationship. A picture was worth a thousand words. A couple of us wondered to each other, 'Who do they think they're fooling?'"

On December 2, Patsy played Atlanta's "Dixie Jubilee," a weekly program broadcast locally. "Crazy" was number one and getting strong country and pop airplay in Atlanta, so there was an enthusiastic welcome. Patsy opened her segment with "Come On In."

"Oh, I tell you, you're sitting up tonight!" she said. "Oh, dogies [directed to the band], you sound like Pappy [Bob] Wills on them good fiddles. Never heard such a swinging beat in all my life. Howdy, everybody! You having a good time? Well, let your hair down and let's see what you look like. We're having a ball. Here's one that's a kinda true-to-life story." With the crowd in the palm of her hand, Randy auditioned a key for her. "Leave it right in the same gear as that, Hoss, and we'll see what damage we can do to it."

Patsy did "A Poor Man's Roses (or a Rich Man's Gold)." Carnegie Hall was still very much on Patsy's mind. "This ain't like New York, but it's uptown! Talk

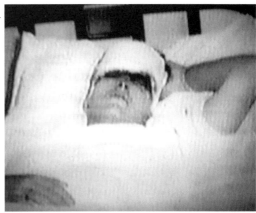

Left: Patsy's June 1961 hometown appearance at Winchester Drive-In, which was marred by a chorus of boos from angry wives.

Right: Less than a week after Patsy's Winchester appearance, she lay near death after she and her brother Sam were struck head-on in Madison, outside Nashville.

(Collection of Pearl Butler)

Below: Patsy returns to the Opry on crutches, September 1961, after miraculously surviving the automobile accident. That night she introduced "Crazy."

(WSM Photo/Les Leverett)

Patsy, three weeks prior to her appearance at Carnegie Hall, helps celebrate the Grand Ole Opry's birthday, November 3, 1961, at the old Maxwell House Hotel.

(WSM Photo/Les Leverett)

A milestone: Patsy appears with a Grand Ole Opry troupe at Carnegie Hall. Singing "I Fall to Pieces" and "Crazy," she had the Carnegie "Hallbillies" clapping, stomping, and yelling for more. (WSM Photo/Les Leverett)

Left: Opry stars arriving in New York, November 30, 1961, aboard TWA's "Grand Ole Opry Liner" (clockwise from top): Minnie Pearl, Jim Reeves, Faron Young, Bill Monroe, Grandpa Jones, and Patsy Cline. (WSM Photo/Les Leverett)

Right: Patsy backstage at Carnegie Hall with manager/guitarist Randy Hughes. (WSM Photo/Les Leverett)

Below: November 30, 3:00 A.M., at LaGuardia Airport following the Carnegie Hall concert. Patsy kicks up her feet while waiting to board the return flight to Nashville. Randy Hughes, holding cigarette, speaks with *Tennessean* reporter Red O'Donnell. (WSM Photo/Les Leverett)

Above left: Throughout her career Patsy affected many different looks. This sophisticated candid was snapped in May 1962 at WSM Radio. (WSM Photo/Les Leverett)

Above right: Patsy, 1962, with children Randy, born January 22, 1961, and Julie, born August 25, 1958. (Collection of Ellis Nassour)

Below left: Patsy with gospel singer and two-time Louisiana governor Jimmie Davis at the 1961 Country Music Festival. (WSM Photo/Les Leverett)

Below right: Julie Dick, soon to celebrate her fourth birthday, summer 1962, at Berryville, Virginia's Watermelon Park, where Patsy was performing. (Forrest P. McCarty)

Above: A replica of Patsy and Charlie's den/music room at their Goodlettsville home was constructed in the Grand Ole Opry Museum.

(Ellis Nassour)

Left: Patsy moved into her "dream house," "bought with my blood, sweat, and tears," hoping for a new beginning with Charlie. She spent a fortune decorating and furnishing. The dining room with the much-talked-about mural was her pride and joy. So was the guest bath, which had gold sprinkled into the tiles . . . so was her den, which she dubbed the music room.

(WSM Photo/Bev LeCroy)

Below: Loretta Lynn takes advantage of Patsy's famed bathroom with gold-sprinkled tiles.

(Les Leverett)

Above: Patsy rehearses with Ernest Tubb and his Troubadours for an August 1962 appearance on WSM-TV's *Pet Milk Show*. (WSM Photo/Bev LeCroy)

Below left: Owen Bradley, a proficient music director and pianist, rehearses with Patsy in 1962 in the Decca Records studio. (Country Music Foundation)

Below right: Patsy, October 1962, wins *Cash Box* magazine's Most Programmed [country] Album. She was also named *Billboard*'s Favorite [country] Female Artist. (WSM Photo/Les Leverett)

Another milestone: Patsy plays Las Vegas. Pictured at the Mint Casino, November 23, 1962, in a Town and Travelwear gown embroidered with three thousand sequins. She was accompanied by Tompall and the Glaser Brothers (whose name is misspelled on the sign). (Kathy Hughes)

Above: Patsy onstage at Mint Casino with the Glaser Brothers (standing, left to right: Tompall, Jim and Chuck). Randy booked Patsy in Vegas for over a month so she could pay for her Goodlettsville, Tennessee dream house. (Kathy Hughes)

Below: A trade magazine ad in conjunction with the Country Music Festival, November 1962, reads: "My Heartaches to see and thank you personally for my greatest year in the Music Business."

Patsy as a bobby-soxer—part of Decca's campaign to increase her popularity among teens.

(MCA Records Photo)

about a hen out of a coop! I really felt like one up there. I'm a telling you! But you know what? We made 'em show their true colors. We brought that country out of 'em if anybody did! They was sitting up there stomping their feet and yelling just like a bunch of hillbillies. Just like we do! I was real surprised. Carnegie Hall was fabulous, but, you know, it ain't as big as the Grand Ole Opry. You couldn't get 'em in there! We were awfully proud of having the opportunity to go that far up in high cotton. Well, I guess, I'd have to say that's the cream of the crop. And, believe you me, it really did my ole heart good because little did I know who was sitting in the audience a-watching me. 'Cause if I had, I wouldn't been able to go on, I'll guarantee you!

"They had Jimmy Dean and Jack Benny. I guess he come to see Tommy Jackson play the fiddle. He was there anyway.[1] Above all, and the most inspiring thing of the whole thing that excited me the most, was Princess Manassia, who is the sister of the King of Persia,[2] was there in the box to my right. And after the show was over, she came to the fella who was in charge of all the doings, Dr. Brooks of the musicians union there in New York, and she told him—well, I haven't gotten over it yet—she said, 'The girl that knocked me out—all the acts were tremendous, but the most tremendous thing on the show as far as I'm concerned was the Cline girl.' Talk about it. Well, I was all shook up! They couldn't hold me. I said, 'Well, why didn't you tell me?' We had WSM's photographer there. I'd-a took a picture of me and her and hung it on the wall."

Patsy sang her swinging rendition of Hughie Cannon's standard "Bill Bailey, Won't You Please Come Home," and then, without any introduction, she went into "I Fall to Pieces."

Following a commercial break, the announcer commented on her recovery and Patsy received a burst of warm-hearted applause. "Thank you so very much," she said. "You're wonderful. The greatest gift a person can have, regardless of hit records or not and I have been very fortunate in the last six to eight months—but the greatest gift that you folks could have given me was the encouragement that you gave me right at the very time when I needed you most.

"You came through with the flyingest colors! I received over two thousand cards and letters and a lot of 'em were from here in Atlanta. I just wanna say, you'll never know how happy you made this ole country gal! And I just hope I don't try to live up to this 'Crazy' bit like I did the last one. We'd like to do the flip side of 'Crazy' for you right now. Gimme about a B-flat, boys, or just gimme a B and I'll put the flat to it." She sang "Who Can I Count On?" and "Fool Number One" and closed with "Crazy," which received a standing ovation.

Over the next few weeks Patsy was to commute to New York for Dick Clark's "American Bandstand" and "The Tennessee Ernie Ford Show," both on ABC. She did the Ozark Jubilee and regional shows, such as Buddy Dean's in Baltimore. In *Billboard*'s issue of December 5, "Crazy," while in the country top-5, peaked at number nine on their pop chart. "As you might expect," informed Ralph Emery,

1. In fact, he wasn't on hand.
2. It's unclear whom Patsy means, though the sister of Muhammad Reza Pahlevi, the late Shah of Iran, was in the audience.

"Patsy evoked quite a lot of jealousy in town. When a new artist, and she was relatively new, has a hit, it's not unusual. Then that artist has another, which Patsy did, and there's more jealousy. The third time, when she has another hit, then everybody wants in. Suddenly Patsy was found to be very acceptable. Some of the jealousy faded because she was steamrolling the business like no one we'd ever seen.

"She was making great inroads in pop with a new type of country, one with a contemporary sound. So, the attitude went, if you can't beat 'em, join 'em. It was that way for Patsy. She found a lot of respect in Music City. Success does that."

Patsy, determined not to have another dry spell, maintained an excruciating schedule, working far too much, too soon, and too hard. Her new motto was "I want to see some results!"

"When an artist or writer has a number one," said Hank Cochran, "there's no money for at least a year. Patsy and Charlie were still having a hard time. I left Mom Upchurch's and moved my wife Shirley and the kids into a three-room trailer. I was writing at breakneck speed for me. When I finished a song I thought was right for Patsy, I'd call and either she'd come over or I'd go there.

"At her house, I'd waltz in and very coyly say, 'Gal, do I have a hit for you!' I did, but she didn't always like them. Patsy was striking while the iron was hot. Owen was getting ready to record her again around the middle of December, and they were looking for a special song for a new single. I didn't know of anything really good floating around. She said, 'Hoss, I need a smash, especially now, so look around. And, God, if you find one, holler!'

"I couldn't get that thought out of my head. I went to the Pamper Music studio in Goodlettsville and worked. I was still there when everybody left for home. I got to knocking around with the guitar. Then something hit me. I worked it up in about fifteen minutes."

Cochran immediately rang Patsy. "I found the son of a bitch!"

"Who?" she asked.

"What."

"What?"

"I'm a fucking genius! I found the son of a bitch you been looking for! I got a hit for you!"

"Well, get your ass over here with it pronto!"

"I'm on my way!"

"Hank!"

"Yep?"

"On your way, stop and get us a bottle!"

Cochran called home to say he'd be late, grabbed his guitar, then hopped into the 1962 Falcon owned by the music publisher. He zipped from Goodlettsville into Nashville, made the stop at a package store and headed to Hillhurst Drive. Patsy and Dottie were preparing supper.

"Hold everything!" Hank announced as he walked into the kitchen. "Whose fat ass is that sticking outa the refrigerator? Hell, I knew it was you, Dottie!"

"Okay, where is it, you fucking genius?" snapped Patsy.

"Hello, Patsy!"

"Cut to the chase." She turned the gas on the stove off. "This better be good!"

"It is."

"Did you pick up a bottle?"

"Yes, ma'am."

"Let's have it!" Patsy went to the cupboard, pulled down three glasses and poured. "Hoss, let's hear this goddamn masterpiece!"

Cochran took his guitar and began:

I've got your picture
That you gave to me;
And it's signed "With Love"
Just like it used to be.

The only thing different,
The only thing new,
I've got these little things,
She's got you . . .[3]

"Wait! Start over."

"I told you you were gonna love it!"

"Modesty becomes you. Where's that bottle?" She poured another round of drinks. "Sing it again!" Then she poured another round and ordered, "Hoss, sing it again! I wanna learn it this time."

When they finished the bottle, Patsy was still singing. She and Cochran were in tears from the emotion she brought to the song. Patsy phoned Randy and sang "She's Got You" as Cochran accompanied.

"Hey, we found it!" Patsy raved. "We've found us a knockout!"

The next day Patsy and Cochran went to Bradley's studio and did it for him. He liked it right away.

"We'll cut it next week," Bradley decided.

It was a rare occasion. The very first time Patsy Cline *and* Owen Bradley agreed they'd found the perfect song for her B-flat voice.

At 7:00 P.M. on Sunday, December 17, Patsy recorded Cochran's stirringly simple masterpiece. It was the perfect merging of singer and song. If "I Fall to Pieces" accomplished nothing else, it proved that it wouldn't be the beat that would keep Patsy eating but poignant ballads.

"She was a hurt individual," observed Lightnin' Chance, "a great cut-up on the outside but hurting on the inside. Some of it went back to her childhood when her father deserted the family. We got into this minutely, talking in the back of those cars, going from date to date. The secret behind Patsy was how she lived every note and word of her songs. When we cut 'A Church, a Courtroom and Then Good-bye,' there was a line—it's the only one I remember—that told how she hated the sight of that courtroom where man-made laws pushed God's laws aside.

3. "She's Got You" by Hank Cochran; © 1962, Pamper Music, Inc.; copyright renewed by Sony-Tree Music Publishing; all rights reserved; used by permission.

You could feel the hate and bitterness, her own experiences. Patsy had a story to tell, and nobody ever knew what it was. If there were parallels in her music, she had a way of identifying with them."

The session ran three and a half hours, an unbelievable amount of time for one song and one-take Patsy. She did the song again and again. Everyone was thrown off a bit. Finally Bradley, over the microphone from the control room, frantically said, "Okay. Go. Go. Go!" And Patsy got it. She was having problems. This time they weren't physical but emotional. In fact, on doctor's orders, Patsy shouldn't have been in the studio at all.

Personnel on the recording include the Jordanaires; Floyd Cramer, piano; Bill Pursell, organ; Harold Bradley, electric bass; Bob Moore, bass; Randy Hughes, guitar; Walter Haynes, steel guitar; and Murrey "Buddy" Harmon, drums.

As Christmas approached, it appeared the Dicks had more to celebrate that year than at any other time. Patsy had back-to-back hits. "I Fall to Pieces" may have started slowly but it finished at the top. *Billboard* ranked it number 2 for the year among the top 100 pop singles. The house was decorated. There were gifts galore under the tree for Julie and little Randy. But it was far from a joyful occasion.

"I LOVE YOU SO MUCH, IT HURTS"

PATSY CLINE: "All right, little Sheriff, you always wanted
to make out. Tonight you're going to get some!"
FARON YOUNG: "Get your ass outa here!"
PATSY CLINE: "No, let's make all of Charlie's wildest
dreams come true!"

*P*atsy Cline knew the feeling of pain on both sides of the microphone. The disillusionment and loneliness she sang of had become part of her life. She told some friends, including Dottie and Del Wood, "Charlie's drinking his misery away and I'm working mine away. His hug is his beer in a frosted mug. And I lie in bed wanting and waiting." On December 16, 1961, she was at home writing Christmas cards, which heralded under a bough of decorated ivy, "From the Four of Us." Whatever the chain of events that occurred—an argument with Charlie, little Randy's crying, Julie simply not listening when told something—it was devastating.

A bundle of frayed nerves, Patsy began shaking and crying uncontrollably. She went to the doctor, who informed her that she was in the throes of a nervous breakdown. As he'd done earlier to no avail, he warned that she was taking on too much responsibility and work during her recuperation. He prescribed medication and a long period of concentrated rest and relaxation.

That evening Dottie came to be with Patsy, who seemed to be in a daze. "Patsy, can I get you anything?" It took a moment before Patsy realized Dottie was in the room. "Hon, why didn't you call me sooner?" Dottie said.

"Oh, Dottie. Thanks for coming. Sister, I didn't even know. It just hit me."

Dottie caressed Patsy. "Honey, I can't believe it."

"Well, it's true. The doctor says I've had a nervous breakdown. I ain't my old self for sure. I feel like I've had the hell beat outa me. He says I gotta stay home and rest. Wouldn't that be funny?"

"What?"

"Me, leading a normal life! Dottie, I gotta work. I have to keep this family together. The kids need new clothes and I—"

"Hon, all that can wait. Tell me what happened."

"Blackouts. They just started. Last night I laid in bed shaking with the walls coming in at me. I got on my knees and prayed that God would let it pass."

Patsy sat at her dressing table and removed her wig, revealing the cloth pressure band she wore around her head and the still highly visible scars from the auto accident. Dottie went to assist her and started to remove the headband.

"No. Leave it. It relieves the headaches. They've been so bad, all that helps is laying my head against the cold bathroom tiles." Patsy stared in the mirror. "You can count the years on my face."

"Oh, Patsy—"

"Sister, I ain't lookin' for pity."

"And you won't be getting any from me!"

There was always music at Patsy and Charlie's house and the radio was playing softly in the background. "Crazy" came on.

"That's your big one," said Dottie softly.

"You know what? I still can't stand it."

"It's made you the biggest crossover star in the business."

"That don't help when I'm laying in bed being ignored."

"Charlie drinking again?"

"Yeah, but when did he stop? It's funny, ain't it?"

"What?"

"I've become a captive of my own ambition."

That night, after Dottie left and Charlie was at work, Patsy sat at the dining room table and wrote Louise Seger in Houston a Christmas card:

Hi Gal,

I'm still kicking but slow.

I haven't forgotten you for a minute but I just don't ever do anything but go, go, go and the Dr. just put me to bed with a nervous breakdown for 2 wks. You all be good & tell all at KIKK *Thanks* & Howdy.

Hope to see you all soon.

Love, Patsy Cline & Family

Two nights later Patsy was in the recording studio.

Patsy always had her "buddies," as she fondly called Dottie, Brenda, and Loretta, who now rallied around as she had often rallied around them. Along with Pearl and Roger Miller, they would gather to entertain her. There were daily gatherings of the "henhouse brigade" on Hillhurst Drive, where the women would sing, cook, clean, discuss their career ups and downs, and gossip.

"When I think back," said Pearl Butler, "I can't remember seeing Patsy sad. But she was a great person for hiding things—her feelings, her problems with Charlie. Patsy could laugh, kid around, and carry on as if nothing was the matter even if something was bothering her bad. Maybe she'd be crying on the inside. You wouldn't know it, though. She never let that part of herself show."

To others—often total strangers—she revealed everything. Louise Seger and Patsy had countless midnight long-distance phone "sessions," in which, said Louise, they would discuss their most personal problems. "If I wanted to, I could crucify Mr. Charlie Dick! He didn't always treat Patsy right."

Did Patsy and Charlie have a sound marriage? Not by normal standards. "It was rocky solid," said Del Wood. "Patsy was always saying, 'I shoulda met the bastard sooner so I coulda left him sooner!' But she could've never left Charlie. Fighting was a way of life and, if you dared say anything negative about either, there'd be hell to pay. If ever any two people needed each other, it was them."

"Every time I saw Patsy and asked how things were," reported Jimmy Dean, "she'd say, 'I'm leaving that no-good bastard!' But she didn't. Maybe her name was most misleading. She wasn't anyone's patsy—with the exception of Charlie. They were stormy as thunderclaps and all in love. He'd slap her. She'd go crying to friends about what a brute he was. Then, in two flashes of a duck's tail, they were back lovie-dovie as all get out till the next time."

Faron Young recalls, "She'd explode, 'Get the fuck outa here. You're just in everybody's goddamn way. I don't need you here. You're nothing but a tax write-off.' He'd be waiting for her when she got home and they'd run into each other's arms. Figure it out! Beats the shit outa me."

Did Patsy ever say she loved Charlie? "I don't know that she ever did. She told me she hated him. But sometimes hate can be love in an insane sorta way. She used to say, 'Charlie's favorite pastime is making me feel blue, but this is the last time I'll cry over him.' It was *always* the last time."

"I never saw Patsy bruised, beaten or upset, or heard Charlie berate her," said Pearl. "He may have been the strongest man in the world, but if he ever took a notion to hit Patsy, I imagine he lived to regret it. But I heard things, and got curious enough to make some serious girl talk. Patsy told me they were in *love*, and after that I knew better than to utter a peep!"

Teddy Wilburn reported, "She'd do something he didn't like, and he'd take retaliation. They'd call each other names and break each other up and down the wall. They'd put each other down, then turn around and pick each other up. I used to think, 'What are these two doing married?' But they had something. Had to!"

"Patsy and Charlie were so in love," said Dottie, "especially for two who could be at such odds. Sometimes Charlie forgot that above all else Patsy wanted and needed stardom. Maybe Patsy expected a little too much from him. Maybe he wanted too much from her. Their marriage was a roller coaster ride—up and down, off track and on.

"Patsy was the one who changed. Charlie was *still* good ole Charlie. She'd say, 'I want to get rid of him' but couldn't live without him. It made me sad to see

Charlie drink too much. He became a different person. They'd end up hurting each other. Both had healthy tempers and it could get dangerous being around them."

Hank Cochran laughed that Patsy and Charlie could have been a number one song—with a bullet. "They were the most amazingly in love persons I knew. But I saw Patsy knock hell out of Charlie with a damn iron and anything else she could get her hands on. They'd go a few rounds and she'd have Charlie arrested and thrown in the drunk tank. Then Patsy'd call everyone in town and tell them about it. And first thing the next day she'd go down to get him out."

Charlie doesn't deny he and Patsy had fights. "When we went at it and a stranger walked in, he may have thought we were going for the shotguns. But when we finished, we didn't go around carrying chips on our shoulders. They were forgotten."

He pointed out that Patsy only had him arrested once, that he only hit Patsy "once or twice," and that he never hit her with enough impact to throw her to the floor (as depicted in the biographical film *Sweet Dreams*).

Friends claim it was heartbreak that drove Patsy to work so hard after the accident. Others said she never got the type of support she needed from Charlie. He refutes this. "I don't know what more I could've done! I gave up my job to be with Patsy on the road and to help with the kids."

Young said that stardom affected Patsy and Charlie's marriage. "Where he used to say, 'Patsy, go get me a beer' or 'Fix me something to eat,' she now turned right around and put the fire to his ass."

Observed Pearl, "Patsy was career-minded, though. Driven. She'd say she wasn't gonna let another baby stand in the way of her doing personal appearances, TV and so on. She said she had two and that was enough. Patsy was gonna have the operation so she wouldn't have any more. Charlie loved her enough that he wouldn't let her do it. He went and had it done himself.[1] Don't that prove something?

"Now, nothing meant more to Patsy than her kids. She was always thinking of their future. It almost killed her, leaving those young'uns at home. On the road, Patsy'd make Carl pull over whenever she saw a phone. She'd say, 'I've got to call my babies and go to the bathroom—in that order!' "

"Her boisterousness and you-think-I-give-a-goddamn come-on was a coverup for a heart as big as the world and as soft as jelly," said Lightnin' Chance. "But Patsy could be meaner than hell, and I'm not just blowing smoke. Sometimes that boy deserved a crown!"

Patsy was once a woman in search of a dream. When that dream became reality, neither she nor Charlie could handle it. Suddenly the girl he was so in love with and sharing every intimate thought with was the center of everyone's attention. There was little private life with the phone ringing incessantly: people wanting Patsy here, there, everywhere; recording sessions; writers wanting to audition songs; personal appearances; promotions; photo shoots; interviews; and working on this deal to get to the next. Charlie no longer played a dominant role. He was no longer number one.

Stardom, whether the husband's or the wife's, can be devastating to a marriage.

---

1. Perhaps Charlie only spoke of doing this, since he did father a child in his marriage to Jamey Ryan.

☆

Was Patsy faithful to Charlie? Was he faithful to her? There is an array of spins on those questions.

Patsy and Porter Wagoner worked several package shows together. "I can truthfully say Patsy was a beautiful, great woman. She lived and breathed her music. As an artist, she was dedicated to the business. Patsy and I had a lot of common ground. I did everything the best I could, and so did she. We were never satisfied with second best. Neither of us could live knowing we didn't give something the very best we had.

"Patsy enjoyed having a good time and so did I. I have wonderful memories of Patsy when we worked the road. One of the funniest things involved Patsy, Lew Childre[2] and me. We were in the West Virginia hill country and, in those days, people you met would invite you fishing or to dinner. I took Patsy and Lew along to one of these families. By the time we got to their place way back in the woods, it was dark.

"We drove up and walked into the yard. Patsy bumped into something and jumped like crazy. There was this boy hunkered down relieving himself and just a-going to town doing his thing. He shot straight up, grabbed his overalls, and pulled them up as best he could. He gave us this wild look and blurted, 'My brother Wiley's inside. He's got a gitar. He plays the hell out of it!' Then he ran inside.

"Lew and I nearly fell out. Patsy broke up screaming. 'I don't know who that was, but he's got something, too, and he plays the hell out of it!' All through dinner that poor boy tried to avoid looking at Patsy, 'cause whenever he did she'd give him this sly smile and wink.

"Traveling in the car caravan with someone you liked to be around didn't often happen. I looked forward to being with Patsy, who you could depend upon for entertainment. Nobody was a stranger around her. I'd known Patsy a long time and was quite attracted to her. There was an affinity between her and me. We enjoyed each other's company and, after a while, one thing led to another. It was beautiful and special.

"But I wouldn't say we were in love or that we had any torrid romance.[3] We were sharing what we felt at the moment, two people alone who'd grown fond of each other. It was a communion of two spirits who found they had more in common than friendship. In each other's arms, it made a few lonely nights on the dismal road more bearable."

Were there also lonely nights on the road with Faron Young? "Hot damn!" proclaimed Young as he gave a unique overview of Patsy and Charlie's relationship.

"When Patsy was out working with me," Young stated, "Charlie'd get drunk and call to accuse her of things. And he'd be home doing just what he was accusing Patsy of."

One of these occasions was a series of dates that landed Patsy and Young in

2. One of the original stars of the Wheeling, West Virginia, Jamboree and later a member of the Opry.
3. Wagoner has claimed several of those: with Norma Jean, Tammy Wynette, and a lengthy affair with former singing partner Dolly Parton.

Wyoming. She came to his hotel room, where he was in bed watching TV. "Patsy was about half snookered from the pint of whiskey she kept in her bag. She told me she'd been on the phone with Charlie and he was berating her again."

Patsy sat on the edge of the bed and they talked and watched TV together. Suddenly, Patsy got really heated about what Charlie was accusing her of. She started taking her clothes off.

"What are you doing?" asked the stunned Young.

"All right, little Sheriff, you always wanted to make out with me! Well, tonight you're gonna get some!"

"Honey, are you nuts? Get your ass outa my room!"

"Naw! Tonight's your night!"

She proceeded to get in bed with Young.

"Hey, what you doing?"

"Hoss, let's make all of Charlie's wildest dreams come true!"

Of that incident, Young simply stated, "What the hell you gonna do? We laughed about it the next day."

Patsy and Randy. It kept coming up. Some said "definitely," others "never in a million years."

Kathy Hughes said her marriage was solid and there was no romance between her husband and Patsy. "She had a strong dependence on Randy and theirs was more than a client/manager relationship. They were best of friends. Why's that ugly to some people? Randy was there for Patsy at all hours. Two-thirty one Sunday morning, Patsy called. She was in tears and told Randy, 'It's a knock-down, drag-out fight! You better get over here quick.' And he did. Just like that, got out of bed and went.

"Patsy was always threatening to leave Charlie. But anything Patsy said about getting a divorce, she wasn't leaving Charlie for Randy!"

Billy Walker reported, "Patsy and Charlie separated for a while, and Patsy and Randy made overtures but resolved it. Randy was my manager. I was with him a lot. If a romance was there, I didn't know it. They had a crush but it didn't go further. It had long waned. He knew she'd be hell to live with and he was very much in love with Kathy. *And* nothing could've broken she and Charlie apart."

"To Patsy," explained Gordon Stoker, "Randy was the greatest. He was stuck on her and she was stuck on him. I kidded him, 'Don't get too interested in your merchandise.' Randy got tired of me bugging him and finally said, 'I was told to never put your cock in the payroll.' He made that remark firm and sincere."

"The subject never came up between us," noted Dottie. "They were so close, it made you wonder. Patsy loved Randy. It was love for the man who helped achieve her dream. I never saw them even embrace. Patsy was never unfaithful, but that didn't stop Charlie from accusing. He wanted to say something to hurt. He'd yell, 'You ought to be home with me and the kids!' And Patsy'd yell back, 'If I was, there wouldn't be anything to eat. Somebody's got to make a living!' "

Though she was to suffer the consequences, Patsy, in pursuit of money to pay bills and the realization of her dreams, didn't allow her nervous breakdown to put a damper on the new year. Charlie was now lending a hand on the road and with the business affairs.

On January 10, 1962, Decca released Patsy's new single. The label's ad in *Billboard* read: "Don't Fall to Pieces but you'll be Crazy about Patsy Cline's newest two-sided smash 'She's Got You' c/w 'Strange.'"

"I was living in Madison the first time I heard 'She's Got You,'" Loretta recalled, "and was on my knees waxing our hardwood floor. The radio was on. Peggy Sue, my sister, was with me, and I told her, 'Well, this is gonna be a smash record.' And it wasn't long before it was."

Patsy had been a friend of June Carter (with whom Cash was having an intense affair while still married to his wife Vivian) for nearly ten years. Patsy now became a favorite of Cash, whose star had soared since he entered the business in 1956. He selected her to appear on one of his star cavalcades.

Patsy was feeling down on January 22, while en route to Kansas City on a two-week whirlwind tour of Canada, the northern states, and Midwest, because she wasn't home to celebrate little Randy's first birthday. All she did was pack, travel, work, unpack, and then a few days later, repeat the process. Even now that she'd made it, there was no resting on her laurels. Was this what she'd had in mind when she yearned for stardom?

That night, she continued a letter to Louise that she had begun several days before in Nashville:

No, I'm not dead and I'm still thinking of you, but just don't get time enough to write. I'm in the car now on tour trying to write you. This tour is with J.R. [Johnny] Cash, Carl Perkins, George Jones, Gordon Terry & Johnny Western and what a bunch! Ha. They really are a swinging bunch of nuts.

Got a 12 year old girl who plays steel guitar out of this world. My ole ears have never heard anything like it. She also plays sax & sings. Looks like a blonde doll. And, boy, what a show woman. She's great. Her name is Barbara Mandrell. Wish you could hear her.

Hope this finds you and yours well and not snowed in like I've been so much lately. . . . There's been so much snow, you can hardly move. I'm sick of it.

Guess you've heard my new record "She's Got You." It's going into Billboard next week at Number 60 in the Top 100 pop. So hope it will get into all the charts. In some places the other side is taking off, "Strange." But "She's Got You" is the side. I wish you'd call the station where Hal works and thank him for me for 1961 and I appreciate every spin of my records. . . .

Well, I've got to finish this tour. Ends in about seven more days and then I go home for 3 days, then to Toronto Canada for 2 days & then home for about four days then start another tour. So see why I don't have time to write much?

Hope to be able to work Houston again soon but don't know when it will be. Sure would like to see you & talk awhile.

Well, I guess I'll close as we are almost to the hotel anyway. So write soon and take care.

Love, Patsy Cline

Tired of the low-key ballads Bradley had been selecting for her recordings, she was seriously looking for "some good story stuff in a good uptempo" and, backstage in Omaha on the tour, Patsy heard Carl Perkins running down a song. "I was composing it ["So Wrong," written with Donny Dill and Mel Tillis] as I went along," he said, "jotting the lyrics on a paper towel. Patsy hollered, 'Perkins, whose song is that?' I replied, 'It's mine, I guess. I'm writing it.' She came to the door and looked me straight in the eye and told me, 'Hell, no. It's mine! I'm recording it.'"

Patsy Cline product was everywhere. She was big with everyone, die-hard country fans, pop audiences, and an ever-growing teen audience. On January 29, the label released a colorful EP package of "Crazy," "Foolin' 'Round," "Who Can I Count On" and "South of the Border (Down Mexico Way)." Her back-to-back hits created great demand. Randy was asking top dollar, but his phone never stopped ringing. As in 1957, after the success of "Walkin' After Midnight," the better part of Patsy's day was spent talking on the phone doing interviews and speaking to deejays. She told Dottie, "I feel like a piece of meat everybody wants a piece of."

Toronto in early February was Minnie Pearl's second tour date with Patsy. "We shared the same dressing room. I was impressed with the way Patsy treated her fans. She was extremely kind and patient, and that always gets to me." On that date, Roy Drusky and a very young Bill Anderson saw how Patsy championed all the stars on the program.

"Patsy was a real spunky lady," Anderson pointed out. "Then she could be as feminine as you wanted. She was smart enough to know the difference between the two. We worked one night for this particular promoter and hadn't been paid."

"When no money appeared forthcoming the next day, we discussed what to do," Drusky said. "We needed a volunteer to make the point that we wouldn't be able to work unless we were paid. Patsy said, 'Hell, leave it to me. I'll take care of this.'"

Patsy called the promoter over and told him, "No dough, no show."

"He told Patsy he couldn't come up with the money right away and would send it later," Anderson said. "Patsy walked onstage to great applause. She quieted the audience and asked for the house lights to be turned up.

"She told them, 'Folks, we've been working for this promoter and we've not been paid. Country folks have to eat, too. Since we aren't being paid, I'm sorry to tell you, as much as we love you, we just can't perform for you tonight. I hope you understand.'"

The audience started booing, cursing, and stamping their feet. Patsy waved and walked into the wings. Within a few minutes, the promoter came running backstage with a couple of grocery sacks filled with the artists' money.

"That's more like it, Hoss," Patsy exclaimed. "Somebody count it to make sure it's all there!"

Owen Bradley wasn't letting Patsy burn too many bridges. He had her back in the studio on February 12, 13, 15, and 28 and she recorded fourteen tracks. While she was soaring, Decca wanted a third album for release before the end of the year.

The songs, evenly balanced between country and pop and simple orchestrations versus heavily stringed, show Bradley's genius as a producer and Patsy's versatility: "You Made Me Love You (I Didn't Want to Do It)," recorded by Al Jolson on Decca in 1913 and later a huge smash for Judy Garland; 1931's "Heartaches" and "That's My Desire"; 1920's "Anytime," also a 1940s hit for country's Eddy Arnold and pop's Eddie Fisher; and the Kay Starr hit "You Were Only Fooling (While I Was Falling in Love)," a favorite of the teenage Virginia Hensley; Hank Williams's hits "I Can't Help It (If I'm Still in Love with You)" and "Your Cheatin' Heart"; "Half as Much" and "You Belong to Me" from 1952, co-written by Pee Wee King and Redd Stewart.

The new songs were: "Lonely Street," a Four-Star copyright "cowritten" by the infamous W. S. Stevenson and already a hit for Andy Williams, Kitty Wells, and its cowriter Carl Belew; Harlan Howard's "When I Get Thru with You (You'll Love Me Too)"; Justin Tubb's "Imagine That"; and "So Wrong." In addition, Bradley chose to completely remake "You're Stronger Than Me" in a pop style. The arrangers were Bill McElhiney and Bill Justis.

"I visited with Patsy on as many sessions as I could," Dottie remembered, "and afterward Owen would have us to his office for a little ritual. Sometimes Charlie'd be with us. We'd listen to the playback and drink champagne. Patsy'd make a toast and then he'd make one. To the next hit was always the first, and after that it was up for grabs.

"As the tapes played, Patsy'd ask around to me, Teddy [Wilburn], Hank, Jan, and whomever else might be there, 'Do you think it's all right?' We'd say it was fantastic, which it was and which she knew all along. But she'd ask, 'Do you really think it's all right?' Maybe she needed reassuring."

Bradley surmised, "The success of 'Crazy' might have scared Patsy. When I wanted to use strings, she was in a dilemma over whether she was breaking out of the country mold. Patsy's voice was romantic and had a magnificent, wide range. She could master anything, but she wanted to be a country singer.

"She kept saying, 'I want to yodel.' She thought if she did, she'd have one big country hit. I'd cry, 'Oh, no, Patsy! No more yodeling.' The next thing you know she was wanting strings. As she progressed as a singer and stylist, Patsy attempted to get deep into her musical roots instead of going along with what everyone thought would sell. She was at the forefront of the innovators, and there weren't many then."

Though Patsy loved anything Howard put in front of her, she seemed to have second thoughts about "When I Get Thru with You." "It was kind of a teenybopper song," he explained. "The lyrics were aimed at young girls, high school kids—the type of following Patsy had a large sampling of. She recorded the heck out of it, but afterward she was a little embarrassed because it wasn't your conventional 'Your Cheatin' Heart' kind of country ballad. Owen chose to back it for release with Justin's 'Imagine That.' Patsy'd go on the Opry and plug the A-side but sing Justin's. I used to get mad at her!

"When we talked about it, Patsy said she felt she might be betraying her country fans. She was quite concerned about not letting them down, and them not putting her down."

Patsy had complete trust in Bradley. Theirs had developed into a father-daughter relationship. However, she still couldn't overcome her fears about changing too quickly.

"By fighting her fears," Jordanaire Ray Walker said, "Patsy put a certain depth in her singing. She found as she cooperated more and more with Owen that there was nothing to fear and nothing to be ashamed of. She could start singing songs that her heart really felt. Patsy sang them with such positive conviction because they were nothing more than a remake of her life.

"Patsy was complex, with a fiery temperament. She even called herself a hell-cat! But she never used her temper unless there was a reason. If you disagreed with her, you had to put your side of the argument in front of her. She wanted the right answer. She lived in fear of not getting that answer, I feel, because of the downward spiral in her career after making such a splash with 'Walkin' After Midnight.' She didn't want to lose again."

On March 3, "She's Got You" entered the *Billboard* country chart and had already started a slow climb on the magazine's pop chart. The next weekend, Patsy was on a series of dates in the Northwest and Canada with old friends Jimmy Dean and George Hamilton IV. "Jimmy had a smash with 'Big Bad John' and was riding high with 'P.T. 109,'" Hamilton said, "and Patsy was on her third consecutive hit. We worked for Marlin Payne, a Montana promoter, who had a friend drive us from date to date in his limousine. The old gang was reunited.

"Patsy sat on the right, Jimmy on the left, and I rode in the middle. We had a couple of hundred miles to go in blizzard conditions. It was early on a Sunday morning and one of them produced a bottle. There was no mix. They were drinking straight out of the bottle, passing it back and forth across me. Before I knew it, I was sitting between two people who were alternately laughing and crying, and becoming increasingly intoxicated. I had a low tolerance for whiskey so didn't partake.

"But Patsy would take a drink and start reminiscing, then Jimmy'd take one and start telling a story as only he can. They told about the years in Washington on the 'Town and Country Jamboree,' their comings and goings, the good times and the bad. It was sentimental, funny at times, and poignant.

"Jimmy had gone his way with the CBS show and split from Connie B. Gay, who was bought out by the network. Patsy was making headlines as the female country innovator of the time. And I had left rock 'n' roll behind."

Patsy kept passing the bottle to Hamilton and finally succeeded in shaming him into joining in. She and Hamilton talked about how they got their big breaks on "Arthur Godfrey's Talent Scouts," reminisced about the Jamboree, and told of their families. By early afternoon, they were thoroughly out of it.

"We weren't stoned or unable to walk," Hamilton said, "but we were feeling no pain. I was amazed at how well they held their liquor. I was the drunkest. And we had a matinee to do. We were in rare form!"

Patsy was to see a lot of Jimmy Dean. Just after the Northwest and Canada dates, they coheadlined the annual firemen's benefit in Houston. Backstage to meet Patsy upon arrival was Louise Seger.

"It was like I'd seen her just the other day," Louise said. "She reached into her travel bag and waved this gorgeous silver fox, saying, 'Look what I bought in Canada! Ain't too shabby! I want you to hold it for me while I'm onstage. I don't want anyone making off with it.' Patsy was phenomenal. She did all the hits. When she sang 'Crazy,' there was a hush. Afterward, when she took off her wig, even with all the makeup Patsy was wearing, I could see the scars from the wreck. I hated to think what she'd gone through.

"She invited me back to the Montague Hotel with her and Jimmy Dean. We had drinks and I was looking forward to a long conversation with Patsy. But they seemed to have something else in mind. They looked pretty wrapped up in each other. They said good-bye and headed out. Patsy looked back over her shoulder and winked—I'll never forget it—and said, 'Keep in touch, Louise.' I replied, 'You bet.'"

Randy's business was booming. His artists were successful, and the commissions were rolling in. Tired of long hauls in the crowded cars of the caravans and having to work around the schedule of commercial airlines, Randy decided to buy a plane. Roy Drusky recommended a pilot friend for flying lessons and was on the lookout for a four-seater plane for him.

In April, after the release of an EP of "She's Got You," "Strange," "The Wayward Wind," and "I Love You So Much, It Hurts," Patsy and Dean coheadlined WIRL Radio's Shower of Stars in Peoria, Illinois. Patsy did an interview with the *Limelight,* a school newspaper. Asked if her life had been affected by her success, she answered, "I never have any time to spend with my family. I'm very nervous due to my automobile accident last year. Many times I have to leave a crowd and take a fifteen-minute rest."

She spoke of the children and claimed "her two greatest buddies are Jimmy Dean and Ferlin Husky." Discussing her goal to become a star, she acknowledged, "I've gotten more than I asked for. All that I ever wanted was to hear my voice on record and have a song among the top 20."

Patsy advised teens interested in a show business career, "If you can define in life what you want to do, set your goal and don't change it. Work toward it and listen, above all, to your parents because you never have but one set. Make them proud and you will achieve your greatest wish in life."

"When times got good," Charlie said, "all Patsy talked about was the day she'd build her dream house—a real showplace. One time or another, we must have looked everywhere. Randy told us of a particular house that was just what Patsy wanted—with lots of room and grounds.

"We went cruising around Goodlettsville off Dickerson Pike, a section of Highway 41. We were on Nella Drive in an area overgrown with beautiful trees, searching for the house Randy'd mentioned. Suddenly, Patsy hollered, 'Charlie, stop the car! Turn around. That's it, baby!' I made a quick turn, parked, and we got out. There was this huge house under construction.

"It was red brick, with spanking white shutters, and had this small portico with a laced wrought-iron support. We looked it over, and I could see Patsy was in love with it. She traipsed through it. I couldn't get her to leave. She said kinda aloud to herself, 'Just goes to show you if you wait long enough, it'll all come your way. Oh, baby! This is gonna be fantastic!'"

Charlie laughed that the only thing more fantastic than the house was the price tag. "It was thirty thousand dollars, which was a lot to swallow. But Patsy didn't care. She said, 'We can afford it and if we can't, I'll get Randy to book me some big dates so we can. Nobody's gonna deny me my dream house. Let's take it!' The lady got her house."

Patsy had reason to be optimistic. "She's Got You" reached the number one position on the *Billboard* country chart, as well as on the charts of the other trades and radio stations. It managed an impressive nineteen-week reign. On *Billboard*'s pop chart, the song peaked at number 14 before sliding. It was pop-listed a total of ten weeks. The B-side, "Strange," made it into the top 100, to number 97. On May 7, Decca released "When I Get Thru with You (You'll Love Me Too)" c/w "Imagine That." It didn't take long for both sides to begin to make noise on the country and pop charts.

The tri-level house sat back off the street, and "within shouting distance of the backyard" there was a rustic farm. Until the housing development started, the area was farm and grazing land. The first floor had huge living and dining rooms, a bedroom, a bath, and a large state-of-the-art kitchen with a serving counter/cabinet that separated it from an adjoining informal dining nook. The children's rooms and a guest bedroom were on the second floor.

The basement, which opened onto a stone patio, had a spacious den with a wet bar. Patsy dubbed this the music room. There was an adjacent garage. The lower floors had fireplaces. An intercom system was installed throughout.

"Patsy wouldn't hear of using decorators," Charlie commented. "Day and night she threw herself into designing every inch. Patsy's dream house had to be the very best. She could drive a hard bargain. If something wasn't just so, she wouldn't have it." She ordered custom-made furniture, drapes, and carpeting. In most of the house, she wanted an American Heritage touch, so she bought lots of colonial furnishings. She even had a tree brought in.

When the specially designed white satin three-piece sectional arrived, Patsy told Charlie, "Honey, the arm's in the wrong place here. It's on the left. I wanted it on the right. Call the store and tell 'em to come pick it up and make it right.' When I reminded her how many weeks it took to get, and how many more we'd have to wait, she brushed it off, saying, 'I don't care. I paid for it, damn it, and I want it the way I ordered it!'" When it returned, she placed a portrait of herself over it.

There was a fancy dining room table that expanded to seat eight and ten. She had a mural painted on a nearby wall. Below it was a solid mahogany credenza. Another table in colonial design was purchased for the kitchen breakfast room. Julie's room upstairs had a canopied bed and curtains decorated with ballerinas. Little Randy's room had bunk beds.

For the downstairs master bath, Patsy bought the kind of gold-speckled wallpaper she had seen in a Hollywood movie years before and "sprinkled gold dust all over the place," Charlie recalled.

George Hamilton IV and his wife, Adelaide, were often at the Goodlettsville furniture store where Patsy shopped. "Adelaide was a friend of the owner," Hamilton said, "but when we saw what a hard time Patsy was giving the poor man, we didn't say too much about knowing her. We didn't want him to hate us! Patsy was very precise in what she ordered, and God help him if the store wasn't."

Brenda Lee has vivid impressions of the house. "Whenever Patsy was in town she was a-fussing and a-fixing up. I visited them so often, I felt it was a second home. Some items Patsy bought, like her lamps with the frilly shades, were kitsch, but she wasn't out to impress anyone. This was her prize. She figured she owed herself something. I used to tease her, 'Hey, big sister, what did you buy for the house today?' And she'd tell me! I felt good for her.

"Patsy and Charlie's bedroom was beige. The centerpiece was this large rug in the shape of a gold record. There was a short half Louis XIV, half Regency-style chest of drawers festooned with acanthus leaves."

Her closets were filled with sweaters, slacks, dresses, western costumes, boots, spike heels, and slippers, among them her gold lamé "chug-a-boots" slippers. In a place of honor were her silver fox stole, a sparkling rhinestone tiara, and several formal gowns. She'd hold the tiara to her head and say, "Introducing the new Queen of Country Music!"

There was a collection of wigs. Since the accident, Patsy hadn't followed through on the plastic surgery. She began collecting wigs in blonde and brown. She had a beautician style the bangs to help hide her forehead scars.

"Of course," said Brenda, "if nothing was too good for that house, that went double for those kids. They had to feel special. Patsy'd say, 'They're all I'm working my butt off for anyway.' Their rooms were really lovely and crammed full of toys and, for Julie, precious dresses. I watched Patsy play with the kids and admired how she doted on them.

"That 'music room' was one of the nicest and most comfortable rooms I'd been in. You felt right at home at Patsy and Charlie's, just the way she sang in 'Come On In.' It had a beautiful parquet floor with all different shades of wood. There was a bar padded in red Naugahyde with the words 'Patsy and Charlie' studded into the leather covering. A covered-wagon planter with a huge snake plant and a cowboy-boot cigarette lighter sat on the bar. Patsy displayed her collection of salt and pepper shakers and her ceramics. She had a black cougar, a Brahma bull, a toy poodle, and I don't know what all."

There was a couch that turned into a bed, an overstuffed recliner, and a hi-fi on a rollabout table. Patsy had record albums everywhere. On the wall she hung her two album covers alongside those of Webb Pierce, Red Foley, Burl Ives, the Wilburns, and Brenda Lee's first.

"We loved that kitchen!" Brenda laughed. "A little too much! Patsy and I had one thing in common. We gained weight so easily and we were always on a diet. I have wonderful memories of Dottie and Loretta coming over. They'd exchange recipes and cook. We'd sit in there and eat and talk about the road, which didn't help our diets one bit.

"I felt Patsy had a trait common among show business folk. In spite of fame and her newfound wealth, she was lonely. Maybe that was another reason Julie and Randy were the light of her eyes. God, she was a terrific mother!"

Dottie so looked forward to Patsy's return from the road that she sometimes waited for her on Nella Drive. "I'd help her clean and cook. I'd do anything just to be with her. I had her on a pedestal. She used to kid me about that, saying, 'Sister, you know what birds do to them things!'

"That house was her mansion, the sign she'd arrived. Patsy loved to shop for that house and was *always* surprising Charlie with some new piece of furniture or an appliance. That gave her such pleasure."

Arriving one day as furniture was being delivered, Dottie commented, "Well, it looks like you cleaned out that store on Donaldson Pike."

"Didn't I!" Patsy agreed. "What do you think?"

"Honey, it's all gorgeous."

"*And* expensive! That salesman looked at me in my gold lamé pedal pushers and said, 'This piece may be out of your range.' I told him, 'I don't care how much it costs, I want it.' He said, 'Mrs. Dick, you have good taste!' I told him, 'Yeah, it's called money!'"

Nothing was ever out of place. "When you walked in the front door, there was a small foyer," Dottie said. "Patsy'd wax it and wax it. I'd kid her, 'Aren't you afraid you'll wear through it?' If someone walked on it, she'd grab the dustmop and touch it up. Once Charlie was standing there and laughed, 'Dottie, can't you make her stop?' Patsy snapped, 'Not till I see my face!' He said, 'Honey, we have mirrors! Dottie, what are you gonna do? Patsy helps the help!'

"When she was home, you couldn't get Patsy away from her babies. That's what she called them. How she loved doing things for them, like buying clothes and toys and giving them birthday parties. When she'd go on the road, she'd say, 'I feel guilty every time I go off and leave them, but I know they understand.' I wanted success and dreamed of being a star, but I had children and I saw how the business tore her up when she left them. It made me stop and think."

Just after Patsy and Charlie moved to Nella Drive, Dottie and Loretta were getting the grand tour. Patsy was mopping the foyer. She put the dustmop aside and said, "Y'all come outside with me." They walked into the front yard. Patsy went up to the curb, turned, and looked at her house with tears pouring down her face.

"Patsy, what's the matter?" asked Dottie.

"I just love this house, Hoss. I waited so damn long. I was so naive."

"What do you mean, Patsy?"

"Y'all, I thought I wanted the future, when all along it was the past I was aching for. Tell me, what happened to yesterday?"

"Why are you down, hon?" Dottie admonished her. "Look at what you have!"

"Right. I have something that's made the waiting worth it. This is my castle, my blood, sweat, and tears. Now that I have it, I wonder if it'll bring me happiness. I'll never be happy till I build Mama one just like it. When I die, tell 'em to lay me out right there in the living room!"

"Patsy, for God's sake!" Dottie exclaimed.

"Hoss, I mean it!"

Roy Drusky found Randy his plane, a green-and-white Piper Comanche. He considered the identification number, N7000P, a good omen. "Seven's your lucky number," he told Randy, "and that P's for papa." Randy made a down payment and that May they flew to St. Louis to take delivery.

Harlan Howard reported that on those rare days Randy allowed Patsy off, usually early in the week, he helped her relax by taking her flying. Leaving the car at Cornelia Fort Air Park, they flew off someplace warm and sunny for the afternoon. Pensacola was a mutually favored destination.

"Ain't this a hoot," Patsy said one day, "flyin' to Pensacola for lobster on the beach!"

"You said you been working too much," Randy answered, "and I need to get as much experience in this thing as possible."

"This is the first time since Christmas I'm doing something I wanna do."

"Great. I'm glad you're enjoying it."

"Hoss, I got some news for you."

"Shoot."

"I'm slowing down." Randy remained silent. "Maybe you couldn't hear me," Patsy shouted. "I said I'm slowing down."

"I heard you!"

"That's it? No argument?"

"Patsy, we've been through this before. You're riding high! We're demanding big money and getting it. You've had four hits in a row, and Decca's banging the drums on your third album. We got everything going! Now's the time to work."

"We're raking it in, all right, but there ain't a minute to spend it. I'm working more than I should and feeling the worse for it. And I hate going out on the road four and five days a week and leaving behind my babies."

"Charlie's good with the kids, and now you have that colored woman to help when you're on the road."

"Guess I was wrong."

"About what?"

"I thought you were the only sane man I know. If you were, you'd know nothing's as good as their mother! The kids're all that's left of what was right. I hate to think what goes on in that house as soon as I'm out the door."

"You and Charlie. He promises to stop drinking, but can't. You have him arrested, then go bail him out. You threaten to leave, but don't. Seems y'all are always through forever—till tomorrow."

"By the time I make up my mind to leave, my mind's already gone. Charlie's made his choices. There ain't nothing I can do 'bout 'em. Anyway, mind your own business."

"You are my business."

"Dollar signs are all I mean to anyone!"

"Now wait a goddamn minute! Didn't you tell me to keep you working so you could pay for your dream house?"

"Yeah. And I'll keep working, but I'm just gonna put albums out."

"Listen, it don't work that way! You got to go out and meet your public or they soon forget you. If we play our cards right, we can make more money and sooner on public appearances than we can on record royalties. Remember, you ain't the only woman in this business anymore."

"Randy, did you say you gonna land this bird right on the beach?"

"Patsy, they've got an airport in Pensacola. And that's right, change the subject!"

"Oops! Steady there. You're sure you know how to fly this thing?"

"Yep—"

"Just checking. Don't forget, I gotta be home before the stores close. Julie'll be four Saturday, and since you got me working all weekend, I'm giving her party tomorrow."

"No problem. I don't have a license to fly at night anyway. Get your bib ready, we're coming in for a landing!"

In the June 5 issue of *Billboard*, "When I Get Thru with You" ranked number 10 on the country chart. The flip side, "Imagine That," came one notch away from the top 20. Both tunes performed respectably in pop. The A-side made it to 53; the B, to 90. Though promoters balked, Randy shot Patsy's asking price sky high, elevating her to her own special place in the business. No longer would she play taverns, roadhouses, or high school auditoriums.

Patsy coheadlined on June 15 with Johnny Cash at the Hollywood Bowl in an event billed as the "Shower of Stars" and "the first and largest combined spectacular of folk, country and western, and bluegrass performers to be held on the West Coast." The lineup included George Jones, Don Gibson, Mother Maybelle and the Carter Family, Leroy Van Dyke, Gordon Terry, Johnny Western, and Hank Cochran. Backup was provided by Cash's band, the Tennessee Three.

In the vast audience was Patsy's mother, whom she'd flown out. "Patsy never accepted the fact that she'd made it. She liked to have me with her for the big shows and, of course, it was a thrill. She was so insecure, she'd make me sit in the audience so I'd tell her what people said. I'd hear a man say she was great and then a woman say she didn't think Patsy was so hot.

"At the end of the shows, before she'd close with 'Lovesick Blues,' Patsy'd say from the stage, 'One of the best friends I have in the world is here tonight. I want you to meet her—Mrs. Hilda Hensley from Winchester, Virginia, my mother.' I'd just sit there, but Patsy'd say, 'Mom, if you don't stand up and take a bow, I won't go on with the show!' When I'd stand, the people around me were more embarrassed than me. Nobody said another word the rest of the evening."

Jan and Harlan Howard surprised Johnny, June, and the Carters and Patsy by coming out for the show with their family. "It was a show I'll never forget," Jan insisted. "What a lineup! It was memorable. We were seeing less and less of each other, so we had an extensive 'yak' session. I remember that night for another reason. It must have been one of the coldest nights in Los Angeles history, and in June!"

Patsy stayed with the "Shower of Stars," playing Phoenix on the sixteenth, Tucson on the seventeenth, then Douglas and Safford, Arizona, El Paso, and Albuquerque.

When she returned home on July 8 after a rigorous five days of holiday shows, she and Charlie headed from Nashville to Florida. Randy had gotten Patsy a job that had new career potential: She joined Webb Pierce, Sonny James, and Dottie in De Land to star in a country musical film.

According to Dottie, "The plot was simple and built around the artists making personal appearances, where they'd do their big hits. It was a copy of the rock 'n' roll formula movies. It was fun. We had expenses paid and several days on the beach to relax. In the end, it was one of those stories you used to hear about a lot in country. The producer ran off with our money. We were never paid, and the movie, or what was made of it, never saw the light of day."

Decca continued to push Patsy. On July 16, the label released her single of "So Wrong" backed with "You're Stronger Than Me."

On July 25, Patsy's friend Jo Ann Thomas got a call from her. She would be working the Richland Fire Company Carnival, one of the oldest in the state of Pennsylvania, and wanted to stay with Jo Ann and Gus. Jo Ann picked Patsy up at the Harrisburg airport. On the way to Richland, they got tied up in a traffic snarl.

"There'd been a train wreck," Jo Ann explained, "and traffic was moving very slowly. I counted thirteen ambulances, and we were kind of shook up."

The scene brought back painful memories to Patsy. She said, "Whatever you do, please be careful. I'd rather be late for the show than in another accident. I still ain't completely healed from my car wreck. I've seen enough of the hospital to last me a lifetime!"

For the carnival concert, for which Patsy was being paid in excess of a thousand dollars, admission was seventy-five cents for adults, and children were admitted free. Close to seven thousand fans jammed the bleachers, waiting, hoping Patsy would make it. Night came, and she still hadn't arrived. Finally, Jo Ann's car pulled in. When Patsy went onstage, the audience gave her a standing ovation.

The next day, Jo Ann took Patsy to her parents' farm for Sunday dinner. Her mom prepared a huge ham and one of Patsy's favorites, fried chicken. Jo Ann's father couldn't get over having Patsy Cline in his house.

"He was following Patsy around like a puppy," Jo Ann recalled. "I was getting irritated. I told Patsy I was sorry for the way he was acting. She said, 'Please don't be ashamed of your daddy—at least he stayed with your family and took care of all of you. My father deserted us when I was small and I had to sing on street corners for coins people would throw me. When I had enough money, I took it home to Mom to buy food with.'"

That afternoon, on the way to the airport, Patsy saw a roadside fruit market and wanted to stop. She bought a large bag of cherries. She and Jo Ann ate them, throwing the pits out the car window.

"I'll do one thing before I die," Patsy exclaimed, "and plant cherry trees from Hershey to Harrisburg."

"Oh, Patsy," admonished Jo Ann, "don't talk like that! It makes me feel creepy."

At the airport, just before Patsy boarded her plane, Jo Ann stopped her and requested one last photograph.

"As I stood there looking at her through the viewfinder," noted Jo Ann, "I felt real strong that I'd never see Patsy again."

That Monday night, Dottie's phone rang. It was Patsy calling to say that she and Charlie had had a violent argument. "She sounded terribly frightened," Dottie said, "so I offered to come over and spend the night. When I got there I figured, as usual, everything would be all right. It wasn't." When she arrived, she and Patsy hugged. "Honey, you're shivering," said Dottie. "What in the world's wrong? Patsy? Patsy, what happened? Where's Charlie?"

"He's gone out for the evening, *and* that son of a bitch won't ever be coming back in this house!"

"Patsy, look at me. Are the children okay?"

"Oh, yeah. He's a damn dick but he wouldn't dare do anything to them. He knows I'd kill him!"

Dottie calmed Patsy down. "Now, honey, what happened? Where's Charlie?"

"He was drinking heavily and started pushing me around in front of the kids. I called the police and had him arrested."

"Oh, Patsy. I'm sorry."

"I'm not! Speaking of drinks, Sister, let's pour one!"

"Should you?"

"Best medicine in the world."

"I'd love to, but Bill'll be home any minute looking for his supper."

"Let him look! It's amazing what they find when they're good and hungry. Maybe it'll make him appreciate you a little more."

They went to the music room. Patsy put the glasses and ice on the bar and Dottie started to pour. Patsy grabbed the bottle.

"Whoa, hon! That's too much!"

"I want a drink, not a swallow! Here's to those who wish us well and those who don't can go to hell! Sister, it seems all I do is lose. It's like I just fell off the turnip truck! Every time I try to make this marriage right, it gets worse. And I get burned!"

"Patsy, why do you always blame yourself?"

"You're right. Why can't I find the love I sing about in my songs? Girl, our men don't understand and don't wanna. Men are men and, no matter how hard you try, you can't make gods of 'em. I can never forgive Daddy or Charlie for not being gods. Yeah! We're in this on our own. It's really hard out there for us girls. The amount of damn work you do and still have nothing to show for it. We work, work, work, and still we're not accepted like the goddamn men."

"The men sure have it easier," Dottie agreed.

"And they lord it all over us! It's bad enough for a girl trying to make it, but it's really difficult when the girl's married."

"To someone in or out of the business."

"That's the honest-to-God truth, Hoss. Don't matter what we do, we ain't nothing but sex to them."

Patsy got up and mixed another round of drinks. She pulled down two bulging scrapbooks that she and Dottie had been constantly compiling with articles about Patsy, her chart listings, sheet music of her songs, the Decca trade ads, Trudy Stamper's WSM newsletter, and photos of Patsy with Husky, Young, and Elvis. Patsy loved Elvis and kept "my special portrait" inside the back cover. It was a huge picture from a magazine. She told Dottie, "Here's another great one—Danny Thomas, Ann-Margret, Jane Russell, Bob Hope, *and* Elvis at this Memphis fundraiser for St. Jude Hospital. It was one of the greatest moments in my life."

Patsy and Dottie thumbed through the pages. Dottie had a good laugh. "I've never seen this clipping!"

"Which one? Oh, my goodness. That! " Patsy cracked up laughing. "'Patsy Cline Is Back in a Big Way.' I shoulda called that newspaper. I wasn't even pregnant! I'd just gone back to the Opry after the car wreck."

"It says, 'You can't keep a star away from those hit records.'"

"That's the truth, which you'll soon find out now that you're signed to RCA. I'm so proud of you, Sister!"

"I owe you a lot. You've brought me a long way!"

"Naw. You done it! You've pushed and shoved and stayed with it."

"You showed me how."

"Yeah, and now here I am wondering if it was worth the pushing and shoving I had to go through."

They came to a photo of Patsy and Jimmy Dean on the "Jamboree." "Jimmy was a taskmaster," Patsy declared, "but we had some fun. And that's where I got my feet wet and learned about TV."

Dottie pulled out a 1957 article from the Winchester *Evening Star* about Patsy on "Arthur Godfrey's Talent Scouts."

"That show was responsible for really putting the Cline on the map!" Patsy noted. She pulled clippings of *Billboard*'s chart listings. "'I Fall to Pieces' made it to number one on the country charts, but remember that song 'Michael (Row Your Boat Ashore)' by the Highwaymen? That kept me out of the top ten. But, here's the week it got to number twelve. Enough about the Cline."

"I enjoy it. It makes me happy to see you happy. I'd rather see you laughing than crying."

"How're things with you? Bill staying busy?"

"We're keeping our heads above water."

"You need to do some more writing."

"I am, Patsy. I'm working up a new song now."

"Great. Then take it right into the studio." Patsy got up. "Hoss, excuse me a second. I've got to go to the 'conversation piece (as she called the upstairs bath speckled with gold).'"

Patsy went upstairs into the dark living room to the picture window that looked onto the lawn. She pulled back the drapes and peered into the early morning darkness. A strange mood overcame her. She felt alone and helpless. During her hospitalization, she told Dottie, "If there's only one effect nighttime can have on you, it's to make you feel more helpless and cut off from everyone—those you love—than you really are."

Tonight, as she stared into the void, she understood those words more than ever. What all she had sacrificed to fill those scrapbooks! She was a star with fancy furs, expensive cars, and her dream house. She had adulation, thunderous applause. But now there was nothing except her children.

Patsy went to her bedroom, got some paper, and began writing. She then folded the paper into her hand and returned downstairs, where Dottie had put one of her records, "Honky Tonk Merry-Go-Round," on the hi-fi.

On the stairs, she paused for a moment as a slight feeling of uneasiness came over her. It was a fleeting glimpse, a vague, distant, very far-off perception that something wasn't right.

"Patsy, are you okay?" inquired Dottie. "You look so pale."

"It's nothing, Hoss. I'm fine."

"I thought I'd play something to brighten our mood."

"We could use that!" Patsy picked up the scrapbooks. "Dottie, I want you to have these—"

"Oh, Patsy, I couldn't. They're your memories."

"I'll remember 'em the way I wanna. I want you to have 'em and keep 'em for me."

"I just couldn't."

"You gonna argue with the Cline? Anyway, they ain't gonna do me no good, 'cause I'll never live to see thirty—"

"My God, Patsy! Don't talk like that."

"It's the truth."

"Patsy, I just put some music on to lift our spirits, and now you're talking like this! Let's change the subject."

"We can if you'll take 'em."

"Okay, Sister, I'll keep them for you. You know where they'll be."

"Thanks, Hoss."

"I'll keep them for your grandchildren—"

"Grandchildren? Imagine the Cline a grandma! Thank God for the young'uns. They're my hope, the only things that matter. They're what keep me going."

"The kids are compensation, but I wish we had more."

"Tell me about it! When I hit the road, they know I'm gonna be gone a while. It tears my heart out when Julie starts crying and pulls on my dress. She says, 'Please, Mommy, let me come with you. Please, Mommy, don't leave me. Please, Mommy, I'll miss you.'"

"And each one of those 'Please, Mommies' is a stab in the heart."

"You know, it's nearly daylight?"

"No! I've got to go. You'll be okay?"

"I'll be fine. Thanks a bunch for coming over. I needed to talk."

"Charlie coming back in the morning?"

"Oh, yeah, he'll be back."

Dottie drove home, sat down at her kitchen table with the scrapbooks, and thumbed through the pages. "I started to cry—for both of us. I wondered what on earth possessed Patsy to give up her cherished scrapbooks. She was real down because of the argument and fight with Charlie. She kept trying to be a good wife and mother, but it seemed no one appreciated it.

"I admired the picture of Patsy and Jimmy Dean, then turned the page. There was this piece of paper folded up. I didn't know what to think, so I opened it. It was a check for seventy-five dollars with a little note saying, 'I know you're having it hard and that you're not working. You can use this to pay the rent. Love, Patsy.'

"I don't know how Patsy knew. She had so many problems of her own, I didn't want to bother her with ours. That night I had just enough money to put a dollar's worth of gas in the car to get to Goodlettsville. Bill and I had been trying to get enough money together to pay the rent and hadn't been able to."

Patsy still hadn't forgotten her roots. The next weekend she and Charlie took Julie and Randy to Winchester for a visit with Mrs. Hensley. On Saturday afternoon she played Berryville's Watermelon Park. That night the couple visited the Charles Town, West Virginia, Moose Lodge where Bill Peer and the Melody Boys happened to be playing.

Band member Joe Shrewbridge said, "Patsy and Charlie were in a booth at the back of the hall. They didn't come up and say hello to Bill, but he knew they were there. He couldn't help it because everyone made such a fuss. But he ignored Patsy because he didn't want to upset Dolly. I felt pretty bad for Bill and Dolly."

During one of the breaks, some of the musicians who worked with Patsy went over to say hello. Guitarist/vocalist John Anderson brought back word that Patsy wouldn't mind getting up to do a number. When Bill told Dolly, she said, 'No way!' To the folks who wouldn't let up, Bill said, 'She's relaxing. We shouldn't bother her. Let her enjoy herself.'"

That night, as she waited on pins and needles to be invited onstage, Patsy was finally able to enjoy her privacy.

"NEVER NO MORE"

SAM HENSLEY: "Hey, I told you that Patsy is not on any
plane!"
HILDA HENSLEY: "Wait a minute! Patsy *was* on a plane!"

The cover of Patsy's third album, *Sentimentally Yours,* pictured Patsy reclining on pillows in one of her new boutique wigs, heavy makeup, and a paisley print dress. The album, released August 6, 1962, featured "She's Got You," "Strange," and songs from the first three of the four February sessions.

Harlan Howard and Hank Cochran were in a heated race to write Patsy's next number one hit. That neither succeeded was due to fate and a miscalculation of what would sell. They did compose two of the most mesmerizing tunes Patsy recorded, "That's How a Heartache Begins" and "Why Can't He Be You?" In fact, the September 5 and 10 sessions were crammed with superb material: Cochran's "When You Need a Laugh," Roy Drusky's "Your Kinda Love" and Wayne Walker and Webb Pierce's "Leavin' on Your Mind." The uptempo numbers, Marijohn Wilkin and Fred Burch's "Tra Le La Le La Triangle" and Bob Montgomery's "Back in Baby's Arms," aptly summed up, respectively, Patsy's early life in the Brunswick Triangle and the Dicks' marriage.

At the first "champagne playback" party, Patsy and Bradley hosted Dottie, Cochran, Drusky, and agent Hubert Long. When Bradley ran the tape of "Why Can't He Be You?", Cochran was so moved by Patsy's reading of his material he cried.

Patsy's thirtieth birthday was September 8, and Sunday, September 9, was the occasion of Patsy and Charlie's first big party in the dream house.

"That night, as everyone celebrated," Dottie reflected, "don't think I wasn't relieved that whatever kind of premonition Patsy had didn't fulfill itself. I didn't forget what happened, but she was continually moving on to a newer plane, and it was no more than a fragment of a memory."

"Parties," Billy Walker said, "have always been a prevalent thing in Nashville music society, but back then we were a close-knit community, always on the go. So they were, more or less, spirited 'family' reunions. That night, however, it was an occasion. Patsy was celebrating more the debut of her house than her birthday. And, let me tell you, *that* bathroom had some visitors."

The guests included the Hugheses, the Wests, the Lynns, the Howards, the Cochrans, Wayne Walker, Del Wood, the Wilburn Brothers, singer Wilma Burgess and, among seventy-five others, Faron Young.

"Like at all parties," Faron recounted, "we sat around and had some drinks and then someone grabbed a guitar and we'd take turns singing. There was a little to-do later when Charlie pulled out a set of forty-fives and started showing off. I looked real close and realized they were my guns from one of my movies. He'd 'bought' them from me, saying 'Sheriff, I'll pay you later.' That son of a bitch never did. When I tried to get 'em back, he said he lost them. I told him, 'What you mean is you lost the money you owe me.'

"That night Charlie, Mooney Lynn, and all of us did some drinking but ole Charlie really put away some stuff. He mooned us. It was downright funny, but Patsy was embarrassed. Everybody laughed up a storm. There was no way you could stay angry with Charlie."

A few nights later, Patsy asked Dottie to sit with her again.

"Well, Hoss, we've shared a lot of secrets, haven't we?"

"I guess," said Dottie, understating the case.

"I got another one for you tonight."

"Okay. What is it?"

"Naw."

"Come on, let's hear it!"

"You sure you can keep a secret?"

"Cross my heart!"

"Well, I been putting aside something for a rainy day. Something that's just mine. I don't want even Charlie to know about it."

"Not even Charlie?"

"Nope. This is between me and you."

"Patsy, what the heck are you talking about?"

"My stash."

"What do you mean?"

"I got me a stash."

"A what?"

"A stash."

"Oh, my God, I don't believe this."

"Believe it. 'Cause it's the honest truth. If found me this hiding place behind one of the bricks in the fireplace in the music room. I've been putting money in there every week. Don't you dare tell a soul. You're the only other person that knows. I just want you to know about it in case anything happens to me."

"There you go again! Patsy, why do you feel you have to hide money?"

"It's my business, Hoss. It's for that rainy day Grandpa [Jones] is always telling me about. Remember, now, mum's the word."

An EP containing "So Wrong," "You're Stronger Than Me," "Heartaches" and "Your Cheatin' Heart" came out September 24. "Heartaches" and "Why Can't He Be You" were issued as a back-to-back single October 8.

The 11th Annual WSM Country Music Festival got under way on November 7, and the visiting disc jockeys were set loose on the stars for interviews to air on their stations. At the taping sessions in WSM's Studio B were Flatt & Scruggs, Roy Drusky, George Hamilton IV, the Butlers, Skeeter Davis, Jim Reeves, Faron Young, Jimmy Dean, and Patsy.

Nashville's new country darling did at least a hundred interviews. She was asked how it felt being hospitalized for thirty-five days. Her in-depth answer: "Awful!" Asked why she went back to work in a wheelchair, she replied "'Cause I couldn't walk!" What about on crutches? "'Cause I just couldn't stay home."

At ceremonies in the Maxwell House Hotel, Patsy came away the big female winner. She took home ten honors, including *Billboard*'s Favorite Female Artist; *Cashbox*'s Most Programmed Album of the Year, *Patsy Cline Showcase,* and Most Programmed C&W Female Vocalist; *Music Reporter*'s Female Vocalist of the Year and Star of the Year; and *Music Vendor*'s Female Vocalist of the Year for "Crazy" and "She's Got You." For the second year in a row, Patsy unseated Kitty Wells.

"It's so unbelievable," cried Patsy, attired in a gold brocade evening suit, her silver fox, and spike heels. "My new house is gonna have wall-to-wall awards! It's wonderful. You're wonderful! *But*—what am I gonna do next year?"

She was finally receiving the recognition she had sought so eagerly—and the money that went along with it—but was more pleased that, once again, Loretta, with *Cashbox*'s Most Promising Female award, was moving up.

Faron Young noted, "Patsy was attracting so much attention and was in as much demand on the pop music circuit as she was in country. She finally realized she could be hotter copy without a hayseed image. She became a real city slicker in her high-fashion gowns and fancy dresses. And, oh, my God, she started wearing hats. Not Stetsons! Church hats, social-gathering hats. I wondered, 'What next, hillbillies playing golf?'

"She was also getting the big head. Patsy and I worked a lot of concerts together. When you're hot, you're hot, and Patsy was hot. And loved every minute of it! We were driving along to some date and we'd take turns running up and down on the car radio, trying to see if we could find our songs."

Patsy tuned in "Crazy," then "She's Got You." Young yelled, "Goddamn it! Ain't they playing my record of 'Sweet Dreams'?" Patsy tuned in "So Wrong" and "Heartaches," laughing with great glee each time she heard one of her tunes.

"Where's 'Hello, Walls'?" Young exclaimed. "They haven't forgotten me, have they?"

"You're old hat, Sheriff! They don't wanna play you no more."

"You better watch it, or you can get out and walk."

"I won't have no problem getting a ride," she replied, playfully hiking her skirt.

"Patsy, you ain't conceited. You're convinced. Don't wallow in hog heaven just yet. 'The Yellow Bandana' is bigger than anything you ever had!"

"I don't hear 'em playing it!"

Young frantically tuned the radio.

"I betcha I'll find 'Have I Waited Too Long?'"

"Get real, Sheriff! They don't play oldies."

"Five dollars!"

"You're on!"

Young turned the dial again.

"Oh, is that it?"

"Hell, no! It's 'I Fall to Pieces.' Hell and goddamn!"

"Everybody's playing my records! Now, how much was the bet?"

For someone who seemed so sure of herself, Lightnin' Chance found Patsy to be the opposite. "Before we went onstage, Patsy was nervous. She'd have knots in her stomach and would keep a handkerchief in her hand because her palms would be moist from sweating. Offstage, she smoked. After the accident, things got worse. She had frequent headaches. Patsy was always so fidgety. Maybe that's why she moved around so much. When she was having those scars worked on, she'd keep some type of band around her hairline to apply pressure and to keep her stitches in place.

"Onstage, no one could come close to Patsy. She was amazing, a star. That's such an overused word, but Patsy was the epitome of what it used to mean. I worked with her when she wore those cowgirl outfits and when she wore fancy dresses. And, you know what? It didn't make a damn bit of difference what Patsy wore or didn't wear, because when she opened her mouth at that mike not only did she get attention, she demanded it.

"When Patsy finished a show, she was wrung out like a washrag. She could be testy, but it was a joy and a privilege to have known and worked with her. She didn't go in for a lot of audience rap. The funny things that happened involved her snide remarks to the guys in the band—her 'dogies.' I developed this applause-milking gimmick with my bass by making it squeak—some say I made the damn thing cry. I used it for musical comment and, sometimes, to pick at an artist. Patsy got a kick out of it. She'd act real scared and say, 'Little dogie, you trying to scare the boss lady?'

"I saw artists stand on their heads, gobble peanut butter from a ceiling fan, pee in a vest pocket and all kinds of stuff, anything to be different. Patsy didn't have to go for that. She was unique. She had showmanship."

Patsy often called the dream house "the house that Vegas built." Since Patsy's Decca earnings were coming in slim royalty payments because of hefty advances, she needed financial security to keep the house. True to both their dreams, Randy booked her into the Merri-Mint Theatre of the Mint Casino, which was owned by the Sahara Hotel on the strip. It was to be for thirty-five days.

Teddy Wilburn received a call at the end of the D.J. Convention. "She was beside herself about playing Vegas. Elvis and Johnny Cash had gone there and conquered it. Patsy had spent five thousand dollars on arrangements and was learning dance steps from a choreographer. She was set to work with the Glaser Brothers—Chuck, Jim, and Tompall, who'd also won the Godfrey show. They were a

Decca act. Patsy was upset that they wouldn't rehearse. They told her it wasn't in their contract.

"Doyle, Loretta, and I played there and knew the hotel where she'd be staying, Ferguson's, had a couple of big rooms where she could rehearse. 'There's nothing to worry about,' I said. 'Throw away those arrangements and forget about the choreography. Just get everybody there a couple of days early and plan what you want to do. That way, it'll be fresh in everybody's mind. And, if all else fails, just get up on that damn stage and sing and you'll knock 'em dead like you always do—even the high rollers.'"

Charlie stated that Patsy made $6,300 a week, "but that included the band and Randy's commission. He also noted that he felt Patsy didn't really want to go. "I think she was scared." The first night they arrived, Patsy went on a crying jag. "Patsy wanted to go home! I don't know whether she thought she wasn't prepared, or that she'd heard so much about Vegas and all the big names out there and it frightened her."

"Patsy started to show some real fears," said Gordon Stoker of the Jordanaires. "You'd never think she was fearful of anything. She confided in me, 'How can a nothing like me even be doing what I'm doing?' I told her, 'Because you realize you're nothing. We all are, say, compared to Christ. And she shot back, 'Well, you gotta start somewhere!'"

Patsy opened on November 23, with Hilda and Charlie in the audience. The Merri-Mint wasn't a Vegas showroom as they are known today. It was tacky and seedy. Patsy Cline was the classiest thing it had seen. And the casino got their money's worth out of their star. She worked seven nights a week. To the Las Vegas press and audiences, Patsy was a major record star. "So Wrong" made it to number 14 on the *Billboard* country chart in August and to 85 in the pop top-100. Surprisingly, "Heartaches" wasn't making any country waves but was number 73 on the pop chart. The powers in Vegas saw her potential as a regular, and Randy negotiated to bring her back to town, but not downtown.

A few days into her run, Patsy encountered that disease dreaded by all entertainers who play Vegas—dry throat. Charlie noted that for a couple of performances, she had to mime her own records from a music system rigged behind the curtains. Despite this problem, the Sahara entertainment executives who came several times to hear her loved her and moved to book her for a one-nighter in their main showroom on the strip. When Randy broke the news to her, she balked.

"Hoss, that's too uptown for me. I don't wanna wear fancy gowns. I want to wear my cowgirl outfits."

"Here we go again! Those days are finished. Look where you are!"

"Yeah, and I'm miserable. Listen, Randy, I'm tired and I don't want to hear any more about it. I miss my kids."

"Yes, ma'am, Miss Cline. Anything you say. Let me arrange for your supper. Something with a lot of sugar."

"It won't help!"

"And we can continue this conversation tomorrow."

"It won't do no good, so you can *dis*continue it right now!"

As Christmas approached, Patsy tried to do her shopping for the children's presents, but her heart wasn't in it. She called home twice a day to hear Julie and little Randy's voices. Onstage Christmas Eve, she broke out crying in the middle of "Am I a Fool?"[1] When she came off, she said the lyrics really got to her.

"No matter what, I'll never do this again," she swore. "This is a time to be with your family, not away from them."

Randy made no mention that he had been continuing to negotiate with the Sahara for Patsy's return in early 1963. The engagement ended on Friday, December 28, so he had to get Patsy to the Sahara for a trial run. The day after Christmas he broke it to her.

"Patsy, we won't be going home Friday."

"What?"

"As soon as we finish here, we're doing one night at the Sahara. I just sewed it up. They want to see you on their stage."

"I keep telling you I wanna slow down, that I gotta slow down. But you don't hear me. No one listens to what I want. I have to go out there and do the work."

"Patsy, we can't stop now!"

"Tell 'em I said thanks but no thanks."

"No way, baby!"

"Goddamn, don't it matter what I want?"

Randy rushed out, and standing in the doorway was a man from Patsy's past.

"Hello," he said quietly. "Is it okay to come in?"

"Donn Hecht! My God, what a wonderful surprise!"

"I had to see your show. Las Vegas is the big time, and so are you!"

"Yeah, so I been hearing! You look great."

"A little dusty. We just drove in from L.A. Let me look at you!"

"No. No. Please don't. All I can say is that I'm alive! I'll look better after the show. One more less to do."

That night Patsy brought Hecht onstage. "I'd like you all to meet a really fine country and pop writer who's played an important role in my career. Ladies and gentlemen, Mr. Donn Hecht, the cowriter of my first number one hit, 'Walkin' After Midnight.' Donn, take a bow."

After the performance, Hecht said, "We visited backstage for quite a while. Though she was dressed to the nines, Patsy didn't look better. She was exhausted, pale, unsure. Only the heart was there. At first, I thought it was overwork, but the lines on her young face spelled much more. She was only thirty, but looked so much older. She, Randy, and I were going to eat that night, but Patsy canceled abruptly, saying, 'I need some rest more than I need any food.'

"She told me how much it meant to her that I'd come so far just to see her. Patsy persuaded me to say and talk to her. She complained of not feeling well, which she attributed to the flu bug. While she was fixing her hair, looking at me through the mirror, she brought up Bill McCall. Patsy was still bitter. When she went to get up, she had a slight wobble. She complained of some tight, aching muscles over her shoulders and neck. She wanted to know if I couldn't do anything.

"I stood in back of her, folded her arms over her chest, and gently lifted her bear-hug fashion to stretch her back. I heard a pop and said, 'There. That should

---

1. The 1957 Bobby and Violet Lord tune.

relax you. It works. I do it to my wife.' Patsy told me, 'I feel better already. Okay, you can unsqueeze me now.' So I let her go, hoping she didn't take it the wrong way.

"In a manner that appeared somewhat ominous, she began talking softly about her life and things she had to take care of when she got home. It was like she was going through the eerie motions of settling accounts."

"I don't understand it, Donn."

"What's that, Patsy?"

"I know people who have schooling and all but don't have half my talent. Yet they seem to have everything good happen to them without half trying."

"Yeah, I've seen that."

"Hell, all my life it's been uphill! Even now. I tried to do everything without stepping on or hurting anyone—even when it meant hurting me. But all that's gonna stop. Experience is a hard teacher. She gives the tests first—"

"And the lessons come after."

"Right. I've got a lot of living to do with people I wanna do it with. And for *once* in my life I'm damn well gonna do it. You remember in 1957 I recorded your song 'Cry Not for Me'?"

"I sure do."

"And that son of a bitch McCall wouldn't release it until 1959. He didn't want to spend any money promoting it."

"That was Bill's Patsy Cline insurance. He got wind you might fly the coop, so he sat on it."

"Well, there's a story in that song about my life."

"How, Patsy? This is no time for crying. You've reached a place hundreds of would-bes envy."

"Don't kid yourself. I don't. Every time I've had what I wanted here—"she held out the palm of her hand—"something pulls the rug out from under me. Sickness, accidents, hospital bills, *McCall.* I'd like to do that song again. Listen, 'Cry not for me / when I am far away / there's nothing more to say / cry not for me.'"

"God, you still remember the words!"

"Sure, but I don't want anybody to cry for me."

"What do you expect those who love you to do?"

"Listen to the songs and how I did my damnedest to sing them right."

"You're a songwriter's dream!"

"Or nightmare!"

"Patsy, you've got a lot of songs to sing before you join 'Hillbilly Heaven.'"

Patsy laughed. Hecht said it was the first time all night. "If there're a bunch of hillbillies up there, you can be damn sure I'll get in." She continued to talk. "And I owe you a lot."

"How's that?"

"Your way of thinking things out. About music being music and crossing fences to see what people and things are really like."

"Thanks, but you don't owe me. We learn from relationships we have along the way. I feel proud to share in your career."

"There was nothing for me musically before 'Walkin' After Midnight.' My one regret was that it had to be shoved down my throat! It musta been like giving medicine to a baby! The baby doesn't want it—"

"But I keep saying, 'But, baby, it's good for you!'"

"Donn, I want to record more of your material!"

"We can work that out, make that same spark happen again. If I have another song I really think you can do, I'll submit it to you."

"My manager. There, I've got a problem. Not the kind you may think, but he's the decisionmaker in the family."

"Family?"

"You know what I mean."

"I'm not sure I do. But I'll go over some new material for you."

"I'd like that."

"I could use the money from a Patsy Cline hit."

"So could I!"

"If it's in the cards, as they say in Vegas, it's in the cards! You know, I've never been to Nashville."

"You're kidding?"

"No. Just never got around to it."

"Think we could get rolling soon?"

"In about a month."

"Great."

"It's late, Patsy, and I'm going to have to head out."

"Come on, let's find Randy and we can all go."

Outside on East Fremont Street, Patsy and Hecht hugged.

"I'll see you in Nashville, Hoss!"

Patsy and Randy crossed the street. Then Patsy turned, waved, and said, "Donn! Goodbye, Hoss. Have a safe trip!"

Upon reflection, Hecht commented, "I can't arrive at any other conclusion than to say logic followed that Patsy and Randy were more than client/manager, and that things hadn't been going well in her marriage. They walked down the street in a way that suggested much more than a business relationship. Perhaps, at last, she had found the man in her life."

Not long after Patsy's single of "Leavin' on Your Mind" and "Tra Le La Le La Triangle" was released on January 7, 1963, Patsy and Loretta spent the day together. "She and Charlie had a fuss. Patsy came over to pick me up, and we were going into town to pick up a bunch of long gowns for Patsy.

"She'd been talking about what was going on between her and Charlie so I said, 'Well, it looks like you're leaving, girl!' And we broke up laughing. She weren't going anywhere. They had their squabbles, but there were pressures from several directions."

After Christmas, Mrs. Hensley said, Patsy spoke quite seriously about divorcing Charlie and had an attorney draw up trust papers for the children.

Charlie refuted this. "That simply wasn't true. Patsy talked about trust funds for the children and I agreed, but we never got around to it. I told her, 'Heck, we've got plenty of time. We can do it the next time you have a breather.' And if Patsy was considering a divorce, she had a funny way of showing it. She wanted me with her constantly, and I was there."

Jean Shepard summed up, "I heard the rumors. I wasn't privy to Patsy's confidences, but that was never the case. To say it was the happiest marriage in the world would be telling a lie. When you see people day in and day out, you get a gut feeling. And Patsy was trying to have another baby. We had the same doctor, Homer M. Pace. One day he was telling me, 'That Cline woman has some temper! You know, Virginia Dick.' I said, 'Oh, Patsy.' He went on, 'She came in here and couldn't be bothered waiting. She had an appointment and demanded to be seen immediately. I told her I'd be with her as soon as I could. And she waited.'

"Dr. Pace finished examining me, and as I was about to leave, he said, 'And if you see Patsy, tell her to come in as soon as she can. That dame has the most screwed-up female problems of anyone I know.' "

In mid- to late January, Patsy and Charlie were returning in the car from an engagement. "Jackie DeShannon came on the radio singing the old Bob Wills song 'Faded Love,'" Charlie recalled. "I thought Patsy was in the back asleep, but she popped up, scaring the devil out of me. She said, 'Everybody's modulating down these days. I wonder why Jackie did it?' I told her, 'Probably the song's not in her key. If it's too high for her, it would be hard to do without bringing it down.'

" 'Oh, no, it wouldn't,' she replied. 'I can do it.' I answered, 'Oh, you can, huh?' She said, 'Yep. I sure as hell can.' "

On January 15 Patsy did an armed forces broadcast on "Country Music Time" that is telling in its content. Delivering a moving rendition of "Leavin' on Your Mind," she followed it with "Tennessee Waltz." After the recruitment pitch, she warmly introduced new artist Clyde Bevis, who sang "Still Loving You." Patsy then made a special comment about the musicians, singling out "ol' Lightnin'" Chance. For her finale, she sang her favorite, the old gospel hymn, "Life's Railroad to Heaven," accompanied by the Jordanaires.

Life is like a mountain railroad
With an engineer that's brave.
We must make the run successful
From the cradle to the grave.

Watch the curves, the hills and tunnels;
Never falter, never fail.
Keep your hands upon the throttle
And your eyes upon the rail.

Blessed Savior, Thou will guide us
'Till we reach that blissful shore
Where the angels wait to join us
In that great forever more.

As she signed off, tears ran down her face.

From February 4 through February 7 she recorded. Bradley surrounded his star with his brigade of regulars—Floyd Cramer, piano; Harold Bradley, electric bass; and Grady Martin, electric guitar; and the Jordanaires. Randy, as usual, played guitar. The producer used ten violins instead of the usual six or seven. Again he brought musician Bill McElhiney in to arrange.

Patsy called Jan Howard Monday morning to ask her if she was coming to the studio. "I don't honestly know," Jan replied. "But I don't think so."

"Why not, damnit?" Patsy assailed her.

"I've got things I need to take care of, and, really, Patsy, I don't want to bug you when you're working."

"Ah, shit, Hoss, bug me!"

"Are you sure?"

"Oh, God, yes! I'd kinda like to have you there."

Jan and Harlan attended along with Dottie.

That first night Patsy recorded "Faded Love"; the Jimmie Hodges classic for the Mills Brothers in 1946, "Someday (You'll Want Me to Want You)"; and the 1931 standard "Love Letters in the Sand," a 1957 hit for Pat Boone.

Charlie, whose printing plant job was nearby, dropped into the Quonset hut studio on his supper break. As soon as he walked in, Bradley urgently waved for him to come to the control room.

"I want you out of here!" Bradley said loudly.

"What did I do? I just got here," replied Charlie.

"You and Patsy have a fight or something?"

"No. Why? What's the matter?"

"I don't know, but she's cried on every song she's done. I *don't* want to break the mood. I don't want her to see you, so get out of here." Charlie left.

"When Patsy finished her takes of 'Faded Love,'" Jan commented, "I couldn't talk. It was common politeness to say something nice. But I was spellbound, dumbfounded. When Patsy sang, she got you right in the gut, but never more than that night on that song. She sang it straight from the heart. It gave me cold chills. I stood there in awe of her."

The following day, Patsy cut the session's token country-sounding tune, Bill Monroe's "Blue Moon of Kentucky"; did her classic swoon rendition of Don Gibson's "Sweet Dreams (of You)," already a hit for the writer and Faron Young; and Irving Berlin's "Always."

The next day's tracks were "Does Your Heart Beat for Me?," cowritten by Russ Morgan and Mitchell Parrish in 1936; and the ever-popular Hughie Cannon standard "Bill Bailey, Won't You Please Come Home," which Patsy gave a new dimension with her sexy, slow build.

Teddy Wilburn found Patsy in Bradley's office about 10:30 and, after listening to the playback, asked Patsy about Las Vegas. She took photos out of her purse and showed him.

"But," Teddy probed, "you haven't told me how it went."

"It was fine," she said. "We knocked 'em out, Hoss. Knocked 'em out!"

"Did you do what I told you?"

"There weren't no problems. Things came off real well, *but* I ain't going back!"

The new songs came the following day: Harlan Howard's "He Called Me Baby" and "You Took Him Off My Hands"; "Crazy Arms"; and "I'll Sail My Ship Alone."

"At the end of the session," Jan noted, "Patsy complimented the Jordanaires on a great job and, for once, was actually elated at how well things had gone. Afterward, as we went through the champagne ritual of listening to the playback in Owen's office, Patsy went into Harry Silverstein's office—he was Owen's assistant and a Decca producer who died very young—and came out with a forty-five rpm record."

Patsy said, "Well, here it is." She held up the record.

"What are you talking about?" asked Owen.

"The record."

"What record?" inquired Jan.

"Here's 'A Church, a Courtroom and Then Goodbye.' It's the first and the last."

"Oh, Patsy, don't say that," Jan scolded.

"Hoss, what I mean is here's the first record that came out and here we are listening to the last one. What a difference!"

Jordanaire Gordon Stoker pointed out, "From some of the strange things Patsy said, I didn't think she was planning on being around long. It went back to a coupla things. During 'Crazy' she walked in on her crutches and said, 'Fellas, the third time is charmed.' I asked her, 'What in the world are you talking about? You've got a cat's nine lives!' We all laughed, and Patsy got to talking about an illness when she was ten, about the car wreck she survived, and said again, 'The third time is charmed. The third time I go. It'll be all she wrote!'"

On February 9, Patsy was one of three featured guests on the 10:45–11:00 segment of the Opry, hosted by Cowboy Copas, who sang two of his famous recordings, "Alabam" and "Signed, Sealed and Delivered." Patsy, with Randy on guitar and Lightnin' Chance on bass, performed "Bill Bailey, Won't You Please Come Home."

Two nights later, an incident involving Pearl Butler showed Patsy's fragile state. For years, Pearl had sung only at Sunday gatherings. Admirers of her raw, natural talent encouraged her—after a few drinks and eating all her food—to sing more often. When she finally grew tired of being a tag-along on husband Carl's shows, she moved into the show business arena to duets with Carl and eventually even a solo spot (though several who loved her dearly described her voice as "one of the worst in country music history").

"We were booked to do our first tour together, a two-week tour in California," Pearl said. "Carl had costumes. I didn't. Goldie Hill[2] told me, 'Patsy don't want her costumes no more. Why don't you call her and see what she's gonna do with 'em. I think she's planning on giving 'em away.' I figured if she was gonna be giving things away, I might as well be on the receiving end.

"We were in Goodlettsville at Les and Dot Leverett's—he's the WSM/Grand Ole Opry photographer—not far from Patsy, so I called. I told her, 'Hon, I ain't got nothing to wear, and I can't let Carl out-spangle me! Could you let me borrow a couple of your old things?'"

Patsy got real angry. Pearl had to hold the receiver from her ear. "Listen,

2. The Decca star from the Louisiana Hayride. After marrying country star Carl Smith, she retired to their quarterhorse and cattle ranch.

Pearl," she admonished her. "I'm ashamed of you for even thinking you have to ask! Get your tail over here and we'll go through the closets and see what we can come up with. But, I have to warn you, my things are old and pretty worn. But if you see anything you like, it's yours!"

Pearl felt funny going to Nella Drive by herself and couldn't get anyone to go with her. Finally, a friend said she'd go. The women arrived about twenty minutes later. They drove down the driveway to enter Patsy and Charlie's music room from the patio. As they got out of the car, they heard loud voices. Patsy's mood had changed drastically. Charlie and Randy were in the room along with Julie and little Randy. The kids were screaming and crying. Patsy was alternately castigating Charlie and the children.

"What kind of goddamn man are you?" she rebuked Charlie. "Don't you have any balls?"

"Patsy," replied Charlie, "I'm sorry."

"You sure are!"

To the friend, it was obvious Patsy and Charlie had been drinking. When the kids, in the middle of the floor surrounded by all manner of toys, tried to escape the commotion, Patsy grabbed them by the sleeve and shouted, "Where are you going, damnit? Didn't I tell y'all to stay put? And shut that crying up!"

The visitors edged closer to the open door.

"You no-good mother!" ranted Patsy. "A simple thing like I asked and you can't do it. Must I depend on Randy for everything?"

As the women began creeping back to the car to leave, Julie saw Pearl and got up.

"Young lady, what'd I just tell you?"

Julie, crying, pointed to the door.

"What?" Patsy wanted to know.

"Mommy, Auntie Pearl."

Patsy spun around, and suddenly it became quiet.

"Oh, howdy, Pearl!"

"Patsy, hon, if we've come at a bad time—"

"Naw! Y'all come on in! We was just having a little business meeting. Some things needed straightening out."

It was all smiles. Patsy brushed past Charlie and took Pearl and her friend upstairs to her huge closet.

"Pearl, you can have anything you want," Patsy offered, opening the closet. "I'm real proud of 'em 'cause Mama made them." Pearl picked out six outfits.[3]

"Is that all you want?"

"Oh, honey, it's more than enough. They'll do me fine. I don't know how to thank you."

Patsy slapped Pearl across the back and exclaimed, "Now, Hoss, don't go and get sentimental on me. You of all folks don't have to thank me. I'm glad I can do something for you. You can have 'em all—boots and everything."

"Oh no, Patsy, I couldn't."

"I don't know why not."

3. She donated these to the Country Music Hall of Fame in 1981.

"Thank you so much, but I really just couldn't."

Patsy gave Pearl a tight squeeze and said, "I'm so happy you're making your dream come true."

"Wish me luck!" Pearl replied.

"I do, but you won't need it. Just go out there and be Pearl!"

They said their good-byes.

"All the way home I couldn't get that scene out of my mind," Pearl sighed. "It was pitiful and sad, not the type of thing you'd ever want to see again. I felt such deep pain for Patsy and Charlie."

The friend told Pearl, "That was the most awful woman I've ever seen in my life! Please don't ever ask me to go back to that house again!"

Several times that winter, Ralph Emery tried to interview Patsy when she dropped by his all-night WSM radio program, but it never worked. "Patsy would be with Charlie and some of their buddies. It was around midnight and they'd be cutting up and making inside jokes. It was frustrating. I was at the end of the party. But this particular Wednesday night [February 13], Patsy dropped in by herself. She and I began rapping, and it was really good. We covered the spectrum of her career, and she was real down, but in a talkative mood.

"She told me, 'I played hard, but I worked hard.' I kick myself every time I think about not rolling the tape. But my previous attempts to interview Patsy had been disasters."

Music publisher Al Gallico, a friend of Patsy's since before Arthur Godfrey, was in town that weekend. "I saw Patsy and Charlie at the Opry and they invited me over to their new home for a party. Randy and I got to talking about road dates. He was bragging about his plane. I told him, 'Hey, do me a favor, please. Give up that shitbox you fly in before something happens.' He shot back, 'Hey, Al, don't worry. I don't take chances.'"

The following Friday, Billy Walker worked a country package show with Patsy in Lima, Ohio. "Charlie and Randy were on that trip, and we were talking about the benefit the next weekend in Kansas City for Cactus Jack Call. Charlie'd been drinking quite a bit, and he became quite abusive to Patsy. It got so embarrassing, Randy and I tried to do something, but you just had to hope Charlie'd go off by himself.

"The next night in Toledo the whole show was simply Patsy and the orchestra. It wasn't unusual for Patsy to play a country gig one night and then turn around and do a pop concert the next, all in the same area. I was coming along to be in the audience. It was a two-hour program, and Patsy came to Randy and said, 'What do I do?'

"She could have done it—before the accident. Since then she'd been plagued with aches, pains, and headaches. She'd get so nervous, she'd stop what she was doing and go rest. I asked, 'You want me to help out?' I had some pop crossover, especially with 'Charlie's Shoes.' Patsy replied, 'Hoss, would you?' I told her, 'Sure. You don't need to ask.' I opened for an hour, then she did an hour and fifteen minutes.

"Afterward, we waited and waited as Patsy posed for pictures and signed autographs. We kept looking at our watches. Finally, I said, 'Well, are you coming or are we gonna have to stay here till you sign autographs for every last person in the hall?'"

En route to dates in Massachusetts after Toledo, Randy reminded Patsy that she still hadn't done her taxes. She told him she was preparing everything—which meant she was "trying to force the top down on my shoe box of receipts and bills." Patsy wanted to know if she could deduct the expense of her new dresses and gowns. In the hotel Sunday morning before she was scheduled to leave, Patsy wrote Herman Longley, her cousin and a public accountant in Elkton, Virginia, that she desperately needed his help. She wrote, "I've got this benefit to do in Kansas City, but as soon as I get home I'm picking up Charlie and the kids and heading to Winchester. I'm bringing everything you'll need to do my taxes, but I'm warning you now it will take you and two Philadelphia lawyers to figure this mess out."

On Wednesday, February 27, Patsy dropped in to visit Trudy Stamper at WSM Radio. "She sat in my office and told me all about the last session. She was so excited about what she'd accomplished. At the time, we had a group of senior citizens on a tour of the station. They were in Studio C, and I asked Patsy if she wouldn't like to go in and sing for them. She said, 'Sure. I'd love to. You think they'd like "Bill Bailey"?' I replied, 'Yes, of course they would. That would be great.'

"Patsy went into the studio. Everyone made such a fuss over her. I'll never forget how those folks gathered around, showering her with love and affection. It was beautiful, and for a brief moment I realized why Patsy wanted so desperately all those years to be a star. She had so much to give and loved the recognition. After she signed autographs and posed for pictures, without any rehearsal or anything, she just sang. And sang her heart out and with lots of soul."

Teddy Wilburn recalled the next day. "Patsy had a seamstress make some drapes for Loretta and Mooney's little Goodlettsville farmhouse. She'd also had two of those big ottomans made to resemble a pair of dice. Patsy surprised them and helped Loretta put the drapes up. The ottomans were late coming in, and she planned on delivering them another time."

Loretta recounted the story of that evening: "Patsy called me and Mooney and asked us to come over to listen to the sessions she'd just completed a bit over a week ago. We got up out of bed and went over. She was all excited and proud. Patsy told us, 'Now, I want y'all to listen to this and see if you think maybe I'm getting out a little too far from country.' Patsy had been worried about that. Me and Doo sat in Patsy and Charlie's music room and listened to the tapes as Patsy embroidered a tablecloth. Her little boy Randy was on a rocking horse.

"When the tape finished, I told her, 'No, Patsy, it's beautiful.' What else could you say? That's what it was. It was fantastic! But, of course, Patsy was fifteen to twenty years ahead of her time in her singing and her music.

"Patsy told me she'd give me fifty dollars if I'd go with her on that Kansas City benefit date Sunday, but I told her, 'I have a date Saturday that pays seventy dollars, so I better go on and take that one.' We made plans to go shopping when she returned from the weekend. Just before we left her house around midnight Patsy said she had something for me. Then she gave me some long dangly sparkling earrings and a whole big box filled with clothes.

"When we went out to the car through the music room, I said to Doo, 'Oh, I forgot to say good-bye to Patsy.' He told me, 'Well, hurry up and go ahead and tell her. It's midnight and we need to be going.' I set the box down on the hood of Patsy and Charlie's Cadillac and went back in. I hugged her and kissed her and as I went back out the door Patsy hauled off and hit me a little bit. She said, 'We're gonna stick together, aren't we gal?' That was the last time I saw Patsy."

You didn't say no to Harry "Hap" Peebles, the Midwest's largest and best-known show promoter. He took care of the acts he booked, was honest and, as a founding member of the Country Music Association, respected. And this was a good cause. Since 1956, Jack Wesley "Cactus Jack" Call was Kansas City's most popular deejay. In January 1963, he was the driving force behind station KCMK-FM switching to an all-country format. Days later he lay unconscious at St. Joseph's Hospital after his car collided with a transport truck. On January 25, he died, leaving a wife, two young sons, and little money.

Peebles contacted Hawkshaw Hawkins and Billy Walker, devoted friends of Call's, to ask if they'd organize a benefit. "Anything for Cactus Jack," Hawkins told him. "He always went overboard for us." In 1961 Peebles was Hawkins' best man at his marriage to Jean Shepard onstage in Wichita before a performance headlining Tex Ritter.

Walker phoned Randy, for assistance. "Sure," Randy pledged. "What can I do?"

"Get Patsy."

"My God, how can I do that when she's in such demand?"

The date was set for Sunday, March 3 at the Kansas City, Kansas, Memorial Auditorium. An impressive array of artists signed on: Roy Acuff; Randy's father-in-law, Cowboy Copas; Opry favorites Wilma Lee and Stoney Cooper with their Clinch Mountain Clan; George Jones; Dottie West; Opry announcer and WSM deejay Ralph Emery; Hawkins; and Walker.

In mid-February, with few tickets sold, Peebles was frantic. He asked Walker, "Since Patsy was such a favorite of Cactus Jack's, won't she do it?"

Walker pleaded with Randy. "But that weekend," Randy explained, "we're in New Orleans on Friday and Birmingham on Saturday. You know how important her Sundays are."

When Randy asked Patsy, she replied, "Hoss, if you can get us there, I'll do it."

"Well, Miss Cline, ain't you forgetting we got a plane? That ole Comanche will get us there with time to spare."

Patsy's Birmingham date was booked as "I Fall to Pieces" hit the charts, two shows for four hundred dollars. Then the promoter canceled. He rebooked when the song was number one, still offering only four hundred—"take it or leave it." Randy took it. The date was canceled again. When the promoter called a third time to rebook, Patsy had "Crazy" and "She's Got You" on the charts. Randy asked for five thousand dollars and settled for three.

MARCH 2

Patsy, Randy, and Charlie left New Orleans in the four-seater after breakfast. They arrived in Birmingham to find the two shows sold out and five hundred waiting outside. Tex Ritter, Charlie Rich, Jerry Lee Lewis, and Flatt & Scruggs were also on the bill. The promoter wanted Patsy to do a third show.

"Hell, no!" said Randy. "Not at this price."

"I gotta have Patsy. How much?"

"Another thousand."

"I can't do it."

"Hoss, what's the problem?" Patsy wanted to know.

"He wants another show but won't pay," Randy replied.

"What do the others say?"

"They'll do it," replied the promoter.

"If everyone else's going to," said Patsy, "I'll do it."

Randy was furious but held his tongue until the promoter left. "Goddamnit, Patsy. This ain't no way to do business! He's making big bucks, why shouldn't we be paid?"

"Did you see the look on his face?" she asked. "He was desperate. We'll get it back double the next time. He's always treated us right. He'll come through. Just you wait and see."

Mr. and Mrs. Bill Holcombe of Alabaster, Alabama, were at the show. "I first saw Patsy on Arthur Godfrey and heard all her records," Helen Holcombe said, "and I wanted to see her. With two babies, we were barely able to scrape together the money for tickets. My mother-in-law babysat the oldest, but we had to take our one-year-old. When we got to the auditorium, I asked Bill to buy me a Patsy Cline photograph so I could get it autographed. He said, 'Honey, we can't afford it.' I didn't push. I knew I was lucky to get the tickets.

"For me, the show began when Patsy came on. She wore a beautiful white dress with rhinestones and, at the waist, she had this huge rhinestone brooch. She sang all her hits, but when she did 'Walkin' After Midnight,' the place went wild. When she finished, Patsy got a standing ovation."

"Any of you gals have weight problems?" asked Patsy. There was a loud roar. "I been busy trying to lose weight and this is the first time in a long time I've been able to wear white." She said how much weight she had lost and the audience applauded. "I'm a-telling you! Don't it just look good? Of course, now I got another problem. I can't look any food in the eye."

At the end, Patsy quieted everyone. She was genuinely touched by their response. "I've really had a good time with you," she said. "God love you! I've done a lot of things that I'm not happy about, and, in the short time God gives us on this earth, I'm doing something about changing all that. I sure do appreciate you sticking with me and buying my records. Y'all been good to ole Patsy!" The audience applauded and jumped to their feet.

"In spite of my child squirming," said Mrs. Holcombe, "it was an evening I've never forgotten. And Bill's never forgotten he didn't get me that photo. I kid him all the time, 'It was only a dollar!'"

After the third show, as Patsy, Charlie, and Randy were leaving, the promoter handed Randy an envelope with a thousand dollars in it. "There," he said, smiling, "you got what you wanted. Thanks for coming through."

Charlie reported that Patsy gave Randy "a look that had 'I told you so' written all over it!"

That same night in Brunswick, Maryland, Bill Peer and his Melody Boys took an intermission at the Moose Lodge. Peer said hello to Fay Crutchley.

"Oh, God, Bill, I miss Patsy," Fay sighed. "Don't you?"

"Sure I do!" he replied.

"Have you heard from her?"

"Are you serious? As far as I'm concerned, Miss Patsy Cline can fall to pieces!"

MARCH 3

The lights went on early that Sunday morning at 4413 GraMar Lane in the Inglewood section of east Nashville. Kathy Hughes received a call from Randy late Saturday to let her know the plane would arrive around 8:00 A.M. at Cornelia Fort Air Park. Walker took a commercial flight to Kansas City Saturday after the Opry. Hawkins, who hated flying, would take his place in the Comanche but come back on his return ticket. Hawkins and Jean Shepard lived a few blocks away, so he came to the Hughes's house to meet Cowboy Copas.

"While Mother and I prepared fried chicken for everyone to eat on the plane," said Kathy, "Hawk and Dad sat in the middle of the kitchen floor, having the time of their lives with our son Larry's gyroscope."

Kathy and her mother got Larry ready for services at Grace Baptist Church, then drove to the airfield. Soon they spotted Randy's plane.

"While Randy refueled," Kathy explained, "Patsy and Charlie told us how well Birmingham had gone and gave Dad regards from Tex Ritter. I gave Patsy a bag with the chicken and a loaf of white bread. She took a piece and joked, 'Can't think of the last time I had fried chicken for breakfast!' Charlie had the weekend receipts and stayed to take care of business. Dad and Hawk got on the plane."

Patsy had stayed in touch all weekend with her maid. Little Randy was running a fever when she left for New Orleans and she was still worried. She asked Charlie to head straight home. Good-byes were exchanged and Randy taxied off a little after nine. He flew northwest, crossed the Mississippi River, and landed at approximately 12:30 P.M. at Fisher Flying Service, Kansas City, Missouri.

There were shows at 2:00, 5:15, and 8:15. Now Patsy had a cold and was exhausted, but there was time enough only to check in at the Town House Hotel, change, and get to the auditorium, which was three blocks away. As they arrived, Anne Call was thanking the artists for their loyalty and introducing them to her children. She asked to meet Acuff and Peebles told her he had missed his flight.

"He told me his wife, Mildred, got this funny feeling about his making the trip, so she didn't wake him." Emery, too, canceled at the last minute because of prior commitments.

Peebles began the show with a tribute to Call: "Cactus Jack earned a reputation as one of country and western music's great Midwestern voices. The entertainers of this Grand Ole Opry show are here because of the respect and affection they felt for him. It doesn't seem right doing a country show without Cactus Jack in his western shirt and string tie interviewing and bringing on the stars. Rest assured, Jack is with us in spirit as we celebrate his memory and dedication to country music."

A festive mood filled the hall. Avid fan Marie Kerby was there: "As they waited to go on, I visited with Billy, whom I'd known three years, Patsy, Hawkshaw, Cowboy, Dottie, and everyone. Fans weren't allowed backstage, so when we'd spot one of the artists we'd run down the hall that led to the stage to say hello. I rushed over to Patsy. In spite of her success, she was [still] the sweet person I'd met two years ago.

"Although she'd flown from Birmingham and Nashville and had been up since early morning, Patsy didn't seem tired. She posed for pictures, talked about her next album, which she told us was her best one yet. When she spoke about Las Vegas, she insisted, 'I definitely don't like Vegas. I never worked so hard in my life. I dread the thought of going back, but it's one of the necessary evils of being in show business.'"

Marie noted that Copas was the most introverted of the stars. "But when he and the others weren't on, they stood on the sidelines and applauded, cheered, and whistled like the rest of us. During the intermission, Hawkshaw even took his guitar and played for some of us. When it came time for him to do his new record 'Lonesome 7-7203,' he didn't know all of it. At the second show he apologized and said, 'I found a copy of the lyrics in my wallet.' The audience went wild. He had George McCormick of the Clinch Mountain Clan stand next to him and hold the paper as he sang.

"Hawk's main topic of conversation was about Jean and their baby, Don Robin, whom they'd named after Don Gibson and Marty Robbins. He described his trick horses and how he'd just built a darkroom in his basement to develop pictures. Then he took pictures of us. Hawk said Jeanie was expecting another baby 'any minute.'"

Patsy felt awful and complained to Randy, "The way you froze us in that plane only made me worse." Peebles prepared a place for Patsy to rest between shows but, with so many fans wanting to meet her, she barely got to sit down.

"Patsy and me sat in the dressing room after the second show," Dottie said. "She was ironing the blouse she had worn with a lace dress her mother made. I said, 'Why don't you let me do that and you get some rest? You already have a bad cold, and you know how easily you get tired.' But Patsy wouldn't listen. That night she closed the show. I never missed the opportunity to watch Patsy perform, but I didn't stand in the wings. I went out front and saw the whole set. As usual, Patsy was magnificent. She never gave an audience short shrift. No matter how late it was or if the show was running overtime, she did all her big songs."

She sang "She's Got You," "Heartaches," "Am I A Fool?" and, from her February sessions, "Sweet Dreams" and "Faded Love." Then she chatted with the audience.

"I've got the flu," she apologized. "I think I caught it in New Orleans Friday night. It ain't getting better, so don't be disappointed if my singing's not up to par."

Patsy sang "I Fall to Pieces" and "Crazy." Marie remembers Patsy pressing a finger to her right ear when she was reaching for high notes. She closed with her favorite song from the last session, "I'll Sail My Ship Alone."

"She had the audience on their feet screaming for more," Dottie remembered. "I was in this ocean of humanity pouring their heart out to Patsy the same way she'd done for them. She was moved to tears and thanked them. Patsy said how much they meant to her and that she'd be nowhere without them."

Randy planned to leave immediately, but KCMK-FM was hosting a press party. Peebles told him it was important for all of them to be there. Departure was put off until Monday morning.

MARCH 4

It was bitter cold. Bad news was the omen of the day. There'd been intermittent rain storms throughout the evening. Randy awoke to rain and dark clouds, then he got word that Fairfax Municipal Airport was fogged in and their morning flight would have to be scratched.

During the night, Billy Walker's phone rang. His dad had had a heart attack. He phoned Hawkins to tell him, "They don't expect him to live. Randy doesn't know when we'll be able to leave and I've got to get home as soon as possible. Can I talk you into going back in Randy's plane and letting me have that airline ticket?"

Hawkins met Walker a few minutes later and gave him the ticket, saying, "Kid, I wouldn't do this for anybody else. I hope your dad pulls through."

Patsy was stirring in her room, irritated after Randy's call informing her of the delay. Her flu was no better. She'd coughed most of the night. She desperately wanted a cigarette but knew it would make her cough worse. Her phone rang.

"Yeah?" It was Dottie. "Hello, Hoss! Cheer me up. Ain't heard nothing but bad news."

"This'll cheer you up. Hap's going to buy everyone breakfast!"

"Sister, I couldn't eat a thing."

"At least come and have coffee."

Patsy put on a wig and tried to make herself presentable.

"Hap, don't expect me to be cheery," she said to Peebles in the coffee shop when he greeted her. "I'm sick as a dog, but when I heard you was buying, I couldn't miss it."

Everyone was stunned when Peebles announced that only three thousand dollars had been raised. Dottie recalled someone exclaiming, "It looks like somebody had their hand in the till." Peebles promised to recheck the proceeds.

Dottie tried to entertain her but could see Patsy's heart wasn't in making conversation. "Hon, what's bothering you?" she asked.

"We can't take off. The airport's fogged in! Randy has no idea when we'll be able to leave. Goddamn! This would happen when I'm in a hurry to get home."

"What's the hurry?"

"I miss my babies. I haven't seen them in three days."

"I know what you mean. I miss my boys."

"Little Randy's sick, and I don't like leaving him for long periods. And I got to get back to take care of that business with the lawyer."

"If that's what's worrying you, why don't you drive back with Bill and me?"

"You mean it, Dottie?"

"Get your things. We'll be leaving in about twenty minutes."

"Let me find Randy and get packing."

Dottie yelled to her husband, Bill West, "Patsy's going back with us."

Bill asked Hawkins if he wanted to return by car. "I do and I don't," he replied. "I hate to see Randy and Cowboy go back alone, but if it won't be too crowded."

"You can stretch out in front and the girls can have the back," Bill said.

"You got a deal!" Hawkins went to find Randy.

About ten minutes later, Patsy and Dottie met at the elevator. They got in with their bags and Dottie pushed the button. When the doors opened to the lobby, Patsy leaned over to pick up her suitcase, then suddenly blurted out, "Naw. Forget it. I'll wait it out with Randy. I think I'll get home quicker."

Hawkins arrived in the lobby. "Where're your bags, Hawk?" asked Bill West.

"I've changed my mind," he replied. "I'm going to wait it out." He put his arm around West. "Heck, this stuff's gonna lift and we'll beat y'all home." Bill gave him a hug.

Dottie attempted to change Patsy's mind, but Patsy said she felt a loyalty to Randy.

"I don't want y'all riding in that small plane in this weather," Dottie told her. "It might crash."

"Don't fret."

"I can't help it. I'll be worried."

"Hoss, don't worry about me 'cause when it comes my time to go, I'm going. If that little bird goes down, I guess I'll go down with it."

"Sure you won't change your mind?"

"Sister, you know my mind!"

The two hugged and kissed. "And that's the way we said our last good-byes," Dottie sighed.

An hour later, as Peebles left the hotel, he ran into Randy, Patsy, and company loading their luggage. "Where y'all going?" he inquired. "I thought you were grounded."

Randy said, "It's starting to clear. We're going to the field so we can take off as soon as the airport opens."

They exchanged farewells and drove to the airfield where owner Eddie Fisher apprised Randy of the weather bulletins warning small craft against flying.

"I thought for a minute," Fisher stated, "he'd attempt to fly in that weather. In the end, he decided against it and they headed back to the hotel."

As soon as she got into her room, Patsy called home and spoke with four-year-old Julie, who wanted to know when she'd be back. Then she talked with Charlie about little Randy. "Is he any better?"

"He still has a fever," Charlie told her, "and is crying a lot. He misses his mommy."

"His mommy misses him, too. We're going to get out of here as soon as the weather clears, but no one knows when that'll be. I'll let you know what we do. Charlie, if the baby gets any worse, call a doctor." She ended the conversation as she always did, "Well, I'll catch you later."

That night Patsy confronted Randy. "Country music, they keep saying, isn't a business but something that's in your blood. That's a crock of shit! And I'm going to kick the next person who tells me that. I want some time off."

"After this, you got almost two weeks!"

"I'm talking something longer. I think you remember our previous conversation."

"Hey, Patsy!"

"No, Randy. It's my career! Look at me. I'm making the dough and not having a goddamn minute to enjoy any of it. The baby's home sick and I'm stuck in Kansas City. And you shoulda heard Julie crying on the phone—"

"Are you feeling guilty again?"

"Things just ain't right."

"Look at it the other way! At what you're giving those kids. And tell me how the hell can you lay off when 'Leavin' On Your Mind' is climbing the charts and you're gonna have two, maybe three singles from the last session. You worry too much. Just let me handle everything."

"You have been and look at the mess you've got us in!"

"Hell, even I can't predict the weather!"

"Driving home," Dottie said, "I kept thinking of what Patsy said about if that little bird goes down, she'd be going down with it. It was raining like it would never stop. It was a thick, murky rain. Sometimes Bill and I couldn't see the tops of the telephone poles. I kept repeating to myself, 'Now, I hope they don't get crazy and decide to try to leave in this weather.' I must have driven Bill insane saying, 'Honey, you do think they'll wait, don't you?' and 'I wonder how the weather is back in Kansas City?'

"Even with both of us driving, it took sixteen hours. Bill's mother was staying with us, taking care of the children. We hardly got in the door good before we said good night. We were exhausted. I lay in bed wondering what time Patsy and Randy had gotten back. I wanted to call but I figured she was sleeping, too."

MARCH 5

Early that Tuesday Patsy called her mother. "Here I am still in Kansas City. The fog's cleared but there're thunderstorms all over the place. Seems every time I stick my neck out, I get my foot into something else." They discussed the benefit and the pittance raised. "Nobody knows what happened. We worked for nothing but expenses and it looks like the wrong person got helped."

She told Mrs. Hensley little Randy was having another bronchitis attack and how both children were crying.

"Don't you go worrying about the kids," Mrs. Hensley advised.

"Mama, I can't help it."

"I know, but Charlie will make sure everything's fine."

"Charlie?"

"No matter what, when it comes to the children you can depend on him. He loves them as much as you. I want to know how you are."

"I think the worst of my flu's gone. I just want to get out of here. It may not be until this afternoon. If I'd gone with Dottie, I'd be home now. I miss my babies!"

"Don't y'all take any chances."

"We won't, Mama. My next date's March sixteenth in Baltimore. Just think, eleven whole days to rest and to spend with the kids."

"You sound like you need it. Now, call me before you leave. If I don't hear from you, I'll know you're still there."

"Okay. I'll catch you later."

Just before noon, the group checked out of the hotel. Back at the airfield, Randy talked on the phone to the weather bureau. "There'd been a clearing in our area," Fisher reported, "but there was bad weather at Springfield, throughout the river and lake region south of Vichy and along the Mississippi from St. Louis down. But Hughes said to get the plane ready."

When the group boarded, seating arrangements were discussed. "Patsy, I know the co-pilot's seat's always yours," Randy said, "but Hawk's too tall for the back."

"I don't like it any more than you, honey," said Hawkins, "'cause the less I see the better I'll enjoy the flight! But it's these long legs."

But they didn't go anywhere. The plane's window kept fogging up from moisture from their breath. "Okay, everybody," Patsy said, laughing, "there's one way we can make it home. You gotta hold your breath!"

The four went to Fisher's office, sat and talked. "They were full of life," he noted. "Nice, down-to-earth people. Hawkins and Copas asked if I had any parachutes. I told them, 'Yeah, but they're old, and y'all better not fly into anything where you'll need one.'"

A half hour later, Randy tried again but it was no go. When the temperature warmed a bit, he tried once more. "This is it!" he yelled. Hawkins phoned Jean Shepard and Randy called Kathy. "We're on the way," he told her.

Hughes seemed levelheaded to Fisher. Still, he advised him, "If the weather gets bad, turn around. We don't want another casualty like the one Sunday. Someone crashed into the side of a bluff between St. Joe and Omaha."

"I won't fly into anything bad," he replied.

"I sure as hell hope not," Hawkins bellowed.

Randy declared, "If I can't handle it, I'll come back and fly west or go someplace else."

The takeoff at 1:30 P.M. went smoothly. The flight distance to Nashville from Kansas City is five hundred statute miles. The Piper Comanche could clock a hundred and twenty miles an hour.

Randy kept in contact with weather stations as he traveled across Missouri and down into Arkansas, following a storm front all the way. When conditions got bad, he'd find an airstrip, land, wait for the front to get sufficiently ahead of him, then go on. At Little Rock there was rain and sleet. Randy called Kathy to let her know they were leaving there and would make a final stop in Dyersburg, just across the Mississippi River in Tennessee to refuel. He landed at the Dyersburg Avionics strip at 5:05, only slightly behind schedule. Randy reported his afternoon-long adventure to the manager, Bill Braese.

"The news I have for you isn't much better," Braese told him. "We've had thunderstorms off and on all day. There's flooding in some parts. We're getting all this precipitation because of a front hanging over Kentucky Lake and the Tennessee River."

"I been across there a hundred times," Randy said.

"You'll have that storm right on your path. Get on the horn to the Atlanta weather bureau for an update while I refuel the plane."

The weather in the area was described as "extremely turbulent." According to the Federal Aviation Authority, at least one commercial liner saw fit to change course. The information did not deter Randy.

Mrs. Braese remarked that everyone appeared exhausted but, even under the circumstances, were nice and friendly. In the Dyersburg Airport coffee shop several locals, stopping by for supper, were stunned to find three Opry favorites. No one could remember when there'd been that many stars in town at one time. The trio was asked for autographs on napkins, even on a matchbook cover.

"How much further?" Hawkins inquired as Randy entered.

"I need to discuss the weather with y'all. I don't know if we should chance the flight."

Just before 6:00, Randy called Kathy. "Hey, honey," he told her, "check and see if it's raining there." She said it wasn't. Kathy told him that a beloved musician had died. "The family's asking if Dad can be a pallbearer tomorrow." Randy assured her they'd be home in "no time flat." He asked Kathy to call Cornelia Field so they'd turn on the runway lights.

When Randy hung up, he told Braese, "Everything's going to be all right. You can see the moon and stars in Nashville. It's clear."

Braese took Hughes outside as the sun was setting. "Look to the east. See those dark clouds? Your wife's seeing the eye of the storm. You're going to be fighting high winds. Are you instrument-rated?"

"No."

"Figured that, since you leap-frogged all the way. You shouldn't attempt it in this weather. Take my car or stay the night. Got a nice motel nearby."

"Hell, I've already come this far. It's only another ninety miles. We'll be there before you know it."

"You're taking a chance. I'll bring your plane down tomorrow and pick up the car."

"That's nice of you, but we're going on."

"How long will it take in the car?" Patsy wanted to know.

"Yeah," Hawkins said.

"I'm going to take care," Randy replied. "If I can't handle the situation, I'll turn around."

"The car'll be waiting," Braese told him.

Randy signed the receipt for the gasoline and put his copy in his money bag. There was enough fuel to stay in the air three and a half hours. They taxied off at 6:07 P.M.

Braese was so certain they'd return, he had his wife call a motel and book three rooms. About an hour later, he told her, "They didn't come back. They must have made it."

Randy had no flight plan. He charted his course east toward and across Highways 51 and 45, past Huntington, Bruceton on the Tennessee River, then slightly northeast to Waverly, and on over Nashville to Madison. The winds were high and probably slowed their time considerably. Time was of the essence. It was getting darker and darker. Near Bruceton and the farming region of Camden, some eighty-five miles west of Nashville, he ran into dense clouds over the river and south of Kentucky Lake. Heavy rain rocked the plane. Witnesses reported seeing a plane turning one direction, then another; flying low, then higher. Randy was either trying to find his way back across the river or scouting for a landing spot in a field. There was a twisting rural road amid the woods of these northeastern Tennessee hills, but it was too narrow.

He searched for a highway. Clouds engulfed the plane, but the rain finally stopped. Suddenly, from nowhere, a fire-prevention lookout tower loomed through the cover at the top of a hill. All indications point to the fact that Randy spotted a possible site and was attempting to land.

Sam Webb, whose farm was located nearby, saw a plane circling his home a few minutes before seven. "It was revving up its motor," he recollected, "going fast and then slow, like it was attempting to climb. then I couldn't see it anymore. But I heard these loud thumping noises, then nothing."

As he made his ascent, it's assumed by aviation experts that Randy flew right into a dense cloud. Amid mounting panic from Patsy, Copas, and Hawkins, he undoubtedly became confused, then disoriented. Randy didn't know if he was flying level, upward, or downward. Not trained to read the instrument panel, he desperately tried to make some sense of the numbers and letters in the near-dark.

Trees began coming at them. Randy frantically worked the wheel, left, right; left, right; left, right. The plane swerved violently. The Comanche propeller tore into the trees and sawed off their tops in such a way it's all but certain the plane was flying upside-down. The thick, hard branches grabbed at the tiny craft, tearing gaping holes. One wing and then another was ripped off. The remnants of the plane and its tightly packed passengers and contents bounced and skidded the tree line.

There was no way out. Finally, the plane dove straight into the ground.

The major road Randy was looking for, Highway 70, lay not quite one mile away.

There were no survivors.

When Kathy Hughes hung the phone up after speaking to Randy at Dyersburg, she alerted Charlie and Jean Shepard that the plane was on the way. Then the phone rang.

It was Billy Walker. "I'm really worried about Randy," he told Kathy. "They were supposed to leave yesterday, and they're still not back. Have you heard anything?"

"He just called, Billy. They only just left today and were refueling in Dyersburg. They'll be leaving any minute."

"Thank God. I didn't know what to think."

"I'm on the way to Cornelia Field right now to have them turn on the runway lights."

"Okay. tell 'em I'm happy everything worked out and they made it back safe and sound."

"Thanks, Billy."

Kathy and her mother, Lucille, went to the field about seven and asked to have the lights on. "We sat in the car and waited and waited. It shouldn't have taken Randy more than forty-five minutes to get home. We began to suspect something had gone wrong. We asked the attendant if he'd heard anything. There was no word. Then something snapped in me. I knew immediately something had, indeed, gone wrong. The attendant suggested it might be better if we went home and waited for further news or in case someone was trying to reach us. All we could think of was that Randy might have turned back. Everything but the most obvious thing ran through my mind.

"We came home and turned the radio on. A little after eight, there was a report that the plane was missing. Another said the plane had gone down. The phone started ringing at about eight-fifteen, and it never stopped. Then friends started to come over."

Grant Turner went on WSM: "It pains me greatly to announce that a plane bearing Patsy Cline, Hawkshaw Hawkins, and Cowboy Copas is late arriving at Cornelia Fort Air Park en route from Dyersburg. At this point, the plane is presumed missing. Stay tuned for further bulletins."

Charlie was getting ready to leave to pick up Patsy. "I was playing with the kids. Around seven-thirty, when no one called from the airport to say Randy and the gang had landed, I got worried. I made a couple of calls. Nothing. Then some friends came over around eight. They'd heard the news on the radio."

"An hour after Kathy's call," Jean said, "I took my baby, Don Robin, and put him in the kitchen sink to give him a bath before bed. I was eight months pregnant, so the sink allowed me to stand up. A little after seven this weird, completely weak feeling came over me for about ten minutes. I was afraid to move away from the sink, because I thought I was going to faint. Don was splashing water, but I kept bathing him. My first thought was, 'Oh, my God, the baby!' I froze and held onto the edge of the sink. Then I said out loud, 'No, Jean, the baby's not due for another month. What's the matter with you?'

"A cold sweat broke over me, then it passed, and I said, 'Oh, Hawk, get home pretty soon!' When he wasn't home by nine, I began to get upset."

At 9:10 the phone rang again at the Hughes home. It was the Civil Aeronautics Board office. Randy's departure from Dyersburg had been confirmed from the gasoline receipts. The officer asked who was on board and wanted to confirm the plane's identification number. The CAB was planning to broadcast a search query over the radio to see if Randy responded. Kathy remarked, "After that, I was never contacted by any official spokesperson."

"When it got to be ten," Jean said, "I told myself, for the safety of the baby and my health, I'd better get to bed. I wasn't overly concerned, because Kathy had told me if the weather got bad Randy might turn back to Dyersburg. I was nervous but not upset. I laid in bed and thought, 'Well, maybe they did go back.' Then I fell asleep.

"I woke to the phone ringing. I got out of bed slowly to answer it. I looked at the clock. It was eleven. It was Eileen, one of Hawk's fans from Minneapolis who'd become a friend. I was still half asleep. 'What are you doing, Jean?' she asked. I was a bit upset at being woke up. I replied, 'My God, I'm doing what every sensible person would be doing at eleven o'clock at night. I was sleeping.' She asked, 'Are you in bed?' I told her I was. She wanted to know if I had the radio on. I answered I didn't. Then there was silence. I heard her starting to cry. Eileen said, 'Oh, my God, Jean!' That's when I knew. I knew what was wrong. I knew the plane was down.

"Eileen was so upset I couldn't get her off the phone. I finally said, 'Hon, I'm by myself. I've got to call somebody. Let me get off.' I stayed pretty cool for about an hour. I called Smiley and Kitty Wilson, two of our closest friends in the business, who'd once played and sang for Ferlin Husky. Their line was busy. When I got them, they'd heard from Kathy and were trying to call me. They came right over. It was an all-night vigil. No authorities phoned or came to the house to say, 'Your husband is missing.' It was a nightmare. It was hell!"

The Wilsons called Jean's doctor. He informed them he was on his way. Governor Frank Clement sent a highway patrol car to the houses of each of the families and stationed it there through the night.

Jean explained, "A woman I didn't know walked into the house before the patrolman arrived and started asking me questions. People were milling around the house, and I was in a daze. My doctor finally had to sedate me. He asked the patrolman to stand duty outside my door and not let anyone disturb me. Minnie Pearl and her husband came as soon as they heard. They asked to see me. The patrolman knocked on my door and said, 'Ma'am, I don't know what to do. Minnie Pearl's here to see you. Should I let her in?'

"The doctor was monitoring the baby's heartbeat every half-hour. I asked if it would be all right to see Minnie and Henry, and he said yes. She was pretty broken up. Hawk was one of her dearest friends. It was like that all night."

On Nella Drive, Charlie was awaiting word and jumped each time the phone rang. Julie and Randy kept asking him where their mother was. "Is Mommy coming home tonight?" Julie asked. "She promised me she'd be here. When's she coming?"

Charlie asserted it was a tough situation. "I hadn't given up hope, and I didn't want to burden them. They wouldn't have even understood. I didn't want to lie, either. I didn't know what to say."

MARCH 6

It was just past midnight that Wednesday morning. Jan Howard was sound asleep. The phone woke her.

"Jan?"

"Yes."

"Oh, thank God. Jan, this is Hank [Cochran]. Are you all right?"

"Yeah. I was asleep, Hank."

"Then it's Patsy."

"What are you talking about?"

"If you're all right, then there's something wrong with Patsy."

"Hank, what on earth are you talking about?"

"I'm in Fred Foster's office at Monument [Records], and a few minutes ago two albums fell off the shelf—one of yours and one of Patsy's. I just had a gut feeling that something was wrong."

"Where's Patsy?"

"I don't know. Don't you worry. I'll call you back."

"Hank, please let me know if something's wrong with Patsy."

"I'll talk to you later."

Roger Miller heard the news. "I used to cruise around town in my 'forty-nine Dodge to think and write music. I was everywhere at once. I tuned in to WSM, and Grant Turner was saying that the plane carrying Patsy, Cowboy, Hawk, and Randy was late arriving at Cornelia Fort Air Park and presumed missing. That was about one A.M. They hadn't announced that the plane had crashed, only that it was overdue. Then Grant announced the flying time from Dyersburg to Nashville and pinpointed an area around Camden where a farmer had seen a plane that looked like it was in trouble and may have crashed. A communications check by radio failed to locate the plane or bring any response. The Civil Air Patrol was forming a search party."

Shortly before midnight, a party of fifteen men began a search in a three- to four-mile radius of Sandy Point, a village about four miles west of Camden. The police dispatcher there said several farmers saw or heard a plane circling with its engine cutting out. A few minutes later they heard a strange noise, which sounded like a crash. Most of those phoning in pinpointed the possible crash around one particular object, the fire tower off Mule Barn Road in Sandy Point, approximately five miles west of the Tennessee River.

A discrepancy exists in the exact time of the crash, and no one will ever know the facts. A report listing results of the CAB investigation said that the crash occurred "about 20 minutes after [the plane] took off." But residents who came forward to Sheriff Loyce Furr had placed the crash at another time. R. C. King of Route 2, Camden, told Gerald Henry, the staff correspondent for the *Tennessean*, the next day: "I heard a plane backfire around 7:30, then I heard it hit the bushes." Mossie Miller of Route 1, Camden, stated to Henry: "I heard something pop a little after seven. The dogs ran out. My wife heard a roar and a pop and then nothing." Patsy's watch stopped at 6:20, Randy's at 6:25.

When Miller got word of the search party, "I suddenly realized that I had to go there. The blood came rushing to my head and I speeded around town, going from door to door, trying to get someone to go with me. It was raining, and I had visions of Patsy, Randy, and the guys maybe hanging from the seats, not able to help themselves. Me and another boy, Don, whose last name I can't remember, headed straight there."

Carl Perkins was about to set out fishing when he heard the news. He left his boat and headed for Camden. Since he had priority license plates, he was able to get his car through the police checkpoint. Perkins drove along until he stopped his car in disbelief. "There was Patsy's bloodied red slip hanging from a tree and Hawk's white cowboy hat standing as tall as it would have on his head."

Miller drove north of Camden, out along Highway 70. "Then I stopped. I looked out and there was this farmhouse standing right there. I can see it clearly even now. It was about two-thirty or three o'clock in the morning, but the lights were on. I knocked on the door. A lady opened it and I asked about anything she or her husband might have seen or heard that might be a plane in trouble.

"She told me, 'No, we ain't heard no plane crashing. We been up here watching this storm and seemed to me I heard a noise that sounded like a clap of thunder a few hours ago right here behind the house. I thought it went with the rain.'

"Don and I went running into the woods just a-yelling and a-screaming their names—Patsy! Randy! Hawk! Cowboy!"

At 3:00 A.M., Jan's phone rang. She was awake, tossing, turning, hoping, praying. It was Hank Cochran again.

"Oh, Jan," he told her, "this is horrible. Randy's plane is missing, and he was carrying Patsy, Hawk, and Cowboy Copas. It's been confirmed on the radio."

Jan was stunned. She couldn't speak. The words wouldn't come out.

"Jan. Jan! Are you there? Are you okay?"

"Yes, Hank," she finally replied, "I'm okay. This is quite a blow. I can't believe it. There are no other reports? Where did it happen?"

"Hon, I've got to see what I can do. Turn your radio on. I'll call you if I find out anything else."

Jan kept thinking that somehow there'd been an error. She turned the radio on. The reports didn't say anyone had been killed. "That night will live in my memory forever. I can never forget it. All I could do was pace and pray. Then I thought of Jeanie and realized I had to be with her. Just a day or so before Hawk left for Kansas City, Harlan and I were at their house. We played a game of Crazy Eights until Jeanie, who was big with the baby, became uncomfortable. Hawk took us out to see his show horses and ran them through some tricks."

At 4:00 A.M. in Winchester, Virginia, the phone at the Hensley home rang and rang. Patsy's brother Sam finally ran to answer it.

"Hello. Who is this?" He heard someone talking but wasn't especially attentive. "I'm sorry, what did you say?" It was a friend of the family trying to relay what he'd heard on the radio. "Hey, is this some kind of joke? Patsy's not on any plane. Why don't you go back to sleep?" He slammed the phone down and started back to his room.

"Who was that?" asked Mrs. Hensley, who'd come to the living room.

"Some crackpot!"

The phone rang back at once. Sam grabbed it. "Hey, I told you that Patsy is not on any plane!"

"Wait a minute," exclaimed Mrs. Hensley, snatching the phone from her son's hand. "Patsy *was* on a plane!"

Mrs. Hensley fell into Sam's arms. She was moaning. All sorts of thoughts ran through her mind. She kept saying over and over again, "My God, how can this be, when they waited out the storm?" She turned on the radio. Moments later Joltin' Jim McCoy called her from station WINC to confirm that the plane was missing.

It was now 5:30, and for nearly two hours Roger Miller and his friend Don had been running through the woods yelling at the top of their lungs. "The briar was so bad it had torn our clothes," related Miller, "and we'd been cut here and there. But we kept at it. Then we came to this clearing, and I spotted the fire tower. I climbed to the top and there it was, about twenty yards away. The trees had been chewed up. Debris hung from the branches. I went back to the main road, where the search party was gathering, and informed the highway patrol. An officer asked me to lead the way. As fast as I could, I ran through the brush and the trees, and when I came up over this little rise, oh, my God, there they were."

The Butlers were returning from their California dates. The utility trailer behind their Cadillac was packed with instruments, amplifiers, and Carl and Patsy's costumes.

"I can't tell you, having known Patsy all those years, how proud I was to be wearing those outfits," Pearl said. "I felt like a million dollars on those shows!"

It was about daybreak. The Butlers were almost home, driving through the "Tennessee sticks" in an intense rain and windstorm when Grant Turner played one of their songs. "No matter where we were," Pearl explained, "we'd call the disc jockey at the particular station to thank him for playing our record. They got a kick out of that, and played more of your records! We kept looking for a phone booth, but you could hardly see a thing in front of you.

"'There's one, Carl!' I yelled. 'Pull over so we can call Grant.' He got as close as possible so I wouldn't get wet, but the wind was blowing so bad I could barely get the door open. I dialed the operator, who heard the wind howling. She said, 'Ma'am, if the booth starts to blow over, don't worry about hanging up. Just get out.' I told her I appreciated her advice, but that I'd probably be in it!

"When I got through to Grant, he asked, 'Pearl, where are y'all?' I told him and said, 'What do you wanna know that for? You gonna come meet us for coffee and doughnuts?' He sounded excited. 'Pearl, just whereabouts are you?' I replied, 'Heck, I don't know. Not far from Nashville. Just a minute. Let me yell to Carl.' I yelled, but he didn't hear me. I told Grant, 'Hon, I think we're someplace right outside of Camden. Know where that is?'

"He said, 'That's about where the plane crashed!' My first instinct was to look out of the booth, but I couldn't see noplace. That's how bad the rain was. I asked, 'What plane are you talking about? Who crashed? Somebody we know?' Grant answered, 'Oh, honey, you don't know?' I said, 'Don't I know what?' He told me, 'Yes, you know them.' 'Them?' I asked. And he told me what happened, and I couldn't believe it. The receiver just hung in my hand. I prayed to God it wasn't so. I didn't how how to tell Carl. He loved Hawk and Cowboy and adored Patsy."

Dottie was in a deep sleep. She didn't hear the phone ringing. There was a knocking at the door.

"Grandmother West?"

"Yes, honey."

"Come on in." Dottie was half asleep but could see she was quite upset. "Grandmother West, what's wrong?"

"Oh, Dottie, wake up! Their plane is down!"

"What plane?"

"The plane Randy Hughes was flying. It's crashed, and they think for sure it's the one Patsy's in!"

"Oh, no! That's not possible." She threw the covers back and hurled herself out of bed. "What do you mean?"

"Honey, that plane Patsy, Hawkshaw Hawkins, and Cowboy Copas were coming home in has crashed somewhere up in the hills."

"No, that can't be true. Randy wouldn't do anything foolish!"

Dottie woke her husband, and they turned the radio on. They lived an isolated life in the country. Dottie wanted more information. There had to be survivors. They started making frantic phone calls.

"I had to know," said Dottie. "And, my God, it was true."

When Miller arrived at the crash site, he wanted to turn back. "It was ghastly. The plane had crashed nose-down. It plowed into the earth on this steep hillside. The engine lay at the bottom of a five- or six-foot-wide crater that was filled with water. The explosion people had heard was not from a gasoline explosion. There had been no fire. It was the sound of the plane's impact. It was all twisted metal and pieces of bodies. There was more of Patsy's body left intact than there was of the others. It was a maddening experience. I saw people already picking through the wreckage, and I screamed at them. Souvenir hunters, scavengers! It was impossible to comprehend. Especially when you loved those folks the way I did." Miller surmised that Randy was in the clouds and thought he was climbing at full power and instead was going down.

Published reports in the local press credit members of the search party arriving first at the fire tower and sighting the crash through field glasses. On the ground, however, W. J. Hollingsworth and his twenty-year-old son Jeners, who farmed corn and cotton off Sandy River Road, and Louis and Carl Bradford, who farmed nearby, happened upon the scene.

An investigation lends credence to the fact that the Hollingsworths, Bradfords, and Miller and his friend, because of the fall of the rugged terrain, possibly passed within feet of each other at the same time and didn't know it. The site was eerily quiet. The elder Hollingsworth was walking south along a ridge to the upper end of an area called Fatty Bottom—a succession of woods, hills, hollows, and swamp.

He got to the site at 6:00 A.M. "I almost had a nervous breakdown when I saw the bodies," Hollingsworth told the *Tennessean.* "I had to sit down and then walk out to the road till help came." Jeners Hollingsworth got word to the search party.

State Trooper Troy Odle, who was up all night helping to organize the ground crew, was the first official at the scene. He shook his head. "I've never seen a wreck as bad." Odle found the tail and radioed the identification number N7000P to confirm ownership by Hughes. Civil Defense official Dean Brewer, asked whether all four bodies had been located, replied, "There's not enough to count ... They're all in small pieces."

Because of the delay in getting the search party started, due to the weather, terrain, and darkness, the final verdict was slow in coming.

"Everybody was calling to express their concern about Patsy," Mrs. Hensley said. "They kept telling me not to give up hope. 'There's still hope,' they'd say. But nothing helped. The waiting was unmerciful."

Then the Hensleys' and Dicks' phones rang again. It was the news no one wanted to hear.

The wire services ran the story, and stations everywhere interrupted programming to report the tragedy. It was a black day in Nashville history, losing three beloved record stars and prominent members of the Opry. Grant Turner went on WSM and, with his voice breaking, said, "Ladies and gentlemen, this is the hardest thing I've ever had to do. The plane bearing Patsy Cline, Hawkshaw Hawkins, and Cowboy Copas has crashed, and all of the above have perished. Patsy Cline, Hawkshaw Hawkins, and Cowboy Copas are dead."

The Butlers continued on down the highway after speaking to Grant Turner. When he came on and made the official announcement, Carl turned off the highway onto a gravel and dirt road.

"It twisted and turned every which way," Pearl remembered. "I finally said, 'Hon, where are you going?' and he stopped and we tried to pull ourselves together. All I could think of were Patsy's costumes in the trailer. And something Patsy had told us one night when we all were driving back from a date. She'd been in Winchester visiting her mother and said, 'Everyone wants me to sing for nothing. That's especially true back home. They think they own me. I want you both to remember this, because one day you'll be able to tell it. The next time I go to Winchester, everyone in that town'll know that Patsy Cline has been there!'

"When I recall that and the last time I saw Patsy, it makes chills run all over me. When they took her back there for her burial, I said to myself and in tribute to her, 'Well, girl, everybody sure did know it!'

"Anyway, when Carl started up the car, we were lost. He turned around and headed back till we hit the highway. I've tried and tried to find that road and, to this day, I've never been able to. I used to think, 'My goodness, did we go on a road that didn't exist?'"

The Butlers had turned onto Mule Barn Road. Had they proceeded another mile, they would have encountered the hundred cars from the search party waiting to go into the area.

☆

Loretta Lynn tells her reaction to Patsy's death. "I had gone to bed early Tuesday night instead of listening to the radio as I usually did. I got up real early Wednesday to clean my house so I'd have plenty of time to get ready and be able to go shopping with Patsy. We had a date for Tuesday, but I heard they would be late coming back. I wanted to be ready for her now.

"I thought, 'I'll call that lazy thing and get her out of bed.' Just as I lay my hand on the phone, it rang. I said to myself, 'I wonder who the heck this is? It's Patsy. She must have come in last night.' But it wasn't Patsy. It was [agent] Bob

Neal's wife calling to tell me the bad news. I froze. I said, 'What? What are you saying?'

"I'll tell you how I felt when I lost her. I felt that probably I wouldn't make it 'cause she was my buddy. I went to her for advice and she'd give it. When she was killed, the thought ran through my mind, 'What am I gonna do now?' When Patsy died, I lost the most wonderful friend I'll *ever* have."

Hank Cochran was driving back into Nashville late Tuesday when he heard the news report. "I was pretty shook and had to pull over. I really loved that gal. I was supposed to be on that plane with them. Patsy had asked me if I wanted to go and I said yes, but at the last minute a meeting came up with Timi Yuro, who was in town looking for material. So I stayed home and wrote all weekend."

Cochran followed the WSM broadcasts into early Wednesday. When he heard that it all was true, he ran outside and went berserk, screaming through the trees, "It's not true. It's not true! Please God, don't let it be true!"

Around the crash site, a multicolored jigsaw puzzle littered the landscape. There were scattered pieces of instruments, guitar strings, sheet music, Patsy's cosmetics, wigs, and clothing. A soft slipper, gold and muddy, from the pair Patsy was reported wearing in Dyersburg, pointed to the impact spot. On a piece of note-paper in red ink was written "Boo Boo Hoo Hoo." Someone picked up Patsy's beloved "Dixie" cigarette lighter. A black sock and western shirt fluttered in tree branches.

Among the broken bodies was Hawkins' cowhide belt, with his name tooled across the back, his famed hawk jacket, his Stetson, and one of a pair of his boots. A few feet away lay the broken black-and-silver neck of his Gibson guitar. Under-neath the torn guitar strings, in pearl inlay, were letters spelling "Hawkshaw." Nearby was Patsy's fringed cowgirl jacket and western hat and, several yards away, her white belt, inscribed with the black-tooled lettering "Patsy Cline."

The beautiful white dress with the rhinestone accent she wore at the last show in Kansas City was never found, nor were the matching shoes. Randy's money bag was never found. Reportedly it was picked up by a local woman, who came to the scene with her baby in her arms.

Randy was thirty-five; Cowboy, forty-nine; Hawkshaw, forty-one; and Patsy, thirty.

She had lived to see her thirtieth birthday after all.

"TODAY, TOMORROW AND FOREVER"

SAMMY MOSS: "The last resting place for the late, great Patsy Cline is Shenandoah Memorial Park. Any time you're in the area, stop by!"

From the Paul Harvey News broadcast on March 6, 1963:

Three familiar voices are suddenly silent today. And over an ugly hole on a Tennessee hillside, the heavens softly weep. No more mournful ballad was ever sung on the Grand Ole Opry than the one which was hammered out on the nation's newsprinters this morning.

The Nashville country music stars Hawkshaw Hawkins and Cowboy Copas and Patsy Cline and her manager. They'd flown in a one-lung Comanche to Kansas City for a benefit performance. For the benefit of the widow of a friend who'd been killed in a car wreck.

And they were returning to home base—Nashville, Tennessee. They'd refueled at Dyersburg. Some severe thunderstorms had been raking the area along the Tennessee River. At least one commercial airliner had detoured. Precisely what happened thereafter will be subject to conjecture forever. And what terror there was toward the end we'll never know. But there was pain. When they found the plane this morning its engine had entered the earth straight down.

Somebody will write a cow-country classic about this night ride to nowhere. Because hill folks are a sentimental lot. But the highest compliment their eulogies are likely to include is that the somber citizens who converged this day on that ugly scar in the woodland where pieces of four bodies lay, that there are real tears in their whispered words. And that they refer to each of the suddenly deceased by his or her first name.

For none of them ever thought of Randy and the Cowboy, Hawkshaw, and Patsy any other way than as homefolks, kinfolks, friends.

Brenda Lee was in Germany and heard an Armed Forces Network broadcast. "It stunned and hurt me. Patsy was gone just like that. It seemed so unfair after all she'd gone through. I called Owen and asked what I should do. He told me even if I could cancel my dates, I'd miss the funeral. He said, 'Hon, Patsy, would understand.' The thing I kept saying to myself was, 'She hadn't even seen her peak.' Probably, had she lived, Patsy'd be bigger than even she ever dreamed!"

Donn Hecht and his wife were driving from Los Angeles International Airport, where he'd just purchased his ticket for the trip to Nashville. "I was tuned to a country station absorbing all I could. Suddenly, they interrupted with the news. I was too overcome to drive. I pulled onto the shoulder of the freeway. My wife was trying to comfort me. I recall looking up through my tears and seeing the cars whoosh by and thinking, 'How can they go along as though nothing has happened when part of my world has ended?'

"Then the deejay inappropriately put on 'I Fall to Pieces,' and I was rendered completely incapable of operating the car. My wife drove us home where I consumed a third of a bottle of cognac. She said, 'It's none of my business since it was before you knew me, but I'd like to know. Was there anything between you and Patsy?' I said, 'Why do you ask?' She replied, 'I've never seen you like this. You're about ready for the hospital.' My answer was a truthful one, 'Honey, there was *everything* between me and Patsy!'"

In Frederick, Maryland, Fay Crutchley called bandleader Bill Peer. "My God, Fay," Bill exclaimed, "I can't believe this. I had no way of knowing. I was only kidding Saturday night. I didn't mean anything."

"I had forgotten all about what he was talking about," said Fay, "then I remembered when I asked him if he'd heard from Patsy, he said, 'As far as I'm concerned, Patsy can just fall to pieces!'"

Louise Seger had left Houston and was living temporarily in Manaus, Brazil. "When I heard the news of Patsy's death, it was something I wouldn't let myself believe. There were a lot of people around the hotel from Oklahoma who worked the oil rigs and they liked country music. We'd get a few under our belts and we'd start singing. I'd always do Patsy's songs. A man from New York came in from the airport and we got real friendly. I sang 'I Fall to Pieces.'"

"Louise," he asked, "who'd you say sang that song?"

"Patsy Cline."

"My God, that's the girl that was killed in a plane crash, isn't it?"

Louise went absolutely cold. "No, you must be talking about somebody else. It couldn't have been Patsy."

"I'm almost sure it is."

"I said it couldn't have been. No, you must mean somebody else. You don't mean Patsy Cline."

"I'd almost swear to it. I was reading about it in *Life* on the plane coming down."

"I don't care what you were reading, you've got to be mistaken."

"The magazine's in my room. Here's the key. If you don't believe me, go see for yourself. Honey, I'm not lying to you."

Louise went to the room, found the magazine, and started turning the pages until there it was. He hadn't lied. Patsy Cline had been killed. Louise broke down.

Granville "Shorty" Graves, fondly known around the Phillips-Robinson Funeral Home in Madison, Tennessee, as "the last man to let you down" because of his job as an assistant funeral director, went to Stockdale-Milan Funeral Home in Camden Wednesday morning to bring the bodies to Nashville.

"I paid four hundred dollars in charges for the work they did, swapped bags, and headed back with a Tennessee Highway Patrol escort. Each time I'd cross a county line—from Dickson, to Cheatham, to Williamson and so on into Davidson County—there'd be another car waiting to take me on."

Hubert Long helped the families with final arrangements. Friends from inside and outside the music community gathered at the homes of the deceased bearing cakes, pies, fried chicken, baked hams, potato salad, stuffed eggs, biscuits, soft drinks, and bottles of beer and liquor.

As Patsy wanted, Charlie brought Patsy home for one more night to the house she loved so much. "Since she'd gotten to spend so little time in it, I wanted her to enjoy it for as long as she could." He had her gold-finished casket placed in front of the now-draped picture window in the living room. He put a photograph of Patsy on top. WSM and the Grand Ole Opry sent a huge casket spray.

"At first," said Ann Tant, "I thought it a bit morbid having the casket at the house with the kids and all, but Patsy did love that house, and everything was handled in the very best of taste."

Alexander Groves, the young sailor who dated Patsy during the summer of 1953, was living in Massachusetts. "Country music wasn't very popular in New England," he explained, "and I was unaware of the incredible career Patsy had carved for herself. When I picked up the newspaper and read about the accident that took her life, I read the article and reread it. I said, 'This is Pat Cline, the girl that I dated!' But no one would believe it."

Five years later, when he was married and had started to follow country, his wife came home one day with an album she bought him. It was *Patsy Cline's Greatest Hits*.

Dottie West was in bad shape. She even found herself angry at Patsy. "I was at the kitchen table crying and staring into nowhere. My face was a mess, but I didn't know, didn't care. I was sipping black coffee and saying, 'Damn it, Patsy, why didn't you come with us? You always had to be so hardheaded. Had to do everything the way you wanted it!'"

Bill West tried to get Dottie out of her stupor. "Dottie, you've got to pull yourself together and get dressed. We've got to go to Kathy, Lucille, and Jeanie. Then we've got to go to Charlie. He needs us. We have to help him. There are people who need us. We're their friends. We need to be with them. Think about what they're going through."

"Charlie. Oh, my God, Charlie!" Dottie snapped back to life. She got up. "Bill, here I am feeling sorry for myself, and I'd forgotten what Charlie and those poor children must be going through."

When they pulled up and Dottie saw the house, she couldn't get out of the car. Her husband opened the door and waited.

"Honey?"

"Bill, I can't."

"You've got to." He took her arm and helped her out. She slipped. He thought she was fainting, but Dottie suddenly stood erect. She looked at the house and Patsy's words about bringing her back to her castle when she died came to mind. Dottie put her arms around Bill.

When they entered, Dottie and Charlie embraced, shaking. She turned and saw the casket.

"Oh, Charlie, I know she'd be happy."

And they both fell apart.

If things hadn't been traumatic enough for Charlie, they quickly became worse. He was so distraught, there was fear among close friends that he might kill himself. "Let there be no mistake about the fact that Charlie loved Patsy," Del Wood said. "I only wish all those doubting Thomases had been there to see how broken he was and the exemplary way in which he conducted himself. My heart went out to him. He looked drained, pale. Like a lost soul."

Explaining Patsy's death to the children was an ordeal. "Randy had only just turned two that January," he said, "but telling Julie, who was four and a half, oh, God, that was one of the hardest things I ever had to do. Our friends were terrific with the kids, trying to keep their minds occupied, but they knew something was not right. Especially Julie.

"She didn't quite understand what had happened, but she knew it wasn't the normal, everyday thing. She'd ask me, 'Daddy, is my mama ever coming home again?'" Randy was still sick. "There was no way I could make him understand. He kept running through the house crying for his mother. That made it doubly bad."

On Wednesday evening, Mrs. Hensley arrived with three carloads of family and friends, including Charlie's mother, Mary, who'd grown devoted to Patsy. Mrs. Hensley said she'd tried to accept her daughter's death. When she got to the house and stood before the closed casket, the full impact hit her and daughter Sylvia Mae.

It was a horrifying experience as one would pass out, then come to, only to have the other pass out.

"People told me they were talking to me and I seemed to be in space," recalled Dottie. "I was. I was a zombie. I couldn't bring myself to believe Patsy was gone. Bill didn't know what he was going to do. He was afraid he'd have to call my doctor and put me to bed. Patsy was my friend. Heck, she was more than that! It wasn't easy accepting her death, nor would it be easy to go on without her. But I had to.

"Charlie was getting upset with me. He and Bill forced me to get away from the casket. I was on Patsy's gorgeous white satin couch. I rubbed my hand across the fabric and said, 'Charlie, this is the sofa Patsy just had made.' He answered, 'Yeah, Dottie.' I said, 'She was so proud of it.' Charlie said, laughing, 'She shoulda been 'cause she drove 'em crazy till they got it the way she wanted it!'

"Next to me was Loretta. Oh, she was upset and shaking. I looked on the wall and saw the portraits of Julie and Randy that Patsy had done the week before. I started to cry about those kids not having their mother, and so did Loretta."

At the various homes, friends gathered en masse—from the stars of the Opry, industry executives, and neighbors to devoted fans and, in Charlie's case, his buddies and poker mates from the printing plant.

On Nella Drive, everyone took on chores. Minnie Pearl and Pearl Butler stood watch at the door. Anita Carter and Jan Howard went into Madison and bought a Barbie doll for Julie and toys for Randy. Dottie and Loretta carved ham while Skeeter Davis served potato salad. Del Wood and Mooney Lynn scrambled eggs and bacon. Hank and Shirley Cochran kept the trays full of sandwiches, ham, and chicken. Roger Miller and Ann Tant kept hot biscuits coming. Teddy Wilburn and Wilma Burgess made iced tea. Billy Walker and Owen Bradley filled glasses with ice. Faron Young spiked drinks when asked.

Dottie and Loretta thought playing with the children would help not only them but the kids. "But it didn't," said Dottie. "Julie and Randy kept running to Charlie, hugging his leg and asking, 'Daddy, where's Mommy? Isn't she coming home tonight?' Every time they'd start to cry, Loretta, Hilda, and me would would go to pieces. And Hank was taking it real bad."

As the night wore into morning, Charlie had spent very little time just being with Patsy. He wanted that very much. Finally, he asked everyone but Mrs. Hensley and the immediate family to leave. "I want to be alone with my girl," he said.

A prayer service was set for Thursday afternoon at five at Phillips-Robinson. Patsy's friend from Madison Hospital, the Rev. Jay Alford, officiated. Afterward, her remains were flown to Winchester on a Tennessee National Guard plane for services on Saturday afternoon. Interment, at the request of Mrs. Hensley, was to be in the new Shenandoah Memorial Park on Route 522 South outside Winchester.

Joint services for Randy and his father-in-law, Cowboy Copas, were scheduled for 10:00 A.M. Friday, with Hawkshaw Hawkins's rites to take place at 3:30. A framed photograph of each was placed on top of the closed caskets. Even though the services were at different times, all four caskets were displayed together.

The attendance for the services was the largest in Nashville history. Streets near the funeral home had to be closed to traffic. Over one thousand mourners were jammed into each of the rites. Loudspeakers were placed outside to supplement the home's permanent porch speakers. By Thursday morning, 615 flower sprays were received, prompting the funeral home to request florists to take any further orders directly to Forest Lawn Cemetery on Dickerson Road. At Charlie's directive, Patsy's flowers were to go to the local cemetery. Telegrams poured in from across the nation and throughout the world.

Teddy Wilburn said of the prayer service for Patsy, "You had to fight your way through the surging crowds in the street and inside the funeral home. We were milling around, talking in low, hushed tones waiting for the Reverend Alford to begin. Suddenly there was this commotion and word filtered in that Jack Anglin of the Johnny [Wright] & Jack duo had been killed. He'd been to the barber shop for a trim before heading to the service. On the way he was involved in an accident.

"I broke down, absolutely lost control. People were upset and horrified at the news. It was too much. Now we'd lost a fourth star, in addition to Sleepy McDaniel from Hank Snow's band. I'd known Patsy, Cowboy, and Hawk well, but Doyle and

I went all the way back to the Louisiana Hayride with Jack. I was wiped out from Patsy's death and had two funerals to go to, and now Jack. I fell apart. Two people finally had to help me outside. Someone sat me down in the front seat of a car so I could pull myself together. I don't think I did for several days."

Dottie remarked that Anglin's death totally nonplussed everyone. "Bill was holding me up and I heard people gasping. I looked up and someone said, 'Jack Anglin's just been killed.' The news raced through the crowd. What a shock. Another shock! Johnny was there with [his wife] Kitty [Wells] and when he heard the news about his partner and brother-in-law,[1] he became hysterical. A black cloud had fallen over Music City."

Over 600 cars were in the Copas and Hawkins processions.

Teddy Wilburn reflected on the impact of the deaths. "The country music industry had gone for almost ten years without any tragedy. Everyone was living on and on and on, and no one tremendously important in the business had died since Hank Williams. And his was a natural death, so to speak. It was amazing, especially in view of the way we traveled—no buses, everyone driving cars or limos and pulling equipment trailers. The law of averages caught up with us. But that didn't make it any easier to accept."

Ralph Emery compared that bleak week to something akin to the assassination of President John Kennedy later that year and the incredible feeling of loss it generated. "The impact was hitting everyone and some got the idea to commercialize on it. At Hawk's funeral, one of the record executives told me he was asking me and disc jockeys at all country stations not to play any records that might attempt to morbidly commemorate what had happened."

Each of the stars killed in that March 5th crash and in the March 7th accident was beloved by fans and industry folk alike. WSM and many of the Opry members debated whether or not to cancel the Saturday performance of the Opry. It was finally decided to go on with the show as the stars would have wanted. "Then we pondered how to handle the deaths on the broadcast," Emery explained. "It was a sad, sad night. Things were quite subdued. People were talking, but I honestly don't think they knew what they were saying. Something about there being a jinx on the Opry began circulating. Someone spoke of a hex on Patsy—you know, to have recovered from the car wreck and then to be involved in another horrible accident."

Beginning at 7:30, the stage was filled with music, laughs, and pure Opry entertainment. At 8:34 Opry manager Ott Devine began a simple spoken tribute after the evening's performers and all Opry members on hand gathered onstage: "We won't be having no big to-do. They sure wouldn't have liked that. Patsy, Hawk, Cope, Jack, and Randy would want us to recall the happier occasions. What do you say when you lose such friends? We can reflect on their contributions to us through entertainment, their acts of charity and love. We can think of the pleasure they brought to the lives of millions and take some comfort in knowing that they found fulfillment in the time allotted to them. They will never be forgotten."

He asked for a moment of silent prayer. Throughout the great hall, 3,500 fans stood and bowed their heads. The Jordanaires at center stage then began a moving

---

1. He was married to Wright's sister Louise.

rendition of "How Great Thou Art," accompanied by a lone piano. Audible sobs broke the stillness.

In a much more jovial voice, Devine exclaimed, "Patsy, Cowboy, Hawkshaw, Jack, and Randy never walked on this stage without a smile, and they'd want us to keep smiling now. Let's continue in the tradition of the Grand Ole Opry!"

Roy Acuff and his Smoky Mountain Boys stepped to the footlights at 8:39 and struck a rousing fiddle tune of celebration, attempting to turn a sad occasion into one of joyous remembrance. The stars filed off with long faces and tears.

Minnie Pearl was next to go on, but she was upset and crying. Emery motioned to let her have another minute to compose herself. She swallowed hard, wiped her eyes, signaled she was ready, and Acuff brought her on to wild applause. She rushed out with her famed greeting, "Howwwwddddeeee! I'm so proud to be here." And what, a few minutes earlier, had been an ocean of sad humanity dabbing their eyes with handkerchiefs was instantly transformed into a sea of howling laughter. But their sadness was not forgotten. Waiting in the wings, Minnie had turned to Emery and said, "Oh, Lordy, we lost some good friends!" Across the nation that night, her sentiments were shared by countless country and pop music fans.

It would be polite to say that Patsy's funeral on Sunday was a three-ring circus. Since Charlie had to attend the services for the other deceased, Patsy's funeral was moved to Sunday afternoon to give him, Mrs. Hensley, and members of the family time to get safely to Winchester. The burial attracted thousands of fans and a mass of media personnel. They quickly became an unruly mob that city and Virginia state police could barely handle. Members of the family were disgusted with the conduct of a majority of the crowd, but Mrs. Hensley and Charlie were too distraught to know what transpired. The situation became so unmanageable that old friends of Patsy's, such as the Crutchleys, the Deytons, Jumbo Rinker, even Bill Peer couldn't get into the funeral home.

Sammy Moss, a Winchester disc jockey and bandleader who'd also known and befriended Patsy early on, noted on his annual Patsy Cline memorial broadcast in 1972: "This country DJ had never expected anything like this. I had been asked to be a pallbearer along with other friends of Patsy's.... As I arrived ... about two forty-five it looked as though something big was about to happen. Streets were jammed with people. Traffic was almost at a standstill, and when I arrived at the Jones Funeral Home I could see what all the commotion was about. It was the general public wanting to participate in the final rites of Patsy Cline. The Jones Funeral Home was a large establishment with two large rooms, and both rooms were filled to capacity with persons seated and standing. The doors were locked quite a while before services began because this place was filled beyond expectation."

The memorial leaflet distributed by the family quoted Tennyson:

Sunset and evening star,
And one clear call for me!
And may there be no moaning of the bar,
When I put out to sea,
But such a tide as moving seems to sleep,

Patsy shows off her beloved fox stole. (Country Music Foundation)

Above left: Patsy at the Opry in May 1962. Randy Hughes, left, plays guitar. On bass is Lightnin' Chance, also Hughes's business partner.

(WSM Photo/Les Leverett)

Above right: Patsy, Johnny Cash, Don Gibson (who wrote "Sweet Dreams (of You)"), and George Jones bonded during Cash's nationwide Shower of Stars tour. Old friends June Carter, Carl Perkins, and Leroy Van Dyke were also on the show.

Right: Patsy at Tootsie's Orchid Lounge between Opry shows, February 16, 1963—sixteen days before her death—with Randy Hughes (back to camera) and recording artist Billy Walker.

(WSM Radio Archives)

An alternate shot from a photo shoot at the Decca Records studio on August 6, 1962, for Patsy's third album—the last to be issued in her lifetime.

(MCA Records Photo/Hal Buksbaum)

Left: Patsy at WSM Radio studios a month before she died. She wore a wig styled to hide scars from her automobile accident.

(WSM Photo/Les Leverett)

Below: Patsy performs "Bill Bailey" with WSM Radio's Waking Crew Band for a senior citizens group two and a half weeks before the fatal plane crash.

(WSM Photo: Les Leverett)

Patsy at her last New York photo session at Decca Records, February 1962. House photographer Hal Buksbaum said that several times when Patsy stopped to freshen her makeup she told him, "I'm just not destined to live a long life."

Above: Cowboy Copas (top) and Hawkshaw Hawkins. (WSM photo)

One of the last photos taken of Patsy in Kansas City at Memorial Auditorium, March 3, 1963. (Alfredda Rhoades/Collection of Ellis Nassour)

The crash site near
Camden, Tennessee.

(Nashville *Tennessean* Photos/Gerald
Holly © 1981, 1993, 2008 Ellis
Nassour; Used with permission)

Roger Miller, whom Patsy adored because he could make her laugh, rushed to the crash area in his car and searched throughout the night. He was one of the first to come upon the crash.
(Nashville *Tennessean*/Joe Ruddis)

Opposite: Grand Ole Opry memorial service held March 9, 1963. Opry manager Ott Devine is at the announcer's podium. Some of the stars onstage: Roy Acuff, June Carter, Jack Greene, Marvin Hughes at piano, Sonny James, the Jordanaires at WSM microphone adjacent to piano, Merle Kilgore, agent Hubert Long, Lonzo and Oscar, Minnie Pearl in hat and partially obscured, Cal Smith, Stringbean, Buck Trent, Opry announcer Grand Turner, Porter Wagoner, Doyle and Teddy Wilburn, Smiley Wilson, and Del Wood. (WSM Photo/Les Leverett)

Memorials and curiosity seekers at Nashville's Woodlawn Cemetery following funerals for Cowboy Copas and Hawkshaw Hawkins. (Nashville *Tennessean*/Joe Ruddis)

Patsy and Charlie's daughter, five-year-old Julie, accepting the Cash Box Magazine Award naming Patsy the Most Programmed Country Female Vocalist from editor Bob Austin at Nashville's Country Music Festival, November 1963.

(WSM Photo/Les Leverett)

Plaque from the gateway erected in 1964 at Winchester's Shenandoah Memorial Park by Charlie and family members.

(Ellis Nassour)

THIS ENTRANCEWAY IS dedicated in remembrance of PATSY CLINE one of America's best beloved singers, by her husband Charles Dick, their children Julie and Randy and her family 1963

| DATE 19 63 | FLIGHT FROM | FLIGHT TO | EQUIPMENT FLOWN | | | | CLASSIFICATION | DURATION OF FLIGHT |
			AIRCRAFT MAKE AND MODEL	CERTIFICATE NUMBER	ENGINE	H. P.		
2-15	Nashville	Local	Comanche	7000P	Lyc.	250		30
2-16	"	Dresden Ala.	"	"	"	"		45
2-16	Dresden Ala.	Tifton Ga.	"	"	"	"		2 00
2-17	Tifton Ga.	Stephenville Tifton Fla.	"	"	"	"		2 30
2-18	Tifton Ga.	Dresden Ala.	"	"	"	"		1 50
2-18	Dresden Ala.	Nashville Tenn.	"	"	"	"		45
2-24	Nashville	Local	"	"	"	"		45
3-2	"	Birmingham Ala.	"	"	"	"		1 15
3-3	Birmingham Ala.	Nashville Tenn.	"	"	"	"		1 15
3-3	Nashville Tenn.	K.C. Kan.	"	"	"	"		3 00

THE RECORD ON THIS PAGE IS CERTIFIED TRUE AND CORRECT:

PILOT_____ ATTESTED BY_____   CARRY TOTALS FORWARD TO TOP OF NEXT PAGE

The flight record from Randy's Piper Comanche shows that on March 2, 1963, he flew from Nashville to Birmingham and back, then to Kansas City. He never entered data for the flight from there, through Arkansas and into Dyersburg.
(Civil Aeronautics Board/Photo by Mark Willix)

Dottie West, October 1980, reviewing one of the scrapbooks Patsy gave her in July 1962. (Les Leverett)

Hilda Hensley, Patsy's mother, in 1985 with one of the Western costumes she made for her daughter. The bronze plaque she had made for the foot of Patsy's grave reads, "Death cannot kill what never dies."

(People Photo by Stanley Trettick © 1985; Licensed by Ellis Nassour; Used with permission)

Opposite: Another milestone: Patsy Cline becomes the first solo female named to the Country Music Hall of Fame. Johnny Cash makes the announcement on the 1973 Country Music Awards on CBS TV. (WSM Photo/Les Leverett)

United States Postal Stamp, issued September 1993, celebrating 60th Anniversary of Patsy Cline's birth.

Virginia honors Patsy with a Department of Historic Resources marker at her childhood home, 608 South Kent Street, dedicated September 3, 2005, five days before the anniversary of Patsy's birth. Charlie Dick, daughter Julie Fudge, and then–Celebrating Patsy Cline president Philip Martin attended the dedication.

(Rick Foster/Winchester *Star*)

Two of the costumes handcrafted by Patsy's mother, Hilda Hensley, that were auctioned at Christie's New York in 2003 after a lawsuit between Sam Hensley Jr. and Sylvia Wilt over their mother's will. (Ellis Nassour)

Chester "Chet" Brannon,
twenty-seven, possibly Patsy's
father, living the good life in
San Juan, Puerto Rico, 1939.
(Collection of Charlotte Brannon Bartles)

Charlotte Brannon, who claims Patsy
is her half sister, in 1949, age fifteen.
(Collection of Charlotte Brannon Bartles)

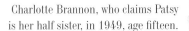

Woman said to be Hilda Hensley
in 1932 with Bill Henesy, whose
daughter claims he sired Patsy
Cline. (Collection of Barbara Henesy O'Donnell)

COUNTRY MUSIC
HALL OF FAME
ELECTED 1973

PATSY CLINE

SEPTEMBER 8, 1932   MARCH 5, 1963

BORN VIRGINIA PATTERSON HENSLEY IN VIRGINIA, PATSY WILL LIVE IN COUNTRY MUSIC ANNALS AS ONE OF ITS OUTSTANDING VOCALISTS. TRAGICALLY, HER CAREER WAS CUT SHORT IN ITS PRIME WHEN SHE WAS KILLED IN A PLANE CRASH. HER HERITAGE OF RECORDINGS IS TESTIMONY TO HER ARTISTIC CAPACITY... BIGGEST HIT, "I FALL TO PIECES," HAS BECOME A STANDARD. CATAPULTED TO FAME BY AN ARTHUR GODFREY TALENT SCOUTS APPEARANCE IN 1957. JOINED GRAND OLE OPRY 1960... REALIZATION OF A LIFELONG AMBITION.

COUNTRY MUSIC ASSOCIATION

Country Music Hall of Fame plaque. Patsy Cline was a star when she left us, and a star she remains. (Les Leverett)

Too full for sound and foam,
When that which drew from out the boundless deep
Turns again home.

The Reverend Nathan Williamson conducted the Winchester service and delivered the message when the service began at 3:30. Gerald Cline attended the funeral and went to Mrs. Hensley and Charlie afterward to extend his condolences. At 4:30 the pallbearers, all save one area disc jockeys—Joltin' Jim McCoy, WHPL Radio; Moss, WRFL; Bill Alison, WINC; Dick Dovel, WFTR (Frederick); Eddie Matherly, WKCW (Warrenton); and Billy Graves, a Nashville producer—began moving with the casket toward the hearse. As the doors of the funeral home opened, a burst of excitement thundered through the throng. "There she is!" people screamed. "There's Patsy!" The crowd surged forward, and the pallbearers couldn't maneuver the casket. Cameras clicked, flashbulbs popped. One person, then another yelled, "Let us through. We want to see Patsy!"

It was thought that Mrs. Hensley fainted, but no one could get to her. Then, in the mass of people, she was there, being held by her daughter and son. A path opened, and the casket was hurriedly placed in the hearse. The funeral route wound some four miles from downtown to Shenandoah Memorial Park.

When Patsy's old friends from Brunswick, Maryland, Fay and Harry Crutchley, arrived at the funeral home after being stuck in traffic for nearly two hours, they found the doors locked. They started for the memorial park, but found traffic so congested they pulled off the road a mile from the cemetery.

Jack Cummins described the funeral in the Winchester *Star*:

And people who knew her, knew of her or just wanted to see the affair out of some morbid curiosity, packed the area. ... Cars were lined up from the edge of the city all the way to the cemetery. ... A small fortune in flowers of every description was delivered at graveside.

And before Patsy—the small-town girl who made good as the number one country music singer—was in the earth, the people who trampled and jammed the soggy cemetery field were beginning to steal sprigs of lilies and roses or other flowers.

The effect of the first stolen flower hit the crowd like an electrical shock. The people—jammed in close to the small tent over the grave—began snatching, literally from the side of the grave, everything and anything they could lay their hands on, short of the gold-finished coffin.

Several women surveyed the racks of flowers and wreaths with a critical eye, and began a methodical selection of the items they wanted—as if it were dollar day at the department store.

One blondish woman, perhaps in her early forties, managed to pick several wreaths clean of decorations and plastic emblems, and even made herself a little collection of cards from the various wreaths and garlands of flowers, banked high beside the grave.

But it's unlikely that Patsy ... would have minded. These were "her people," her fans, the people who made her famous. One of the honorary pallbearers, speaking of the thousands of people, probably summed it up

☆ 243 ☆

best when he said, "It's like a religion with them. They're very emotional and that's one of the reasons so many people are here."

Those who came to see only the celebrities who were supposed to be on hand were disappointed. According to another of the honorary pall-bearers, none of the people named to serve in that capacity was notified of his obligations. Consequently, he said, they apparently didn't know they were supposed to have been there.

After the services, as the people flooded back to their parked cars like a tide rolling out . . . a colossal traffic jam developed, tying up autos and trucks for miles on either side of the cemetery. Many of the onlookers appeared to have just slipped into any old clothes they could find for the trip to the cemetery. They ranged from infants to bent, wrinkled elderly men and women . . .

And it seemed nearly everyone at the cemetery had a camera of one kind or another—movie cameras, expensive 35 millimeter models, and $5 box types. Occasionally, while a solemn-faced pastor intoned the words of ritual over the casket, the crisp buzz of a movie camera could be heard in the hushed mob.

Several hundred yards away, on the side of a big white barn, a photographer had perched himself halfway up, apparently by scaling the side of the wall. At a restaurant a few hundred yards north of the cemetery the proprietor, in white apron, was surveying his driveway, packed with cars of onlookers. In exasperation he called to a state policeman to "Try and do something about getting my driveway cleaned out."

When it was over—about an hour later—the highways were still jammed for hours. A squad of state policemen was sent to important inter-sections and remained there, directing the crush of cars through the early evening.

But apparently the drivers and their passengers didn't mind too much—they had seen what they wanted.

Patsy got a funeral worthy of royalty.

On his 1972 broadcast, Sammy Moss stated: "The last resting place for the late, great Patsy Cline is Shenandoah Memorial Park just a few miles from Winchester, Virginia. Any time you're in the area, stop by! Tributes have been paid by many of Patsy Cline's followers, but the place and the name will remain forever. Remember it's Patsy Cline, Shenandoah Memorial Park, Winchester, Virginia!"

Someone said that time heals sorrow
But I can't help but dread tomorrow,
When I miss you more today than yesterday . . .[2]

The letter dated March 6, 1963, and received by the Country Music Association on

2. "I Miss You More Today," by Lorene Allen and Loretta Lynn, © 1972 Sure-Fire Music Company; all rights reserved; used by permission.

March 13 from Shaun Gooderham of Middlesex, England, was a typical fan reaction to the cataclysmic events of the preceding week.

> I have just learned of the death of Miss Patsy Cline, Cowboy Copas, and Hawkshaw Hawkins, a great and tragic shock to all.
>
> Each of these truly great artists have made their mark on the music scene, and they will be sorely missed by every "country fan."
>
> Miss Cline seemed fated from the start. It is such a pity that after her motor accident this should happen, just when deserved success was coming her way. She had so much to live for.
>
> Cowboy Copas, perhaps the best known, was a veteran in the true country style. He will be missed most of all, I think. Hawkshaw Hawkins in my opinion was the best singer of country ballads next to Hank Williams. He had a voice of amazing depth, quality and realism which could sing a country song better than anyone else.
>
> That this terrible tragedy should happen just now, when country music had a real hold on the music world is a blow from which, if it wasn't country music, it would perhaps never recover. . . . Let everyone know that they will be missed just as much in Britain as in America.
>
> Finally may I say how sorry I am for the relatives. The hearts of many people go out to them I am sure. One thing, they have the satisfaction of knowing their loved ones died for a cause, "Country Music." They lived and died country music. To them country music came first, and it was there at the last.
>
> May God always keep their memory alive.

Immediately after the accident, Billy Walker told the Nashville *Banner,* "God was on my side. Else how can you explain my being here and Patsy, Copas, Hawk, and Randy gone? No, I was not scheduled to ride the plane. Actually there wasn't enough room for me in the four-seater. So I went out and back on a commercial flight."

There was nothing said about his dad having a heart attack, or Walker calling Hawkins and asking him to let him have his plane ticket—thus putting Hawkins on the plane in his place.

Walker set the record straight. "For a long time, I was in a deep depression because I thought I was partially responsible for what happened since I had encouraged everyone to come to Kansas City to help the Call family. The benefit cost Patsy, Cowboy, Hawk, and Randy their lives.

"I realize there was no way I could have foreseen any of what happened. That didn't help me then, however. I was thankful I was alive, but, of course, I certainly had guilt feelings. They were gone, I was still here. Cowboy was a dear friend, and I had gone a long way back with Hawk. And Randy and Patsy were like family. He was like a brother to me and, gosh, I just adored Patsy more and more the longer I was around her. I had a terrible time coping with my feelings and couldn't talk about it. I know now it just wasn't in God's plan for me."

One thing soon became quite clear. If everyone who said, and many continue to, that they were asked by Patsy to go on the Kansas City benefit in that Comanche had in fact gone, Randy would have to have taken a cargo plane to get them all there.

Hap Peebles and Tex Ritter led a moving tribute on Sunday, March 17, at the Kansas City Memorial Auditorium. Peebles spoke of the good deed Patsy, Hawkins, Copas, and Randy Hughes performed. Ritter sang "Hillbilly Heaven," mentioning the deceased stars by name.

Vocally, Patsy had majesty and poignancy. She could segue from yodels to sweeping high notes, from hoedown to Irving Berlin, and from Cole Porter to rock 'n' roll.

At the twelfth annual Country Music Festival in November 1963, Patsy was selected *Billboard*'s Favorite Female Country Artist. For a second time, *Cashbox* magazine honored her as Most Programmed Female Vocalist. In quite an emotional moment, Julie accepted the award.

Faron Young observed, "Patsy had power and sincerity. Had it not been for her, there wouldn't have been opportunities for girl singers. Her driving ambition was to be a star, then a bigger star. She would have declared no quarter. Patsy'd be hotter than Hades, a giant. Patsy had it and would've continued to have it. No other singer could put a damn niche in her ass!"

Noting the scarring after Patsy's automobile accident, he said that "Max Factor was doing a job on her" and that she planned to have dental work.

Lightnin' Chance boasted, "Patsy had charisma. She was like Red Foley when he did the gospel hymns and Hank Williams with his heart broken and bleeding. Patsy was at her finest when she sang the 'you-done-me-wrong-dang-you' type tunes. She was telling her story and the story of the ladies in her audience. She was damning those men for doing her and those ladies dirty."

Loretta Lynn spoke of her friend: "Patsy was probably the first country female who dared to speak what she felt, the first to be different. No one has come close to singing as she did. Patsy was twenty-five years ahead of her time."

Former Winchester WINC Radio manager Philip Whitney pointed out, "Patsy was part of her music, in it all the way. The music was her life, and that's the way she lived it."

While during her life many had mocked Patsy's innovations and brassiness, and the fact that she was "going pop," after her death she was immediately canonized. Suddenly, crossover wasn't so bad if it meant record sales like Patsy's.

"There was even a campaign to develop another Patsy," stated Charlie. "Decca had loads of gals who tried to imitate her. They were standing in the wings! None came close to touching Patsy."

Even Charlie would attempt to find another Patsy.

In spite of impressive sales, Patsy never achieved Gold Record status. The Recording Industry Association of American (RIAA) seldom recognized Nashville artists, but in Patsy's case, Decca may have been at fault. As opposed to its Universal Pictures and pop music divisions, the company considered the country division a stepchild. Patsy's sales audits were never submitted.

"Gold Records were unheard of in country then," noted Charlie. "Only Patsy Montana had one. But if anybody had bothered to check, Kitty Wells would've received one for 'It Wasn't God Who Made Honky Tonk Angels,' and Patsy would have been awarded them on the strength of 'Walkin' After Midnight,' 'I Fall to Pieces,' and 'Crazy.'"

He's probably not referring to LPs. The bulk of Patsy's sales were 45s and EPs with four tracks in a photo sleeve.

In 1964 the Civil Aeronautics Board claimed the probable cause of the crash was a "Non-instrument pilot attempting visual flight in adverse weather conditions, resulting in a loss of control. Judgment of the pilot in initiating flight in the existing conditions was misguided."

Their investigation concurred with the observations of witnesses at Dyersburg airport that there was no engine malfunction. Exact details will never be known, but it's been surmised that the plane may have been flying upside down or, because of how it came down, flipped on impact; that it shifted hard to the left as the wings were torn off and nose-dived into the ground. It's said Randy was thrown from his seat, and Patsy, directly behind him, was ejected with more impact. Because she was partly shielded by Randy, more of her body remained intact.

If he'd been flying two miles to the east, Randy would have come out of the clouds over Camden and found the highway, maybe even a flat stretch where he could land.

Kathy Hughes took issue with statements claiming she'd told Randy she could "see the moon and stars . . . it's clear [in Nashville]." She recalled instead, "It had poured most of that day. The rain had stopped. I didn't tell him the sun was shining, only that it looked like it was trying to quit raining."

Sturvesant Insurance Company of Allentown, Pennsylvania, filed for a "declaratory judgment," stating that it wasn't liable for damage or personal liability because Randy hadn't flown enough hours to pilot solo without an instructor. Randy was issued his license in May 1962, and his logbook showed he'd flown one hundred sixty hours—just over three of those at night.

Rumors circulated that Randy lived and flew his plane dangerously, but Mrs. Hughes said, "I'm certain Randy felt he was doing the right thing. The CAB reported pilots with hours of flying get in the same predicament." She noted, "There was talk he and the others had been drinking," but the autopsy of recovered remains backed up Mr. Braese's statement that "there was no smell of alcohol and everyone appeared to be sober."

Mrs. Hughes filed a $2.5 million suit, with the three estates filing claims of $750,000 each. A settlement was reached, awarding $33,333 to each of the families and $15,000 for the plane.

Months after the crash, Patsy's Confederate flag / Rebel soldier cigarette lighter and Hawkins's rhinestone-studded "Hawk" jacket and Western hat, pilfered from the wreckage, were donated to the Country Music Hall of Fame. Carl Perkins presented items he'd found, including Patsy's mascara case and hairbrush. Gordon Stoker of the Jordanaires turned over a piece of the plane's floorboard he'd been given. Ralph Emery donated the plane's cockpit dashboard clock—with the hands stopped at 6:20 P.M. The beautician who dressed Patsy's hair and wigs donated a wig.

In 1964, a memorial entrance to Shenandoah Memorial Park, where only simple markers were allowed, was completed. Inscribed on a giant granite slab are music notes and these words: "This entranceway is dedicated in remembrance of Patsy Cline, one of America's best beloved singers by her husband Charlie Dick, their children Julie and Randy and her family."

"When Charlie began dating," said Faron Young, "it was ironic that he found a gal who sang just like Patsy. She worked for Del Reeves, Porter Wagoner, and me. Of course, she was a knockout!"

He spoke of petite beauty Jamey Ryan. It was amazing how reminiscent her vocal talents were of Patsy's, but the rub was that she was just eighteen.

Mrs. Hensley wasn't pleased that her grandchildren's mother figure was still in her teens. Charlie was eleven years older. He felt his children's most important need was a mother. He loved Jamey, she got on well with Julie and Randy, and gossip be damned.

Assuming she had a trump card, Mrs. Hensley filed Patsy's handwritten will in probate court in Davidson County, Tennessee; but Charlie managed to have it over-turned. However, when it proved impossible for him to work and care for the children, he made a temporary truce and allowed Mrs. Hensley to keep them, as per Patsy's will. They remained with her for a year and a half, spending holidays and summers with their father, who supported them financially.

Charlie and Jamey married in 1965. Mrs. Hensley contended that when she came to Nashville with her grandchildren, "I was not welcome at Charlie's home."

"Not true," claims Charlie. "That was just Hilda talking. She knew she was wel-come. If she chose to stay in a motel, it was her own doing. There was a misunder-standing between Hilda and Jamey, but that was cleared up. We were all very, very good friends."

Julie and Randy spent the summers of 1963 and 1964 in Nashville and returned to Winchester Labor Day weekend. In 1965, they never came "home" to Hilda, who said that when she rang Charlie to protest, he gave the phone to five-year-old Julie, who told her she wanted to live with "Daddy" and that "We have a new Mommy now."

Of her marriage, Jamey explained that Mrs. Hensley "felt mixed emotions. I was still a teen and marrying the twenty-nine-year-old father of her two grandchildren. Her attitude was, 'What kind of kid is coming in here and taking care of my grand-babies?' It was hard for her to give the children up, but after a couple of years, she saw I loved and cared for them as if they were my own. I didn't talk to her on a reg-ular basis, but we did stay in touch and were friends."

Charlie and Jamey had a son, Charles Jr. (Chip), in 1966. They divorced in 1972.

"I remained close to Julie and Randy," Jamey said. "Lots of things happened between Charlie and me. It was sad our marriage didn't work. It's one of those things we all have to learn to live with. But we have a son and now grandkids, so good, bad, or indifferent, I have to accept Charlie. I know he did try. It wasn't easy. He has been a good father."

Many assert Charlie's drinking, carousing, and preoccupation with Patsy's memory were contributing factors in the breakup.

Jamey's Patsy-like clarion voice would later come in handy. She provided the vocals for two songs in *Sweet Dreams*: "Bill Bailey (Won't You Please Come Home)" and "Blue Christmas," a song Patsy never recorded.

It puzzles or irritates some that Patsy's daughter calls Jamey "Mom," but Julie was not quite four and a half when her mother was killed, so Jamey was in fact Julie's mother figure during her formative years.

"I've written some songs since Patsy's death," said Hank Cochran, "and I've just cried because she wasn't around to sing them."

Patsy could still be climbing the charts just on her ability to deliver songwriters' lyrics so poignantly. Some call that tear in her voice a gimmick; however, according to Bradley, it was natural.

It's a rare country awards show that an artist fails to mention being influenced by Patsy. Such artists include Emmylou Harris, k.d. lang, Reba McEntire, Barbara Mandrell, LeAnn Rimes, Linda Ronstadt, and Trisha Yearwood.

"It's wonderful that whenever Patsy Cline's name is mentioned," poet Maya Angelou observed, "people's voices fall and they become right sentimental. And rightly so."

"I never met her, and that is certainly my loss," regretted late country legend Tammy Wynette, who sang her share of songs about heartbreak. "Patsy Cline is and perhaps will always be the standard bearer for all female country singers. She truly was my inspiration."

A gift of Patsy Cline albums to k.d. lang on her twenty-first birthday was a transforming experience. "I was just blown away by her interpretive quality and the timbre of her voice. It was pretty powerful stuff."

When Trisha Yearwood became an Opry member in 1999, Charlie and Julie presented a necklace that belonged to Patsy. "Patsy's voice was big," Yearwood attested, "but it's also very emotional. On 'Faded Love,' you hear her breathe. It's like she's in the room with you."

At Reba McEntire's early Nashville sessions, related Harold Bradley—Owen's brother and a well-regarded bass player on Patsy's records—she kept asking him, "What was it like to record with Patsy Cline? What was she like?" At her Hall of Fame induction, McEntire performed "Crazy" and observed "Patsy was larger than life! . . . She taught me emotion—raw, sincere, unashamed. On her recording of 'Crazy,' you can almost hear her cry from her guts. I wanted to create that kind of emotion when I sang."

In 1979 she recorded "Sweet Dreams (of You)"; and until a 1991 tragedy in which the plane transporting her band crashed, McEntire ended concerts with it.

Terri Clark's love for Patsy turned her to crime. Upon arrival in Nashville, she so admired a photo of Patsy that hung on the wall at Tootsie's that she decided she had to have it as a good luck charm. The "theft" made news, and Clark vowed "when I make it, I'll return it." In 2006, upon being made an Opry member, she kept her promise.

With her ability to sustain high notes, LeAnn Rimes is the closest anyone has come to sounding like Patsy. Her 1996 debut recording, "Blue," made when she was fourteen and which won her Grammys as Best New Artist and Best Female Country Vocal Performance, was written by Bill Mack, a Dallas disc jockey and record promoter. He'd written the tune for Cline and sent her a demo.

Rimes's early recordings, which included "I Fall to Pieces" and "Crazy," were produced by Bradley. "Being compared to Patsy Cline," said Rimes, "was the biggest honor, because I always looked up to her."

When Dolly Parton invited Loretta and Tammy to join her sessions for the album *Honky Tonk Angels*, Parton and co-producer Steve Buckingham created a quartet on Hank Williams's rockabilly classic "Lovesick Blues" by overdubbing Patsy's rendition.

In 1988 Bradley removed Patsy's vocals from ten songs on the three-track master tapes and merged them with contemporary arrangements for a larger orchestra. The results were less than satisfying.

Bradley, in conjunction with the Cline and Jim Reeves estates and RCA producer and recording artist Chet Atkins, created duets on "I Fall to Pieces" and "Have You Ever Been Lonely (Have You Ever Been Blue)?," recorded by the singers in almost the same key.

In 1991 MCA released *The Patsy Cline Collection*, with over one hundred songs Patsy recorded or sang live or on the radio. The following year, Patsy and Willie Nelson were honored with induction into the Grammy Awards Hall of Fame for "Crazy."

Discovery!, released in the U.K. in 1994, was an apt title. It contained seventeen Patsy vocals from Arthur Godfrey shows, including the never-recorded "Down by the Riverside" and "The Man Upstairs." The U.S. release has dialogue between Godfrey and Patsy.

A long-lost tape surfaced of Patsy singing live in Tulsa. It was cleaned up and released in 1997 as *Patsy Cline Live at the Cimarron Ballroom*. Amid thirteen tunes, including "Stupid Cupid," which Patsy had sung on Armed Forces Radio and in Las Vegas, and "Shake, Rattle and Roll," there's rare chatter with the audience.

In 1999, *Patsy Cline Duets* was released with Crystal Gale, Glen Campbell, Waylon Jennings, and Willie Nelson singing with Patsy. In 2005 Natalie Cole, George Jones, Norah Jones, Diana Krall, k.d. lang, Martina McBride, and, among others, Lee Ann Womack, did renditions of Patsy's songs for *Remembering Patsy*.

Recording artist Mandy Barnett portrayed Patsy in 2006's *Crazy*, the biopic about electric guitarist Hank Garland, who played on Patsy's sessions from 1957 through the 1960 "I Fall to Pieces" recording, when, following disagreements, Bradley stopped using him. Session logs don't list him playing on the "Crazy" sessions.

March 1963 proved to be one of the grimmest months in country history. Besides the deaths of Patsy, Cowboy, Hawk, and Randy, and the loss of Jack Anglin, Texas Ruby, one of Patsy's early influences, passed. President John F. Kennedy would be assassinated that November.

One of the most poignant tributes to Patsy was Jimmy Buffet's in his song "I Miss You So Badly":

I've got a head full of feelin' higher
And an earful of Patsy Cline.
There is no one who can touch her;
Hell, I hang on every line.[3]

3. © 1977, Outer Banks Music Company. All rights reserved. Used by permission.

For Joltin' Jim McCoy's annual March 5 Patsy Cline memorial broadcast, he received the following poem, "Leaning on Heaven's Gate," from Mrs. Hensley:

I wonder if you've ever stood beside a casket flanked with flowers
And asked the Lord to help you thank Him for the hours
When she was a child at your knee.

For your tender loving care,
For a voice that was filled with laughter and a will to do,
For all the little things that meant so much.

And when she came home late,
I'd be waiting at the window
Or leaning on the gate.
Yes, I remember that day forever, when God said, "It's moving day."
He knew my darling daughter was already on her way
To a new home with Him in heaven.

And now when we come home late,
She'll be waiting at God's window
Or leaning on heaven's gate.

This classified ad appeared in the October 15, 1980, edition of the *Winchester Star*:

CEMETARY lots (4)
Shenandoah Memorial Park,
Adjoins Patsy Cline.

A phone number was given. Within days, the lots were sold.

Patsy Cline's grave is marked with a simple bronze plaque that reads: *Death cannot kill what never dies, love.*

She was a star when she left us, and a star she remains.

AFTERWORD
"DON'T EVER LEAVE ME AGAIN"

Strange,
You're still in all my dreams.
Oh, what a funny thing,
I still care for you.
How strange.[1]

Since this book's initial publication twenty-seven years ago and then after the 1993 edition, a number of fascinating details about Pasty Cline's life have surfaced.

The saga of Patsy and Charlie and the spectrum of their marriage—from unbridled passion and wedded bliss to their struggles to make it as a family and eventually bouts of great turmoil—could fill volumes.

Rose Marie ("Ree") Flynt became one of the shoulders Patsy could cry on. "We met on music gigs back when they were living in Fayetteville [North Carolina] and struggling," she observed. "I assisted Patsy with driving, wardrobe, hair, selling records and photos, and making sure her pay was accurate. Traveling so many roads, so many hours—cracking up laughing or singing our hearts out—we bonded. She helped me with my phrasing and taught me how to breathe from my diaphragm. She

---

1. "Strange," by Mel Tillis and Fred Burch, © 1961. Cedarwood Publishing Company; all rights reserved; used by permission.

also taught me about showmanship, saying the 'trick' to grabbing an audience was a song that socks it to them and leaves them wanting more."

According to Flynt, problems flared early in the couple's marriage. She recounted the time she returned Patsy home after some club dates to find a strange car parked out front. "Patsy caught Charlie red-handed [with a woman]. There was hell to pay!"

Another time, "after shopping for groceries and liquor, we got to the house and there was Charlie's car. Patsy became livid. 'That bastard should be at work!' He was asleep. She woke him up and they got into it pretty bad. I was in the kitchen putting things away. Patsy ran in with Charlie yelling, 'If you don't shut up, I'll slap the hell out of you!' He saw I had a whiskey bottle in my hand. I told him, 'If you don't want me to splatter your brains with this bottle, you better not put your hands on her.'"

Juggling career and marriage was difficult, but Patsy made great attempts to be the ideal wife. Yet the reputation of the "old" Patsy—especially in the "Brunswick Triangle"—was hard to shake.

Flynt told of Baltimore disc jockey Ray Davis, who bragged that he'd taken Patsy home after a gig and slept with her. "I dressed him down, saying, 'You didn't sleep with Patsy—I did.' Then it dawned on me what he might think, and I explained. We were just girls in our twenties and didn't think anything of it—especially if we could save money on hotel rooms."

When Ree's husband, Pat Flynt, a Private First Class at Fort Hood, Texas, caught scuttlebutt of Davis's boast, he called his wife and told her he didn't want her hanging around "that woman."

"What do you mean?" his wife demanded. "Ray's full of crap. He didn't sleep with her that night, I did!" Pat wanted an explanation. When Ree gave it, they laughed.

Flynt described carefree times when she and Patsy would enjoy "downing a few," with Patsy's choice being bourbon and Coca-Cola—a few times sans Coke, "just picking up the bottle and drinking."

With Godfrey and "Walkin' After Midnight," Patsy was hot. Flynt drove her to so many dates, often they didn't know where they were. "En route to Berryville, Virginia, for a show at Watermelon Park, I got lost," she recollected. "By the time I found it, Patsy missed two shows. The head honcho got mad and I took the blame. He said he'd have to dock her fee. She told him how badly she needed the money and promised an extra-long show.

"In the dressing room, I laid out her gold lamé pants suit. Patsy was exhausted, but she got dressed. It was so tight, she couldn't sit. I looked around and there she was leaning against the wall taking forty winks."

When they went to collect, "the bum not only shorted her fifty dollars but demanded 25 percent from the sale of records and photos. Patsy was steaming mad, but had another date the next day and didn't want to argue. 'Do it,' she said. I threw him a few bills and change."

In the car, Flynt told Patsy to look in the glove compartment. She pulled out an envelope and, waving a handful of dollar bills, screamed, "Ree, you didn't!"

"Yes, I did," replied Flynt. "That bastard wasn't going to screw you twice in one night."

In 1962 Patsy's biggest road "haul" was twelve hundred dollars for an Alabama show featuring rock 'n' roll stars. The fee would have been much less, but Randy asked the promoter, if the rock artists got paid more, why shouldn't Patsy?

Patsy and Ree Flynt began a correspondence—an archive of over twenty letters—in October 1959 that spanned four years, to February 5, 1963, a month before Patsy's death. (The excerpts from Patsy's letters to Rose Marie Flint appear here as Patsy wrote them, uncorrected.)

In her handwritten (except for one typed) letters, Patsy's voice jumps off the page as she discusses her marriage, love for the children, career, songs, and the grueling travel as she began another hit streak. In letter after letter, she went on about either how much she loved Charlie and hated being away from him, or how she couldn't get out the door fast enough.

Of the letters, Lisa Flood, creator of www.patsified.com, stated, "At a time when Patsy was meeting the goals she'd dreamed of, she was falling apart. She couldn't find peace in her life. The letters make it plain that Patsy despised Charlie much more than she loved him. She writes that he beats her and leaves her lying in the hospital to go drinking."

A friend of Mrs. Hensley's who read letter excerpts found that "Patsy never refers to Charlie by name, but uses 'he' and 'him.' I'm stunned he didn't buy the letters and burn them. Patsy makes her case against him in her own handwriting. They should convince the doubters who believe all his tiptoeing that he only hit Patsy once; and that [when they fought] Patsy gave as good as she got."

An August 1960 letter is particularly poignant. Patsy, on tour and fearful of losing her second child (Randy), wrote of being in a Los Angeles hospital. Two days later, however, she was heading to Oregon, planning to return to California for a TV segment, and to do shows in Illinois—all the time concerned that "I'm gonna lose this young'un yet. But guess I'll leave it to the Man upstairs."

After her near fatal 1961 accident and breakdown, Patsy was often hyper and, as one letter put it, "wound tight." Anxious about paying over one thousand dollars for her thirty-three-day hospitalization, doctors, and planned plastic surgery, she went back on tour too soon. Patsy wrote of being "sick in health, happiness & my mind & nerves are shot," to the point that you might think the person who was so laid-back, carefree, and a bit of a hell-raiser in earlier times was now a barely contained explosion waiting to happen.

Patsy's determination to be front and center was such that on Saturday, July 29, five weeks after her surgeries, she returned to the stage in Tulsa at Leon McAuliff's huge Cimarron Ballroom, with Charlie to help. McAuliff, a Western swing bandleader with hits of his own, and his Cimarron Boys accompanied.

The ornate showroom, built in the 1920s by the Tulsa Shriners, had a capacity of two thousand and a studio for KVOO Radio.

Patsy's timing was perfect. "I Fall to Pieces" was at the top of the trade charts and getting crossover play. There was one show—tickets priced at $1.50—and it was sold out.

Some of those who saw Patsy up close, such as club secretary Romana Ellison, were shocked at the extent of the scars. She told the Country Music Foundation's

Paul Kingsbury, "Patsy was pretty sore, but it didn't affect her singing." Since she was on crutches, the stage manager accommodated with a stool.

Patsy's ad-libs provided juxtaposition between the poignancy of her vocalizing and, as evidenced in her letters, her lack of education. Referencing her accident, Patsy kidded that she looked "beat up" because of "what women drivers does for you." After a beat she added, "Not all!" complimenting the local gals. It was also interesting that in her banter she showed she kept up with current events when she got political and threw some brickbats at then–Soviet Premier Nikita Khrushchev.

There were several ovations and, quite moved, Patsy sobbed, "Bless your heart! . . . When 'I Fall to Pieces' became #1, it took six nurses to tie me to that bed!" Weeks of dates were canceled, but, she said she told Randy, "Don't cancel Tulsa! I'm gonna be there if I gotta crawl. And I made it." The audience went wild.

On August 21, still badly bruised, Patsy recorded "Crazy." "It was one of the few songs Patsy didn't get on the first take," Willie Nelson said. "I realized she was attempting to sing it the way I had recorded the demo. I told her, 'Make it your own.' Back at the microphone, Patsy sang the lyrics instead of speaking them and got it."

In two letters that month, one sent the day after a recording session, Patsy and Bradley were already planning a second album, but she wasn't happy about the direction of her career. "I could spit dust I'm so mad. . . . He wants to put violins (you heard me) on my new session. [He's] still trying to get me in the pop." She complained not of pain or depression but of having to do so many ballads. "I'll die & walk out," she wrote, "before I'll go all the way pop." She argued that the sessions proved she could sing pop music, which she already knew.

Patsy made no mention of "Crazy," which she still evidently disliked. She seemed to come to like "I Fall to Pieces," bragging it was climbing the country and pop charts and concluding "Now don't that blow your hat in the creek?"

On September 8, 1961, Patsy turned twenty-nine. Hobbling on crutches, she was back on the road. In a letter dated two days earlier, she was at wit's end, complaining Charlie was causing havoc, forcing her to think more seriously about divorce: "It's the same ole thing . . . he proceeded to get drunk every dam night . . . I get so dam fed up I could scream. I'm at that point again where it don't matter where he is to me anymore."

She was frustrated over Charlie "not being man enough to take it"—accepting her as his wife and "having me where I am now," a reference to her stardom. She said she was putting away as much money as she could "& then when I get sick enough of it I'll be able to live with out my dam man."

In an October letter, Patsy is ecstatic not only over having two hits but also over her black and white "all power" Cadillac. Working New York, Michigan, and Florida and planning a stop in Nashville, she says she found two weeks to relax with Julie and her mother at the Washington apartment she rented. But by page five, trouble rears its head. Patsy writes that on a tour Charlie "got loaded & cussed & knocked me around in front of people." She described his leaving her at the hospital to go drinking, stating "Ree, my life is the most up set. I'm fed up [and] don't care if I ever see this man again. [I'm] unhappy, tired of trying, sick, and tired of being hurt & used." She revealed she was seeing a divorce lawyer and that, "for the first time," Charlie believed her. "He's begging me to stay with him, but I'm finished with trying, crying, begging and there's nothing left to be hurt any more. . . . I've had it!

I'm almost out of my mind worrying what to do. Leave or stay here. . . . The children are the only reason I'm here."

But it wasn't so cut and dry. Overnight, with pleas for forgiveness, things may have brightened, for Charlie remained in the picture. He also has adamantly denied a pattern of abuse. The marriage, according to him, "was not all a bed of roses. . . . We were hardheaded and hot-tempered." But, he alleged, their blowups were "more verbal than physical. . . . We never had a slugging fight. . . . You'd think all hell was going to break loose when we got going good. But we had a lot of fun making up." Of *Sweet Dreams,* in which Charlie (who along with Mrs. Hensley received a sizeable fee) is portrayed as abusive and a drinker, he quipped, "It's good, if you like fiction."

Friends came to accept them as a volatile couple, with Charlie drinking or cursing her and Patsy bad-mouthing and demeaning him.

In 2007, when a tourist at Winchester's Visitor and Convention Bureau asked about Charlie, a volunteer, someone Charlie had grown up with, stated "Charlie was a nice, pleasant fellow until he discovered booze at eighteen."

Del Wood asserted, "They were up one day, down the next. It didn't take a rocket scientist to see they were heading for disaster. But a coupla days or a couple of hours after Patsy would sob he was an s-o-b, they'd be happy and lovey-dovey and you wondered if you heard Patsy right. If Charlie did to Patsy what that movie [*Sweet Dreams*] portrayed, there wouldn't have been a grease spot left of him. Patsy would have really cleaned his clock."

Dottie laughed, "Their fights were always interesting to watch because you knew Patsy would win!"

Close friend Faye Morgan, then a record promoter, shared times at Tootsies with Patsy and Charlie. "He was shameless, always drinking and flirting. She was used to him crawling in at all hours but never felt she was in danger of losing him. Patsy's only comment was, 'Who cares? He needs me. I don't need him.' She never mentioned divorce."

In Patsy's letter of February 26, 1962, there was no talk of domestic trouble, only her excitement on receiving a royalty check for $23,000 as she sees her struggles finally being rewarded: "I can't get used to it yet. First I cried, then I laughed, then I prayed & thanked God, then cried & laughed some more. Boy! What a feeling!"

Patsy was enjoying huge record sales and was in demand for concert and TV appearances. For a TV show outside Los Angeles, Charlie decided to take a leadership role. Always the spiffy dresser, he showed up "very Hollywood"—dressed to the nines and wearing an ascot—and began making suggestions, even to the lighting director. Patsy was so put out she berated him in front of the crew. The only thing Charlie abhorred more than being called "Mr. Cline," was being a laughingstock.

With success, Patsy became unrelentingly ambitious and more determined to break the stranglehold men had on the business. Charlie enjoyed the financial riches of her success but was unwilling or unable to adapt to Patsy's stardom. When marital problems flared, Patsy attempted to get Charlie to toe the line by threatening him with divorce or cutting him off financially—knowing full well he couldn't live the life he was enjoying on his own salary.

☆

It's been alleged that Charlie had numerous affairs, and Patsy hasn't been left out of the gossip mill. There are persistent rumors about Patsy and Randy Hughes. Because they spent so much time together, it's easy to believe that she fell in love with him. Randy was the one man she could depend upon. He may have been attracted to her, but more than anyone other than Dottie, he knew Patsy's strengths and weaknesses, moods and demons—and didn't want to rock his marriage.

Several friends said Randy loved Patsy, "but not that way." Patsy's regular bass player and one of Randy's closest friends, Lightnin' Chance, wasn't sure whether they were involved but had his suspicions. "I knew Randy like a brother," he said, "and, by that time, I'd gotten to know Patsy. I thought if they got involved it would be a train wreck." Chance had a couple of "man-to-man talks with Randy to warn him there could be trouble ahead if he thought with his heart and not his head."

Ree Flynt said that she became aware they were more than just manager and client during one visit with Patsy. "She felt Randy was the man she needed in her life. It may have gone further than most suppose, because at the house once when I was returning to the room, I caught them in an intimate embrace and kissing."

Faron Young agrees Patsy and Randy shared some "monkey business." He went so far as to say, "Randy was going to divorce Kathy." Others claim it's doubtful he ever seriously contemplated that. His wife said the subject never came up.

Then there's Porter Wagoner's claim of a brief fling and Young's own admissions of indiscretions.

A good ole boy with a potty mouth, Young was handsome and had the caché of having hit records and being in movies. Women were never a problem, but many scoffed at his claim of an affair with Patsy—especially since he and Charlie were close. Ree Flynt wasn't one of them, however, since she witnessed one blatant incident in which Charlie was only a few feet away.

April 28, 1962, Patsy was headlining at Bristol, Tennessee's Motor Speedway with Young and Ray Price. When the Flynts arrived at the Sandman Motel, Patsy was going through her elaborate makeup ritual, applying a layer of pancake makeup over her scars. A victory celebration was going on for "Fireball" Roberts (NASCAR pioneer Edward Glenn Roberts Jr.), who'd won the big race in his souped-up Pontiac Catalina.

"There was a knock at the door," remembered Flynt. "There was the Sheriff. When he spied Patsy, he had this shit-eating grin and went right up in her face. She introduced us, but it was like I wasn't there. I had the impression Patsy thought of him as a brother or sidekick, nothing more. He wanted to sing a new song. I was so taken by him, I hadn't even noticed his guitar. He sat on the bed and, as Patsy rolled her hair, he entertained us."

Flynt's husband rushed in, excited that he'd met "Fireball," and asked who wanted "highballs." He and Rose Marie went for drinks. "When I returned," she said, "the door was partially closed. I pushed it open and there was Faron all over Patsy, laying a long kiss on her. They weren't kissing like no brother and sister I knew. I was tongue-tied. Finally, I mustered up the words, 'I see y'all ain't thirsty anymore—at least, for something to drink.' Patsy raised her head and bellowed, 'Whew, yeeeeha, doggies' and laughed."

A second later, Charlie stormed in, seemingly oblivious to Patsy and Young on the bed. "He grabbed Patsy's purse," Flynt said, "took some money, and snapped, 'I'm going to buy booze.' Maybe he knew more than he was letting on because he went and grabbed Faron's guitar and told him, 'If you want to hear a gal sing, Sheriff, listen to Ree.' Charlie pushed the guitar on me. 'Here,' he said, winking, 'sing something.' I told him he was full of shit and to go get his booze. Patsy and Faron roared."

The Flynts and Young rode to the track in Patsy's Cadillac with Charlie behind the wheel. He had no idea where the entrance to the stage area was, and Young was telling him, "Turn here! Turn right, damn it! Turn left, damn it!" Then Patsy would chime in "No! Not here, damn it!"

"We came over a ridge and there was the track," quipped Flynt. "Faron hollered 'Gun it, damn it! Gun it!' And he did, and Patsy was yelling, 'No, Charlie! No!' but, egged on by Faron, he kept bad-assing. We raced around the track to be met by police cars, sirens blaring, and folks frantically waving their arms. An army of very upset people surrounded us. The guys from Faron's band came running. Patsy shouted, 'Get out, damn it! Hurry up and get out!'

"One of the cops wanted to know who'd been driving. On cue, Faron's boys raised their hands. I stood there stupefied. Patsy took the head officer aside, sweet-talking him that they had a show to do. Could they discuss it later? Thank goodness, they didn't smell Charlie's breath. By the end of the show, it was forgotten."

The partying resumed around the motel pool. "One of the drivers kept coming on to Patsy," reported Flynt, "and she kept ignoring him while not ignoring him. He was hard to ignore—good looking, great build, in his twenties. I kidded her that the only man she cared about was Charlie. When she ignored the guy's advances again, I razzed, 'Just as well. You probably couldn't get him if you wanted to.' Patsy shot back, 'You wanna bet?'"

Flynt was about to put up "good money" when Young arrived. "For a change he wasn't drinking, but he was making an ass of himself over Patsy by really hitting on her, I mean really hitting on her, and right in front of Charlie. She was saved by Ray, who asked her if she'd loan him some money. Without even wondering what he'd done with what he'd been paid, Patsy pulled a fifty out of her billfold. He was intoxicated, but argued that it was too much. Patsy told him it was the smallest bill she had and to pay her back when he could."

A jam session erupted. Patsy yelled to Young to play something fast, and one of the musicians started doing the twist. Patsy went into her room on the pretense of freshening up her makeup. Young followed.

"Next thing you know," Flynt stated, "this fellow came huffing and puffing and yelled, 'Patsy, some guy's stealing your car!' It took her a moment to open the door. She yelled to Charlie to do something. He ignored her. Pat and another guy stopped the culprit, who was drunk and pulling a prank. I gave Charlie hell, saying 'It'd be funny if you had to walk home.' He smart-alecked, 'Don't worry, she's got plenty damn insurance.'"

Flynt recalled another incident from that road trip, when Patsy was trying to make a call to her friend Trudy Stamper at Nashville's WSM Radio and kept getting the wrong number. She hadn't been up long and may have been a tad hung over. On the phone with the long-distance operator, "Patsy got louder and louder, repeating the station's name over and over, but the operator just didn't understand her. She got real huffy and said, 'No, Hoss, it's WSM. W-S-M! That's S! S! You know, as in s-h-i-t!' To her credit, the operator didn't hang up, and Patsy got her number.

Patsy admitted to Flynt and other close girlfriends that she had one "real bad crush." He was strapping South Dakota rancher Bill Lane, owner of Rapid City's Dan's Bar & Ballroom, where she appeared in 1961 and summer 1962. A former club employee said, "Patsy was always talking a blue streak about Big Dan."

Lane was head over heels too, and often surprised Patsy by showing up at dates or sending orchids—after kidding her about a line she sang on "Why Can't He Be You?"—including an orchid he brought her at Carnegie Hall. Lane says that he and Patsy had a "very deep friendship" and that he wanted more, but Patsy "wasn't going there."

☆

June Carter, back on the tour circuit with Johnny Cash, pushed him to book Patsy on his summer 1962 Shower of Stars tour. He agreed, and gave her star billing. Cash was married, but in name only, to wife Vivian, whom he used to call his "Snookie Pootsie." Now, he had a new Snookie in Carter. It wasn't the most discreet affair. He pleaded for a divorce, but Mrs. Cash said no. Carter vowed: "Vivian, he will be mine." It took four more years.

During the tour, Charlie visited Patsy on weekends. According to Carter, he and Patsy were often at each other's throats, especially if Patsy found him throwing her money away drinking or playing poker with the musicians.

Cash and Patsy had a brother/sister relationship, but neither that nor his relationship with Carter stopped him from trying to hit on her. In his autobiography he told of the night he had to check her out. "[I] knocked on her door. The response came back immediately: 'Get away from my door, Cash!' I did that, and never hit on her again. To her credit, she was still nice to me."

Observed Cash, "Patsy could cuss like a sailor. I'd hate to have gotten in a fight with her, but she was kind to everybody who treated her right. . . . She had the heart of an angel to go with her voice."

JR, as Patsy called Cash, wasn't fond of Charlie's disruptions, and Patsy sent him packing. But, remembered Carter, "every night they'd spend long periods on the phone, ending up arguing, trading insults, or accusing the other of something."

Patsy couldn't have been happier than in July 1962. She met her idol Elvis Presley again, this time in Memphis at a fundraiser for St. Jude Hospital, then in its fifth year of operation. When Patsy told Flynt she and Elvis were friends, Flynt doubted her. Flynt recalled, "So she picked up the phone and called Elvis. My heart was beating with excitement, which proved to be short-lived. He wasn't home, but whomever she spoke to told her he'd call her."

Not long after, things between Patsy and Charlie imploded. "I got the hell beat out of me," Patsy wrote Flynt, adding she had Charlie's "a—locked up to get sober and cool off. Then I slapped him with devorice papers and he moved out for two weeks." She relayed Charlie's "pleading" and his promise of "no more drinking and no calling me names," admitting she went soft and let him come home. But there was a caveat to make sure he knew she meant business. "The devorce hasn't been dropped," she stated. To renew the proceedings, all she had to do was "pick up the phone & say [to her attorney] 'go ahead with it' & it's over in four months."

Patsy's cousin Herman Longley claimed that in the incident where Charlie was arrested, he'd hit Patsy so hard a scar had broken open and bled. He noted that when being charged, the judge had told Charlie, "Come before me again for laying your hands on her and you're going to the penitentiary." Charlie dismisses that, saying he only spent a few hours in jail and that "the judge made Patsy come to court and drop it, so I got my revenge."

It appears that with so many threats to leave him, Charlie may have read the writing on the wall. The remainder of the letters Patsy sent Flynt are filled with career and baby talk. Somehow Patsy and Charlie managed to live more peaceably. And romantically.

On August 4, 1962, Patsy wrote Flynt that she was "p.g." and worried she might have a miscarriage: "I'm in bed now trying to keep it. Had the Dr last night and he said he thought I'd lose it yet. . . . I've got low blood and it's kinda early after losing all that blood from the wreck. . . . I sure didn't want to get this way but . . . I might have to go to the hospital." That stipulated, Patsy said she was busier "than a one arm man with an itch."

Two weeks later, she was boasting to Flynt that her "Showcase [album] sold 60,000 copies. . . . That's not bad, heck, at 18¢ each for me? And this new [album] they say will do better than that. Honestly Ree, I can't believe that I'm at long last able to make a little money. . . . I never got a check for records for 7 years. . . . Now it's like a dream. But I sure am grateful . . . & thank God for all these great things." Complaining of having to record another ballad, she wrote, "Decca says that's what they want, that that's my way of getting thru to the people. . . . But I sure would like to change the pace once in a while."

A week before her birthday, Patsy underwent a makeover to partially cover her scars, writing her friend: "Don't be surprised if you see a blonde living at my house. I am a blonde now with real long hair. It's a little funny at first when you see me but now every one says they like it better than my real hair. It's a wig. . . . Crazy Baby!"

On September 2, 1962, Flynt arrived for a week at the new Dick home in Goodlettsville. "When I got there, a boy was cutting the grass. Inside, Patsy was writing a check for him and crying. She said she couldn't get Charlie to cut the grass or do anything around the house, that with the medical bills and her need for plastic surgery, he wasn't even trying to save money. I boomed, 'Well, what good is he?' and she replied, 'No damn good.'"

Minutes later Patsy was in the throes of decorating, deciding what to do for the Labor Day weekend, and mopping and polishing to get the house ready for their first party.

Monday, Patsy and Ree picked up nearly twenty demos of songs Bradley had selected from various songwriters for the scheduled September 5 and 10 sessions and spent the rest of the day in the "music room" listening to the submissions.

"When Patsy went up to feed the kids and start dinner," said Flynt, "I threw her new LP *Sentimentally Yours* on the phono. It wasn't long before Charlie came home. He greeted me but when he realized what I was listening to he roared, 'Don't you ever get tired of listening to that bitch?' I asked what the hell was the matter with him. He didn't answer and proceeded upstairs."

The next day Patsy and Flynt went sightseeing and attempted to visit Cash, who wasn't home. Loretta Lynn, pregnant with twins, her husband, and friends visited that night. "We sat around talking shop and, except for Loretta, drinking," recollected Flynt. "Loretta whined that nobody liked her and that she'd never make it big. Patsy kept fluffing her up, telling her not to pay attention to the gals because they were just jealous."

On September 5, Flynt accompanied Patsy to Decca's studio, where Patsy was to lay down four tunes. "Patsy confronted Owen over how much she hated 'Tra Le La Le La Triangle,' which was on Monday's schedule. It certainly was in a pop vein, but another reason for her dislike might have been how close to home the song was." It was about a wife's tough choice between her lover and husband. Bradley calmed Patsy down, suggesting, "Why don't you wait until you hear the arrangement before you hit the ceiling?"

In the studio, said Flynt, "Owen dimmed the lights. Patsy's mood totally changed. When she finished 'Why Can't He Be You?' I tiptoed around the partition. Patsy was wiping her eyes. I whispered 'What's wrong, kid?' and she waved me off." Later, they gathered in the control room. Even Patsy was pleased with the playback. Bradley couldn't resist. He quipped, "Maybe now you'll like 'Tra Le La Le La Triangle'!"

The next morning, Patsy reached her mother, who had been picking apples all week.

From a poor family in Opequon, outside Winchester, Mrs. Hensley had picked apples as a child with her sister and parents Goldie Lavinia [Newlinger] and James Arlington Patterson. In 1916, at age thirty-one, Patterson fell from a roof and suffered a smashed leg. Because of an infection, a decision was made to amputate. In apple season, Hilda was in the orchards to earn money to support the family. Patterson died in the 1918 influenza epidemic. In 1929, as the nation slipped into the Great Depression, Goldie married a former prison guard, Frank Allanson, with whom she had five more children.

On the phone with her mother, Patsy, incredulous, wanted to know "Why have you been out in the fields all day?" Mrs. Hensley responded it was because she needed money.

Asserts Flynt, "Patsy was having none of it. She reminded Hilda she'd just sent her five hundred dollars and asked what the hell she'd done with it. She argued, 'Mama, if you need money, why didn't you ask me? I don't want you doing back-breaking work at your age.' Hilda shot back that she was only forty-five. She knew how to manipulate Patsy. She promised to send another five hundred!'"

Patsy slammed the receiver down and was silent for a few moments. Then she went about making a deposit slip for the bank, but told Flynt she didn't feel like going.

"I volunteered. Patsy handed me the keys to the Cadillac and a bag with cash and checks. I glanced at the deposit slip. The amount was twenty thousand dollars. I joked, 'Well, it was nice knowing you!' Patsy replied, 'Ree, I ain't worrying about you, Hoss! I'd trust you with my life.'"

☆

By her letter of November 22, Patsy's career was soaring. She bragged, "I got 6 awards . . . more than any other female or male. I'm so proud & happy I could bust.

. . . [T]he greatest of all, Ree, was [the] Star Award . . . the greatest anyone can get [She was the first female recipient] . . . [and] they gave it to me." She claimed a total of fourteen awards, nine of them Gold; and that every time she looked at them she cried. She expressed surprise that people were stopping and congratulating her. "I didn't dream so many people would know me."

On January 3, 1963, Patsy described a belated family Christmas gathering and an inauspicious beginning of the new year to Flynt. Referring to her husband by name, she reported that at the end of the Vegas engagement, Charlie left at 2:00 A.M., "drove 2,500 miles with only 11 hours sleep . . . and arrived in Winchester at Noon on December 27. . . . Both eyes looked like a wild man, but he wanted to be with me and the kids," whom she said got "a carload of stuff."

Charlie gave Patsy a silver tea and coffee service from Henesy Jewelry of Charles Town, West Virginia, a sweater, pants suit, and gold watch. Patsy presented him with a tape system with four speakers for his car (she gave another system to Randy for his plane).

Patsy reported that Mrs. Hensley would be "getting married to a fellow" as soon as "he can keep her in fine style and buy her a nice home," but soon she was ruminating in her letter about feeling used by her family, noting "The love and closeness we used to have will never be again."

In blow-by-blow detail, Patsy describes a brouhaha that broke out when her mother; her mother's "new Husband to be," Hale (last name unkown); Patsy's sister, Sylvia Mae, whom she referred to as Sibby; her brother, Samuel Jr.; and the siblings' dates returned "drunk" in the wee hours New Year's Day to Mrs. Hensley's home.

Patsy pointed out that she and Charlie were "stone sober" and with Julie and Randy, but that Sylvia and her boyfriend "had the damest bloodiest fight you've ever seen." In the scuffle, furniture and a door were damaged. Mrs. Hensley was holding Sam off, and the fiancé was kicking him. Patsy called the police, then she and Charlie hurriedly packed, grabbed the kids, and "left for good"—swearing she'd never return because "there just isn't any home there anymore. . . . None of them has ever helped to care for the place and I have done and done and paid and paid and bought and bought and paid their bills."

She decided to "live my life the best way I can, keep my troubles and mind my own business. See how they like it now without 'The BIG STAR sister' that can do anything she wants with all her money."

From comments Sylvia made, Patsy felt her sister was jealous. "I was never so hurt. . . . I have cried and cried and done all I can when life and living is easier for them now than its ever been."

She inferred Sylvia felt she'd been held back from a life of her own because she was the baby and, if she were to get married, there'd be no one to take care of their mother. She resented that with Mrs. Hensley planning marriage, she'd be left to work and pay household expenses.

Patsy's sense of humor wasn't missing: "Sibby's boy crazy, going with one fellow & nuts over another she can't get. [She] bought this fellow she's flipped over a diamond ring for Christmas and she's never went with him . . . and the fellow got the girl he's been dating an engagement ring."

She mentioned Charlie again, saying "he sees things a little clearer and sees how I worry and I'm beat to begin with and been sick for 6 weeks with sinus trouble and head colds and couldn't talk half the time. . . . Such is life, I guess."

In a sign that things had improved in their marriage, Patsy was hopeful that Charlie "will straighten out now. He sure was good to me in Vegas," helping with everything.

Mrs. Hensley and Sylvia called Patsy in Goodlettsville to apologize, begging her not to keep her promise. Patsy told Flynt that if she did return to Winchester, "they can come see me anytime but I will not ever spend another night in that place I used to call home."

Things may have been going smoother in Patsy and Charlie's marriage, but Sylvia kept informing friends of what Mrs. Hensley had insisted—that Patsy was leaving Charlie, planning to file for divorce following her July royalty payment, when she'd have money to cover legal and living expenses.

Sylvia told a friend, "Patsy still loves Charlie. She just can't live with him any longer." Other intimates observed Patsy had outgrown him. Charlie counters that they remained together until the end.

In Patsy's February 1963 letter, her last to Flynt, she doesn't mention Charlie but announces she'd "been busyer than a one arm man in a nest of bees" selecting a babysitter and recording. Of the next LP, she stated Bradley and Decca thought it would be her best yet, "and I sure hope they are right because I had 22 musicians . . . 4 nights in a row. But I believe we got a little something different this time." She closed with a list of what she had to do before leaving to do a show. It included washing, ironing, and fixing dinner.

In March 1963, according to Federal Aviation Agency [FAA] testimony reviewed in 2007, Randy's Piper Comanche had sixty gallons of fuel upon take-off. It was determined that the plane wasn't excessively loaded. Billy Walker noted his friends were traveling lightly: Patsy with only a makeup case and two dresses, "one white, one red," and the men with a change of clothes for the Kansas City shows.

No flight plan was filed as Randy's exact route couldn't be determined. Due to inclement weather, he'd "hedge-hopped" upon takeoff from Kansas City, making a brief stop at 3:15 P.M. in Rogers, Arkansas, to add fuel.

At 4:58 Randy notified the Service Flight Station [SFS] at Dyersburg Municipal Airport that he'd be landing in five minutes.

The restaurant there received a call from the regional FAA center asking if they would stay open because a plane was coming in.

Airport manager William Braese, thirty-five in 1963 and now in his eighties, recalls Randy "remarking how tiresome it had been traveling all day. He wanted to top off the fuel tank and be weather briefed." Braese found the landing gear door flapping, and Randy assured him it would be fixed.

As Patsy, Cowboy, and Hawk entered the restaurant, Carolyn Fay Jones, a twenty-two-year-old waitress, had just dropped a dime in the restaurant jukebox and selected "Crazy." Patsy made a beeline to the restroom.

Records show twenty-seven gallons of one-hundred-octane fuel were pumped into the wing tanks and the oil brought to the proper level. Paying the bill, Randy made small talk with bookkeeper Evelyn Braese, the manager's wife, who asked if he wanted to tie the aircraft down. He replied, "Let me first check the weather."

He was briefed by SFS specialist Leroy Neal that visibility was five miles with winds of twenty knots per hour and gusts of thirty-one knots, some rain, light snow, and overcast skies. Neal assessed conditions as "marginal" under Visual Flight Rules. He cited weather concerns throughout the area and pinpointed observation markers, such as highways and streets with lighting, though he warned these might not be visible because of clouds. Randy asked for the time of sunset and was informed it would come early due to the clouds. He inquired if the runways would then be lighted in case he had to return. Neal said they would be.

Randy made the call home. On hanging up, he informed Mrs. Braese, "My wife told me the sun just broke out, so we are going on.'"

He apprised Neal of the call. "The sun at Nashville most likely is going to be brief," he replied.

When Fay came to take the orders, Hawkins asked, "Do you know who's singin' that song?" She replied, "Why, that's Patsy Cline."

Patsy joined them and Hawkins, ever the practical joker, waved Fay over. "How would you like to meet Patsy Cline?" he wanted to know. She replied, "I'd love to!" He blurted, "Well, this is Patsy Cline!"

"I almost fainted," gasped Fay years later. "It was a good thing I wasn't holding a pot of hot coffee! Patsy was dressed all in red—red coat, red dress, red shoes. I asked her for an autograph and she complied." Fay remembered what everyone ordered: Hawkins and Copas had corned beef and cabbage, a special saluting upcoming St. Patrick's Day; Patsy had shrimp salad and iced tea.

Randy joined them, ordering only coffee, then left to check again with Neal. When Braese heard Randy was going on, he became quite concerned. "It boiled down to Mr. Hughes not having enough training to fly into weather. He wasn't aware of the thunderstorms that passed through, which was puzzling since he told me how rough flying had been."

On a map, Braese pointed out to Randy that as he ascended to two thousand feet, Kentucky Lake, four miles east, would be his "fade out point"; and that there were few visual guidance points in the sparsely settled area. In his Civil Aeronautic Board (CAB) report, he made no mention of offering Randy his station wagon for the continuation of the trip.

Ten minutes prior to takeoff, Braese overheard Randy and Patsy conversing. He says it might have been Patsy who was anxious to get back. "She didn't want to be late for some appointment. She told Mr. Hughes, 'If you want to stay, we'll stay. If you want to go, we'll go.'"

Randy did a thorough preflight check. The passengers entered—Patsy in the left rear, Copas [whom Braese referred to as "the youngest and smallest man"] at right. Randy entered over the wing. Hawkins had the co-pilot's seat. Randy revved the engine a few minutes to get the oil to takeoff temperature.

Braese called the takeoff at 6:07 normal. "I don't know what more I could have done. They were just in a hurry to get home."

At 6:30, Samuel Ward, an experienced pilot, was in his office four miles west of Camden. He heard an aircraft engine and went to investigate. He didn't see the plane but, from the sound, estimated it was traveling in a northerly direction. "It was running perfectly, just above the tree tops [about three hundred feet]. I thought the pilot must be lost and trying to orientate by the lights and highways. Then, I saw a white light going toward the ground at a forty-five-degree angle. The engine was cut and there was a dull crash and thereafter complete silence."

He contacted the Highway Patrol and a few minutes later gave trooper Troy Odle the estimated location as two miles north of Sandy Point village.

The crash site is five miles west of Camden off US 641 and Mount Carmel Road. Wreckage was spread over three hundred feet.

In 1979, Faron Young, discussing Randy's attempting the flight's last leg, surmised, "He was hardheaded. The Randy I knew as my sideman and manager would never have done that. It wouldn't have happened if he didn't have such a big head. Money and success managing Patsy changed him. Suddenly, he thought he was Colonel Parker [Elvis's manager]. The reason Randy bought his puddle jumper was envy. I had a plane, so he had to have one. He needed flying lessons. I warned him that when you spot dark clouds or a storm, don't think you can fly around it; just turn back."

☆

Rose Marie Flynt vividly remembers an incident on March 16, 1963, ten days after Patsy's death. Faron Young was headlining at the Washington, D.C. Coliseum (where the Beatles performed their first North American concert) with Don Gibson and Connie Smith. It was a show Patsy had been scheduled to do. Dottie West filled her spot.

"Patsy had sent me tickets," explained Flynt, "so I went, assuming there'd be tributes from Faron, Don, Connie, and Dottie. Backstage, I was stunned to see Charlie. As broken up as I'd heard he was, I thought he'd be in mourning. He asked me if I wanted a drink. I replied, 'You know I don't drink.' Faron was pretty snookered. His guitar cases were crammed with whiskey bottles. Charlie wasn't too far behind, but he could walk and talk. Dottie, my sister, and I had pushed Faron out of the dressing room and up a steep flight of steps to the stage. He kept saying, 'I can't do it. I can't go on.'"

It was too late; the MC had introduced him. As the women strained to get Young on, he was still whining. The promoter panicked, saying "The place is sold out. If he doesn't go on, I'll have to give everyone their money back!"

As screaming fans stomped their feet, the guitarist in Young's band stepped to the microphone and told them, "Folks, the Sheriff's gonna be out in a few minutes—as soon as he sobers up." The audience, thinking it was part of the show, howled.

"God bless Dottie," Flynt remarked. "She was trying to pump Faron up by saying, 'Sheriff, get it together so you can do the show or else no one's going to get paid!' He muttered, 'Hell, yeah, I'm gonna do the show. Nobody's gonna stiff me!'"

When the announcer introduced Young a third time, the women gave him a push and out he went—smack dab into the microphone, knocking it over.

"Faron stumbled to his guitar," Flynt laughed, "and, by some miracle, started his hit 'Hello, Walls.' I don't know how he did it, but he got through the show. Maybe he'd done it so many times, it was automatic."

After they got Young onstage, all shared a laugh. Charlie told Flynt, "You need a drink after that!"

☆

In February 1964, almost forgotten now, Loretta Lynn, wanting to explain Charlie's desperation, wrote and recorded the poignant ballad "This Haunted House":

> I watched you leave, that's how I know you're gone;
> But this heart of mine keeps telling me I'm wrong.
> I see your face before me ev'ry night
> In this haunted house when I turn off the lights.
> Sometimes I hear you walk across the floor
> And my arms reach out to hold you like before.
> I live for all the things we used to do
> In this haunted house I filled with love for you.
> This haunted house I'm living in is killin' me
> And the ghost of your love won't set me free.
> Each morning finds me crying and alone
> In this haunted house we used to call our home.[5]

True to Lynn's song, living in Patsy's "dream house" became too much for Charlie. He sold it in 1965 to singer Wilma Burgess, who accidentally discovered Patsy's "rainy day" stash in the bricks of the fireplace. She also discovered much more.

When Charlie departed, he'd left behind an archive of acetate radio transcriptions saying he would return for them. When he didn't, Burgess sold or gave them away to relatives and friends. A cousin ended up with the transcription of Patsy on *Arthur Godfrey's Talent Scouts*. Acetates of Patsy live at Tulsa's Cimarron Ballroom ended up in the hands of artist Tommy Overstreet.

Burgess swore the house was haunted: "There were strange occurrences. You'd be upstairs and the toilet downstairs would flush. Doors would open and slam. I'd be downstairs and it would sound as if a bowling ball was rolling down the upstairs hall. Sometimes, I'd hear music as if Patsy was singing."

Owen Bradley, who also produced Burgess, told her he could account for what was happening. "If Patsy's anywhere," he laughed, "she's in that house!" Dottie agreed, saying the house represented Patsy's "blood, sweat, and tears."

When her career slowed, Burgess sold the house. It was eventually purchased by the H. R. Nash family, who were careful to keep the dining room mural Patsy was so proud of and those specks of gold in the downstairs bath. Mrs. Nash also made quite a find: Patsy's diary from the 1950s. As excited as Patsy must have been about winning *Talent Scouts* and being hired as a regular, her entry for January 22, 1957, reads simply: "Started on Godfrey show. Saw Godfrey & talked." The next day, making her professional debut on national TV, she penned: "Was on morning show of Godfrey. Went to Decca. Got $25.00 from Paul Cohen."

Many consider Foggy Bottom to be Patsy, Cowboy, Hawk, and Randy's grave and their respective Winchester and Nashville cemetery sites symbolic mourning places.

The property owner deeded the area to Camden and an etched boulder was placed near the impact point.

W. J. (Jeffrey) Hollingsworth and his son Jenners, among the first at the scene, squirreled away the plane's tail section with part of the identification number and the belly. In 2001, the *Winchester Star* reported two brothers had secured the belly and attempted a sale to the Country Music Hall of Fame, which rejected the offer. Later, they purchased the tail section. The pieces were put on eBay, stated one of the brothers, "so the whole world could kind of get in on it." After protests, the items were pulled. The brothers informed eBay that they had cleared the sale with family members, and the auction was reinstated. The original low bid was $100,000, later reduced to $50,000; but the pieces didn't sell.

Charlie told the *Star* he had no desire to own any part of the plane: "It's just two pieces of tin. We have things of Patsy's . . . mementos we will cherish and keep forever."

In 2005, when Kathy Hughes visited the site, one of the brothers brought the tail section to display. Another brought the mangled propeller.

There have been efforts to honor Patsy as befits a star of her legendary status. At the forefront was Harold "Doc" Madigan, owner of Gaunt's Drug Store, who long ago restored the fountain and counter from which Virginia Hensley used to dispense ice cream and soda, though now it's used solely as a tourist attraction.

Charlie, daughter Julie, and Dick's brother Mel organized the Always Patsy Cline fan club.

There was a campaign for a sign to denote Winchester as Patsy's hometown. In 1986 the Frederick County Board of Supervisors endorsed having a street named after her. Mrs. Hensley was ambivalent about the honor. "I have kept quiet. I thought my absence in these things would convey my feelings. . . . It's a very nice gesture, but I think it's way too late. . . . If they wanted to do something in her memory— let's face it, they can't do anything for Patsy now."

The street naming never occurred. A year later, however, the developer of a new mall named an entrance road Patsy Cline Boulevard.

Since 1987 fans from around the globe gather in Winchester over Labor Day weekend to celebrate Patsy and the anniversary of her birth with a fan club–sponsored Saturday picnic and Sunday graveside service.

Helped by donations from family, fans, and the owner of the cemetery, a fifty-five-foot, $35,000 bell tower was dedicated that year. That same day the Virginia State Department of Transportation placed two markers on U.S. 522 South, designating the area between Winchester and Double Tollgate as Patsy Cline Memorial Highway.

In the beginning, Mrs. Hensley shied away from events; but later she began a music scholarship fundraiser banquet and was always present to meet Patsy's fans. She told the *Star*, "I realized how much people really love my daughter. Some had ridden the bus from Canada. I feel I'd be letting my daughter's fans down if I didn't help."

The Chamber of Commerce established a committee in March 1993—the thirtieth anniversary of Patsy's death—to create a museum. That entity became Celebrating Patsy Cline, Inc. (CPC). Museum plans have been afoot for some time but the project has consistently failed to get off the ground, to the chagrin of many fans.

After the 1998 fundraiser, Sylvia told several fans how difficult it was for her to listen to Patsy's final recordings, such as "Sweet Dreams (of You)" and "Faded Love," because of the hurt she heard in Patsy's voice. Even at that time, with little love lost on Charlie, Sylvia was still telling friends and fans that Patsy had planned to divorce Charlie.

That day CPC unveiled a model for the Patsy Cline Museum—a $4 million "Hollywood/Vegas–style monstrosity," as a fan put it. The exterior would feature a sixty-foot-high neon Patsy that winked. Sylvia, none too happy, was overheard complaining, "Four million dollars would pay for a lot of scholarships." The design was set aside.

A fan who attended several weekends said Charlie made appearances on Friday night, then hosted a small coterie of fans at his ground-floor hotel suite, "where everyone would hover over him and hang on every word. They worship him like he's a god from Nashville."

Charlie's suite has been dubbed "the party room" because it's BYOB with the bathtub filled with beer. Fans often spill into the courtyard, causing complaints about the noise. The party ends when Charlie goes to bed.

Appraised another fan, "I came to notice how odd it was that Patsy seemed absent from these events. Once, someone put on a Patsy CD. Charlie, in a bit of a stupor, hollered 'Turn that shit off!'"

Former fan club member Mark Willix sent Julie a 2003 e-mail inquiring how dues were spent. "She made it public," he decried, "and on Memorial weekend people were pointing and whispering behind my back. Charlie spotted me in the party room, came over, put his arm around me, and grumbled, 'If you ever say anything about Patsy or my life with her again, I'll knock the shit out of you.'"

Charlie would be at the picnic and grave service, but it was rare to see any interaction between him, Mrs. Hensley, and Sylvia. He's been notably absent from the scholarship banquets.

Julie, with current husband Richard Fudge and their four children, rode in a vintage convertible in the 1993 Apple Blossom Festival parade; but, except for 2003, she never attended the fan club events because of family and business obligations.

Jim Gibbons of Canada met Hilda Hensley at her first fundraiser, a meeting that blossomed into a deep friendship. "Hilda was a humble woman, living only on a pension, rent from the house across the street, and money she made as a seamstress."

On their last visit, Mrs. Hensley fixed supper and they watched footage of Patsy that had been transferred to video. "Watching Mom H watching Patsy sing, you could see the love in her eyes, the memories flashing through her mind." He was on an elite list of those to enjoy a sleepover at Mrs. Hensley's "with Patsy's outfits, costumes, and numerous personal items just a few feet away. More than anything, Hilda wanted a museum to honor Patsy. A reason she never sold the house across the street was because she hoped it would be it."

When the city seemed ready to assist in making that hope a reality by changing zoning laws, etc., Mrs. Hensley suddenly wasn't interested in working with them.

"Hilda's idea of a museum," explained Gibbons, "was a place for fans to see Patsy's memorabilia and costumes, which would be a source of income for her, Sibby, and Sam. With the city taking it on, income would go toward operating expenses and tourism."

Mrs. Hensley was excited about the prospect of a movie being made about her daughter and cooperated with the producers. However, she didn't want to meet the stars of *Sweet Dreams*, namely Jessica Lange, who played Patsy, and Ann Wedgeworth, who played her role.

Charlie wasn't the only one disappointed with the film. Mrs. Hensley said, "Jessica [Lange] did a wonderful job with what she had to work with [a performance that won her an Academy Award nomination]. We were told they were going to make a beautiful love story. . . . I saw it one time. That was enough."

At a 1985 family reunion, Dave Hess, son of Hilda's lifelong friend Maud, recalled Hilda going further. "She stamped her cane down and protested, 'Why couldn't they just tell the truth? They made Patsy out to be a cigarette-smoking, bar-hopping, beer-drinking slut.'"

Hilda Hensley died December 10, 1998, at age eighty-two.

"After a steady weight loss of about four months," Sylvia wrote friends, "[Mother] contracted the flu." Reluctantly, on December 7, Mrs. Hensley was admitted to Winchester Medical Center. The diagnosis was cancer, advanced and widespread. "We were in shock," lamented Sylvia, "but never dreamed how quickly things would progress."

Three days later, her mother, whom Sylvia called "the most decent human being I've ever known," closed her eyes "and gently drifted away . . . into a world free of pain, infirmity, or hardship."

Randy remained as silent as ever, but Julie wrote fans: "Grandmother was a very simple person who would always say, 'Don't do a lot for me.'" She was also quoted in the *Star*: "She was always busy cooking and caring for Randy and me. You could not make her slow down." Earlier, she noted, "When I came to visit, I did not come to visit Mrs. Hensley, I did not come to visit Patsy Cline's mother, I visited my Granny."

In Mrs. Hensley's *Star* obituary, there's no mention of another marriage. In the absence of court records it's impossible to know if she ever wed again, but reliable sources assert that she did and that the marriage was brief, ending not in divorce but annulment. If a marriage existed at her time of death, Hilda would have been ineligible for burial in Winchester National Cemetery as a veteran's wife; thus, the annulment. Some claim that she never divorced Sam.

Responding to condolence cards, Sylvia remembered her mother as "the greatest gift God ever loaned us" who "treated everyone the same—with simple respect, with quiet dignity and on occasion, a bit of motherly advice, reprimand, or down-to-earth homespun philosophy."

She described their last moments: "As I held her hand, I did not want to let her go but realized she no longer needed, or wanted, to stay. I thanked God for allowing it to be easy and peaceful; and for allowing us the solace of knowing she was not alone, or afraid . . . Knowing the impact she had on so many varied lives has made this hardest of life's losses a little more bearable. . . . Seeing how much of the intangible she gave to others, when she had so little herself . . . confirms the enormous faith, heart, and generosity which personified her life."

What wasn't acknowledged was what Hilda Hensley had wished for forty-five years. She was being reunited with her daughter Virginia, known to us forevermore as Patsy Cline.

In due time, it would be revealed that Hilda had been keeping a secret and, very early on, had allegedly led a secret life.

Mrs. Hensley didn't live to see her children feud over her estate and auction off the assets she prized and cared for: Patsy's colorful western costumes and clothing.

Through the years, with families of their own, Sylvia (Wilt, now divorced) and Sam didn't seek the spotlight. In fact, Sam showed no interest in the events related to Patsy. "He came once, incognito, to the scholarship banquet," noted a former CPC board member, "when coerced by Mrs. Hensley, but didn't stay long. He never offered to help raise money."

An intimate of Mrs. Hensley observed, "Sam was a mystery. He had issues. He resented never being able to pursue an acting or singing career. Patsy adored both siblings, but she encouraged his dreams of a show business career and helped him financially."

Patsy noted in her January 1963 letter to Flynt that Sam had passed his army physical and was about to be called to duty, "but his recklessness in driving and the records showing he won't listen to anyone" had the army thinking he was a "nonconformist. . . . [I've] talked to him until I'm blue in the face [and] thought [for] sure the army would straighten him out."

A family relation judged that heavy drinking and abusive behavior was responsible for Sam's divorce. "He wasn't a happy man," she related. "He could be brusque, and Hilda was sometimes sick over his behavior, which once, to Sam's great displeasure, caused her to compare him to his father."

Mrs. Hensley's one-page handwritten will, dated March 26, 1988, and filed with the circuit court eight days following her death, bequeathed "all my furniture, clothes, real estate, and assets to my children . . . to share equally in all things . . . in friendship together. . . . They have only each other now. Please keep the family ties. I would like some of Patsy's pictures [to] be given Randy & Julie."

She further stated that her wishes were to be carried out after any bills she owed were paid. After her signature, she had the document signed by a witness.

A family friend noted that Julie rarely visited her grandmother but that Randy came frequently and always brought Mrs. Hensley gifts. Sylvia and Sam's children lived locally and had a closer relationship. However, other than Randy and Julie, the other grandchildren aren't mentioned in the will.

The Kent Street houses were listed for sale in 1999. Sylvia attempted to prevent the sale on the pretense of preserving "the family ties." When that failed, she insisted the houses be sold as a package. That ploy also failed. In January 2000, the 605 and 608 Kent Street houses, assessed at $51,800 and $71,300 respectively, were sold.

The main interest was for 608, with the buyer planning to furnish it appropriately and have it open for tours. After renovations, it was listed for rental, an opportunity for "the ultimate Patsy Cline lover" to absorb her karma for only $625 a month. The rental had one catch: dealing with tourists who might make pilgrimages and knock on the door day or night.

By 2000 the division of other property, such as the costumes and other clothing Mrs. Hensley had made and personal items belonging to Patsy that had been loaned to Nashville's Grand Ole Opry Museum, was unresolved.

At a bank meeting with the estate administrator, Sam complained that he hadn't received an equitable share and attacked on a new front—accusing his sister of removing a trunk from Mrs. Hensley's home that contained a dress Patsy wore at the Hollywood Bowl and a replica of the off-white dress she wore at her final Kansas City performances.

"Things got loud," observed a family friend, "and Sylvia became so enraged, she was forcibly removed. It was always about money with Sam. He often got quite angry with Hilda for giving money away [for music scholarships]. He thought any money made in Patsy's name should go to the family. Sylvia didn't think Sam should get a thing, which led to all the bickering."

The friend also claimed that during this time Charlie insisted that the costumes and awards that had been in Mrs. Hensley's possession since the mid-1960s be returned to him as they were part of Patsy's legacy. "He stated he had only loaned them to Hilda."

In early 2001 Sam and the estate administrator sued Sylvia over the trunk items and division of Patsy's costumes and clothing. Sylvia maintained the trunk contained family photos, placed at her mother's for safekeeping, and that she'd never seen the replica dress.

Sylvia and Sam's private lives became very public as newspaper stories emboldened with graphic headlines detailed petty bickering. Circuit Court Judge John Wetsel attempted to get the siblings to settle. When they wouldn't, proceedings began on February 28, 2002. Very shortly thereafter came a bombshell.

Opposing counsel alleged that among items in Sylvia's unlawful possession was a book that Mrs. Hensley had been writing.

Rebecca Williams, Sam's companion of eighteen years, testified that she had seen and read "at least nine legal pads crammed full of Hilda's writings," adding that Mrs. Hensley wanted the vignettes about her life with Patsy published "so that her children would be taken care of financially for the remainder of their lives." Opposing counsel placed a value of $1.2 million on the manuscript materials and claimed that Mrs. Hensley had wanted the materials back.

Sylvia avowed in court that her mother had given her the pads to destroy in the mid-1990s after she'd informed Hilda that the book brought up painful childhood memories. This was corroborated by three witnesses, including Sylvia's daughter Christine, who testified that her grandmother "wanted to wash her hands of the project and had handed over the work to Mother to do with as she wanted." Sylvia testified that, with her mother's permission, she did indeed destroy the work in her fireplace.

Of the proposed book, Jim Gibbons said, "It was an intimate memoir by a devoted mother. Hilda said she wanted to get the true story out to correct misconceptions about Patsy. She read to me portions dealing with she and Patsy being in New York for the Godfrey show. That was a thrilling time for Mom H, not only being on national TV but also seeing Patsy win. She read another section relating to a time she spent in Canada with Patsy.

"According to what Mom H told me, the bulk of what she was revealing had to do with Charlie's treatment of Patsy. She never read that portion to me, but I counseled her that there was the strong possibility Charlie would be very angry. She said, 'I'm old and probably won't be around when this gets published, so there won't be any fallout for me from him.'"

She advised Gibbons that she had four publishers interested. "She needed the pages typed. Sibby and I offered. Of course, Mom H favored her daughter, but Sibby did nothing for almost a year—using personal issues, such as her pending divorce and her children—as excuses."

On March 1, the court case was handed over to a panel of seven jurors. Considering the convoluted goings-on, everyone expected them to be out for days. As deliberations began, Sylvia, caught up in the fast-approaching anniversary of her sister's death, was becoming visibly upset.

She didn't have to endure pain long. The panel returned their verdict in two hours, noting that the plaintiffs had produced little evidence to support their case. It was unanimous: in relation to the four matters before the court, Sylvia had committed no crime. She burst into tears. It was vindication, but at what cost? Shattered that Sam would sue her, she told intimates that their relationship would never be the same.

There were more than thirty Cline-related items still in dispute. Three weeks later, "after letting the dust settle," Judge Wetsel invited the parties to discuss which items could be sold or he would set another trial date. He explained to Sylvia that the plaintiffs might file an objection to the jury's judgment and that "this thing needs to be settled."

In April 2003, he ordered six of Patsy's costumes to be sold to offset expenses. Almost $10,000 was raised. Over $35,000 was due the estate administrator. Sylvia, claiming legal bills approaching $60,000, said she was unable to pay. The judge ordered 140 pieces of clothing and memorabilia onto the auction block.

The matter dragged on. By late May 2004, with no agreement, Judge Wetsel, "wanting to see the wrangling end," had them meet with a mediator. Using an egg timer to guarantee equal time, they went back and forth until all property was divided.

"Many feel that instead of destroying Mrs. Hensley's memoir," said a family friend, "Sibby squirreled it away. Nearly everyone found the proceedings a sad display of greed and jealously that would have Hilda spinning in her grave. Instead of fighting, Sibby and Sam should have pulled together after their mother's death."

The auctions—held in December 2002 at Beverly Hills' Profiles in History (PIH) and 2003 and 2004 at Christie's in Rockefeller Center, New York—were a devastating blow to fans. They were disheartened that Charlie, who had carefully groomed himself as a different person than the one depicted during his marriage, as protector of Patsy's image and benefactor of millions in royalties, didn't attempt to keep such valued history.

Julie wrote fans: "[it] is sad that my aunt and uncle can't settle this matter."

The auction contained a surprise. Mrs. Hensley had contacted PIH fifteen years earlier about how proceeds from the sale of her collection could go toward a museum. "She was in turmoil because raising the money [for a museum] would mean a sale of her daughter's possessions," said company president Joseph Maddalena.

The auction was a collector's gold mine. Predictions had some lots bringing as much as $100,000. "It will be a win-win situation," Maddalena pronounced, hoping buyers would in turn donate purchases to a museum.

There were eighteen lots—costumes fringed with white leather, casual wear, and cocktail dresses made by Mrs. Hensley but worthy of any top designer. Some lots contained a single outfit; others contained multiple items. The showstopper was the stunning black gown with three thousand sequins and matching purse with rhinestone clasp by Town and Travelwear, which Patsy had bought at New York's Waldorf-Astoria and worn in Las Vegas. It was estimated to go for $30,000 to $40,000 but failed to find a buyer.

Other highlights were a green silk chiffon dress with a cinch-waist belt by Academy Award–winning costume designer Helen Rose and the gold dress with black lace overlay bearing the label "Specially Hand Made and Fashioned by Hilda V. Hensley," created for Carnegie Hall (estimated $8,000–$12,000).

Seeing so many of her sister's items going to the highest bidder, Sylvia tried to prevent the sale of sixteen lots of Patsy's clothing and accessories in Christie's November 2003 Entertainment Memorabilia auction by offering to sell her house.

The auction house estimated sales in the range of $27,000 to $35,000. Among the standouts were Patsy's Western outfits in blue, green, and red—some fringed, some with rhinestones and music notes ($3,000–$3,500 each). In-person and telephone bidding was fierce on Patsy's famed white boots, which fetched $21,000. All total, $124,000 was realized.

For their 2004 auction, Christie's had eleven lots with estimates of $300 (costume jewelry) to $1,500 (clothing, costumes, and accessories). Remaining items included the Vegas gown and a rarely seen, elegant sleeveless black silk chiffon gown with pearl and rhinestone details that had a trailing scarf.

In a grassroots effort, fans raised $3,500 for CPC. Fans and collectors salvaged costumes and clothing worth $21,500, and a white Western hat for $3,585. The fan club/estate paid $2,500 for a Western outfit.

Fan and collector Brad Savage shopped both auctions, taking home seventeen outfits; among those, the Vegas gown for $4,500. Asked why he was buying Patsy Cline collectibles, he replied, "Patsy's name stands alone in the pantheon of country music. There won't ever be a greater female recording artist. Her songs are straight from the heart, from loneliness, from the soul; and with a pathos greater than any other artist. Her voice is something otherworldly, unique, magical."

The final auction realized only $23,000.

Suddenly, it seemed, Sylvia was ready to accept those painful memories she'd spoken of in court. A year after the trial, she was telling people she was writing a book. "Many thought it was really Hilda's notes," claimed the friend. To date, there's been no further mention of it. The November 2003 auction raised enough money to bring closure for Sylvia and Sam and a second trial became moot.

Though he married twice after Patsy deserted him (including once more to his first wife), Bill Peer took his love for Patsy to the grave. His son Larry, a musician living in Berryville, granted, "It was no secret Dad was head over heels for Patsy. She had a spell on him. He saw much potential in her, tried to develop that and go along for the ride. He lavished his inheritance from his mother on Patsy, taking her to New York, Nashville, many other places, getting her recorded locally and paying for her first Nashville sessions. When the money ran out, she left him."

One of the musicians in Peer's Melody Boys surmised, "I don't know if Patsy ever loved Bill. She certainly used him. In 1956 he worked some kind of deal at Goode Motors in Charles Town, where he worked in the parts department, and got her a new Buick. She saw it and bemoaned, 'Oh, I wanted a Cadillac.'"

Patsy got her Cadillac the next year from Charles Town jeweler Bill Henesy, who also had an auto dealership. She was a bit disappointed. It was a convertible, buffed to a high sheen, but nonetheless a used car.

In March 1951 Patricia Virginia was born to Bill and Jenny Peer. She was called Patsy. Many assume Peer named his daughter after Patsy, but, refuted Larry, it was the other way around. "Dad didn't even meet Virginia Hensley until 1952."

He remembers the uproar when his mother discovered the Valentine's card Patsy sent Bill in 1955 with a photo of Patsy in her undies and signed "Love, Patsy." Observed Larry, "That was all the proof Mom needed to prove what she'd suspected."

Even after their professional and personal breakup, Peer kept popping back into Patsy's life when she played local dates and on occasions when Patsy returned to the Brunswick Moose Lodge with Charlie.

As a child, Bill Peer had been kicked in the chest by a horse. Through the years doctors attributed the pain he experienced to that accident. But those closest to him knew better.

In later years, in a blunt father/son talk, Peer told his son that he had made a lot of mistakes and maybe Patsy was the biggest. "Dad never got over what Patsy did to him," said Larry. "He reconciled himself to the fact that she didn't love him, but what he could never forgive was her lack of recognition of what he strived to do for her. That was a worse pain than any kick in the chest."

Equally upsetting was scuttlebutt Bill and Jenny heard about how he used Patsy to advance his career. "That was ridiculous," snapped Jenny. "We'd been so close, great friends. We used to have Patsy and Gerald to our home. We loved Patsy, but I was no fool. Even a blind person could see how much Bill loved Patsy. Bill would have gone to the ends of this earth for her, and a couple of times he pretty well did. Look at the appreciation he got. She never ever mentioned his name. However, bitterness aside, Patsy's death devastated all of us."

As a result of his childhood accident, in the early 1960s Peer developed blood clots in his lungs. For relief, he'd "eat Rolaids like candy," rub his chest, and, sometimes scaring folks, suddenly throw his arms in the air.

Patsy Peer was a three-time winner of the National Championship Country Music competition. When her father took her to Nashville in 1967 for demo recordings, they visited Charlie and his family.

"It seemed strange he'd go there," maintained Larry, "because of so much that happened. But Charlie was working in the music business and maybe Dad thought he would help."

On September 4, 1968, Bill Peer was admitted to Charles Town General Hospital for a hernia operation. Everything that could go wrong did. When the doctor was stitching the wound, he used methylate, some of which flowed into Peer's privates. It was sponged and the wound rinsed, but the methylate caused swelling and incapacitated him. Then Peer developed a clot in his leg. Larry visited his dad the morning of September 19. A few hours later, Peer was dead. The blood clot had passed into his lungs.

Peer was forty-eight. At his viewing, more than one thousand people signed the funeral home register. In his obituaries there was one sentence about his famous protégé: "It was while his band was playing in the Washington [Capitol] arena, that Miss Patsy Cline, who was a member of the Melody Boys and Girls band, began her climb up the ladder of success by being signed by the Jimmy Dean show for Saturday night appearances."

The bandleader and his daughter were set to make demo records in Nashville in October. "Once more, Dad was close to his dream, but came up short."

Patsy Peer, saying it wasn't the same without her father, abandoned her career dreams, married a minister, and sings in church.

With writing partner Lorene Allen, Loretta Lynn again mourned the loss of her "buddy" in 1972 with the poignant "I Miss You More Today (Than Yesterday)."

In her 1976 best-selling autobiography, *Coal Miner's Daughter*, Lynn devoted a chapter to Patsy, recalling their last visit (February 21, 1963), when Patsy came over to hang new drapes. That night, Loretta and Mooney were summoned to Patsy and Charlie's home, a visit she elaborated on in her book: "Patsy embroidered a tablecloth. . . . Randy was on a rocking horse, rocking very hard. I was worried that he'd fall off and get hurt, but Patsy said not to worry." In the box of clothing Patsy gave Loretta "was a little red, sexy shorty nightgown. She told me, 'This is the sexiest thing I've ever had. Red is the color men like.'"

She described the nightie as one "made out of two small Band-Aids, and one a little bigger"; but revealed she could never bring herself to wear it.

Loretta released *I Remember Patsy* in 1977, produced by Bradley, also her long-time producer; it included a seven-minute-plus track on which she reminisced about Patsy. The sessions weren't easy for Loretta. "Memories of Patsy grew stronger within me," she said. "I began crying . . . and the strangest feeling came over me. It was like Patsy herself was telling me how ashamed she was. . . . I felt she was talking to me—telling me to 'go to it, girl'—and I sailed through without a hitch.'"

That year, old friends clashed when Loretta took umbrage to an interview in which Dottie called Patsy "a boozer and a cusser." Defending Patsy, Loretta shot back, "She wasn't like that. . . . Patsy came up rough, sort of jerked up by the hair . . . but she never done anything any worse than anybody else, or as bad as most. . . . Patsy took a lot of my problems with her. I'm going to my grave with a lot of hers."

Dottie was stunned. "Patsy was my idol, one my best friends. She loved life and was so full of love and a good-hearted person. She was a beer drinker and a cusser, which she got from coming up in a hard life, and didn't care who knew it."

Charlie and Dottie maintained a close friendship, and he even wrote three songs with her and Bill: "In It's Own Little Way," which Dottie recorded, "My Heart's Daily Reminder," and "What's the World Coming To." It's been claimed she and Charlie had a fling (which she declined discussing).

In 1978 Loretta spoke of Patsy's hold on her: "Some people will think I sound crazy, but I've had ESP all my life." She added that while performing in Las Vegas and experiencing dry throat, "I felt Patsy's hand on my arm. . . . I could feel her saying, 'Don't you worry, Loretta, it's gonna be fine.' And it was."

In 1963 Patsy's first husband, Gerald Cline, married Sarah Louise Bayer, who gave birth to a daughter, Gina, in 1967. Gina now lives in the family home in Martinsburg, West Virginia. While Cline's three earlier marriages seemed sealed with invisible glue, this one stuck. He settled down because Sarah, who knew his reputation, laid down rules; and because, finally, he'd found a woman he loved and who loved him. Well into the 1970s, Gerald was a driver of sixteen-wheel rigs, but he retired when diagnosed with heart ailments.

"He was a good father," Gina remarked. "He wasn't a hobby-oriented or lets-go-fishing person. We didn't do a lot of things together. He just enjoyed doing stuff around the house. One thing he never did was carve, as his character is seen doing, making a boat, in *Sweet Dreams*. They interviewed him, but I don't know where they got that from. I guess they had to have him doing something!"

Except for a photo of Gerald and Patsy on their wedding, Cline had no other souvenir of his most famous wife; and he never spoke of Patsy to his daughter. "He never shared any memories of that time," Gina stated. "It was not a discussion we ever had."

Gerald died following a 1994 heart attack. He was sixty-nine. Though he and his son Ronnie had never been close, Ronnie did attend the funeral.

Dottie recorded several songs in the early 1960s that had been hits for Patsy, who always had high praise for Dottie's vocal and songwriting talents.

Mrs. Hensley considered Dottie probably Patsy's closest Nashville friend, and she was disappointed when she couldn't make Patsy's funeral and sing in her honor. "She always told me she wanted to visit Patsy's grave," explained Mrs. Hensley. "Finally in 1976, Dottie called and asked if I'd accompany her to the cemetery so she could lay some flowers. She said, 'Be sure and look real nice.' I asked if she was going to have pictures taken. She replied yes. I explained the only way I'd agree to go was if there were no pictures. She said she'd call me back, but I never heard another word."

Years later, Dottie confirmed the call. "I should have known better," she admitted. "I wasn't thinking."

In 1964 Dottie became the first country female to win a Grammy Award and went on to another thirteen nominations.

On January 6, 1969, a fire destroyed Dottie's home. She came within a hair's breath of being killed. Three things survived: her first engagement ring, a watch, and Patsy Cline's scrapbook.

Dottie underwent a makeover in an effort to shake her country image. She had plastic surgery, wore tight-fitting and revealing costumes (some by Bob Mackie), and posed for a men's magazine, which resulted in backlash from conservative fans.

She recovered to enjoy a second career with a number of top-selling duets with Kenny Rogers. She had numerous charted singles and albums and a massive crossover 1973 hit with Billy Davis's "Country Sunshine" (originally recorded for Coca-Cola commercials). That year, she and husband Bill West divorced. Dottie made TV appearances, was a frequent club headliner, and toured in the Broadway musical *The Best Little Whorehouse in Texas*.

Dottie married twice more, with both marriages ending in divorce. Following lawsuits by two managers and a series of bad investments, Dottie borrowed heavily. At the time her bank was forclosing on her home, the IRS came after her for $1 million in back taxes. All but destitute, she filed for bankruptcy protection.

More trouble ensued when Dottie was found hiding belongings. The FBI entered, criminal charges followed, and an auction was held. Several friends donated purchased items back to her. Rogers gave her one of his cars. Charlie and Julie, worried that Patsy's scrapbook would be sold, were given permission to rescue it.

Between 1990 and 1991, Dottie toured with her daughter Shelly, a rising country star. Dottie's career was one of country music's longest lasting. Her last record was in July 1991. That August she was badly injured when, en route to the Opry, her car stalled. An eighty-one-year-old neighbor offered her a lift. Approaching the exit at excessive speed, he lost control and the car soared eighty feet across the highway and into an enbankment.

Though badly injured, Dottie pulled the driver out and, as Patsy had done after her 1961 accident, insisted that he be taken to the hospital first. She suffered a ruptured spleen and lacerated liver. On September 4, 1991, during a third surgery attempt to stop the bleeding, she died.

President George H. W. Bush, a longtime fan for whom West had performed at the White House, expressed condolences during an appearance at that year's CMA Awards. Her hometown, McMinnville, Tennessee, renamed Highway 56 the Dottie West Memorial Highway. She's yet to be inducted into the Country Music Hall of Fame.

☆

Country music pioneer Ernest Tubb passed away in 1984; but, due to a family dispute involving his estranged wife, Olene, it took five years for his resting place to get a headstone.

Del Wood was one of the most vocal artists in her disdain for country music's swing toward pop/rock. She was highly critical of Opry officials for giving more exposure to newer stars, whom she would often insult, sprinkling her remarks with expletives. As her career faded, Wood became more and more bitter. She appeared frequently on the Opry through summer 1989. Wood died following complications from a stroke that October.

Patsy's beloved friend Roger Miller went on to win thirteen Grammy Awards and write a Broadway musical, *Big River*, which won him a Tony Award. He died in 1992 after fighting lung cancer. Miller was inducted into the Country Music Hall of Fame in 1995.

Beloved comedienne extraordaire and Hall of Fame inductee Minnie Pearl continued to be a huge presence on the Opry into 1991. She died in 1996 at age eighty-three and was buried with her famed straw hat with the price tag.

Faron Young also died in 1996 at age sixty-four of a self-inflicted gunshot wound after being diagnosed with emphensyma and prostate cancer. In 1993, he'd been ranked by *Billboard* as the twentieth-most-successful Country Singles Artist of All Time. Young was a 2000 Hall of Fame inductee.

Owen Bradley, musical innovator and producer of some of the biggest acts in country music, died in 1998. The brilliant songwriter Harlan Howard passed away in 2002.

Doyle and Teddy Wilburn remained Opry members until Doyle's death in 1982 at age fifty-two. Teddy continued solo. He died in 2003, days before his seventy-second birthday.

Porter Wagoner died of lung cancer in 2007.

Samuel L. Hensley Jr. died, presumably of cancer, in Bunker Hill, West Virginia, November 1, 2004. He was sixty-four. Three daughters survived him. Another daughter is deceased. He had seven grandchildren and one great-grandchild. After his divorce, Sam relocated to California. His partner Rebecca Williams has a son.

In December 2006, Williams sold over one hundred items associated with Patsy from his estate to CPC and Legacy. The sale included a sewing machine of Mrs. Hensley's, several of her design sketches, and framed Gold and Platinum Records from Decca/MCA for sales of *Patsy Cline's Greatest Hits*.

Julie had four children. She named Virginia, from her first marriage (to Michael Connors, which ended in divorce), after her grandmother. Sadly, she was killed in a 1994 auto accident. She was fourteen and had appeared in music videos. Fudge has three grandchildren, making Charlie, at age seventy-six, a great-grandfather.

Randy, who closely favors Patsy, has remained largely unseen and unheard. He doesn't participate in fan club activities. Mrs. Hensley often told of how he'd doted on her and she on him. She observed that he was more like Patsy, and that Julie was daddy's girl. Little is known about him except that he is or has been a musician.

In a message sent to fans, Julie noted that Randy "has played around with drums and guitars, but hasn't done anything professional. He enjoys music, movies, and exotic animals. . . . He likes hunting, usually with a bow. He has been known to go shark fishing. He has never been married, and says he doesn't intend to. He has had some girlfriends, but not a special one that changed his mind."

Among Patsy's relations, singer/songwriter Matraca Berg is a third cousin, and actress Jennifer Love Hewitt, through her grandmother Charlotte Shipp, is a distant cousin.

In a fascinating turn of events, Patsy may be descended from royal blood.

Patsy has often been referred to as the Queen of Country Music. As far-fetched as it sounds, there's the possibility she may be descended from the German royal family. Patsy may have known, which could be why she often wore a jeweled tiara.

Charlie could be "royal" by marriage—consort to Princess Patsy; and Julie and Randy could be a princess and prince.

Hilda Hensley, for nearly half a century as Patsy's protector, was, as one fan put it, "considered a saint." It comes as a bit of a shocker that in her youth she may have been a gal that several men chased until they caught her.

Charlotte Brannon Bartles and Barbara Henesy O'Donnell—unknown to each other—vow that their fathers, Chester Brannon and Darwin Henesy, not Samuel Hensley, was Virginia Hensley's father.

Chester Brannon, a Winchester native, avid fancier of women, racecar driver, and amateur pilot, enjoyed taking Hilda to the local car races.

Darwin Henesy, a nephew of R. J. Funkhouser, one of West Virginia's legendary entrepreneurs, was a Charles Town native, avid fancier of women, racecar enthusiast, industrial spy, Pennsylvania quarry manager, World War II pilot, jeweler, auto dealership owner, and banker.

Where Samuel Hensley—farmer, quarry worker, and later a blacksmith who had a penchant for singing—fits into the puzzle isn't easy to decipher. It will never be known if Hilda Patterson met Sam at a church social, as the story goes, or if she was introduced to him in a last-ditch effort to save face when she became pregnant.

In 2005 Charlotte Bartles, née Brannon, in her book [with Linda Sowers] *Patsy Cline: Our Father's Other Daughter*, revealed that her father, called Chet, was Virginia's father and her half sister. It hadn't been the best-kept secret among close friends and kin of Hilda, Patsy, or the Brannon families. They were cousins, aunts, and uncles by marriage who often visited each other.

Hilda, only fourteen, met Chet, eighteen, in 1931 when, according to Mrs. Bartles, Hilda came from Gore to the farm and apple orchard outside Winchester of Tom Brannon and his wife Lizzie to care for their five kids while she was pregnant with number six.

Chet, whose family spread was across the field, staggered home one night and fell into Tom's hog pen. Hilda found him laying face down, shooed away the hogs, and stayed with him until morning. In the days that followed, Chet jumped the fence between the properties to call on Hilda, and they'd go off, spending hours alone.

Brannon, quite handsome and with a reputation as a daredevil, was shameless, dating Hilda and her Winchester friend Gladys Scroggins [later his wife] at the same time.

"When Hilda came to him with news she was pregnant, Dad wanted to do the right thing," affirmed Chet's daughter, "but her mother, Goldie, and her husband, Frank, were dead-set against it. They said Hilda was too young to get married."

But marriage, literally an old-fashioned hill country "shotgun" wedding, it was. The license from Winchester's United Brethren Church, validated in Frederick County courthouse files, disclosed that Hilda and Sam wed on September 2, 1932—not 1929 as Mrs. Hensley had claimed. Documents and birth certificates on file indicate Virginia Hensley's birth was six days later.

Mrs. Bartles asserted Sam would have known he wasn't the father since Hilda was in her ninth month.

"I can't imagine how frightening it must have been to find herself in such a situation," she empathized, "barely out of childhood herself, poor, pregnant, and unmarried. She or her mother made a decision, and I'm sure they felt it was the best one for her and her unborn child."

But the Brannons, she says, along with relatives and nonrelatives, including

Charlie, "knew who Patsy's real father was. I still hear echoes of Patsy telling me she was going to see Daddy."

One reason Patsy visited Chet, Mrs. Bartles claims, "was because he was generous. I had my measly allowance, but he'd give Patsy and Hilda real money. Patsy said several times she was grateful my father was good to them."

She related that her father was never openly affectionate with her, "but lit up like a Christmas tree and oozed with charm at the sight of Patsy. I was in second or third grade, and it all didn't sink in, but as I grew older I found it embarrassing to constantly hear Daddy tell family members Virginia was his daughter."

On comparing 1950s photographs of Patsy and Charlotte, there is no doubting a strong resemblance.

After the family moved to Hancock, Maryland, and Virginia became Patsy Cline, Chet informed Charlotte, "Patsy's your sister. You look just like her and you act just like her." She laughed that she didn't know whether to take that last part as a compliment.

It wasn't uncommon for her father and mother to discuss Patsy and what she was doing careerwise "as anyone would talk about a member of the family."

Her parents rarely missed going to Washington on Saturday nights to catch Patsy perform with Jimmy Dean on the Town and Country Jamboree at the Capitol Arena. With Sam out of her life by 1957, Mrs. Hensley invited the Brannons to Patsy and Charlie's wedding. They opted to attend only the reception.

Hilda and Patsy would drive the family car to Brannon's Mobil Oil station for check-ups and repairs. They also visited his home with his wife and family.

On one occasion, Mrs. Bartles told a friend that Patsy and Hilda often came to visit. "She said, 'Don't you hate Hilda?' I replied, 'Why would I hate her?' And I loved Patsy."

Chet Brannon told his daughter that there was jealously on her mother's part concerning Hilda and Patsy. "If there was," she said, "she hid it well. I never heard Mom badmouth Hilda. Whenever she came to visit, she welcomed her with open arms."

Even after her rise to fame, Patsy didn't deny Brannon was her father. Mrs. Bartles reports a friend trumpeting to Patsy in a Winchester restaurant, "You're Patsy Cline, aren't you? You're Chet Brannon's daughter." Patsy purportedly replied, "Yes, but I'm not allowed to speak about it."

"If anyone were to look at our father's facial features," argued Mrs. Bartles's brother Bob, "you can see Patsy had a lot of them, especially the nose and jawline."

A memorable day for Bob was in 1957 after Patsy had won the Godfrey show. "It was a Saturday afternoon. I was getting home from basketball and about to put my gym bag in my room. Mom told me, 'Be very quiet. Patsy's taking a nap on your bed.' I went in on my tiptoes."

Later, Patsy came to the kitchen, where Bob was sitting with his mother. Patsy told jokes and stories. "She'd let a cuss word slip and glance at Mom and me with a look of apology," he recalled.

Her cursing might have been something she inherited from Sam. When he joined Hilda at another relative's home for dinner, Sam stunned his host "not only insulting Hilda but also with incessant cussing and blasphemy."

Bob said that Patsy had a wonderful laugh. "After she finished the punch line of a story, she'd stomp her foot hard on the floor. Once, when she did that, the heel of her shoe broke off. I tried to fix it and Patsy shrugged, 'Hell, I'll get another pair. They were only eighty dollars.' That kind of struck us. At the time, women paid twenty to twenty-five dollars for a pair of heels."

When Chet came home from the station next door, he and Patsy were all smiles. He was delighted when word spread that Patsy had come to visit. Mrs. Bartles divulged, "Cars would line up outside with folks hoping to get a glimpse. Daddy was proud of her success and he'd invite people in to meet her."

One taker wouldn't forget the introduction. Patsy was getting dressed when Brannon yelled, "I got someone I want you to meet." Recalled Bob, "She stunned everyone, coming out wearing this big grin and nothing more than a red bra and half-slip. They stood chatting for ten minutes."

After a visit when Hilda, "looking very attractive and slender though she had curves like Patsy," came with Patsy, Charlie, baby Julie, and Sylvia for a fried chicken dinner, Mrs. Bartles's mother did something rare. "She had been observing Patsy and I sitting next to each other on the couch and she said, 'I saw how much you favor each other.'"

There were arguments over the attention Chet paid Patsy. After one very heated exchange, Mrs. Bartles said her mother was very upset and scolded, "You didn't claim Patsy when she needed you, so why are you claiming her now?"

Mrs. Bartles didn't meet "my half sister" until 1955, when "Daddy took me to see Patsy sing at a carnival. He was very eager to hang out with her, but the feeling was mutual."

Until he was halfway through college [1961], Bob never knew Patsy was considered his half sister. Mrs. Bartles spilled the beans, and the story started coming out in drips and drabs.

In later years, when Patsy played locally, Mrs. Bartles made a point to catch the shows. When Patsy knew she and her husband were there, she would either join them at their table or invite them backstage.

Mrs. Bartles, always struck by Patsy's compassion, remembered a show where a family walked six miles to see her perform, "Patsy was so moved, she insisted on taking them home." Mrs. Bartles went along on the ride and, on the return, was tempted "to broach the subject of how we were related, but I couldn't bring myself to do it."

She said that Mrs. Hensley or her Aunt Maud called to inform her family of Patsy's death. Chet told Mrs. Hensley he'd take her to Nashville. "Daddy put some things together," said Bartles, "went to his friend and barber Oscar Truax, and asked if he could go to the head of the line. He told Oscar, 'I just got news my daughter was killed outside Nashville and I have to drive her mother there.'"

Her father and family members tried to attend Patsy's funeral, but were stymied by miles and miles of backed-up traffic.

After Patsy's death, noted Bartles, her father "was quite subdued and evasive when people asked him about being Patsy's father. However, he never denied it."

Chet Brannon died in 1984 at age seventy-two.

In 2007, asked why she never discussed the paternity issue with her father, or in a later visit with Mrs. Hensley in Winchester, Charlotte Bartles lamented, "It was out of fear of his reaction. He had a dark side others never saw. As far as Hilda is concerned, Patsy was dead and I simply couldn't muster the courage to talk about those long-gone days."

Darwin Henesy, called Bill, of Charles Town, was a descendant, by way of his uncle, the thrice-married industrial visionary R. J. Funkhouser, of the royal house of Saxe-Coburg, with lineage to Prince Albert, consort to Queen Victoria.

A Republican, Funkhouser ran losing campaigns for governor of West Virginia and for the senate. On retiring, he became a prodigious philosophical writer and, with wife Peggy Morningstar, a preservationist for the homes built by Charles Washington, brother of the first president.

Henesy's daughter Barbara O'Donnell believes her father and Mrs. Hensley had an affair while he attended Shenandoah College in fall 1931, a month before his eighteenth birthday. "He went one semester and flunked out. He only took three subjects. His main interest was women."

She claims Henesy fathered Patsy Cline. "He didn't want to settle down and marry Hilda when she became pregnant. He was young, had money, and enjoyed playing the field. But he had to do something. Daddy knew Sam from Winchester and arranged for him to marry Hilda and give her baby a name."

Mrs. O'Donnell, a former interior decorator and wholesaler of objects of fine art, was born in 1946 and resided in Charles Town into her teens before relocating with her mother and younger sister Billie Jean to Arizona and Florida.

She has no correspondence between Mrs. Hensley and her father, but possesses snapshots from 1933 purporting to be of Hilda, seventeen and married about a year, with shoulder-length hair, being embraced by the handsome, dapper Henesy, and some from 1938 in which her hair is in a bob. When shown the photos, friends of Hilda Hensley's, including Jim Gibbons, said the woman bears a likeness to Hilda but didn't believe it to be her.

Mrs. O'Donnell recalled Hensley family fishing trips well into the 1950s where, she claimed, her father rendezvoused with Mrs. Hensley. She also recollected being with him at the Hensley home for Sylvia's high school graduation party while in her teens.

In 2007, when asked why she'd waited so long to come forward, Mrs. O'Donnell responded, "No one wanted to hear my story. Publishers replied that without conclusive proof, such as DNA, they wouldn't touch it. All I have are my recollections."

Mrs. O'Donnell reported that in younger years she was often mistaken for Patsy. In side-by-side photos of the two, a resemblance cannot be doubted.

Before joining the military in the 1940s Henesy helped run several Funkhouser companies, including a mine quarry where he employed Sam and Randolph, his son from his first marriage. He later threw his hat into the political ring, running a losing campaign for state senate.

Mrs. O'Donnell recalled waking up in the wee hours of March 6, 1963, "with a premonition that Daddy had been killed. I was crying and wanted to call him. Mother said if something had happened, we would have been notified."

When she rang the store later, she recalled shop assistant Ruby Shewbridge informing her that her father was alright but quite broken up over Patsy's death.

"What?" she responded. "Patsy's dead?" When she asked for her father, she was told he was getting a flight to Nashville.

Many claim that some statements Mrs. O'Donnell made are improbable, such as her father attempting to have Patsy buried in the Funkhouser or Henesy plots in Winchester Cemetery.

She said that when she wanted to discuss all this with Mrs. Hensley, friends advised against it. "Even Charlie said not to bother," she admitted. "I spoke with him on the phone. We had a very interesting conversation. There were things about his family he needed to know."

No one interviewed mentioned a relationship between Henesy and Hilda Hensley. Those who might know are no longer alive to verify O'Donnell's account. She admits that her father never out-and-out said that he was Patsy Cline's father. However, she firmly believes it to be true and alleged that besides Patsy, Henesy sired five other children out of wedlock, including two who went on to international fame as singers.

Henesy died in 1970 from head injuries suffered when a car hit the vehicle he was a passenger in. He was fifty-six.

Patsy told Dottie and Del that Sam had molested her. When the *Sweet Dreams* production team interviewed Mrs. Hensley for their film, she informed them that Sam didn't so much desert his family in 1947 when Patsy was thirteen but was asked to leave.

Dottie revealed to Patsy that she'd been molested by her father from age twelve to eighteen. When she reported the abuse to authorities, Dottie testified against him, resulting in his serving forty years in prison.

Until early December 1956, Patsy and Sam were estranged. However, when Mrs. Hensley told Patsy the news that Sam had been diagnosed with lung cancer, they visited him at the hospital. With Mrs. Hensley present and as a witness, she called him "Daddy." This was their last visit. He died a few days later.

Well into the 1980s things were often tense between Mrs. Hensley and Charlie. A friend mentioned once that when she was upset, Mrs. Hensley "gritted her teeth and swore that if she could, she'd get rid of him. She was expressing how she felt after the many things Patsy told her and how he treated her. The pain went deep."

This dislike had to be difficult for Mrs. Hensley because she and Charlie's mother, Mary, had been longtime, devoted friends.

The friend, like many, "found Charlie to be a likable guy but his dark side bothered me. When you hear things over and over, that usually confirms it. He hurt Hilda over the years, and it was a challenge for her to be civil. She only did it for the sake of Julie and Randy."

Mrs. Hensley alleged that when she requested Charlie send her Patsy's awards, costumes, and clothing, he shipped them C.O.D. Mrs. Hensley, caught unawares, didn't have enough cash. Peeved, she left the deliveryman on her front porch and went to her bank.

In her will, Patsy was leaving Mrs. Hensley "all money which is in my possession at the time of my death or any income to follow . . . to use in any way to bene-fit and educate my children Julia and Allen Dick . . . [with] any royalties paid to me . . . to go to the care and education of Julia S. and Allen Dick."

The only things Patsy bequeathed to Charlie were "my western designed den furniture, a hi-fi stereo record player and radio, records and albums and tape recorder and blond floor model television set . . . [and] whatever make car we have at the time of my death."

He got Patsy's Cadillac—and a lifetime of huge royalties.

Patsy Cline's fans now number in the millions and come from every walk of life. Many never intended to become fans. They came across Patsy accidentally, liked her, but thought it would just be a phase; then they couldn't tear themselves away.

One of those is Lisa Flood. "I got hooked so easily. It's amazing that I still feel the same excitement with each song. Patsy's voice is something you hear once in a generation. She appeals to the teenage angst that lies within some of us long after our teenage years. Her vocals sound bruised, loaded with pain and feeling. It's raw, not processed or polished. She's lived it and her hurt acts as a healer. Even though ninety-nine percent of us never had the chance to meet her or attend one of her shows, we cling to her memory and cherish it."

Rose Marie Flynt, remembering her friend, said "Patsy valued loyalty and hon-esty above all else, but the thing I admired was that she knew what she was capable of and wasn't jealous of anyone. That's evidenced by the fact she helped Brenda, Dot-tie, and Loretta.

"During hard times, Patsy could be dying on the inside, but when she went onstage and took that microphone in her hand, a smile came across her face. There's no doubt her talent was God-given. When she sang songs like 'Faded Love,' the emo-tion was so real she made me cry."

Interest among fans hasn't abated. There's no end to discussions of how Randy Hughes's plane crashed, what Patsy was wearing at Dyersburg, what their hurry was to get to Nashville, why film from the movie Patsy and Dottie made or more TV-show footage hasn't been discovered.

Some speculate that Charlie is hiding a stash of photographs. However, he's said family photos and mementoes were destroyed due to water damage after a pipe rupture. Others think Mrs. Hensley had never-released recordings.

In 2007, CMT Television reported on a 1963 press release from PR Wire International:

NASHVILLE, March 1, 1963/PRWireIntl/Cline lead

Singer Cline Announces Custom Bus Tour

Singer Patsy Cline has announced that she will undertake a new tour, trav-eling exclusively by specially customized bus. She had previously traveled by automobile and private airplane, but had grown more concerned about travel after a near-fatal car crash in 1961. Her first tour date is March 3 in Kansas City.

Best laid plans. Sadly, that didn't happen. If only it had.

Patsy Cline was wrested away much too soon. She endures as a great artist not because of her tragic death at an early age, but because she's the key, the link to a fabulous past. As long as we have her music, Patsy lives inside of us, immortal.

PATSY CLINE
DISCOGRAPHY

O nly three of Patsy Cline's albums were released during her lifetime: *Patsy Cline* (Decca 8611), August 5, 1957; *Showcase* with the Jordanaires (Decca 4202), November 27, 1961; and *Sentimentally Yours* (Decca 4282), August 6, 1962.

Following her death, on June 16, 1963, Decca released *The Patsy Cline Story* (Decca K88-7176), complete with a handsome gatefold biographical sketch and photos. It contained the hits "Walkin' After Midnight"; "I Fall to Pieces"; "Crazy"; "She's Got You"; Patsy's January 1963 single "Leavin' on Your Mind," cut September, 1962, which had made it into the country top-10; and "Sweet Dreams," from the February 1963 and last sessions. The latter had been released as a single April 15, 1963, and climbed to number 5 on the *Billboard* country chart. There were two additional cuts from the September 1962 sessions, "Back in Baby's Arms" and "Tra Le La Le La Triangle"; and sixteen previously released tunes.

A Portrait of Patsy Cline (Decca 4508) was released November 2, 1964. On March 13, 1967, Decca issued *Patsy Cline's Greatest Hits* (Decca 4854).

Since then, there have been numerous albums from Decca, its budget label Vocalion, and parent MCA Records, which eliminated the Decca imprint in 1970; as well as repackagings of Patsy's Four-Star songs from such budget labels as Nashville's Hilltop, which leased their LPs to Pickwick International, and other compilations on Accord, Allegiance, Design, Hallmark, Highland, Roller Skate, Sears, Roebuck special products, and VJ International.

Because of Britain's Decca Records label, Patsy's product in the United Kingdom was on the Coral label.

The Everest albums in the following list contain only Patsy's Four-Star material.

Upon release of *Coal Miner's Daughter,* MCA reissued Patsy's early and later material, some of it remastered, in restyled packages or using original Decca art.

The Patsy Cline Collection (MCA 4-10421), compiled by the Country Music Foundation and released in October 1991 by MCA Records, is a four-compact disc or tape cassette boxed set containing 104 of Patsy's recordings, radio transcriptions, and live performances, such as her December 1961 Atlanta "Dixie Jubilee" appearance. It features a sixty-four-page souvenir booklet with photographs, remembrances, and information on Patsy's recording sessions, along with personnel used by producer Owen Bradley. In the following history of Patsy's recording sessions, all songs *except* "Ain't No Wheels on This Ship," "Cry Not for Me," "Dear God," "Fingerprints," "He Will Do It for Me," "Hidin' Out," "I Cried All the Way to the Altar," "Stop the World and Let Me Off," and "Walking Dream" are in this set.

ALBUM KEY

(To find the album on which specific songs are featured, see the Album Key column of The Recording Sessions, which follows; # denotes availability on compact disc)

A.	Patsy Cline	MCA 25200#
B.	Showcase with the Jordanaires	MCA 87#
C.	Sentimentally Yours	MCA 90#
D.	The Patsy Cline Story	MCA 4038#
E.	A Portrait of Patsy Cline	MCA 224#
F.	That's How a Heartache Begins	Decca DL-4586
G.	Here's Patsy Cline	MCA 738#
H.	Patsy Cline's Greatest Hits	MCA 12#
I.	Country Great	MCA 736
J.	Stop, Look and Listen	MCA 1440#
K.	Today, Tomorrow and Forever	MCA 1463#
L.	*Sweet Dreams*—Soundtrack	MCA 6149#
M.	Walkin' Dreams: Her First Recordings, Volume 1	Rhino R2 70048#
N.	Hungry For Love: Her First Recordings, Volume 2	Rhino R2 70049#
O.	The Rockin' Side: Her First Recordings, Volume 3	Rhino R2 70050#

ALBUMS THAT FOLLOWED
(with original record numbers)

Of posthumously released Patsy Cline product, the following comprise songs that Patsy sang live at the Opry or "manufactured" duets:

Live at the Cimarron Ballroom (1997)	MCA/Nashville D11579
Patsy Cline Duets, Volume 1 (1999)	Private I/Mercury Records 463417097, CD includes nine "duets," including with Willie Nelson, Glen Campbell, and Crystal Gayle, and CD-ROM with onscreen lyrics and photo gallery

Revisited (2006)   Intersound 64550, features two
                                  "duets" with Willie Nelson and
                                  one with an unidentified vocalist

    Concurrent with their U.S. release and distribution, Patsy Cline singles and albums were released in Australia, Belgium, France, Germany, Greece, Japan, Malaysia, the Philippines, South Africa, New Zealand, and the United Kingdom.

    There have been numerous compilation albums that include one or more previously released Patsy Cline tracks. Of interest:

*Greatest Hits of Jim Reeves
& Patsy Cline* (1981)   RCA AHL1-4127
*Remembering Patsy Cline &
Jim Reeves* (1982)   MCA 5319
*Rounding up the Gals, Vol. 1: Great
Female Country* (2001)   by Kitty Wells, Patsy Cline, others
                                  Jasmine Music B00005NNIU, one
                                  Patsy Cline track
Legends of the Opry (2006)   Opry Music OM-0609
Great Ladies of the Opry (2006) Opry Music OM-0611

THE RECORDING SESSIONS

Session Date	Selection(s) Recorded	Album Key	Original Single Number A&B Side	Single Release Date
Coral Records:				
January 5, 1955	"I Love You, Honey"	K	61583A	February 5, 1956
	"Come On In" +	—	61583B	
	"I Cried All the Way to the Altar"	M		
	"I Don't Wanta"	O		
June 1, 1955	"Hidin' Out"	M	61523A	November 5, 1955
	"Turn the Cards Slowly"	J	61523B	
	"A Church, a Courtroom and Then Goodbye"	M	61464A	July 20, 1955
	"Honky Tonk Merry-Go-Round"	K	61464B	
Decca Records:				
April 22, 1956	"Stop, Look and Listen"	J	29963B	July 8, 1956
	"I've Loved and Lost Again"	G	29963A	
	"Dear God"	M	30794A	December 15, 1958
	"He Will Do for You (What He's Done for Me)"	M	30794B	
November 8, 1956	"Walkin' After Midnight"	A,H,L	30221A	February 11, 1957
	"A Poor Man's Roses (or a Rich Man's Gold)"	J	30221B	
	"The Heart You Break May Be Your Own"	—		
	"Pick Me Up on Your Way Down"	—	25732B	RP + +

Session Date	Selection(s) Recorded	Album Key	Original Single Number A&B Side	Single Release Date
April 24, 1957 (New York, Paul Cohen)	"Today, Tomorrow and Forever"	K	30339A	May 27, 1957
	"Fingerprints"	A		
	"A Stranger in My Arms"	M	30406B	August 12, 1957
	"Don't Ever Leave Me Again"	A,I,J		
April 25, 1957 (New York, Paul Cohen)	"Try Again"	K	30339B	RP
	"Too Many Secrets"	A,I,J	25738A	
	"Then You'll Know"	A,I	30504B	November 18, 1957
May 23, 1957	"Three Cigarettes (in an Ashtray)"	A,J	30406A	
	"In Care of the Blues"	A,G,J	25744B	
	"I Can't Forget"	I		
	"Hungry for Love"	A,I		
	"That Wonderful Someone"	A,I		
	"Ain't No Wheels on This Ship"	A,I,J		
	"I Don't Wanta" (Remake)	A,I		
December 13, 1957	"Stop the World (and Let Me Off)"	H,G	30504A	January 13, 1958
	"Walking Dream"	G	30542A	
	"Cry Not for Me"	N	30542B	February 23, 1959
	"If I Could See the World (Through the Eyes of a Child)"	G,J	30846A	September 9, 1958
February 13, 1958	"Just Out of Reach (of My Two Open Arms)"	J	30746A	
	"I Can See an Angel"	K	30746B	
	"Let the Teardrops Fall"	K	30706A	August 18, 1958
	"Never No More"	J	30659B	
	"If I Could Only Stay Asleep"	K	30706B	June 1, 1958
	"Come On In" (Remake)	—	30659A	

Session Date	Selection(s) Recorded	Album Key	Original Single Number A&B Side	Single Release Date
January 8, 1959	"I'm Moving Along"	F,K	30929B	July 20, 1959
	"I'm Blue Again"	F,K	25724A	RP
	"Love, Love, Love Me, Honey, Do"	F,K		
	"Yes, I Understand"	N	30846A	
January 9, 1959	"Gotta Lot of Rhythm in My Soul"	K	30929A	
July 3, 1959	"Life's Railway to Heaven"	G		
	"Just a Closer Walk with Thee"	G	Kapp 659A,B	RP
January 27, 1960	"Lovesick Blues"	F,L	31061A	March 7, 1960
	"How Can I Face Tomorrow?"	G	31061B	
	"There He Goes"	F	31128B	August 1, 1960
	"Crazy Dreams"	F	31128A	
November 16, 1960	"I Fall to Pieces"	B,D,H,L	31205A	January 30, 1961
	"Shoes"	F,J	25694B	RP
	"Lovin' in Vain"	F	31205B	
	"True Love"	B,D	25724B	
August 17, 1961	"San Antonio Rose"	B,D,L	25673A	RP
	"The Wayward Wind"	B,D	25747A	RP
	"A Poor Man's Roses (or a Rich Man's Gold)" (Remake)	B,D		
August 21, 1961	"Crazy"	B,D,H,L	31317A	October 16, 1961
August 24, 1961	"Who Can I Count On?"	E	31317B	
	"Seven Lonely Days"	B,D,L	25686B	RP
	"I Love You So Much, It Hurts"	B,D	25686A	
	"Foolin' 'Round"	B,D,L	25707A	RP
	"Have You Ever Been Lonely (Have You Ever Been Blue)?"	B		

Session Date	Selection(s) Recorded	Album Key	Original Single Number A&B Side	Single Release Date
August 25, 1961	"South of the Border (Down Mexico Way)"	B,D	25673B	
	"Walkin' After Midnight" (Remake)	B,D,H,L		
	"Strange"	C,D,H	31354B	January 10, 1962
	"You're Stronger Than Me"			
December 17, 1961	"She's Got You"	C,D,H,L	31354A	
	"You Made Me Love You (I Didn't Want to Do It)"	C	25738B	
	"You Belong to Me"	C,D		
	"Heartaches"	C,D	31429A	October 8, 1962
	"Your Cheatin' Heart"	C,D,L	31754B	
February 13, 1962	"That's My Desire"	C	25707B	RP
	"Half as Much"	C,L	25694A	
February 15, 1962	"Lonely Street"	C	25699A	RP
	"Anytime"	C	25744A	
	"You Were Only Fooling (When I Was Falling in Love)"	C	25699B	
	"I Can't Help It (If I'm Still in Love with You)"	C	31754A	RP
February 28, 1962	"You're Stronger Than Me" (Remake)	D,H	31406B	July 16, 1962
	"When I Get Thru With You (You'll Love Me, Too)"	C,E	31377A	May 7, 1962
	"Imagine That"	D	31377B	
	"So Wrong"	D,H	31406A	
September 9, 1962	"Why Can't He Be You?"	D,H	31429B	October 8, 1962
	"Your Kinda Love"	E	31588A	RP
	"When You Need a Laugh"	E	31552A	RP
	"Leavin' on Your Mind"	D,H	31455A	January 7, 1963

Session Date	Selection(s) Recorded	Album Key	Original Single Number A&B Side	Single Release Date
September 10, 1962	"Back in Baby's Arms"	D,H	31483B	RP
	"Tra Le Le La Triangle"	D	31455B	
	"That's How a Heartache Begins"	F	31616A	RP
February 4, 1963	"Faded Love"	E,H	31522A	RP
	"Someday (You'll Want Me to Want You)"	E	31588B	RP
	"Love Letters in the Sand"	F	31616B	
February 5, 1963	"Blue Moon of Kentucky"	D,H	31522B	
	"Sweet Dreams (of You)"	D,H,L	31483A	
	"Always"	E	25732A	
February 6, 1963	"Does Your Heart Beat for Me?"	E	25712A	RP
February 7, 1963	"Bill Bailey, Won't You Please Come Home?"	F	31671B	RP
	"He Called Me Baby"	F	31671A	
	"Crazy Arms"	E	25747B	
	"You Took Him Off My Hands"	E	25712B	
	"I'll Sail My Ship Alone"	E	31552B	

(At Decca Records Studios, Nashville, and produced by Owen Bradley, unless otherwise specified; album key denotes compact disc or cassette *currently* available)

N.B.: Single release numbers are listed through 1969. Beginning in 1970, MCA Records issued singles using new master numbers under the MCA label.

+ Radio transcription version on "Live at the Opry," Volume 2

+ + Released posthumously

BIBLIOGRAPHY

Books

Coal Miner's Daughter, by Loretta Lynn with George Vecsey; a Bernard Geis Associates Book, Henry Regnery Company, Chicago; 1976.

The Country Music Encyclopedia, compiled by Melvin Shestack; Thomas Y. Crowell Company, New York; 1974.

The Country Music Story, A Picture History of Country and Western Music, by Robert Shelton and Burt Goldblatt; Castle Books, Secaucus, New Jersey; 1966.

The Complete Encyclopedia of Television Programs 1947–1976, compiled by Vincent Terrace; A.S. Barnes and Company, New York; 1976.

Web sites

www.patsified.com

www.patsy.nu

www.patsycline.info

www.patsyclinehta.com

www.patsyclinemuseum.com

www.patsyclinetribute.com

www.reclinerclub.com

A variety of Patsy Cline television appearances, transferred from film to video, can be found at www.youtube.com.

ACKNOWLEDGMENTS

eep gratitude goes to Mrs. Hilda Hensley, who began this book with me, for sharing her love and memories of her daughter, and to Charlie Dick, the first person interviewed.

The bulk of photographic memorabilia documenting Patsy's career was taken by WSM-Grand Ole Opry cameraman Les Leverett. Without Mr. Leverett's untiring cooperation, drive for perfection in the processing stage, and his loyal friendship, this book could not have been realized to the fullest extent.

For their valued cooperation, thank you to the Country Music Foundation Library and Media Center, the Grand Ole Opry, and MCA Records/Nashville.

For source material I thank BMI; Civil Aeronautics Board; Clark County Library, Las Vegas; Jimmy Dean; the Handley Library Stewart B. Bell Jr. Archives, Winchester, Virginia (Rebecca Ebert); Paul Harvey for permission to reprint a portion of his March 5, 1963, broadcast; the Kansas City *Star*; H. R. and Barbara Nash for access to a former home of Patsy Cline and Charlie Dick and mementoes; the Nashville *Banner* and *Tennessean*; the New York City Library for the Performing Arts; the Paley Center for Broadcasting, New York; Time, Inc.; the United States Departments of the Air Force, Army, and National Guard; the Winchester *Star*; and Vanderbilt University Libraries.

Thanks to Acuff-Rose/Sony-Tree Music, Cedarwood Publishing, Cheerleader Music, Loretta Lynn Enterprises, Sure-Fire Music, and Warner Chappell Music for permission to quote song lyrics.

No words can express my gratitude to those who gave so generously of their time to create an oral history of the lives of Patsy Cline and those closely connected with her. Special thanks go to Kathy Hughes (the former Mrs. Randy Hughes and daughter of Cowboy Copas), Jean Shepard (the former Mrs. Hawkshaw Hawkins), Larry Peer, Joseph and Catherine Shrewbridge, and Jenny Yontz (first wife of Bill Peer).

Deep appreciation is due Loretta Lynn for sharing her memories of Patsy during our association and for remembering Patsy in her autobiography, *Coal Miner's Daughter*.

Thanks are due to Marie Flynt for access to her Patsy Cline correspondence; Alfredda Rhoades and Erma Schonfield, Kansas City, for sharing memories and mementoes of Patsy Cline's last concert; Louise Seger for sharing her Patsy Cline correspondence; and Ronnie West, son of Gerald Cline, for establishing contact with the Cline family.

I greatly appreciate the assistance of James Baroutas, Guy Cesario, Christie's New York (Whitney Richardson), Gina Cline (daughter of Gerald Cline), Bill Cox, Tim Davis, Jim Fitzgerald, Walter Gidaly, Phil Hunter, Jim Kniceley, Linda Lenzi, Philip Martin, Faye Morgan, Michael Nassour, the Rapid City [SD] Chamber of Commerce (Stevie Wessel), and Dustin Watson.

At Chicago Review Press I thank Lisa Reardon, Mary Kravenas, Michelle Niebur, and Jonathan Hahn, with special thanks to senior editor Yuval Taylor.

Photographs, interview transcripts, and research materials from this book have been donated to the Country Music Foundation Library and Media Center and to the Handley Library Stewart B. Bell Jr. Archives, Winchester.

I am truly grateful for the praise so many have given this book, which was a labor of love. I'm deeply humbled that my ability to render the recollections of Patsy Cline by Charlie Dick, Hilda Hensley, Jan Howard, Brenda Lee, Roger Miller, Dottie West, Del Wood, Faron Young, and so many others has moved you. A writer can have no greater goal or honor.

ELLIS NASSOUR
2008

INDEX

Acuff, Claude "Spot," 40
Acuff, Roy, 15–16, 80, 218, 220, 242
"Ain't No Wheels on This Ship," 89
Alford, Reverend Jay, 156–157, 240
Alison, Bill, 243
Allen, Barbara, 86
Allen, Lorene, 244
Allen, Rex, 145
Allen, Rosalie, 86
Althouse, Reverend Paul L., 24
"Always," 213
"American Bandstand," 179
American Federation of Musicians (AFM)
    contract form, 32
Anderson, Bill, 190
Anderson, John, 44–45, 55, 128, 147, 203
Angell, Jimmy, 149
Angell, Mrs. Ruby Nell, 149
Anglin, Jack, 86, 240–241
Anita Kerr Singers, 85, 89, 96
Armel, Bud, 53–54
Armel, Charlie, 99
Armel, Geraldine, 53
Arnold, Eddy, 39, 83, 120–121
Arthur, Charline, 86, 119
Atkins, Chet, 4, 121–122

"Back in Baby's Arms," 204
Bailey, DeFord, 14
Bee, Molly, 86
Belew, Carl, 191
Benny, Jack, 176, 179
Berlin, Irving, 213
Bert's, Winchester, VA, 19

Bevis, Clyde, 212
"Bill Bailey, Won't You Please Come
    Home," 213
Billboard awards, 95, 170, 206, 246
Blair, Joyce, 136, 149–150
Blanchfield, Elias, 18, 29, 39
Block, Alan, 63, 81
Bloomenthal, Sy, 46
"Blue Moon of Kentucky," 213
Boone, Pat, 78
Bowes, Margie, 113–114, 150, 153
Bradford, Carl, 233
Bradford, Louis, 233
Bradley, Harold, 35, 134, 167, 182, 212–213
Bradley, Owen, 35–38, 56, 65–66, 85–89, 91,
    96–98, 101–104, 114, 116, 119, 121–122,
    127, 129, 132–136, 141–142, 152, 160,
    163, 165–170, 180–182, 190–192, 204,
    212–214, 237, 240, 246, 249
Braese, Bill, 226–227
Brewer, Dean, 233–234
Brewer, Teresa, 33, 119
Brown, George, 167
Burch, Fred, 204
Burgess, Wilma, 205, 240, 249
Burrows, Lee, 25, 28, 50–52, 78, 94–95, 153
Butler, Carl, 110–112, 206, 214, 232, 234
Butler, Pearl, 86, 110–112, 127, 154, 169–170,
    184–186, 206, 214–216, 232, 234, 240
Byrd, Harry F., 52

Call, Anne, 220
Call, Cactus Jack, 216, 218, 220–221
Cannon, Hughie, 213

Canova, Judy, 86
Carnegie Hall, Grand Ole Opry at, 175–179
Carper, Bobby, 20
Carroll, Marvin, 47
Carson, Martha Lou, 86, 97
Carter, Anita, 240
Carter, June, 82, 189, 198
Carter, Maybelle, 86, 198
Cash, Johnny, 4, 189, 198, 207
Cashbox's Most Programmed awards, 170,
    206, 246
"Celebrating Patsy," Kurtz Cultural Center,
    249
Challenge Records, 133
Chance, Lightnin', 88, 115, 136–137, 168,
    181–182, 186, 207, 212, 214, 246
Childre, Lew, 187
Chuck and Ray's, Winchester, VA, 19
"Church, a Courtroom and Then Goodbye,
    A," 34, 38, 42, 181, 214
Clark, Dick, 179
Clark, Mrs. Harold, 149, 159
Clark, Roy, 47
Clement, Governor Frank, 229
Click, Mary, 69
Clinch Mountain Clan, 132, 218, 221
Cline, Dorothy, 22–23
Cline, Earl Hezekiah, 22, 47
Cline, Gerald (first husband), 22–29, 32–36,
    41, 44–47, 50–51, 54–55, 68, 70, 76, 82,
    86, 92–93, 97, 243
Cline, Geraldine Hottle, 86, 92–93
Cline, Lettie Viola, 22, 25, 46–47
Cline, Nevin, 22–24, 27, 92
Cline, Ronnie, 22
Clooney, Rosemary, 33
Coal Miner's Daughter (Lynn), 152–153, 159,
    247
Cochran, Hank, 131–136, 139, 161, 163,
    167–168, 180–181, 186, 191, 198,
    204–205, 230–231, 235, 240
Coffee-Dan's, Los Angeles, 61
Cohen, Paul, 32–38, 50, 56, 75, 84–85, 87,
    89, 96, 98, 101
"Come On In," 37, 98–99, 126
Coolidge, Calvin, 82
Cooper, Bob, 176
Cooper, Wilma Lee and Stoney, 86–87, 115,
    132, 218
Copas, Cowboy, 3, 115, 120, 214, 218,
    220–221, 223, 225, 228, 235, 240, 245

Copas, Kathaloma "Kathy," 115, 220
Coral Records, 39, 50, 56, 101
Cosse, Xavier X., 97
Country Deputies, 112, 129, 178
"Country Hoedown," 56
Country Music Hall of Fame
    Connie Gay's election to, 46
    memorabilia at, 247
    Owen Bradley's election to, 35
    Patsy's election to, 4
"Country Music Time," 212
Country Song Roundup, 142, 150
"Country Style, U.S.A.," 120–121, 136
Cousin Emmy, 87
Cramer, Floyd, 167, 182, 212
"Crazy," 163–171, 178–179, 184, 191, 206, 247
"Crazy Arms," 33, 213
"Crazy Dreams," 119–120
Crosby, Bob, 81
Crum, Simon, 116
Crutchley, Fay, 22–25, 28–29, 34, 39, 43–45,
    55, 76, 86, 128, 148, 220, 237, 242–243
"Cry Not for Me," 96, 104, 210
Cummins, Jack, 243–244

Daisy, Texas, 87
"Dakota Lil," 91
Damrosch, Dr. Walter, 14
Darren, Jimmy, 162
Davies, Gail, 246
Davis, Janette, 32–33, 57, 67, 72–73, 75,
    77–78
Davis, Skeeter, 87, 153–154, 206, 240
Day, Jimmy, 119
Dean, Buddy, 179
Dean, Jimmy, 29–31, 44–52, 66–70, 79,
    83–84, 179, 185, 192–193, 201, 206
Dean, Sylvia "Boots," 156
"Dear God," 56, 101
Decca, 31–33, 35, 56–57, 65, 72, 75–76, 80,
    84, 86, 89–92, 96, 98, 101–102,
    119–120, 122, 129, 133, 137, 142, 145, 160,
    165, 170, 189, 190, 194, 197, 199, 207,
    246
Delugg, Milton, 65
Denny, Jim, 14–16, 40, 81
Deren, Jane, 104–105
DeRose, Peter, 167
DeShannon, Jackie, 212
Devine, Ott, 118, 152–153, 176, 241–242

Deyton, Roy, 19–20, 25, 33–34, 36–37, 44–45, 90, 100, 128, 242
Dick, Charlie (second husband)
  courting of Patsy by, 52–57, 65, 67–70, 76–77, 82–84, 86, 89
  death of Patsy and, 3–4, 219–220, 223–225, 227–229, 238–240, 242–243, 246, 248
  marriage to Jamey Ryan, 3–4, 186, 248
  marriage to Patsy, 92, 94–97, 100–101, 103–105, 109–117, 120–121, 123–128, 130, 136, 139–140, 143, 146, 149–152, 154, 160, 164–165, 168–171, 183–189, 193–201, 205, 208, 211–213, 215–216
Dick, Charles, Jr., 248
Dick, Jamey Ryan. *See* Ryan, Jamey
Dick, Julie Simadore (daughter), 95–96, 99–101, 104, 111, 123–124, 127–128, 139, 168, 186, 195–198, 202, 208–209, 211, 215, 223–224, 229, 239–240, 246, 248
Dick, Mary, 53, 69, 239
Dick, Mel, 53–54, 249
Dick, Randolph "Randy" (son), 120, 123, 136, 139, 186, 189, 195–197, 202, 208–209, 211, 215, 217, 220, 222–224, 229, 239–240, 248
Dick, William, 53–54
Dill, Donny, 190
Discography, of Patsy Cline recordings, 251–258. *See also* specific titles
Dixie Jubilee, 157, 178
"Does Your Heart Beat for Me?", 213
"Don't Ever Leave Me Again," 85
Dovel, Dick, 243
Drusky, Roy, 118, 132–133, 168, 190, 193, 196, 204, 206
Dunbar Cave Resort, Clarksville, IN, 40

"Ed Sullivan Show, The," 82
Emery, Ralph, 146, 179–180, 216, 218, 220, 241–242
Ernest Tubb's Mid-Nite Jamboree, 145
Evans, Dr. Hillis, 149–150, 155, 160

"Faded Love," 3–4, 212–213
Farber, Bert, 72, 75
Fisher, Eddie, 223, 225
Flatt & Scruggs, 206, 219
Foley, Red, 51, 90, 92, 95, 99, 246

"Foolin' 'Round," 167–168
Ford, Tennessee Ernie, 115, 179
Foster, Fred, 230
Four-Star Records, 30–38, 51–52, 61–66, 81–82, 84–85, 90–91, 96–98, 102, 104, 111, 114, 116, 119–120, 191
Fowler, Wally, 12–14, 16, 39, 102
Francis, Mrs. Todd, 247
Freed, Alan, 82
Fritts, Doris, 24, 26, 44
Frye, Betty, 18–19
Frye, Bobby, 18–19
Frye, George and Katherine, 18–19
Frye, Sonny, 18
Furr, Sheriff Loyce, 230

G&M Music Store, 12, 37–38
Gable, Dorothy, 247
Gabler, Milt, 31
Gabor, Zsa Zsa, 112
Gaines, Bob, 12, 37–38
Gallico, Al, 71–72, 216
Garland, Hank "Sugarfoot," 102, 119, 121, 134
Gaunt's Drug Store, 11, 13–14, 16–17, 249
Gay, Connie B., 29–30, 46, 49–50, 52, 56, 65–66, 69, 79–80, 83, 192
Gibson, Don, 198, 213, 221
Glaser, Chuck, Jim, and Tompall, 207–208
Godfrey, Arthur, 32–33, 57, 66–78, 82, 84–85, 93, 97, 201
Goldberg, Sidney, 101, 122, 133, 160
Goode Motors, 19–20, 44
Gooderham, Shaun, 244
"Gotta Lot of Rhythm in My Soul," 102
Grammer, Billy, 47
Grammy Awards, in honor of Patsy Cline, 247
Grand Ole Opry
  atmosphere of, 110
  Carnegie Hall appearance, 175–179
  Elvis at, 25–26
  history of, 14–15
  Loretta Lynn on, 150–155
  museum of, 248
  Patsy's appearances at, 39–40, 50–51, 80–81, 96, 104, 124
  Patsy's audition for, 11–15
  Patsy's car accident and, 149–150, 159, 162–163
  Patsy's childhood and, 5

Grand Ole Opry (cont.)
  Patsy's death and, 241–242
  Patsy's membership in, 118, 121, 136, 145, 169–170, 214
Grant, Gogi, 56, 167
Graves, Billy, 243
Graves, Granville "Shorty," 238
Greene, Jack, 157
Greyhound terminal, Winchester, VA, 17
Grimsley, Cliff and Tex, 30
Groves, Alexander, 26–27, 238
Grubbs, Ralph, 11–13

Haddock, D., 37
"Half as Much," 191
Hall, Connie, 87, 150
Hamilton, Adelaide, 194
Hamilton, George, IV, 47–48, 57, 192, 194, 206
Harman, Murrey "Buddy," 167, 182
Harris, Emmylou, 246
Harris, Hal, 142–144, 148
Hart, Freddie, 133–134
Harvey, Paul, 236–237
"Have You Ever Been Lonely (Have You Ever Been Blue)?", 167
Hawkins, Don Robin, 221, 228
Hawkins, Hawkshaw, 131, 135, 218, 220–223, 225–226, 228, 231, 235, 240–241, 245, 247
Hawkins, Hoyt, 102
Hay, "Judge" George D., 14
Haynes, Walter, 167, 182
"Heartaches," 191, 206, 208
"Heart You Break May Be Your Own, The," 65
"He Called Me Baby," 213
Hecht, Donn, 31, 61–65, 71, 73, 76, 81, 96, 104, 116–117, 209–211, 237
Helms, Don, 88, 90
Henry, Gerald, 230
Hensley, Benjamin (great-grandfather), 6
Hensley, Hilda Patterson (mother), 4–18, 23–25, 37, 52, 57, 66–69, 71, 73–76, 78–79, 89, 92, 101, 126, 148–149, 159, 177, 198, 211, 224–225, 231–232, 234, 239–240, 242–243, 248–250
Hensley, Margaret Elizabeth Shifflett (grandmother), 6, 8
Hensley, Randolph (half-brother), 7
Hensley, Sam (father), 7–11, 68–69

Hensley, Samuel Lawrence "John" (brother), 8, 81, 148–150, 155–156, 231
Hensley, Solomon Job (grandfather), 6–8
Hensley, Sylvia Mae (sister), 4, 8, 56, 147, 148, 239
Hensley, Tempie Glenn (half-sister), 5, 7
Hensley, Wynona Jones, 7
"He Will Do For You," 56, 101
"Hidin' Out," 34, 38, 50
Hill, Goldie, 87, 119, 154, 214
Hill & Range (song publishers), 62
Hilliard, Bob, 65
Hodges, Jimmie, 213
Holcombe, Bill and Helen, 219
Hollingsworth, W. J. and Jeners, 233, 247
"Honky Tonk Merry-Go-Round," 34, 38–39
Horner, Ray, 18
Hottle, Geraldine. See Cline, Geraldine Hottle
Houston, Alec, 47
"How Can I Face Tomorrow?", 119–120
Howard, Harlan, 130–133, 135–136, 139, 141–142, 161–163, 167–168, 170, 191, 196, 198, 204–205, 213, 246
Howard, Jan, 130–133, 135, 139, 141–142, 150, 154, 169–170, 191, 198, 205, 213–214, 229–231, 240
Huffmeister, Dolly. See Peer, Dolly Huffmeister
Hughes, Kathy, 125–126, 188, 205, 220, 225–229, 247
Hughes, Marvin, 121
Hughes, Ramsey Dorris "Randy"
  career of, 3, 97, 114–119, 122, 125–126, 128, 134, 147, 156, 160, 162, 167–168, 177–178, 181–182, 188, 190, 193–194, 196–198, 205, 207–209, 211, 213–218
  death of (with Patsy), 219–228, 233, 235, 240, 245, 247
"Hungry For Love," 89
Husky, Ferlin, 39, 84, 112, 115–116, 125, 128, 193

"I Can See an Angel," 98
"I Can't Forget You," 89
"I Can't Help It," 191
"I Cried All the Way to the Altar," 37
"I Don't Wanta," 37, 89, 94
"I Fall to Pieces," 132–138, 140–141, 150–151, 160–162, 165, 169, 171

"If I Could See the World," 96
"If I Could Stay Asleep," 98
"I'll Sail My Ship Alone," 213
"I Love You, Honey," 37
"I Love You So Much, It Hurts," 164–165, 167
"Imagine That," 171, 191, 194, 198
"I'm Blue Again," 102
"I'm Moving Along," 102
"I've Loved and Lost Again," 56

Jackson, Tommy, 39, 89, 176, 179
Jackson, Wanda, 51, 87, 119
James, Sonny, 56, 142, 198
Jean, Norma, 87, 187, 221
Jeans, Mary Lu, 81
Jenkins, Tiny, 47
"Jimmy Dean Show," 83–84, 119
Johnson, Joe, 133
Johnson, Loudilla, 154–155
Johnson, Mark, 44, 50
Jones, George, 127, 189, 198, 218
Jones, Herbie, 47
Jones, Marshall Louis "Grandpa," 118–119, 145, 175–177, 206
Jones, Ramona, 177
Jones, Wynona. *See* Hensley, Wynona Jones
Jordanaires, 102–103, 105, 134, 167, 171, 176, 182, 212–214, 241
"Just a Closer Walk With Thee," 104
"Just Out of Reach," 98
Justis, Bill, 191

Keith, Ben, 134
Keith, Vivian, 153
Kerby, Marie, 221–222
Kern, Henry, 99
Kerr, Anita, 85, 89, 96
Kershaw, Doug, 129
KIKK Radio, Houston, 142–145, 148
Kilgallen, Dorothy, 175–176
King, Pee Wee, 81, 191
King, R. C., 230
Kingsbury, Paul, 119, 134
Kirham, Doug, 134
Klick, Mary, 47
Kountry Krackers, 53
Kramer, Floyd, 102, 119

Lamarr, Hedy, 101
lang, k.d., 246
Lange, Jessica, 53
Lansbury, Angela, 101
Lanson, Snooky, 145
Latin Quarter, New York City, 33
Lavender, Shorty, 132
"Leavin' on Your Mind," 204, 211
Lee, Brenda, 89–90, 101, 120–121, 127–128, 132, 138, 165, 184, 195, 237
Lee, Wilma, 115
Lenhart, Evelyn, 22–23
"Let the Teardrops Fall," 98
Leverett, Les, 111, 176, 214
Lewis, Jerry Lee, 219
Leyden, Norman, 77
"Life's Railway to Heaven," 104–105
Lisell, Richard, 33
Log Cabin Boys, 19
"Lonely Street," 191
Long, Hubert, 114–115, 128, 153, 204, 238
Longley, Herman V., Jr. (cousin), 6–8, 11, 68–69, 217
Louvin, Ira, 159
"Love Letters in the Sand," 213
"Love, Love, Love Me, Honey, Do," 102
"Lovesick Blues," 119–120, 165
"Lovin' in Vain," 133–135, 165
Lynn, Judy, 87
Lynn, Loretta, 150–155, 161, 170, 184, 189, 195–196, 205–206, 208, 211, 217–218, 234–235, 239–240, 244, 246, 248
Lynn, Mooney, 150–153, 155, 205, 217–218

McAuliff, Leon, 161
McCall, Darrell, 132–133
McCall, William A., 30–38, 51–52, 57, 61–66, 81–82, 85–87, 90, 91, 96–98, 104, 111, 114–120, 122, 209
McCormick, George, 132, 221
McCoy, Joltin' Jim, 9–10, 86, 105, 147–148, 159, 232, 243, 248–250
McDaniel, Lulu, 84
McDaniel, Sleepy, 240
McElhiney, Bill, 166, 191, 213
Madagan, Harold, 249
Maddox, Rose, 87
Mandrell, Barbara, 189
Mann, Sally, 5, 7
Maphis, Rose Lee, 87

Martin, Grady, 89, 102, 119, 167, 213
Marvin, Tony, 77
Massey, Louise, 87
Matthews, Neal, 102
Mature, Victor, 101
MCA Records, 247
Melody Boys, 19–21, 30, 32, 37, 53, 128,
    202–203, 220
Melody Lane Club, Martinsburg, WV, 10
Melody Playboys, 9–10, 105, 147
Mercury Records, 157
Merri-Mint Theatre, Las Vegas, 207–209
Metherly, Eddie, 243
Metronomes, 17, 32
"Mid-Nite Jamboree," 26, 40
Miller, Eddie, 37, 56, 62, 89, 119
Miller, Leo, 32
Miller, Mossie, 230, 233
MIller, Roger, 112, 120, 129–131, 138–139,
    157, 178, 184, 230, 232, 240
Monroe, Bill, 175–177, 213
Montana, Patsy, 87, 246
Montgomery, Bob, 204
Monument Records, 230
Moore, Bob, 134, 167, 182
Moose Lodge, Brunswick, MD, 19–21, 23–24,
    29, 34–35, 42–44, 86, 92, 128,
    202–203, 220
Morgan, George, 115
Morgan, Russ, 213
Moser, Ruth, 22
Moss, Sammy, 242–244
Mullican, Moon, 15–16, 115
Music Reporter awards, 206
Music Row, Nashville, 35
Music Vendor awards, 95, 170, 206

National Championship Country Music
    Contest, 29
NBC Radio, 56, 96
Neal, John, 44
Neal, Mrs. Bob, 234–235
Nelson, Pat, 136–137, 141
Nelson, Willie, 112, 163–165, 167, 247
"Never No More," 98
Null, Frances, 39

Oak Ridge Quartet, 12
O'Brien, Pete, 32

O'Day, Molly, 87
Olde, State Trooper Troy, 233
"Old Dominion Barn Dance," 86
Orbison, Roy, 138, 169
Owen, Ruby, 87
Owens, Bonnie, 87
Owens, Buck, 167
Owens, Don, 86, 105
"Ozark Jubilee," 51, 80, 92, 104, 120, 179

Pace, Dr. Homer M., 212
Page, Patti, 246
Painter, Perry, 87
Palace Theatre, Winchester, VA, 12
Palmier, Remo, 77
Pamper Music, 132, 136, 180
Parker, Linda, 87
Parrish, Mitchell, 213
Parton, Dolly, 111, 187
Pastor, Tony, 87
Patsy Cline (album), 91
Patsy Cline Fan Club, 159
Patsy Cline Memorial Committee, 249
Patsy Cline Memorial Highway, 249
Patsy Cline's Greatest Hits, 247
Patsy Cline Showcase, 171, 206
Patterson, Hilda. See Hensley, Hilda
    Patterson (mother)
Patton, Don, 53
Paycheck, Johnny, 131, 139
Payne, Martin, 192
Pearl, Minnie, 81, 175–176, 190, 229, 240, 242
Peebles, Harry "Hap," 218, 220–223, 246
Peer, Clarence William "Bill," 19–23, 25–30,
    32–37, 39–46, 50, 53, 76, 86, 92, 117,
    128, 202–203, 220, 237, 242, 249
Peer, Dolly Huffmeister, 20, 24, 128, 203
Peer, Jenny, 20–21, 25–27, 34, 42–44, 50
Peer, Larry, 50, 249
"Perfect Example of a Fool," 134–135
Perkins, Carl, 189–190, 230–231, 247
"Pick Me Up on Your Way Down," 65, 70
Pierce, Webb, 32, 35, 56, 82, 198, 204
Playboys (Frye Boys), 18–19, 53
"Poor Man's Roses (or a Rich Man's Gold),"
    65, 71–72, 77, 166
Porter, Cole, 166
Posnich, Nat, 176
Presley, Elvis, 25–26, 121, 169, 200, 207
Preston, Terry, 116

Price, Ray, 33, 115, 131
Pursell, Bill, 182

Rainbow Inn, Winchester, VA, 18–19
RCA, 121–122
Recording Hall of Fame, 247
Reed, Jerry, 128, 157
Reeves, Jim, 121, 175–176, 206
Rich, Charlie, 219, 246
Rinker, William R. "Jumbo," 10, 17–18, 20,
    55, 242
Ritter, Tex, 56, 81, 104, 145, 218–220, 246
Robbins, Hargus "Pig," 134, 167
Robbins, Marty, 175–176, 221
Robertson, Texas Jim, 47
Robinson, Randolph "Hobby," 7–8
Rockingham poultry factory, 8
Ronstadt, Linda, 246
Royal, Front, 17
Rumble, John, 88, 119
Ryan, Buck, 47
Ryan, Jamey, 3–4, 186, 248

"San Antonio Rose," 166
Seals, Troy, 246
Seger, Louise, 142–146, 148, 155–156,
    160–161, 184–185, 189–190, 192–193,
    237–238
Sentimentally Yours, 204
"Seven Lonely Days," 167
Shamrock, Winchester, VA, 19
Shapiro & Bernstein Music Company, 71
Shaw, Sergeant Tom, 165
Shelton, Robert, 178
Shenandoah Memorial Park, VA, 243–244,
    248–250
Shepard, Jean, 96, 99–100, 116, 126, 131,
    152–154, 170, 212, 218, 220, 225,
    227–229, 231
"She's Got You," 180–181, 189, 192, 194, 204,
    206
Shifflett, Margaret Elizabeth. See Hensley,
    Margaret Elizabeth Shifflett
    (grandmother)
Shifflett, Polly, 7
Shiner, Gene, 17, 32–33, 44
"Shoes," 134
"Shower of Stars," 198
Shrewbridge, Joseph, 86, 128, 203

Shroyer, Grover, 34–35, 45
Sikes, Bobby, 177–178
Silverstein, Harry, 214
Smalts, Claude B., Jr., 147
Smathers, Ben, 176
Smith, Carl, 113, 145, 186, 214
Smith, Connie, 246
Smith, Hal, 136
Smith, Velma, 134
Smoky Mountain Boys, 242
Snodgrass, Quincy, 47
Snow, Hank, 110
"Someday," 213
Songs by Patsy Cline, 38
South, Joe, 157
"South of the Border," 167
"So Wrong," 190–191, 199, 208
Stamper, Trudy, 88, 158–159, 176–178, 217
"Star Jubilee," 145
Starday Records, 164
Starr, Kay, 48, 63, 119, 165
Stevens, Ray, 157
Stevenson, W. S. (pseudonym for William
    McCall), 37, 89, 119, 191
Stewart, Redd, 81, 191
Stoker, Gordon, 102–103, 169, 188, 208, 214,
    247
Stony Mountain Cloggers, 176
"Stop, Look and Listen," 56
"Stop the World," 96, 98
"Strange," 167, 171, 189, 194, 204, 247
Strickland, Paul, 157
Sullivan, Ed, 82
Sullivan, Phil, 176–178
"Sundown in Nashville," 109–110
Sweet Dreams, 53, 186
"Sweet Dreams," 213

Tant, Ann, 157–158, 238, 240
Taylor, Virginia, 11
Temple, Shirley, 5
"Tennessee Ernie Ford Show, The," 179
Tennessee Three, 198
Terry, Gordon, 189, 198
Texas Troubadours, 39
Texas Wildcats, 29
"That's How a Heartache Begins," 204
"That's My Desire," 191
"That Wonderful Someone," 89
"Then You'll Know," 94

"There He Goes," 119–120, 165
"This Ole House," 33
Thomas, Gus, 120–121
Thomas, Jo Ann, 120–121, 199
Thompson, Hank, 117
"Three Cigarettes in an Ashtray," 33, 84
Tillis, Mel, 127, 139, 167, 190
Tillman, Floyd, 164, 167
"Today, Tomorrow and Forever," 89
Town and Country circuit ("Jamboree"),
   29–30, 32, 44, 46–49, 51–52, 56,
   66–67, 69–70, 79–80, 83, 95
"Town Hall Party," 63, 81, 104
"Tra Le La Le La Triangle," 204, 211
Trask, Diana, 246
Troxell, Lois, 24–25, 43–45, 49
"True Love," 166
"Try Again," 89
Tubb, Ernest, 15, 25–26, 32, 35, 37, 39–41,
   56, 80, 83, 104, 115, 145, 150, 159–160
Tubb, Justin, 139, 170–171, 191
Tucker, Gabe, 40
Tucker, Sophie, 119
"Turn the Cards Slowly," 33–34, 38, 50
Turner, Dale, 47, 49–50, 66, 68, 82, 92, 96,
   105
Turner, Grant, 56, 118, 120, 124, 150,
   162–163, 169, 228, 230, 232, 234

Valli, June, 120
Van Dyke, Leroy, 51, 162, 198
Van Gelder, Lawrence, 83
Vaughn, Barbara, 85
Vee, Bobby, 162
Virginia Gentleman restaurant, Winchester,
   VA, 17

Wagoner, Porter, 39, 89, 118, 187
Wakely, Jimmy, 145
Walker, Billy, 115, 156–157, 163–164, 188,
   205, 216–218, 220–222, 227–228, 240,
   245
Walker, Charlie, 130
Walker, Cindy, 87
Walker, Mrs. Jo, 4
Walker, Ray, 103, 134, 141, 192
Walker, Wayne, 139, 204–205
"Walkin' After Midnight," 63–66, 72–74, 76,
   80–82, 84, 90, 95, 167, 210–211

"Walking Dream," 96, 98
Wallis, Hal and Ginger, 96
WARL Radio, Arlington, VA, 29–30, 46
Watt, Robert W., 176
Wayne, Lou, 15
"Wayward Wind," 167
Webb, June, 153
Webb, Sam, 227
Wells, Kitty, 35, 86, 119, 153–154, 170, 241,
   246
WEPM Radio, 20
West, Bill, 223–224, 238–239, 241
West, Dottie, 49, 137–140, 149, 153, 159, 163,
   166, 170, 177, 180, 183–186, 188,
   190–191, 195–196, 198–202, 204–206,
   213, 218, 221–224, 232–233, 238–241,
   248
Western, Johnny, 189, 198
"Western Ranch Party," 56, 81
"When I Get Thru with You (You'll Love Me
   Too)," 191, 194, 198
"When You Need a Laugh," 204
White, Charlotte, 81
Whitney, Philip, 10, 147
"Who Can I Count On?", 167, 170–171
"Why Can't He Be You?", 204, 206
"Wicked Love," 85
Wilburn, Leslie, 153
Wilburn, Lester, 153
Wilburn, Doyle, 32, 47, 56, 65, 90–91, 104,
   111, 117–118, 152–153, 205, 208
Wilburn, Teddy, 32, 47, 56, 65, 90–91,
   103–104, 117–118, 135, 152–153,
   166–169, 185, 191, 205, 207, 213, 217,
   240–241
Wilkin, Marijohn, 204
Williams, Chickie, 87
Williams, Hank, 113, 115, 117–119, 246
Williams, Hank, Jr., 121
Williamson, Reverend Nathan, 243
Willis Brothers, 115
Wills, Bob, 166
Wills, John, 3–4
Wilson, Smiley and Kitty, 229
WINC Radio, Winchester, VA, 9–10, 147, 232
Wiseman, Lulu Belle, 87
WMAL Radio, Washington, D.C., 29, 46
Wood, Del, 11, 14, 17, 34, 52, 55, 57, 81, 87,
   95, 97, 104, 123–126, 128, 154, 183, 185,
   205, 239
Woods, Harry, 165

Worth, Marion, 87
Wright, Johnny, 86, 240–241
"Write Me (In Care of the Blues)," 89
WSM Radio, Nashville, 13–15, 50, 65, 83, 94,
    96, 103, 111, 142, 170, 176–177, 206, 217,
    228, 234, 241
Wynette, Tammy, 187

"Yes, I Understand," 102, 104
"You Belong to Me," 191
"You Made Me Love You (I Didn't Want to
    Do It)," 191
Young, Donnie, 131
Young, Faron, 39, 41, 56, 84, 112–114,
    116–117, 125, 127–129, 136, 146, 164,

Young, Faron (cont.)
    169–170, 175–176, 178, 185–188,
    205–207, 213, 240, 246, 248
Young, Hilda, 112
"Your Cheatin' Heart," 75, 191
"You're Stronger Than Me," 167–168, 171,
    191, 199
"Your Kinda Love," 204
"You Took Him Off My Hands," 213
"You Were Only Fooling (While I Was
    Falling in Love)," 191
Yuro, Timi, 235

Zero Records, 150

ABOUT THE AUTHOR

*E*llis Nassour is a native Mississippian and New York–based arts journalist. He is the author of *Rock Opera: The Creation of Jesus Christ Superstar*, has written for *The New York Times* and New York *Daily News*, and was associate and contributing editor (music, film, theater) of Oxford University Press's *American National Biography*.

Nassour has developed an original stage musical based on his Patsy Cline biography. The spoken word of the revue *Always, Patsy Cline* is verbatim from interviews with Patsy Cline fan and his family friend Louise Seger. Robyn Archer's Australian and West End revue *A Star Is Torn* also featured excerpts. Nassour is featured with k.d. lang on Bravo TV's *The Voice* segment on Patsy Cline and provided source material for numerous TV and radio tributes including the Virginia Public Television documentary *Patsy Cline: The Lady Behind the Legend*.

As vice president of artist relations for MCA Music, Nassour participated in the development of Tim Rice and Andrew Lloyd Webber's *Jesus Christ Superstar* and the careers of Elton John (supervising his American debut and first U.S. tour), The Who, Bill Cosby, Neil Diamond, Loretta Lynn (and her *Coal Miner's Daughter* campaign), Brenda Lee, Conway Twitty, Florence Henderson, Rick Nelson, and classical guitarist Andres Segovia. At MCA/Universal Studios, he worked with Academy Award–winning composer Alfred Newman on the release of his last score, *Airport*, and on the Broadway revival of *The Boy Friend*, starring Judy Carne and Sandy Duncan. Independently, he worked with disco diva Gloria Gaynor, Broadway composers Jerry Herman and Stephen Sondheim, and crossover star Sarah Brightman.

Ellis Nassour began the St. Patsy's Day tradition at New York's Cowgirl restaurant and was instrumental in getting Patsy Cline named to the Cowgirl Hall of Fame.